Stuttering Research
and Practice:
Bridging the Gap

Stuttering Research and Practice: Bridging the Gap

Edited by

Nan Bernstein Ratner
University of Maryland

E. Charles Healey
University of Nebraska

LEA
LAWRENCE ERLBAUM ASSOCIATES, PUBLISHERS
1999   Mahwah, New Jersey   London

The final camera copy for this work was prepared by the first
volume editor, and therefore the publisher takes no responsibility
for consistency or correctness of typographical style.

Lawrence Erlbaum Associates, Inc., Publishers
10 Industrial Avenue
Mahwah, NJ 07430

Cover design by Kathryn Houghtaling Lacey

Library of Congress Cataloging-in-Publication Data

Stuttering research and practice : bridging the gap / edited by Nan
Bernstein Ratner, E. Charles Healey.
     p.   cm.
Includes bibliographical references and index.
ISBN 0-8058-2458-8 (c : alk. paper). — ISBN 0-8058-2459-6 (pbk. :
alk. paper).
1. Stuttering. I. Ratner, Nan Bernstein. II. Healey, E. Charles.
[DNLM: 1. Stuttering. WM 475S93757 1998]
RC424.S786   1998
616.85′54—dc21
DNLM/DLC
for Library of Congress

                                                  98-28844
                                                     CIP

Books published by Lawrence Erlbaum Associates are printed on
acid-free paper, and their bindings are chosen for strength and
durability.

Printed in the United States of America
10 9 8 7 6 5 4 3 2 1

TABLE OF CONTENTS

Preface

The American Speech-Language-Hearing Association's Special Interest Division for Fluency and Fluency Disorders initiated "annual Leadership Conferences" in 1994. The primary goal of these annual leadership conferences is to bring together clinicians, researchers, and self-help leadership personnel to identify and address current issues in the assessment and treatment of those experiencing a fluency disorder. The Third Annual Leadership Conference held in Monterey, California in 1996 was entitled "Research and Treatment: Bridging the Gap." In retrospect it became apparent that the papers presented at the conference reflected accurately the current and the cutting-edge thinking of leading clinicians and researchers in the profession. The Division's Steering Committee concluded that the inclusion of those papers in a single volume would make a significant addition to the literature in the field.

The Steering Committee of the Division for Fluency and Fluency Disorders is pleased to have participated in the production of this volume. Special thanks are extended to E. Charles Healey and Nan Bernstein Ratner who served not only as editors for this collection of papers but as Conference Co-Chairs for the Third Annual Leadership Conference on "Research and Treatment: Bridging the Gap."

Finally, the Steering Committee wishes to express its appreciation to the authors of these papers, to those who participated in the Third Annual Leadership Conference, and to the many other individuals who made this volume a reality.

Eugene B. Cooper
Division for Fluency and Fluency Disorders
American Speech-Language-Hearing Association
Weston, FL
March, 1998

1 Bridging the Gap Between Stuttering Research and Practice: An Overview

Nan Bernstein Ratner
University of Maryland

E. Charles Healey
University of Nebraska

Despite decades of research and clinical work in the area of stuttering, it is the perception of many that a gap exists between how researchers and clinicians view the disorder. Many researchers claim that clinicians employ practices with dubious roots to either efficacy or basic research in stuttering; that they are "not up on the literature." By contrast, it is not unusual to hear clinicians claim that most published literature appears to have little direct relevance to clinical concerns in the treatment of stuttering. This gap in the appreciation of what clinicians and researchers perceive they can offer each other appears to be an ongoing problem in the field of stuttering.

In May 1996, a conference was held in Monterey, California as a first attempt to bridge the gap between researchers and clinicians. The conference was sponsored by Special Interest Division #4, Fluency and Fluency Disorders, of the American Speech-Language-Hearing Association (ASHA). The program was compiled to allow for a variety of broad perspectives on the nature and treatment of stuttering and how the gap (perceived or real) between researchers and clinicians could be narrowed. For each topic, we endeavored to pair individuals with interests in empirical research methods with scholar-practitioners. Group discussions followed the presentations and the conference ended with a plenary session. In our comments that follow, we note audience response to some of the issues raised by the contributors to this volume.

A broad representation of topics is covered in this text, including general approaches to bridging the gap between research and clinical work. This volume begins with chapters by Conture, Smith, and Yairi, who present a number of conceptual issues regarding the current status of stuttering research and therapy. De Nil and Ludlow provide us with discussions of issues relative to physiological aspects of stuttering that relate to the clinical management of stuttering. Various perspectives associated with the multitude of factors related to conducting research and treating stuttering in children and adults are provided by Guitar, Riley, Gottwald, Hill, Onslow, Siegel, Manning, and Murphy. The volume concludes with two widely diverse perspectives by Ingham and Cordes, and by Starkweather on how treatment efficacy in stuttering should be addressed.

Ed Conture got the conference off to a humorous start with an instructive tour of the rocky voyages undertaken by persons who stutter, by their clinicians, and by those who conduct research in stuttering. His metaphorical description of the voyages of the *U.S.S. Fluency* is apt: fluency research and practice often seem to have navigated the globe, not once, but on numerous occasions, discovering and highlighting anew on repeated voyages the very same themes that caught our attention many years ago. The more that the ship's technology changes, the more the route seems to gravitate toward familiar paths. The student of the field who analyzes its historical roots (Bloodstein, 1993) will note that researchers such as Ludlow and De Nil are current staff bearers for notions about the neurological and specifically, cortical, basis of stuttering first researched by the founding generation of speech-language pathologists in the early years of this century.

His four "sailing instructions" have merit but are not without controversy. For example, his first instruction was to discontinue the "grind to find" research common to our field. According to Conture, throwing out large data nets to catch a few useful research findings does not result in meaningful advancement of our understanding of stuttering. However, Guitar notes later in the volume that some of our most notable scientific advances arose somewhat serendipitously and may characterize clinical discoveries made by a clinician-scientist. But accidental insights into major problems occur in a world where stuttering research is programmatically organized and motivated, as well. An important question is what constitutes irrelevant or unmotivated research. On this question, participants differed widely in their opinions, particularly when it came to deciding the boundaries of the disorder and its relevant aspects for research and therapy. Some attendees professed more interest in discovering effective treatments, even serendipitously, than in understanding how they work. From treatment might come increased understanding of cause. For others, only better understanding of cause had the potential to improve treatment.

An equally important construct for researchers and clinical practitioners in fluency is the distinction among the terms disability, impairment and handicap. Disability has long been a focus for researchers, who in fact are often pressed to address the clinical relevance of their findings in the discussion sections of published journal articles. Conture suggests that even if we understand and can change the disability (i.e., the overt manifestation of the disorder), that this does not necessarily change the handicap of stuttering, a viewpoint supported by Manning and Starkweather (this volume). For some persons who stutter, and the professional who treats them, there is less concern about removing the underlying disability than in remedying the handicap of stuttering (i.e., the disadvantages of living with the disorder). The researcher often seems to avoid such issues, finding them too removed from objective measurement, nontheory based, and too prone to produce heterogeneity in subject performance that vitiates against clear and publishable findings.

At the end of his chapter, Conture notes that our treatment approaches need more careful evaluation, both in terms of furthering the development of more effective treatments, as well as satisfying increasing demands for accountability in therapeutic practice. His concise tutorial provides options for assessing the efficacy of clinical intervention, designs that are functional and realistic. His closing observation is brief but important: It is less important in the short run for us to know whether one approach is better than another than for us to know whether any treatment is achieving its stated ends. For some populations, notably young children, this is a critical issue, as researchers and clinicians tangle with the thorny issue of whether therapy has truly been the agent for recovery in a population known to experience unaided remission from the disorder. Even in adults, the question of whether approaches work, or whether some work better than others, is less than trivial to answer, regardless of design or subject numbers. If one cannot clearly determine what constitutes a positive therapeutic outcome, how can therapeutic efficacy be evaluated?

It was this issue: "What constitutes a positive therapeutic outcome?" that perhaps most polarized the persons who stuttered, the researchers, and the clinicians who attended the conference. Certainly, any post therapeutic outcome that produces perfectly fluent speech that can be utilized in all environments without undue hardship on the patient, and that produces speech-related attitudes and beliefs that resemble those of normally fluent speakers would be considered efficacious. But the use of such a standard to define efficacy in all cases misses our low level of understanding of the tractability of stuttering across patients, even given rather uniform intervention protocols. The medical profession has long recognized that individual response to quite finely controlled pharmaceutical treatments can vary considerably, as well as the fact that a drug may be beneficial in reducing the symptoms of the disorder, but may produce side effects that diminish the drug's effectiveness in treating the patient's original complaint. For many clinicians and patients, this understanding appears tacit: A successful treatment program is not defined as the complete absence of symptoms, but whether the treatment has reduced the disability and handicap of stuttering.

This real-world state of affairs suggests that clinically relevant improvement might remove only portions of the "stutterer's complaint," as one presenter commented, which brings up the thorny issue of deciding what the complaint actually is. One presenter professed that the complaint is obviously the speech disruptions that characterize the observable symptoms of stuttering to listeners; if they are removed, the complaint is solved. This potentially narrow definition of handicap seemed quite palpably inadequate to some clinicians and researchers who themselves stutter. It recalled a past ASHA convention paper presentation that contrasted the therapeutic approaches taken by speech-language pathologists with and without personal histories of stuttering (McFarlane & Goldberg, 1987). Their survey of clinicians showed that fluency-shaping approaches, which tend to concentrate on the elimination of speech behaviors without emphasis on less observable handicapping speech beliefs and behaviors, were most likely to be employed by clinicians with no history of stuttering symptoms. Conversely, stuttering-modification and anxiolytic approaches were most likely to be added to fluency-shaping therapies by clinicians who themselves had experienced stuttering. As Riley notes later in the volume, such observations should tell us something about the depth of the stuttering syndrome that may be less easily appreciated by normally fluent clinicians and researchers.

Perhaps those who have never stuttered have a difficult time appreciating the complexity of the disorder and its effect on the individual. Viewing stuttering as a dynamic rather than a static disorder is the central theme of Anne Smith's chapter. Smith asks us to step back from conventional approaches to stuttering and adopt new perspectives on how best to investigate and characterize the disorder. She cleverly shows how the evolution of scientific investigations of stuttering can be made analogous to the study of volcanoes. She emphasizes that when we concentrate on the overt symptoms of stuttering (e.g., volcanic eruptions), we lose sight of the dynamic process of stuttering in much the same way that classifying volcanoes according to eruption types fails to account for the dynamics of tectonic plate movement underlying volcanic activity. Thus, we can measure the symptoms of stuttering, such as the amount of air flow or tension in the speech musculature via EMG activity, but isolating their primary source is meaningless unless it is placed within the context of a multifactorial model of stuttering. Smith, as do other contributors, emphasizes the multifactorial inputs to stuttering events and to the resulting generalized disorder of speech. She concentrates on system-internal interactions among the motoric, cognitive, linguistic, and affective components of the speech and language production system.

Smith also emphasizes the likelihood that stuttering is best described by nonlinear models. Speakers move from extremely fluent to extremely disfluent moments, seemingly at random. As Yairi notes in his chapter, stuttering rarely develops along the idealized maturational paths described in our literature. Nonlinearity poses extremely interesting problems for understanding the inputs to behavior, and has interesting implications for seeking relationships between external events (such as situation or family interaction) and stuttering. If stuttering is either somewhat quantal (as in the notion of attractor states), or is characterized by other nonlinear patterns of prediction, then contrasting the degree to which X predicts Y may be highly frustrating for clinicians and researchers alike.

Given the high degree of variability surrounding stuttering, Yairi discusses a number of epidemiological factors that have the potential to either greatly inform or cloud the results of stuttering research and studies of stuttering therapy efficacy. He argues that information we have about the genetics of stuttering and phonological disorders in children who stutter is greatly influenced by the interaction of age and gender of children studied. Yairi notes that many individuals who stutter are the products of both genetic heritage and home environments in which stuttering can be observed in family members of the person under study. Yet, few studies that examine the environmental factors that may precipitate or aggravate stuttering take note of this important fact and distinguish parents who stutter from parents who do not in family analyses of stuttering. Children receive a complex heritage from their parents: predispositions to talent (or weakness) in areas of development, as well as an affective disposition from their ancestors that may aid or hinder them in negotiating life's obstacles (Kagan, 1994; Locke, 1993).

Yairi also expresses some concern about how the issue of spontaneous recovery from stuttering in early childhood has been addressed. Although spontaneous recovery has important ramifications for counseling parents about the necessity or wisdom of clinical intervention in early childhood, it complicates the evaluation of the efficacy of therapies for early stuttering. We are just now beginning to appreciate how spontaneous recovery is related to other factors rarely discussed in reporting either research findings or therapy outcome data, such as subject gender, family history of chronic stuttering, and concomitant disorders of communication. Knowing that such factors have predictive value for some aspects of stuttering, such as spontaneous recovery, raises the standard for reporting subject characteristics in our literature. Whether particular factors result in particular patterns of responsiveness to therapy or to differential performance on research tasks is unknown, but should bear scrutiny.

Guitar leads the theme discussion of how one closes a gap between science and practice in a discipline by examining its fundamental causes. Science and practice often attract differing personalities and abilities, differences that may or may not be easily overcome by cooperation between individuals, and that may be difficult to reconcile within a single individual. After evaluating different models for solving this perennial problem, Guitar concludes that we can make great headway in understanding stuttering and its treatment if we provide more outlets for clinicians to more easily disseminate their treatment findings, so that both their colleagues and researchers can examine them. He also argues that some students in training are better suited to be scientists than clinicians and vice versa. In pairing individuals with respective talents but a common domain of interest, the field could reap the benefits of each other's knowledge and expertise.

Following the Guitar chapter, we shift to a discussion of how the neurobiology and neuropsychology of stuttering facilitates our understanding of the disorder. First, Ludlow considers whether or not we can reliably identify persons who have a distinctive profile of stuttering speech ability and performance that discretely distinguishes them from "fluent" individuals. If stuttering is our perceptual interpretation of events (and speakers) that lie on a continuum, rather than in a unique category, most of our research undertakings will be flawed by an inability to specify who the subjects of study should be. Moreover, many medical conditions are characterized by developmental staging that meaningfully affects the symptoms and treatment of the disorder. Our research rarely stratifies populations into the multiple plausible groupings that Ludlow proposes; changing our subject designs in the ways she suggests may cast new light on our understanding of stuttering. Ludlow also notes subject concerns in specification of the genetic/familial history of stuttering (echoed by Yairi in his chapter), the delineation of other speech-language abilities, and information about physical or emotional events proximal to the first symptoms of stuttering. In her view, clumping subjects for analysis may be one of the reasons we fail to produce research with interpretable and clinically relevant findings.

De Nil takes a different approach to the complexity of stuttering. He notes that the neuropsychological and neurophysiological concomitants of stuttering may be far reaching and may interact. Specifically, he tackles the commonly reported differences between fluent speakers and stutterers for lateralization of speech-language functions. He notes that we cannot ascertain how such lateralization differences arise, but provides new and fascinating data to show that they are modified by therapeutic experience.

Clinicians often remark on the effort required to maintain fluency for the person who stutters. De Nil translates aspects of this effort and its associated construct, attention, into new findings that suggest increased activity in the anterior cingulate for people who stutter. Heightened activity in this region may be associated with decreases in automaticity, providing neurological confirmation of clinician and patient reports. Therapy has the potential to create fluent speech that is mirrored by changes in neural activation patterns, suggesting that some neurological correlates of stuttering, whether they are causative, contributive or simply the by-product of fluency failure, are not etched in stone, but are malleable given appropriate intervention.

Ludlow and De Nil provide a neurological framework for learning more about stuttering; Riley's chapter sets the stage for a discussion of clinically grounded research. She discusses the vast heterogeneity of children seen for treatment of their stuttering. Heterogeneity is the bane of experimental design, but is a fact of life we must deal with. Riley lays out possible evaluation and treatment approaches to describing and accommodating the differences among therapy patients. A second theme of her discussion continues a question raised in other chapters: What should the goals of therapy be? From the perspective of a researcher, clinicians should use data-based procedures for establishing fluency, an argument supported by Ingham and Cordes. However, therapy that creates fluency may not solve the problem of stuttering, if the person who stutters finds using fluency techniques cumbersome or if therapy ignores features of stuttering "under the surface," as Manning suggests in his chapter. Riley strongly endorses making the patient an integral part of therapy, allowing the patient to fully describe their concerns, and encouraging the patient to evaluate the outcomes of therapy in multidimensional ways that go beyond the simple reduction of stuttered moments. Her preliminary therapy outcome questionnaires provoke us to consider how patient satisfaction can be objectively described and explained, and how patient outcome reports relate to clinical goal setting.

In her final comments, Riley, perhaps more strongly than any other contributor, notes that progress is impeded when clinicians and researchers cannot mutually respect one another's approaches to stuttering. Researchers dismiss the results of clinical reports, arguing that their designs are flawed. Too many extraneous variables are uncontrolled, statistical analysis is lacking. Clinicians bypass research reports, finding them either irrelevant (or not made relevant) to clinical practice, or too narrowly controlled to be either practicable or effective with the clients on their caseload. The two groups can continue to disregard one another, but the final casualty is the person who stutters. Riley offers examples of how collaborative work can overcome such obstacles. Her examples are echoed by others in this volume, most obviously De Nil, whose work with Kroll has linked subtle changes in cortical neural activity with a form of precision fluency shaping therapy.

Siegel's chapter focuses on the importance of how our understanding of the nature of stuttering has evolved from a long history of research and clinical practice. Through a review of the contributions made by some of the pioneers in our field (e.g.,Travis, Johnson, Van Riper, and Goldiamond), Siegel reminds us that these individuals recognized the contributions and important ramifications the behavioral, affective, and cognitive components of stuttering had for basic research as well as for clinical practice. Consequently, it seems difficult to separate the contributions of one component from the others. Even when strictly behavioral approaches to stuttering appear to work, are they devoid of affective and cognitive manipulation, or are we merely masking such parameters with focused terminology? As Siegel notes, operant approaches to stuttering, such as time out (TO), are particularly fascinating to analyze within alternative frameworks. What constitutes sufficient reward or punishment to change an individual's behavior? Is one person's punishment another person's reward of sorts (such as use of TO to refocus fluency enhancing knowledge)? Moreover, why should response contingencies alter stuttering in the absence of giving the stutterer tools to accomplish this end?

Manning raises a cautionary note when evaluating the effectiveness of therapy. He suggests that different therapies focus on different aspects of the complexities of stuttering, and thus, that all can claim some modicum of success. Yet, effective therapy of any sort must teach active use of techniques, and must enable their use under conditions that are likely to require a rather mature reaction to fear of failure or distraction. Given this, is it any wonder that many of the substantial number of "recovered" or perceptually quite fluent adult stutterers among us report that success for those who did not recover early in childhood was most likely to come during their mid-20s (Hood et al., 1996)? For patients, clinicians, and researchers, understanding probable windows of opportunity, as well as probable stages of life when maximal progress in therapy is less likely to be achieved is as important as which treatment approach is followed. Some of us compare the cognitive as well as the behavioral aspects of fluency therapy to sports psychology in that the technique is nothing if you can't use it under stress. The maturity of the adult patient (and the lack of such maturity in younger patients) may provide an important component of stuttering therapy not easily captured by describing the clinician's goals and strategies, no matter how scientifically sound.

Manning makes another critical observation that directly impacts our ability to judge the therapeutic outcomes of stuttering intervention. He proposes that many cases of therapeutic success become evident only after clients have left therapy — that recovery from stuttering may have its roots during direct therapy, but flower later in the patient's life, as maturity enables control over the behavioral, cognitive, and affective components of stuttering. If this is true, and testimony from many adult stutterers make this quite likely, it becomes even more difficult to ascertain what aspects of therapy or of the therapeutic relationship are most likely to produce lasting change and why certain aspects of any treatment program are effective or not. If therapeutic success is achieved long after therapy has ended, how are we to measure therapy outcomes realistically? It is also difficult to leave Manning's chapter without acknowledging its other message to researchers and clinicians: What we do, when we do it well, makes a difference. No dispassionate discussion of stuttering can capture the essence of therapeutic success.

Manning's chapter provides a logical segue into Murphy's discussion of two emotional scars that appear early in the development of stuttering: shame and guilt. Too often, emotionality has been highlighted (unsuccessfully) as a possible cause of stuttering behaviors. Rather than as a cause of stuttering, Murphy focuses on what stuttering, like other chronic diseases of childhood and later life, does to the emotional well-being of the individual and his or her family. In this regard, he refers us to literature in psychology, a growing literature base that shows how shame and guilt reactions can adversely affect therapeutic success if they are not recognized and addressed. Moreover, Murphy suggests that clinicians who focus too much on teaching a child to speak fluently may actually increase shame and guilt, albeit inadvertently. For some clients, what may be an unrealistic quest for stutter-free speech through a pure "fluency shaping" approach may create or reinforce deep underlying feelings of shame and guilt about stuttering. These emotions can impede a client's ability to use fluency techniques, and can create ever deepening negative emotions when fluency failure continues. Parents also can develop unrealistic expectations for fluency and, in turn, become the "stuttering police" for their disfluent child. This is consistent with Manning's belief that working only with the "surface structure" of stuttering will not produce effective changes. Shame and guilt represent at least two factors that are not dealt with in fluency shaping therapy. Murphy offers suggestions for clinicians that may positively impact these underlying emotional consequences of stuttering.

The next three chapters by Hill, Gottwald, and Onslow and Packman focus on differing approaches to the treatment of preschool-age children who stutter. First, Hill suggests that understanding an individual child's particular strengths, weaknesses, and personal history is critical to optimum treatment. For the children she sees, no single approach to providing fluency skills appears to work unless it is tailored to the child's ability to use language and to coordinate speech gestures, as two examples. Her case studies illustrate how therapy can be customized to the individual needs of children and families.

Hill also tackles some widely held beliefs about the onset of stuttering. Her clinical research protocol has employed standardized assessment of the stressors that children experience near the onset of stuttering. Using such assessment protocols rather than anecdotal reports, she is unable to link the onset of stuttering to unusual trauma or stress in childhood, thus providing some of the first data to evaluate the claim, often made by parents and clinicians, that stuttering is precipitated by high levels of stress in the child's environment. Although preliminary, her data suggest that further inquiry into this topic has the potential to be quite informative for both clinicians and the families of children who stutter.

Gottwald examines the family dynamics of children who stutter. In particular, she is concerned with evaluating the efficacy of instructions given to parents to ameliorate stuttering symptoms. Among these are speech rate changes, alterations in conversational tempo (turn taking), and changes in linguistic demand. As she notes, there are little data to suggest that parental behaviors precipitate stuttering in children, and the few differences that have been noted between parent–child interactions involving stuttering and nonstuttering children are quite likely to be the result, rather than the cause, of fluency disorder in these children. Gottwald calls for increased research into the efficacy of environmental manipulations to facilitate fluency and the use of other populations of communicatively impaired children as comparisons to parent–child interactions in stuttering. She also proposes that there is a need for the differential evaluation of children's and parents' profiles in the prediction of who may benefit most (and least) from such forms of "indirect" therapy for stuttering.

Onslow and Packman report a very different approach to the treatment of stuttering in children. Using behavior modification procedures, they find that stuttering can be greatly reduced by praising children's fluent attempts and acknowledging and correcting stuttered moments. While the approach is couched within a model of response-contingent reinforcement of speech events, readers may detect features from other approaches to fluency enhancement, such as an emphasis on praising the child when he is successful, acknowledging the child's difficulties rather than ignoring them, and guiding the child through successful motor practice of difficult words. The program has produced impressive results that do not appear to result from spontaneous recovery, a complicating factor in evaluating treatment efficacy in children, as pointed out by Yairi in his chapter. Onslow and Packman note that the actual mechanism by which their treatment approach affects change is unknown, and may rest on a number of factors, including broad changes in the child's interactions with parents in the home environment, as well as parents' skill in identifying and correcting stuttering. Having found a technique that appears to work well for children who are in the initial stages of the disorder, Onslow and Packman plan to conduct additional research on the central agents of change, an excellent example of bridging a clinic–research gap.

Although adults may use response-contingent feedback to refocus their fluency-enhancing efforts, it is unclear how untutored children might do the same. James, Ricciardelli, Rogers, and Hunter (1989) noted that adults without fluency-shaping knowledge were much less likely to show positive responses to operant treatment of stuttering, a pattern reversed by providing the missing therapeutic experience. What mechanisms will eventually account for very young children's apparent responsivity to operant programs such as Lidcombe? Such issues are far from academic: Maximizing the effectiveness of existing programs will require us to understand which components produce the optimal gain, and why.

As we bring this volume to a close, perhaps no two chapters take a more diverse perspective on stuttering research and treatment efficacy research than do Ingham and Cordes, and Starkweather. Ingham and Cordes clearly feel that the field is losing its scientific roots, and detect a trend for clinicians to ignore published outcome and speech production data. Few therapeutic recommendations or programs discussed in a recent journal issue devoted to stuttering treatment escape their critical analysis. There were conference attendees who felt their examples were poorly chosen, because contributors to that special journal issue were given the charge to provide tutorials rather than data-based experimental reports.

Nevertheless, the fact that clinicians appear to gravitate toward certain intervention approaches at the expense of others merits careful consideration. Others (Ryan & Ryan, 1996) have similarly lamented the relative unpopularity in the United States and Europe of operant approaches to stuttering treatment, for example, approaches that have clear documented success in experimental as well as in some clinical environments. Ingham and Cordes contend that clinicians are blind to efficacy data. Yet, most of the clinical efficacy data they cite relate to approaches that focus on reducing the frequency of stuttering to some minimal level. In Manning's view, this is akin to treating only the surface structure of the disorder. Starkweather amplifies this perspective by saying that most efficacy studies in stuttering only address what is an observable, measurable manifestation of the disorder and that a reduction in stuttering alone is not enough to define therapeutic efficacy, particularly if what is created (or neglected in treatment) is a host of undesirable avoidance reactions that go unnoticed. More important, Starkweather contends that before we can claim that a treatment is effective we first have to agree on what we mean by effective, a comment that by the end of the volume, has echoes in almost every chapter.

The second half of Ingham and Cordes' chapter tackles a very different but equally important question. When is therapy for stuttering in children warranted? Recent discussion, stemming primarily from Yairi and colleagues' work (see chap. 4, this volume, and Curlee & Yairi, 1997; Yairi & Curlee, 1997), has highlighted an old debate about whether therapy for very young stuttering children should be deferred until after a given length of time since onset of symptoms has passed. Because a significant number of children who stutter will recover, many within a year to 18 months after their first symptoms appear, Yairi and his colleagues question the efficacy, cost efficiency, and ethics of providing therapy to a group of children in which up to 80% will recover seemingly without intervention. Moreover, they question whether delaying intervention for those who do not spontaneously recover impairs the effectiveness of therapy given later.

Such proposals clearly disturb Ingham and Cordes, who present data to suggest that older children do not respond as favorably to therapeutic intervention as do younger children. Delaying therapy appears to have its costs for the individual child, whether or not other children might receive services that might have been unnecessary if clinicians had crystal balls capable of predicting individual, rather than group outcomes. The question of whether therapy provision is warranted, even to children who might recover at some later point without clinical assistance, is also an important concept to contemplate (Bernstein Ratner, 1997a, 1997b). In medical models, solving a problem sooner than later is rarely viewed as problematic: As a trivial example, headaches will go away by themselves, but people usually prefer to treat them with aspirin for quicker results. Moreover, Ingham and Cordes' discussion of the lowered outcome results for treating older children suggests the possibility that persistence of symptoms over time causes changes in stuttering that make it less tractable to intervention. Whether such changes are behavioral (such as increased habit strength of certain speech behaviors), cognitive, affective or an interaction of all three is not clear. What is clear is that we need properly designed, ethical studies to test the merits of early intervention, and the costs of delaying such intervention. As Ingham and Cordes suggest, retrospective analysis is one approach to answering these questions. Unfortunately, prospective studies will become increasingly difficult to design as new information statistically linking chronicity of childhood stuttering to specific diagnostic factors, such as family history, language function and gender, emerge. As we better understand risk factors for recovery and chronicity, how does one randomly assign children to treatment decisions?

A related question is how one determines when "therapy" begins for stuttering, if parental advisement or environmental manipulation are part of a clinical approach to ameliorating the symptoms of early stuttering. Although not addressed in Ingham and Cordes' chapter, other contributors (e.g., Hill and Gottwald) clearly advocate interventions that are not carried out by speech-language pathologists within the clinical setting. Such recommendations are subject to many of the concerns voiced by both Ingham and Yairi, but carry with them additional problems for scientific investigation of the effectiveness of or need for early intervention. In today's electronically linked and increasingly literate world, it is clear that many parents will employ strategies that are advertised as home-based approaches to stuttering treatment. How such unmonitored parental responses will complicate evaluation of the merits of such recommendations and the outcomes of other treatment recommendations/procedures is not easily measurable, but will complicate outcome investigations of childhood stuttering.

Starkweather's position on the merits of strengthening scientific research into the nature of stuttering and its most effective treatment is directly opposite to that of Ingham and Cordes. He offers a number of criteria for determining whether or not a question legitimately falls within the domain of scientific inquiry, and concludes that the highly variable nature of stuttering, particularly as it evolves over a person's lifetime, makes it peculiarly unsuited to scientific inquiry. In particular, many clinicians and persons who stutter will resonate to the self-reference problem Starkweather discusses. At least part of the disorder of stuttering is a result of reactions to the primary behaviors that characterize it. Because such reactions distance us from the understanding of the primary underlying deficit, and because they infinitely complicate and individualize the behavioral characteristics of the disorder, Starkweather is pessimistic about our ability to gain deep insight into stuttering using the scientific method. From his perspective, much of what can be determined empirically about stuttering treatment has no relevance to whether or not treatment is effective — it is the client who is the ultimate judge of whether recovery from stuttering has been achieved. In this regard, he is most similar in his approach to Riley, who asks her clients to define the efficacy of their treatment.

In conclusion, the chapters in this volume paint a broad picture of research and clinical practice in stuttering. Although it may be debatable whether a gap exists between clinical and empirical science in stuttering, there is clear consensus than stuttering is a highly variable, multidimensional disorder. Even as we struggle to understand how stuttering emerges and what the proximal cause of the "first stutter" is, we are increasingly aware that being a stutterer shapes and changes the behaviors we call stuttering. This phenomenon creates great challenges for researchers and clinicians alike. Stuttering produces negative affective, behavioral, and cognitive behaviors, some of which may have their roots in tangible neurological and psychological consequences to living as a person who stutters. The experience of speaking disfluently, with effort and with fear, may well create the intriguing new images of distinctive speech processing observed in recent neuroimaging studies of adults who stutter, rather than telling us important things about the cause of stuttering. More research needs to be done with children who stutter and recover as well as with those who show resistance to our behavioral methods for treating the disorder. The gap between researchers and clinicians will continue unless we all take a new look at how we conceptualize the disorder, how we conduct our empirical studies, and how we define "successful outcomes." This is our collective challenge for the future. It is one we believe that the field can meet successfully.

REFERENCES

Bernstein Ratner, Nan (1997a). Leaving Las Vegas: Clinical odds and individual outcomes. *American Journal of Speech–Language Pathology, 6*, 29–33.

Bernstein Ratner, Nan (1997b). A response to Yairi and Curlee. *American Journal of Speech-Language Pathology, 6*, 86–88.

Bloodstein, O. (1993). *Stuttering: The search for a cause and cure*. Needham Heights, MA: Allyn & Bacon.

Curlee, R., & Yairi, E. (1997). Early intervention with early childhood stuttering: a critical examination of the data. *American Journal of Speech-Language Pathology, 6*, 8–18.

Hood, S., Daly, D., Guitar, B., Manning, W., Murphy, W., Nelson, L., Quesal, R., Ramig, P. & St. Louis, K. (1996, Nov.) *Successful treatment of fluency disorders: Examples of long-term change*. Paper presented at the annual convention of the American Speech, Language Hearing Association, Seattle, WA.

James, J., Ricciardelli, L., Rogers, P., & Hunter, C. (1989). A preliminary analysis of the ameliorative effects of timeout from speaking on stuttering. *Journal of Speech and Hearing Research, 32*, 604–610.

Kagan, J. (1994). *Galen's prophecy*. NY: Basic Books.

Locke, J. (1993). *The child's path to spoken language*. Cambridge, MA: Harvard University Press.

McFarlane, S., & Goldberg, L. (1987). Factors influencing treatment approaches, prognosis and dismissal criteria for stuttering [Abstract]. *ASHA, 29*, 164–165.

Ryan, B., & Ryan, B. V. (1996). Comments on Kuhr (1994). The rise and fall of operant programs for the treatment of stammering. *Folia Phoniatrica et Logopaedia, 48*, 309–312.

Yairi, E., & Curlee, R. (1997). The clinical–research connection in early childhood stuttering: A response to Zebrowksi and Bernstein Ratner. *American Journal of Speech-Language Pathology, 6*, 85–87.

2 The Best Day to Rethink Our Research Agenda Is Between Yesterday and Tomorrow

Edward G. Conture
Vanderbilt University

This chapter won't help me win any popularity contests. Stuttering theory and therapy, in my opinion, have seldom remained flipped when they could just as easily have been flopped. At times, the windshield wiper has served as the main model for much of the theory and therapy development regarding stuttering. To highlight these fluctuations, a little bit of history is in order.

THE U.S.S. FLUENCY

To paraphrase that famous speech-language pathologist, Bob Dylan (1965), individuals who research stuttering "...don't need a weatherman to know which way the wind blows." Tacking between the shores of nurture and nature, and all points in between, has sailed our good ship that I will dub the U.S.S. Fluency. This vessel, often personned by a theoretically whipsawed crew, displays the dings and dents of a ship that has repeatedly sailed through heavy theoretical seas, and has been becalmed more than a few times by no significant differences.

Aboard ship, the ship's crew du jour, good people, straight and true, exhibits the confidence of those that think they can, and here I quote Professor Dylan again, (1965a), "do what has never been done, that can win what has never been won." Unfortunately, our stalwart crew, anxious to get the cruise underway, is sometimes guilty of leaving the harbor just a little too soon, without taking the time to adequately read the ship's logs from previous voyages. So, typically focused on their own journey, our crew frequently sets sail possessing an unhealthy disregard for the past, and thus, often remains doomed to repeat it. Chanting the sailing mantra, "She'll never go down," a catchy phrase one crew member took to heart after seeing it scrawled on the side of a passing iceberg, ship and crew confidently sail right into the path of theoretical hurricanes and therapeutic sand bars, if not the scientifically rudder-snarling effects of nonsignificant differences.

Sailing From Hot Topic to Hot Topic

Setting a course, sometimes seemingly modeled after an arcade game, our vessel pinballs along, here unloading passengers who weary of the voyage, there taking on new ones eager to "get it on" for science and Van Riper, not to mention promotion and tenure, discarding old equipment like a stripper, gathering new like a shop-til-you-dropper, and catching up on the mails in the form of journal publications. In essence, our crew gradually comes to discover that buggy whips, hula hoops, spats, and DAF don't garner market share quite the way they did when they and their ship first left port.

Oh sure, a mutiny occasionally occurs aboard ship, and the ship's steering wheel is personned by young turks and turkettes, but by and large, the crew gets a little older, a bit sea worn, and sort of fed up with the food on board. So, it is little wonder that our crew quickly disembarks when arriving at a new port (read theory). This permits a new crew to come aboard and set sail in search of theoretical booty. Of course, our new crew, much like our old crew—new and old often restricting their ship-to-shore communication to semaphore (better known as yearly poster sessions at national conferences)—has a less than adequate understanding of or concern with the ship's past voyages. In brief, some of our crew has little concern for realities other than their own. Thus, our ship—that sometimes appears more flagging than flagged—sets off again, bound for glory, which, unfortunately, routinely takes off without a forwarding address just before our ship arrives.

Charting a More Purposeful Course

What can be done to encourage our ship to sail in a less pinball-like, more programmatic fashion? Of course, I have no definitive midcourse corrections—true waffle artist that I am—but I think I have met the enemy and he or she looks a bit like thee and me. Without doubt, our stalwart ship will always cruise the uncharted seas of speculation, occasionally spotting islands of facts, and from time to time will land on some solid point of data. And try as we might, it is quite difficult, a priori, to influence the motion of the theoretical ocean. We can, however, build a bit more adaptable ship, and more often rig and sail it in the most efficient, consequential, and productive way possible.

What would be some of the instructions I'd give the crew of such a ship? Well, the following pearls of nonwisdom are submitted for the present as well as future crew's consideration. No, dear readers, you are not about to enter the theoretical twilight zone. Furthermore, this is not a "my way or the highway" manifesto. But I may be a bit strong in my criticisms and suggestions.

Sailing Instructions

Basically, my four-part sailing instructions (i.e., main message of this chapter) are:

    1. Eschew "grind-to-find" research (i.e., throwing out a large net of unmotivated variables, hoping to drag something in with the tide of results) of any kind, but particularly regarding the disability of stuttering.

    2. Stoke up the theoretical fires that underpin and permit testing of possible sources of impairment.

    3. Ask not what treatment efficacy research can do for you and your program but what you and your program can do for treatment efficacy research.

    4. Bring the handicap of stuttering out of the closet, let the sun shine on it, and be not afraid to objectify it.

CATALOGUING OF FACTS DOES NOT NECESSARILY CREATE A KNOWLEDGE BASE

Clearly, if one is to make an omelette, some eggs are going to have to be broken. To begin, let's crack open the product of our collective researches, past and present. What do we find? By and large, a stunning array of facts, a literal cornucopia of data spilling forth seemingly without end. Truly, our cup runneth over with facts. However, such research typically reflects, no matter how elegant, no matter how carefully done, no matter how novel the findings, a mere cataloguing or description of facts. Granted, the influence and significance of past as well as present descriptive research can and should not be disregarded. It has informed us tremendously about the disability of stuttering. Indeed, we owe a great deal to those who have informed us about the disability of stuttering. These facts represent our unique and important contribution to the knowledge bank, from which we all withdraw. Is there more to learn about the disability of stuttering? Absolutely, but what I'd like to advocate, at this time, is charting a course backwards—into full-blown theory development and testing—as well as forward—into objectification and documentation of the handicap of stuttering as well as the efficacy of our treatment for stuttering.

Some Principles to Guide Us

Ideally, our research should flow from ideas about reality, rather than simply describe, catalog, and categorize reality. I mean, we could, if we wanted to, count the number of trees with leaves of a certain shape and report that. But why? Far better, in my opinion, to have a theory that the durability of leaves in wind is affected by their shape, and then test that theory out, in a wind tunnel, with different shapes of leaflike objects and see which leaves last longer than others without shredding, and so forth. Both approaches—description versus theory-driven hypothesis testing—provide us with information. However, the latter goes one step beyond by providing us with *insight*, an enhanced, expanded understanding of the mechanism(s) that create, influence, and so forth, such information. Furthermore, like collagen in a bone-fusion operation, such theory-driven insight provides the bridge on which further information can be gathered and the means by which our field's knowledge base can be expanded and refined.

It is not only theory-driven, hypothesis-testing studies of *impairment* that are needed. We also need studies that relate to the *handicap* of stuttering as well. Although our profession and those related to it need and want to understand the impairment, the public we serve often wants to know and is vitally interested in the handicap. Indeed, it is probably safe to say that it is at the level of handicap that most people who stutter come to most acutely feel and experience the disability of stuttering. Consequently, the need for careful, controlled and objective study of the handicap of stuttering is of paramount importance.

Changing a Disability Does Not Necessarily Change a Handicap

For example, many studies of treatment with adults who stutter strongly suggest that prolonged, slow speech is most effective in terms of behavioral change. That's great, that's fine, that's wonderful. However, what about the effects, if any, of such treatment on the handicap of stuttering? Do the people who stutter who receive such therapy feel, think, or act as if they are less disadvantaged academically, emotionally, psychologically, socially, or vocationally? Unfortunately, this seemingly solid fact (i.e., that prolonged, slow speech increases fluency) has all too often been taken as advice on what brand of therapy to buy. Yes, it is very reasonable to feel, think or believe that improvements in stuttering, the behavior, the disability, lead to improvements in the handicap of stuttering. But how firm is this belief, what is the quantity and quality of data upon which these beliefs are based? What evidence do we have that reduction in the frequency of stuttering, in and of itself, leads to reductions in the disadvantages of stuttering, be they vocational, academic, social, and so forth?

It is clear, changes in one (disability) is related to reductions in the other (handicap), but how and to what degree? For example, can we say to an individual who has just made a significant change/reduction in their stuttering, "You will feel, perceive, and experience no disadvantages stemming from stuttering, from now on, in any aspects of your life"? If we are going to operate from a basis of knowledge all the time, not just when it suits us, then I think a truthful answer to my question has to be as follows: "We do not know enough to unequivocally tell a person who has just significantly reduced the frequency of their stuttering that there will be no further disadvantages in their life related to their stuttering." For now, however, let us turn our attention away from what we don't know, to that which we do know and how we might know even more, in a more reliable fashion.

In the space allotted for this chapter, I really can't, even if I knew, tell you all that we have learned about stuttering from research. I can tell you, however, where I believe that more research seems to be needed and how we might go about meeting that need.

THREE LEVELS OF A DISORDER: IMPAIRMENT, DISABILITY, AND HANDICAP

To provide a framework for addressing these research needs, I would like to quickly review the three levels of any disorder (Curlee, 1993; Prins, 1991; Yaruss, 1988). The first level, *impairment*, involves, in essence, the cause(s) of the disorder; one example of research conducted in this area might be PET scans of cortical activity during the speech production of people who stutter (e.g., Fox, et al., 1996). The second level, *disability*, involves the behavioral manifestations of the disorder. An example of research conducted in this area might be a tabulation of the frequency of stuttering behaviors during the speech of children who do and do not stutter (e.g., Yairi, 1997). The third, or *handicap*, level of the disorder involves the disadvantages (of any kind) imposed by the disorder. One example of research conducted in this area might be the administration of the Inventory of Communication Attitudes (Watson, 1988) to assess how individuals who stutter believe and/or feel their problem has influenced their personal and/or professional lives.

Again, using these three levels of disorders as a frame, we can quickly examine what research has taught us. First, as I've said before, and as a quick review of our textbooks (e.g., Bloodstein, 1995) will show, we have an amazing amount of information pertaining to *disability* (i.e., what stuttering sounds like, looks like, etc.). The quantity and quality of this information is, to borrow a popular phrase, "awesome." Unfortunately, this large repository of information is not always well appreciated by those inside as well as outside the fields of speech, hearing, and language. Why? I believe this is because, despite our valiant attempts to understand impairment, much of what we have actually come to understand is disability. Although it is true that we have islands of facts about impairment (i.e., cause), many of these facts are surrounded by a vast sea of speculation. Further, we have seemingly taken for granted that the disability (e.g., frequency of stuttering) is identical conceptually to the handicap. Of course, it is difficult for someone to experience the handicap of stuttering without the disability of stuttering, but the disability does not necessarily circumscribe or define the handicap. Indeed, the subjective feelings of disadvantage surrounding the behavioral manifestations vary widely in number and nature.

As mentioned earlier, we are, for example, relatively clueless with regard to how our treatment of the disability of stuttering influences the handicap of stuttering. This is a state of affairs that must change for our treatment regimens to grow and be responsive to the entirety of the disorder of stuttering, not just to those aspects of the disorder that are externally observable and where numerically apparent changes are relatively easy to produce. Likewise, although many, many attempts have been made to document *treatment efficacy* for children, teenagers and adults who stutter (e.g., Blood & Conture, 1998; Conture, 1996; Ingham, 1993), considerable uncertainty remains, regarding, among other things (a) the appropriate definition of success (short-, medium-, and long-term) and (b) the most pertinent dependent variables to measure.

What is needed? Well, to answer that, we have to briefly consider how knowledge, in any field, is developed, tested, and refined.

DESCRIPTION, MODEL, AND THEORY: BUILDING BLOCKS FOR ANY KNOWLEDGE-BASED PROFESSIONAL DISCIPLINE

Abstracting from Olswang's (1993) coverage of this topic, there are three inter-related levels of science involved in the development of knowledge. The first (and most concrete) level, *description*, involves the cataloguing of all relevant behavior. As a hypothetical example, we could describe all the semantic, syntactic, and phonologic correlates of instances of stuttering during conversation. The second level, *model*, involves the identification of principles that account for relevant behavior. As a hypothetical example, we could specify how the number and nature of clausal constituents in an utterance underlies or explains apparent correlations between phonetic, semantic, and grammatical elements seemingly associated with stuttering. The third level, *theory*, attempts to test a finite set of principles that concur with (or flow from) the model and, by so doing, reveals the mechanism or processes that account for the phenomenon under study. As a hypothetical example of theory, we might speculate that more cognitive/linguistic planning time is required for longer and more complex clauses and, therefore, if planning time is truncated or interrupted (either externally or internally), the resulting overt speech should contain more errors and/or disfluencies. If we take these three levels—description, model, and theory—and apply them to the three aspects of a disorder (i.e., impairment, disability, and handicap), we may be able to more clearly specify what research has or has not taught us and what it still needs to tell and/or teach us.

IMPAIRMENT, DISABILITY, AND HANDICAP MEET DESCRIPTION, MODELING, AND THEORY

Modeling and Theorizing about Impairment

In terms of impairment, there is a clear need for theory development. Theory is the engine that drives organized, systematic, and motivated assessment of cause. Of course, the more practical reader might wonder: Why continue to study impairment, why continue to develop theories? My answer to this is that our field and our very livelihood may depend on it. If ours is a profession (and I think it is), it is supposedly based on or grounded in a body of knowledge. Such a body of knowledge should not be a mere collection of facts, something similar to a professional-knowledge version of a butterfly or stamp collection. Our body of knowledge needs to be developed, understood, and explained relative to underlying notions about what causes stuttering. Indeed, it is theory rather than fact that we most often rely on when responding to our clients, their parents, the press, and other professionals when they ask, "What causes stuttering"? In essence, a search for impairment is a search for one of the cornerstones of our profession.

Describing Disability

Although description of relevant behaviors may be of value to an understanding of the disability, only through theory will we uncover relations, underlying mechanisms and processes, and rule-governed phenomena associated with cause. We have already collected a great deal of information about disability. Of course, a great deal more needs to be known, but we really need to curtail mere grind-to-find research (i.e., research investigations that measure a large number of variables in the hopes that somehow, somewhere, something will turn up). Our descriptions of stuttering should be motivated by our notions of what we think causes stuttering and/or what we think may be contributing to the handicap of stuttering, and not merely gathering more data with which to further describe the disability.

Describing the Handicap

Stuttering, for someone who stutters, particularly as they grow older, involves more than just speech and speech-related behaviors associated with instances of stuttering. It involves handicap, or the disadvantages that relate to and/or result from the disability. To study handicap, we need to develop principles that may account for why stuttering and/or selected aspects of stuttering are perceived by stutterers and/or their listeners as disadvantages, as negatives. Here, we must not be afraid to be appropriately subjective, to uncover not only the overt surface behavior but the related, at times less overt, underlying thoughts, feelings, and attitudes (see Manning, chap. 10, this volume). It is entirely possible that these relatively covert aspects have as much influence as the more overt, surface aspects with regard to what is and what is not believed to be handicapping. Indeed, if stuttering is not a handicap, why search for the impairment that causes it? Why try to solve something that doesn't warrant solving? The answer is that stuttering often is a significant handicap. Its presence can handicap a person academically, emotionally, psychologically, socially and vocationally. On the surface, such a statement regarding handicap seems quite reasonable. However, it is difficult to assess the veracity of this statement because we lack sufficient objective evidence reported in relevant peer-reviewed literature describing the degree and manner to which stuttering handicaps people across the life span.

Modeling and Theorizing About Treatment Efficacy and Testing Such Models and Theories

Finally, our research must address the *effectiveness* of our treatment, but even this must relate to notions of impairment. If, as some claim, therapy is always effective, why worry about impairment? It's like saying, "if aspirin always works, who cares why?" The truth, however, is that our therapies are not always effective for all people who stutter under all circumstances at all times. And one of the reasons that our therapies are not always effective is that we still don't understand what causes a person to stutter. Rather, in therapy, we most often use what seems to work, at least for a while—but seldom are we really clear why something works.

Instead, what we should be doing in therapy is that which our understanding of cause tells us is relevant to modify and change. Particularly with experimental treatments, we need to employ theoretically motivated treatment procedures, rather than procedures that work but for no known or apparent reason. Likewise, as mentioned before, we have less than adequate understanding of how our therapies influence the handicapping aspects of stuttering. For example, does the life of an individual who stutters become easier, more enjoyable, and so forth as result of our treatments? Our measures, as Blood and Conture (in press) suggest, need to go beyond disability, to the study of handicap, quality of life, functionality (e.g., Franken, van Bezooijen & Boves, 1997), and naturalness (e.g., Onslow, Hayes, Hutchins, & Newman, 1992) of speech.

Designing Ways to Gather Information About the Effectiveness of Our Treatments

Given that space is limited, and that the topic is broad, I must restrict my coverage of this important issue. To do so, I finish this chapter by addressing one aspect of research, studies of treatment efficacy, that touches on all of the above—description, modeling and theory—but from a very practical standpoint: Does what we do work and how do we know that it does? There are abundant reviews of the literature in this field (e.g., Blood & Conture, 1998; Conture, 1996; R. Ingham, 1984; J. Ingham, 1993) and thus, I will not cover that which has already been discussed elsewhere. Instead, what I'd like to do is discuss some of the ways we have gathered and some of the ways we should gather information about the effectiveness of our treatments.

Abstracting from the excellent descriptions of Ventry and Schiavetti (1986), and of Schiavetti and Metz (1996), particularly the latter, one can look at several ways that treatment efficacy has been studied. I use Schiavetti and Metz's symbols to do so: X = administration of experimental treatment and O = observation and/or measurement of dependent variables (e.g., frequency of stuttering). Because this essentially involves designs for studies, I follow Schiavetti and Metz's reasonable suggestions for dividing such designs into (1) weak(er), (2) strong(er), and (3) strongest. Before I describe these designs, I need to provide a bit of terminology.

Treatment Efficacy: Definition of Terms

If at all possible, I suggest that a motivating or theoretically driven principle or reason for using a particular treatment or treatment procedure be established before administration of experimental treatment. Once such a principle/reason is established, the investigator faces a number of methodological considerations. In other fields, such considerations typically involve the use of *clinical trials* or any research activity involving the administration of a test treatment to subjects in order to evaluate the test. Although some of the treatment efficacy research in stuttering could loosely be described as involving clinical trials, much of it would not qualify as *randomized controlled clinical trials* (which have been described by some as the "gold standard" of treatment efficacy research). The randomized controlled clinical trial involves one or more test treatments, at least one control treatment, all subjects simultaneously enrolled and followed up, and subjects randomly assigned to groups. Furthermore, although some describe "therapy studies" in stuttering as involving the assessment of efficacy, efficacy more appropriately refers to the extent to which a specific intervention or treatment produces a beneficial result under *ideally controlled* conditions when administered or monitored by *experts*. Rather, most therapy studies in stuttering involve the assessment of *effectiveness*, or the extent to which a specific intervention or treatment, when used *in the field* (by appropriate but nonexpert professionals), does what it is intended to do for a specific population. In an ideal world, treatment efficacy research in the area of stuttering would be driven by a notion of impairment (i.e., procedures based on theoretically motivated ideas about cause) and would apply clinical trial methodologies while studying how treatment influences both the disability and handicap of stuttering (see Moscicki, 1993 for further discussion of these terms and concepts). This is, however, far from an ideal world and we must consider some of the realities that have shaped past and will shape present and future research in this area.

Typical Treatment Efficacy Designs: Some "Weaker" Designs

As mentioned earlier, much of what follows is based on Schiavetti and Metz's (1996, pp.120-148) excellent, in-depth coverage of designs germane to treatment efficacy research. A common design found in the literature is the "one-time" or "one-shot" case study. Typically, this involves one group of subjects using a *during* Therapy

(X) and *after* Therapy (O_1) design. With this design, success of therapy is determined by subject behavior in O_1. Although the problems with this design may be obvious, one of its more glaring concerns is that it lacks a pretreatment comparison measure as well as a no-treatment control group. In other words, it is hard to know if therapy is of benefit without knowing what the subjects' behavior was before treatment and how a comparable group of subjects would have performed without treatment.

A second, somewhat similar design described by Schiavetti and Metz (1996) is the *one group pretest* (O_1) *therapy* (X) *posttest* (O_2) study. Like the one-shot design previously described, this design also involves one group of subjects. With this design, success of therapy is determined by the difference between O_1 and O_2 (pre- vs. posttest). While an improvement over the one-shot design, it also lacks a no-treatment control group. Unfortunately, far too many treatment studies of stuttering involve either the one-shot or one-group designs.

Typical Treatment Efficacy Designs: Some "Stronger" Designs

Although there are many designs seemingly stronger than the first two discussed, Schiavetti and Metz (1996) suggested two that seem immediately applicable: (1) *matched randomized pretest–posttest control groups* and (2) *ABA time series*. With (1), two groups of subjects are matched for relevant variables (e.g., age, stuttering severity) and then randomly assigned to either an experimental or a control group. The experimental group is tested before therapy (O_1), during therapy (X) and after therapy (O_2) whereas the matched control group is tested only before therapy (O_3) and after therapy (O_4). With this design, success of therapy is determined by comparing the O_1-O_2 difference versus the O_3-O_4 difference. This design allows for comparison of treated subjects to a comparable no-treatment control group, and its index of success involves posttreatment comparison to pretreatment, rather than therapy only, as with the one-group pretest design. Problems (some of which are obvious) with this design include identifying appropriate matching variables (a universal concern for all paired- or related-samples studies), withholding of services from the control group (although this can be remediated, to some degree, by offering withheld services to the control group at the end of the study), and remembering to employ inferential statistics appropriate to related, correlated or paired samples.

The second type of a so-called stronger design, described by Schiavetti and Metz, the *ABA time series* design, which typically involves one group of subjects, eliminates the problem of withholding services, because all subjects receive services (for a general introduction to time series studies, see Gottman, 1981). It does not require a no-treatment control group because every subject is his or her own control. With the ABA design, all subjects are observed several times (O_1 O_2 O_3) *before* treatment (A), then several times again (O_5 O_6 O_7) *during* treatment (B) and then several times (O_8 O_9 O_{10}) *after* treatment (A). With this so-called ABA design, success of treatment can be assessed by examining differences between; before (A)–therapy (B), therapy (B)–after (A) or before (A)–after (A). Although this design allows the investigator to make many, many observations of a relatively small number of subjects (and hence is an excellent source of information about within-subject variability), its ability to generalize to the population as a whole is not always immediately apparent. Typically, investigators reporting the results of ABA studies of treatment efficacy present curves depicting "data trends" between, for example, *A*, *B*, and *A*. Although these graphs or curves clearly describe the trends for one or for a small group of subjects, it is not immediately obvious whether these data trends circumscribe the behavior of the larger population of all subjects of interest.

The generalizability of findings resulted from ABA designs may be strengthened if error bars or confidence intervals are displayed around the many ABA data points (obviously something a bit more meaningful when the data points portrayed come from more than one subject; for further analytical considerations involving time series designs, see Bakeman & Gottman, 1986, pp. 175–189). These error bars or confidence intervals may help provide the reader with some appreciation for the central tendency and dispersion of scores for the particular set of data. On the other hand, probably the best way to insure generalizability of findings resulting from ABA studies of small sets of subjects is to replicate them with another relatively small set of subjects (something that is often done). Such replications increase generalizability to the population at large beyond the small set of subjects studied. Despite these concerns, the ABA design remains one of the more useful designs to study the influence of treatment on stuttering. The ABA design is especially useful, in my opinion, for testing new or modified versions of older therapies, to for assessing whether further study of such therapy with a larger group of subjects appears warranted.

Schiavetti and Metz (1996) cover one last, seemingly elegant, but perhaps unrealistic design for stuttering; the *Solomon randomized four-group* design. This design was developed to control for or to allow study of the influence of pretest (i.e., before treatment) observation on treatment itself as well as after treatment behavioral change. Subjects are matched and then randomly assigned to groups 1–4 as shown in Table 2.1.

With this design, success of therapy might be assessed by averaging O_2 and O_5 and comparing to the average of O_4 and O_6. In this way, not only can the

TABLE 2.1
Solomon Randomized Four - Group Design

	Pretest	Experimental	Therapy	Posttest
Group 1	O_1	X	O_2	
Group 2	O_3			O_4
Group 3		X	O_5	
Group 4				O_6

investigator understand whether treatment was effective, but also how the presence or absence of pretreatment observation might have influenced therapy or posttherapy performance. For example, if the O_2-O_4 difference is greater than the O_5-O_6 difference, then we might suspect such pretest influence.

In Actuality, All Designs are Flawed for One Reason or Another. In truth, no design for the study of treatment efficacy is without its flaws. Some designs require relatively large groups of subjects, something neither practical nor even desirable, especially for exploratory studies of new or experimental therapy procedures. Other designs require withholding of services, something that may be of particular concern, even if such services are eventually offered, with young children for whom timely treatment may be of the essence. Others provide a large amount of data on a small number of subjects, but do not immediately make clear whether these findings would be generalizable to the population at large. As behavior varies, so do clients. The same behavior may come from several sources and these different sources may significantly impact the nature and number of changes different people make. Furthermore, performance variables such as perfectionism, inattention, impulsivity, hyperactivity, and so forth can interfere with learning, and so, presumably with treatment. One size designs will not fit all studies of treatment effectiveness or efficacy.

Indeed, in this writer's opinion, we waste precious time and resources striving for a completely problem-free design. Rather, we need a design that is sufficient for all normal purposes. Our goal should be to use designs that allow us to know, with a reasonable degree of confidence, that this or that treatment is either better, the same, or worse than no treatment at all. We also need designs that will help us develop some idea of why our treatment results look the way they do. I think that these are rather simple and obtainable (but not easily achieved) goals.

CONCLUSIONS

Whereas there must be a physical end to this chapter, there is no end to the topic(s) it discusses, particularly the topic of treatment efficacy/effectiveness. I have tried to highlight the need to (1) increase the development of theory to test cause/ impairment in stuttering, (2) decrease mere description of disability, (3) increase our understanding of handicap, and (4) refine methodological guidelines and standards for conducting treatment efficacy research. Treatment efficacy research, in particular, deserves singling out in these concluding remarks because we must, to survive as a profession, provide at least some of the things expected of us as we become increasingly involved with managed health care.

Developing a Short List of Best-Practices Designs

As mentioned earlier, I think it is clear that a one-size-fits-all design for treatment efficacy research for stuttering is neither possible nor desirable. However, it is just as clear that we could develop a short list of designs and strongly encourage investigators to use one or more of these when conducting their research.

Getting Treatment Efficacy Research Out of the Clinical Closet

Next, although both clinical and laboratory settings provide the control needed to answer various questions, we must face the reality that some of our findings do not generalize well to situations outside the clinic and/or laboratory. Does this mean that we have to abandon our clinical-based studies and favor research conducted in the subject's home? No, for it is just as likely that observations in the home do not generalize to other, equally important settings, such as schools. Rather, we need to know about the relationships between changes in the clinic and changes in other settings. For example, knowing that a 50% decrease in stuttering in the clinic for a given approach will typically result in only a 25% decrease in stuttering at home is valuable information. Putting our collective heads in the sand and pretending, ignoring, or hoping that clinic changes absolutely and consistently mirror changes in the home, school, or workplace may provide us with a degree of comfort, but the problem will still be there once we pull our heads above ground.

Being Able to Routinely Use Somewhat Disfluent Speech May Be More Preferable Than Possessing the Capacity for Fluent Speech That Is Never Used

The purpose of speaking is to communicate our ideas, feelings, thoughts, desires, and wants with others. When an individual cannot speak when, where, with whom, and about what he or she wants, his speech is less than usable, regardless of its fluency. Simply put, we need to keep our eye on the prize: It is utility, not fluency, of speech that is our ultimate goal (see Conture & Guitar, 1993 for a similar discussion). Fluency is a vehicle to obtain the goal; it is not the goal itself. We need to know more, much more, about the utility, usability, and functionality of the fluent speech induced by our various therapies. A perfectly mended, formerly broken leg is of little practical value if the person doesn't or refuses to walk, run, or otherwise use that leg.

Easy Come, Easy Go.

Although changes in fluency shouldn't have to take 5 years, neither should we expect such changes to last if they occur in the space of a weekend. We must, for the good of our field, our clients, and ourselves, resist the urge to produce changes "in the first quarter," and then act as if that constitutes a long-term change. Instead, we must, as a group, conduct the difficult, at times discouraging, but necessary long-term follow-up of our clients to see how their change has or has not lasted. For example, Lincoln and Onslow (1997) provided long-term, 4 years posttreatment follow-up data with preschoolers; this is the type of information we'd like to see more and more investigators report.

So, as a field we are challenged by the public to prove that what we do works, at least sufficiently well to receive adequate reimbursement for our services. The same public increasingly expects us to have some data-based insights into the causes of stuttering. Likewise, the public has become increasingly aware of the fact that there is more to the problem of stuttering than stuttering itself; that is, that stuttering does have social, vocational, and other disadvantages. Can we meet this troika of challenges: (1) reasonable proof that treatment works, (2) theory-driven knowledge of cause, and (3) factual understanding of handicap? Yes, I think we can, but it should be clear that this job will be dangerous before we agree to it. Socrates reportedly said that the unexamined life is not worth living. I submit that the unexamined profession is not worth pursuing. So, our journey to the center of our profession, here in the waning days of the 20th century, will not be for the faint of heart. However, it will be a journey having great consequence, reward, and value. Indeed, if most of us can steer a consequential path, our profession will not only survive but thrive well into the 21st century.

REFERENCES

Bakeman, R., & Gottman, J. (1986). *Observing interaction: An introduction to sequential analysis*. New York: Cambridge University Press.

Blood, G., & Conture, E. (1998). Fluency disorders. In C. Frattali (Ed.), *Outcome measurement in speech-language pathology*, pp. 387–405. New York: Thieme Medical Publishers, Inc.

Bloodstein, O. (1995). *A handbook on stuttering*. San Diego: Singular Press.

Conture, E. (1996). Treatment efficacy: Stuttering. *Journal of Speech and Hearing Research, 39*, S18–S26.

Conture, E., & Guitar, B. (1993). Evaluating efficacy of treatment of stuttering: School-age children. *Journal of Fluency Disorders, 18*, 253–287.

Curlee, R. (1993). Evaluating treatment efficacy for adults: Assessment of stuttering disability. *Journal of Fluency Disorders, 18*, 319–331.

Fox, P., Ingham, R., Ingham, J., Hirsch, T., Downs, J., Martin, C., Jerabek, P., Glass, T., & Lancaster, J. (1996). A PET study of the neural systems of stuttering. *Nature, 382*, 158-162.

Franken, M. C., van Bezooijen, R., & Boves (1997). Stuttering and communicative suitability of speech. *Journal of Speech and Hearing Research, 40*, 83–94.

Gottman, J. (1981). *Time series analysis: Introduction for social scientists*. New York: Cambridge University Press.

Lincoln, M., & Onslow, M. (1997). Long-term outcome of early intervention for stuttering. *American Journal of Speech-Language Pathology, 6*, 51–58.

Ingham, J. C. (1993). Current status of stuttering and behavior modification: I. Recent trends in the application of behavior modification in children and adults. *Journal of Fluency Disorders, 18*, 27–55.

Ingham, R. (1984). *Stuttering and behavior therapy*. San Diego: College-Hill Press.

Moscicki, E. (1993). Fundamental methodological considerations in controlled clinical trials. *Journal of Fluency Disorders, 18*, 183–196.

Olswang, L. (1993). Treatment efficacy research: A paradigm for investigating clinical practice and theory. *Journal of Fluency Disorders, 18*, 125–131.

Onslow, M., Hayes, B., Hutchins, L., & Newman, D. (1992). Speech naturalness and prolonged-speech treatments for stuttering: Further variables and data. *Journal of Speech and Hearing Research, 35*, 274–282.

Prins, D. (1991). Theories of stuttering as event and disorder: Implications for speech production processes. In H. Peters, W. Hulstijn, & C. W. Starkweather (Eds.), *Speech motor control and stuttering* (pp. 571–580). Amsterdam, The Netherlands: Elsevier.

Schiavetti, N., & Metz, D. (1996). *Evaluating research in speech pathology and audiology* (3rd ed.). Boston: Allyn & Bacon.

Ventry, I., & Schiavetti, N. (1986). *Evaluating research in speech pathology and audiology* (2nd ed.). New York: Macmillan.

Watson, J. (1988). A comparison of stutterers' and nonstutterers' affective, cognitive, and behavioral self-reports. *Journal of Speech and Hearing Research, 31*, 377–385.

Yairi, E. (1997). Disfluency characteristics of childhood stuttering. In R. Curlee & G. Siegel (Eds.), *Nature and treatment of stuttering: New directions* (pp. 49–78). Boston: Allyn & Bacon.

Yaruss, J. S. (1998). Describing the consequences of disorders: Stuttering and the international classification of impairments, disabilities and handicaps. *Journal of Speech, Language and Hearing Research, 41,* 249–257.

3 Stuttering: A Unified Approach to a Multifactorial, Dynamic Disorder

Anne Smith
Purdue University

The goal of this chapter is to propose a global, unified strategy that will aid our attempts to understand and to treat stuttering. I do not suggest that all of us will agree about all aspects of stuttering; we will not. What I propose is that, if we could agree on some of the broader issues that drive research and treatment, progress would be more rapid. Furthermore, a widely shared, comprehensive approach to stuttering would provide a critically needed foundation for communicating about the disorder. A shared framework would improve communication among researchers and clinicians, and in turn, communication with individuals who stutter, with parents, with teachers, and with society at large. The myriad approaches to stuttering research and treatment have created a fragmented and confusing literature on the disorder. Papers traditionally were written as if the "answer" to stuttering could be discovered within whatever clinical or experimental approach a particular group believed at a particular time. Those of us who have been in the field for some time have witnessed the recycling of old "answers," for example, the current reemergence of DAF and feedback theories of stuttering (e.g., Harrington, 1988). However, there has been growing agreement among many researchers and clinicians that stuttering is a multifactorial disorder (Conture, 1990; Riley & Riley, 1979; Smith, 1990a; Smith & Kelly, 1997; Starkweather, Gottwald, & Halfond, 1990; Van Riper, 1982; Wall & Myers, 1995; Zimmermann, 1980; Zimmermann, Smith, & Hanley, 1981). The present chapter explores the possible ways in which a multifactorial and dynamic model of stuttering can accelerate and expand progress in our field.

A key to progress is the realization that the traditional, static units of disfluency counts, for example, part-word repetitions or sound prolongations, are convenient fictions that have misled many of us into thinking of stuttering as a static entity (Smith & Kelly, 1997). Stuttering is not a series of "stutter events." Stuttering is a dynamic disorder, and the many processes related to stuttering can be observed at multiple levels, within time frames that range from milliseconds to lifespans, and with many different types of tools. We are not alone, however, in being tempted to simplify a complex, dynamic phenomenon within a static conceptual framework.

As an analogy, consider the scientific study of volcanoes. Anyone who has witnessed a film of a volcanic eruption knows that volcanoes are certainly dynamic. However, the earliest scientific efforts to study volcanoes did not attempt to account for dynamic aspects of volcanoes. Instead, the focus of volcanologists in the 19th century was on counting and classifying volcanoes (Decker & Decker, 1991).

Classification was based on the shape of the landform (e.g., caldera vs. cone) and the type and shape of eruptive materials (see Figure 3.1 for variations in landform and gas clouds). Work on counting and classifying continued until the 1960s, and six major types were identified; Fissure, Strombolian, Hawaiian, Vulcanian, Pelean, and Plinian. However, the shortcomings of this classification scheme were readily apparent.

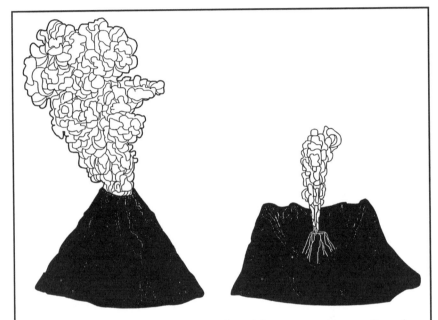

FIG. 3.1. The science of volcanology was focused for many years upon counting and classifying volcanoes. However, the field moved beyond this narrow focus with the introduction of a comprehensive theory of the plate tectonics. Like volcanologists, scientists who investigate stuttering must move beyond classification and counts to a unified theory of stuttering.

> Like all generalities, classification of eruption types and volcanic landforms can be taken only so far. Volcanic eruptions are caused by many factors, ... and the shape of a volcanic mountain may be the end result of a series of eruptions that vary in location, type, size, and sequence... Naming the types of volcanoes, while helpful, is only a beginning in trying to understand them. (Decker & Decker, 1991, pps. 13-15)

A major shift in paradigm for the study of volcanoes occurred in the 1960s when mapping of the magnetic fields of the Earth's seafloor provided convincing support for the theory of plate tectonics. According to this theory, the Earth's surface is broken into 12 major plates that move in relation to one another. This concept explained why the occurrence of volcanoes is not random; rather, they exist in chains along the Earth's surface. Volcanic chains are now understood to occur at the edges of the plates. The plate tectonic theory provided a truly unified account of volcanoes and also explained many aspects of earthquakes. In addition, the processes underlying volcanic eruptions could now be conceptualized in terms of the dynamics of plate movement.

One of the important consequences of this global theory is that the many methods of observing volcanoes and attempting to forecast eruptions could be interpreted within a common framework. For example, McGuire, Kilburn, and Murray (1995) provided a schematic summary of approximately 20 methods currently in use to monitor volcanoes. These methods include magnetic, chemical, thermal, and geoelectrical measures. An important advance for the field of volcanology is that scientists employing magnetic measurements do not have a magnetic theory of volcanoes; those using chemical assays do not have a chemical theory. Rather, the diverse data are brought back to bear on a common account of global plate tectonics.

In an era when we are ready to develop a dynamic, multifactorial, comprehensive theory of stuttering, we are impeded by misguided faith, faith in the reality of the "units" of stuttering and faith in the possibility of finding a simple, single cause of stuttering. A shift in paradigm for research and treatment of stuttering will depend on our taking at least these two steps. The first step is to recognize the limitations of the analysis and explanation of stuttering by the traditional units of disfluency counts. These are the "smoke" of the volcano, and do not in any sense provide the most powerful level of observation or analysis for understanding and treating stuttering. The second step is to express and disseminate the current consensus opinion on the nature of stuttering as a multifactorial disorder. A multifactorial approach is necessary to explain this complex disorder, and dynamic models help us to understand the essentially unreliable nature of stuttering (e.g., Smith & Kelly, 1997).

LIMITATIONS OF TRADITIONAL UNITS OF STUTTERING

The limited utility of disfluency counts in the diagnosis and treatment of stuttering is not a new topic, and we recently addressed this issue (Smith & Kelly, 1997). The central point is that stuttering is a continuous disorder; it is present even when we do not perceive disfluencies. In the research arena there is a troubling trend to use disfluency counts and classifications as the window through which all phenomena associated with the disorder must be observed. For example, results of EMG studies were questioned by Ingham, Cordes, Ingham, and Gow (1995) because, they argued, identification of the onsets and offsets of stuttering events was not reliable. When we indicate that we are analyzing disfluent intervals of speech, this is meant as a relative term. This point was made explicitly in our work: "The methodology employed in the present study was motivated by the consideration that progress in research on stuttering may best be achieved by treating fluency as a continuum of behaviors, and comparing behaviors carefully selected from the extremes of fluent and disfluent speech (Denny & Smith, 1992, p.1227; also see discussion in Smith, 1990b)." The traditional description of observable stuttering behavior is offered only as a landmark to readers to understand where in the stream of speech the data were taken. There is not a necessary relationship between physiological data and the traditional classifications of fluency. Requiring researchers to use these units, to use "reliable means" of classification, and to interpret their data in relation to these units is analogous to asking the scientist who is recording seismic activity around volcanoes to interpret the data in relation to the pattern of smoke rising from the surface of the volcano. There may be a relationship, but the absence of a relationship does not undermine the validity of the seismic data.

Stuttering "events" do not exist; there is not a millisecond or a nanosecond that can be identified as the onset or offset of a disfluency, just as the onset or offset of a volcanic eruption cannot be pinpointed. The dynamic processes related to volcanic eruption occur before, during, and after the "event" that we discern from unaided observation. Likewise, the dynamic processes contributing to relative fluency and disfluency may be quite distant in time and space from the "event" that we perceive as disfluency. These points are made clearer if one examines physiological data. Not only can we not identify the onsets and offsets of disfluencies, viewed at this level, but we cannot pinpoint the onset or offset of "speech." We are fooled often into thinking we can specify the onset of speech when we design reaction time experiments or specify utterances for subjects to repeat. We mark the onset of the acoustic signal as the "onset of speech." We know, however, that many events occurred in the speaker, from CNS activity to respiratory changes, prior to that arbitrary time mark at the speech acoustic onset.

Furthermore, most human speaking behavior occurs in conversation with others. In our laboratory, we have recorded physiological signals during natural conversations from over 60 adults and children who stutter. Examination of these data make it clear that there is not an abrupt, binary switch from listener to speaker role. Fig. 3.2 shows data typical of these experiments: The subject was listening to the experimenter during the first 2 s of the record; then he begins to speak as indicated by the acoustic signal in the bottom trace. The four muscles recorded [two orofacial muscles, orbicularis oris inferior (OOI), and levator labii superior (LLS); and two laryngeal muscles, thyroarytenoid (TA), and cricothyroid (CT)] show different patterns of activity. CT is relatively quiet until approximately 2 s before the subject's speech acoustic signal starts. The remaining three EMG sites show continuous activity that is graded during speaking and listening.

These levels of muscular activity are much higher than that observed in quiet breathing. Such data indicate that both the central nervous system and the muscles are continuously active during conversational speech. Speech muscle systems, that is, the motoneuron pools that innervate the muscles, are receiving a balance of excitatory and inhibitory neural drive in a graded, continuous manner during conversation. This suggests that the speech motor systems of the brain that generate the motor command signals, do not turn "off" and then "on" as a speaker engages in typical conversation. Our working hypothesis is that once in the conversational speech "mode," all of those processes that are necessary for language production, for example, all of the steps outlined in a psycholinguistic model such as Levelt's (1989), occur in parallel.

Returning to the issue of identifying and locating "stuttering events," the data in Fig. 3.2 were recorded from an adult male who stutters. The physiological processes occurring during the time interval depicted generated an acoustic signal that we, as listeners, could classify as containing silent prolongations, sound repetitions, and interjections. These "events", however, are not islands of behavior in which some real boundary or boundaries between fluency and disfluency were

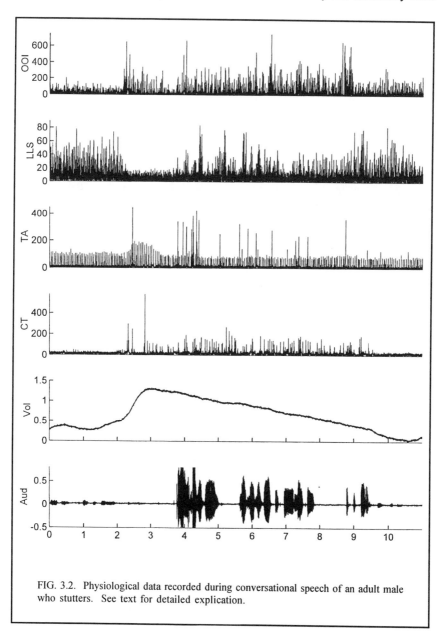

FIG. 3.2. Physiological data recorded during conversational speech of an adult male who stutters. See text for detailed explication.

crossed. Our perception and classification of these "stuttering events" reflect as much or more about the human brain's penchant for categorical perception than the dynamic and multileveled processes that lead to the diagnosis of stuttering.

To summarize this discussion of the units of stuttering, it is suggested that traditional fluency counts and classifications should be viewed as one widely employed level of observation of stuttering, but not as a window through which all other phenomena should be interpreted. Further, to focus discussion and interpretation of data on the precise identification of onsets and offsets of stuttering "events" (Ingham et al., 1995, Armson & Kalinowski, 1994) is to be fooled by imaginary boundaries in the process of speech production, which is essentially a continuous process.

A GLOBAL STRATEGY

Turning to the second step, articulating a global strategy for research and treatment of stuttering, it seems apparent that most workers in the area view stuttering as a multifactorial disorder (Conture, 1990; Riley & Riley, 1979; Smith, 1990a; Smith & Kelly, 1997; Starkweather, Gottwald, & Halfond, 1990; Van Riper, 1982; Wall & Myers, 1995; Zimmermann, 1980; Zimmermann, Smith, & Hanley, 1981). Although single, key factor theories of stuttering continue to appear (e.g., Karniol, 1995), the mainstream of researchers and clinicians who work directly on the problem of stuttering view it as a multifactorial problem. There is compelling evidence for multiple factors underlying stuttering. First, there is the universality of stuttering (Van Riper, 1982). It is difficult to explain the occurrence of stuttering in all cultures and all languages on the basis of a single factor present in all gene pools and/or all environments. Second, there is the heterogeneity of stuttering. A single factor model cannot explain why the behaviors associated with stuttering are so variable within and between individuals diagnosed as stuttering. Third, it is clear that there are a number of variables that produce systematic effects on speakers' fluency, from emotional arousal to syntactic complexity to social context. Thus, there is a good rationale for the range of variables, from linguistic to motor to psychosocial, currently under investigation in relation to stuttering.

In general, our multifactorial account (Smith, 1990a; Smith & Kelly, 1997; Smith & Weber, 1988; Zimmermann, 1980; Zimmermann, Smith, & Hanley, 1981) and other similar approaches (Felsenfeld, 1997; Riley & Riley, 1979; Starkweather, Gottwald, & Halfond, 1990; Van Riper, 1982; Wall & Myers, 1995) implicate cognitive, linguistic, emotional, and motor factors in the etiology of stuttering. These multifactorial accounts also emphasize that the relative weighting of the factors producing stuttering in each individual varies. The concluding statement in Van Riper's (1982) book provides a good summary of this issue:

> Why do some individuals show so many fractured words that they can be said to have the disorder of stuttering? We once hoped that we could identify a single cause of the disruption, but we have unsuccessfully chased that will-of-the-wisp over the hills and far away and in our old age we grow tired. ...Instead we feel that there are multiple factors which

probably determine whether or not a person will tend to have too many broken words. Certain of these factors may be absent or insignificant in their impact on a given individual while other factors may be potent enough to wreck his fluency. ...The point we are making, of course, is that human beings will differ... Each one of them would have his own unique profile and composite score. (pps. 445–446)

In many respects, then, the consumer of the research and clinical literature on stuttering should be encouraged by the significant movement toward a consensus opinion. Also, in the past twenty years, there has been substantial progress in understanding this disorder, due to expanded and improved experimental and clinical efforts to assess the multiple factors that contribute to stuttering. Many long-standing, widely held, but incorrect beliefs about stuttering have been debunked; for example, ideas about the role of parents (e.g., Kelly & Conture, 1992), the nature of the onset of the disorder (e.g., Yairi, 1997), and the physiological aspects of stuttering (e.g., Peters, Hulstijn, & Starkweather, 1990) have changed dramatically.

Despite these positive steps forward, there remains some discomfort with the multifactorial view. At the Munich World Congress on Fluency, one person who stutters expressed the opinion that this was a "cop out." He argued that researchers and clinicians cannot find the real cause of stuttering, so they adopt a multifactorial approach. Similarly, Perkins (1997) indicted multifactorial approaches and asserted that "a scientific solution" to stuttering requires that we find a single "invariant characteristic" that categorically defines the disorder. The logical attraction of a single factor account is obvious: simplicity. However, years of research and clinical experience tell us that stuttering is not a simple, tidy disorder (Smith & Kelly, 1997).

Many disorders, from heart disease to depression, are now understood within multifactorial frameworks. Multifactorial accounts of stuttering are not retreats from scientific solutions; rather, they recognize the complexity of the disorder. Our working model, as illustrated in Fig. 3.3, is open to direct, experimental testing. The core assertion of our approach is that all individuals who stutter experience breakdowns in speech motor processes. Therefore, the multiple factors that impact fluency in those who stutter must directly or indirectly affect speech motor processes. As Fig. 3.3 indicates, the output of the speech motor system can be viewed as occupying a continuum, from the most stable to the least stable behavior. The experimental approach generated by this model is to specify variables that are hypothetically linked to speech motor instability or breakdown; as shown, examples include memory load, syntactic complexity, or speaker anxiety. Experiments can be designed to directly test whether such variables impact the stability and/or perceived fluency of the individual's speech motor output. This approach has been taken in our laboratory, and we have data demonstrating that in adults who stutter, increasing the length and/or syntactic complexity of an utterance produces increased instability in speech motor execution. The increased instability is measured in the absence of overt breakdowns in fluency.

It is proposed, then, that a global strategy for research and clinical practice in stuttering requires the dissemination of the consensus opinion that many factors contribute to the development of stuttering in an individual. The available clinical and experimental literature make it clear that this is the preferred strategy. The alternative is to search for a single characteristic present in all people who stutter, which will then be understood to be the "cause" of stuttering. Returning to the volcano analogy, the latter approach is similar to searching for the single characteristic that all volcanoes have in common. Clearly, the characteristic that qualifies a landform to be classified as a volcano is that it displays eruptive behavior. However, just as one would not claim that disfluencies "cause" stuttering, one

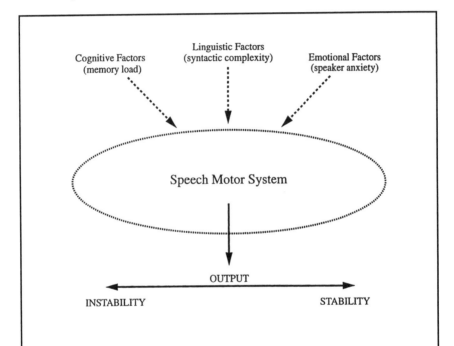

FIG. 3.3. Factors that play a role in stuttering must impact speech motor processes either directly or indirectly. Examples of potentially important factors are shown. The speech motor system produces an output that ranges on a continuum of stability. Speakers who stutter produce motor outputs more often at the extremes of this continuum.

would not claim that eruptions "cause" volcanoes. The task then becomes to define the essential characteristic of an eruption. Is lava flow a necessary condition? Is smoke or a gas cloud a necessary condition? If a fissure in the earth produces smoke but does not have a cone shape or lava flow, is that an eruption, and should the fissure be classified as a volcano? It seems obvious that these types of questions could occupy volcanologists for many years, but that these are the wrong questions.

The preferred strategy is to develop and disseminate a multifactorial model and to assess which variables affect the stability of speech motor processes in individuals who stutter. Real progress in this area also depends on a growing knowledge about the development of language and speech motor skills in childhood. It is encouraging that there is currently much more research focus on the development of fluency and the emergence of stuttering in childhood (e.g., Yairi, 1997). Also, it is important to explore the interactions of the factors that contribute to stuttering. This global strategy will aid us to move beyond the old controversies that have plagued clinicians and researchers in the area of stuttering. The closing two sections of this chapter address the ways in which a multifactorial and dynamic approach to stuttering moves us beyond the "organic versus learned" debate and beyond traditional notions of causality.

Beyond Organicity

A critical foundation for the success of the approach to stuttering proposed here is that we keep in mind that language, cognition, emotion, and, to a large extent, speech motor control, are functions of the brain. As we noted in Smith and Weber, 1988, the central debate in stuttering for many years was on the issue of whether stuttering is organic or learned. Wendell Johnson's (1942) firm resistance to the notion that there was anything "organically" different in those who stutter produced the now classic *diagnosogenic* theory of stuttering. Smith and Weber (1988) pointed to the futility of this debate: Learning is organic. Learning occurs as a result of changes in the activity and connectivity of neurons.

With dramatic advances in the neurosciences and new understanding of brain/behavior relationships, many of us who work on the problem of stuttering hoped that this debate was behind us. However, with the new brain imaging investigations of stuttering (Fox et al., 1996; Wu et al., 1995), confusion on this issue seems to have reemerged. A comprehensive review of the recent brain imaging studies on stuttering is provided by Ludlow (chap. 6, this volume). The concern here is that these studies will be misinterpreted as finally providing proof that stuttering is neurological or organic, rather than a learned disorder. This concern is triggered by reports of the brain imaging work in the popular press and by questions from students and laypersons. For example, at a recent workshop for students and clinicians interested in fluency, one participant suggested that, if there are differences in brain function in persons who stutter, stuttering is really neurological, and that therefore, any behavioral approach to treatment is futile. We have been asked by laypersons if surgery is available to "zap" the area of the brain that "causes" stuttering. The faulty underlying logic seems to be as follows: The structure of the brain is determined by genes. If people who stutter have differences in brain function, such differences must be due to differences in structure, which are genetically determined. Therefore stuttering is neurological (which is equivalent to organic), and the only successful treatments will be surgical or pharmaceutical.

This argument is flawed, and it is critical for clinicians and researchers to communicate to clients and students how it is flawed. As we learn more about the development and plasticity of the mammalian brain, even in adulthood, we understand that, although genes are certainly important in determining the structure of the nervous system, to some extent, structure is function. For example, the visual system might be thought of as a case in which genetically determined codes provide instructions for "hard-wired" connections between neurons in prenatal development. Highly organized and precise connections must be formed in the chains of neurons that connect the retina with the visual cortex. Humans are born with the approximate number of neurons that they will have in adulthood; however, the connections between these neurons in the neonate do not resemble those of the adult (Shatz, 1992). The brain's connections are "remodeled" during development, and this remodeling is dependent on experience (Shatz, 1992).

The classic experiments of Hubel and Wiesel (1970) demonstrated that closing the eyelids of newborn cats, even for a week, altered the formation of the ocular dominance columns in the visual cortex. Later work (Shatz, 1990) refined our understanding of the development of connections in the visual system, demonstrating that neurons not only must fire to complete their connections, but they must have patterned discharge characteristics. "In a sense, then, cells that fire together wire together" (Shatz, 1992, p.64). Paralleling this work on development, recent neurophysiological studies that map the somatosensory cortex of adult rats show remarkable, experience-determined plasticity in the adult brain. After adult female rats nursed a litter of pups, they were shown to have expanded cortical somatosensory areas representing the nipples, with average area increases of 1.6 times those of controls (Xerri, Stern, & Mezernich, 1994). These authors concluded, "These observations are consistent with the conclusion that cortical representations of the skin surfaces are remodeled by our experiences throughout life" (p. 1720).

The research demonstrating the experience-dependent nature of wiring of the brain in development and of the brain's organization in the adult has direct implications for understanding stuttering. In response to the student who inquires about the futility of behavioral approaches to a neurological disorder, it can be suggested that, when the clinician teaches the client easy onsets and/or slowed rate, he or she is "remodeling" the client's brain. By establishing new modes of behavior that the client can produce repeatedly, new modes of neuronal activity are established. When therapeutic intervention targets positive changes in attitudes about speech, the activity of neural systems mediating emotion and their interaction with the neural systems involved in sensorimotor control of speech may be altered. De Nil (chap. 7, this volume) discusses this concept in some detail.

This point brings up the importance of understanding that systems of the brain involved in language production and those mediating the multiple factors involved in stuttering are widely distributed and interactive. When the adult who stutters asks when the locus of stuttering will be found and a surgical cure will be available, the best answer is that it is highly unlikely that a single locus in the brain produces stuttering. The multiple factors that underlie the emergence of stuttering behaviors, linguistic processing, emotional arousal, cognitive components, are not located in a single site in the brain. Indeed, it may prove that group differences in brain function for individuals who stutter will be elusive and unreliable across investigations and imaging methods, as the behaviors that produce the diagnosis of stuttering may arise from the interactions of component neural systems that are essentially normal. For example, studies of autonomic arousal indicate that adults who stutter do not differ from adults who do not stutter in levels of autonomic activity during speech (Peters & Hulstijn, 1984; Weber & Smith, 1990). This would suggest that the neural systems mediating emotional reactivity and autonomic nervous system activity in adults who stutter function normally. However, experimental results and clinical evidence suggest that autonomic arousal can impact fluency (e.g., Weber & Smith, 1990). Thus in the person who stutters, normal activation of limbic areas and sympathetic systems may interact with speech motor systems to alter the probability of the maintenance of fluency.

On the basis of both studies of peripheral neuromotor events (e.g., Denny & Smith, 1992) and the limited brain imaging evidence available to date (e.g., Fox et al., 1996), we know that the neural systems involved in generating motor commands for speech do not function normally in adults who stutter. The multifactorial theoretical framework helps us to understand that the instability and/or failure of speech motor systems in stuttering arises from multileveled, heterogeneous processes, and that it is not an indication that stuttering is "caused" by a lesion in the sensorimotor cortex.

Speech production has an extremely long developmental time course, and there is evidence that speech motor performance may not be adultlike until after the first 10 years of life (Smith, Goffman, & Stark, 1995). Behaviors leading to a diagnosis of stuttering typically begin to appear around 2–4 years of age (Bernstein Ratner, 1997). Given the complex nature of language production, and the extended period over which adult performance is reached, it is likely that language and speech systems of the brain are very much in the "remodeling" stage when the first indicators of a possible stuttering problem appear. When parents ask, "is it organic (or inherited or neurological?)," we can say, " yes, but it is also learned"; to say that a behavior is organic or neurobiological does not mean that it cannot be modified by learning. Indeed, as the child learns to speak, he or she is making new connections between nerve cells, fine-tuning neural networks in the brain. Successful behavioral therapy essentially helps the child to establish adaptive, stable patterns of operation and interaction among the widely distributed neural networks involved in language production. Hopefully, clinical intervention will aid the developing brain to learn and establish neural interactions that produce fluency rather than those that contribute to excessive disfluency.

Beyond Causality

Another recurrent conceptual problem for the area of stuttering lurks behind almost every discussion of experimental results and of clinical practice: the problem of causality. These "chicken and egg" debates are discouragingly familiar. Does stuttering cause abnormal speech movement patterns or does speech motor instability cause stuttering? The ultimate illogic of these questions is embodied in Johnson's (1942) conclusion that diagnosing stuttering causes stuttering. In preceding sections of this chapter, it was suggested that stuttering is a multifactorial disorder. In our multifactorial account, we defined stuttering as a diagnostic category (Zimmermann et al., 1981). We (Smith & Kelly, 1997) suggested that:

> Stuttering emerges in an individual when complex, multileveled, and dynamic processes interact to produce failures in fluency that the individual and his or her culture judge to be aberrant. There is no core factor, a brain lesion, a DNA sequence, a type of disfluency, a phonological buffer problem, that generates all the phenomena associated with stuttering. (p.210)

In updating our model, we emphasized the *dynamic* nature of stuttering. The present discussion focuses on how dynamic theories help us to transcend the causality quagmire that has impeded progress in stuttering for so many years.

Dynamic theories have their origins in the physical sciences and mathematics, but in the past 10 years, nonlinear, dynamic approaches have been applied to a wide range of problems. Especially significant for the problem of stuttering is that dynamic theories have had a remarkable impact on developmentalists who study cognition and action (Elman et al., 1996; Thelen & Smith, 1994). A central concept in dynamic approaches is that of *emergent property*. To explain the notion of emergent property, examples from physics and chemistry are often used. Perhaps the most frequently cited example is the Belousov–Zhabotinskii reaction, in which a few chemicals mixed in a medium in a shallow dish interact to produce a series of patterns of colored waves and spirals. As time progresses, the spirals and waves sweep across the dish until the entire surface is organized in a unique pattern, until finally the "patterns decay and the system dies" (Madore & Freedman, 1987, p.253). Within the tradition of simple, cause–effect models, in which we typically employ reverse engineering to solve problems, "we would wonder how these chemicals *knew* to produce circular and spiral patterns and oscillations of such precise and fixed nature as though driven by a set clock" (Thelen & Smith, 1994, p. 49). Of course the chemicals do not "know" in any sense what the endpoint behavior should be. Instead, the spiral-wave pattern is an emergent property of this complex system. There is no blueprint or plan for the observed pattern, and small changes in the concentrations of the chemicals can produce radical changes in the observed patterns. The traditional approach to stuttering would have us ask, was the pattern "caused" by chemical A or chemical B, or by the nature of the medium in which they were mixed. Clearly, this is the wrong approach.

Thelen and Smith (1994) stated:

> For our approach to development, we use the science of the Belousov–Zhabotinskii chemical reaction rather than the science of our beginning chemistry class. This is a relatively new science that discards simple cause-and-effect models, linearity, determinism, and reductionist analysis. Instead, it is a science for systems with a history, systems that change over time, where novelty can be created, where the end-state is not coded anywhere, and where behavior at the macrolevel can, in principle, be reconciled with behavior a the microlevel. (p. 49)

It is a central tenet of the present chapter that this should be the new science of stuttering. Past work on stuttering has often made the mistake of starting with the end product, the behaviors that we observe in adults who are chronic stutterers, and from that starting point, has used reductionistic approaches to finding the cause. For example, we look for feedback or self-monitoring loops that can cause repetition or prolongation. In our view, repetitions or prolongations are the spirals and waves of the Belousov–Zhabotinskii reactions (or the smoke of the volcano), and the goal of a comprehensive theory of stuttering is to explain how stuttering emerges from the interaction of the complex systems that produce language and speech.

How can we make progress toward the goal of refining and expanding a multifactorial, dynamic theory of stuttering? Thelen and Smith (1994) offered a useful introduction to developmental dynamics, and they demonstrated how principles from this new science could be used to study the development of cognition and action. They asked questions such as "why does change occur" and "why do organisms move from one state to another?" They borrowed heavily from physical theories of nonlinear dynamics to illustrate how *self-organizing systems* produce patterned output. That is, systems with many interacting components can suddenly produce patterns in space and time, and can display nonlinear behavior, that is a shifting from one pattern of output to another very rapidly. We discussed in an earlier paper (Smith & Kelly, 1997) how this feature of nonlinearity is extremely relevant to the understanding of stuttering. The onset of stuttering in childhood can be swift and severe (Yairi, 1997); an adult speaker who stutters may shift very suddenly from fluent to highly disfluent modes.

To understand and model these nonlinear shifts in the output behavior of complex systems, dynamic theorists define *attractor states*, "when systems self-organize…, they 'settle into' one or a few modes of behavior (which themselves may be quite complex) that the system prefers over all the possible modes" (Thelen & Smith, p. 56). As shown in Fig. 3.4, these attractors are often represented as valleys with a ball at the bottom. The more stable an attractor state, the deeper the valley, and more energy is required to move out of that mode or state. During development, the number and depth of attractors change, and Thelen and her colleagues have used such illustrations to depict the ontogenetic "landscape" for locomotion (see Fig. 4.17 of Thelen and Smith, 1994). As suggested in Fig. 3.4, a similar approach could be employed to describe an ontogenetic landscape for the development of speech. As a brief illustration for the present purpose, suppose that, as speech motor skills are emerging, in a typically developing child in the 2–5 year period, attractors are shallow, and production is unstable (top trace, Fig. 3.4). During periods of normal nonfluency in childhood, some of these attractors or modes result in nonfluent speech (second trace, Fig. 3.4). With maturation, these multiple speech attractors or modes eventually disappear and a deep, stable attractor for fluent speech emerges. It takes considerable noise or energy (e.g., extreme fatigue, a large audience) to move a normal adult speaker out of this normally fluent mode (third trace). On the other hand, we hypothesize that some children, as they move through the ontogenetic landscape for speech, continue to have unstable

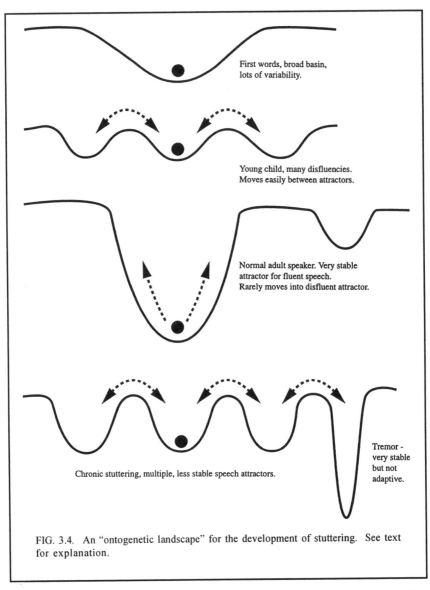

First words, broad basin,
lots of variability.

Young child, many disfluencies.
Moves easily between attractors.

Normal adult speaker. Very stable
attractor for fluent speech.
Rarely moves into disfluent attractor.

Tremor -
very stable
but not
adaptive.

Chronic stuttering, multiple, less stable speech attractors.

FIG. 3.4. An "ontogenetic landscape" for the development of stuttering. See text
for explanation.

attractors that produce disfluent modes of behavior. Ultimately, children who develop
chronic stuttering have these multiple attractor states for speech. They move from
the disfluent to fluent attractors easily.

There is experimental evidence to support the application of such a model to
the emergence of stuttering. In work from our laboratory and from others (e.g.,
Smith et al., 1993), evidence has been accumulating to suggest that, in the intervals
of speech breakdown in adults who stutter, there are stable patterns of
neuromuscular activity. In other words, during periods of time when listeners
perceive the stutterer's speech to contain perceptible disruptions, there tend to be

consistent patterns of activity, and specific muscles repeatedly tend to increase or decrease their amplitude of activity. In fact, an extremely stable form of neuromuscular discharge can occur: tremor. Tremor results when neurons that innervate the muscle fire repeatedly in synchrony. This is a stable pattern of neuromuscular activity, but it is not adaptive. When muscles that must be controlled to produce speech are "locked" in this type of discharge pattern, fluent speech cannot continue. We can think of tremor as a deep attractor from which it is difficult for the speaker to move. In a study of 9 children (ages 2–14 years) who were diagnosed as stuttering (Kelly, Smith, & Goffman, 1995), we found that only the older children who stutter showed tremor in orofacial muscles during their speech breakdowns. Thus, we hypothesized that the deep attractor of tremor develops as the child emerges as a chronic stutterer.

To suggest that disfluent behavior represents a stable, attractor state is a novel idea, which in a sense, seems counterintuitive. We tend to think of stuttering behaviors as "discoordinated," but it has just been suggested that stuttering may be associated with hypercoordination as well as with dis- or hypocoordination. This type of phenomenon is consistent with the activity of nonlinear, dynamical systems. There are many examples of stable attractor states that are not signs of healthy functioning (e.g., EEG rhythms in epilepsy and hyperregularity of heart rate associated with some forms of heart disease; Bassingthwaighte, Liebovitch, & West, 1994; Mackey & Milton, 1987). Thus, the stability/instability continuum for speech motor output (e.g., Fig. 3.3) cannot be interpreted as a good/bad continuum. Some stable behaviors, for example tremor, are not conducive to the forward flow of fluent speech.

How can we reconcile these discussions of chemical reactions and attractors to the axiom we began with, that is, language production is a function of the brain? Dynamical theories, such as that of Thelen and Smith (1994) have been criticized for overreliance on metaphors and analogies drawn from physical systems, which, after all, do not have nervous systems. They are sensitive to this issue and have suggested that their approach is consistent with neural network (also called connectionist) modeling in several important ways, including: (1) The structure of behavior is explained without requiring an "icon of the structure in the head," and (2) that knowledge is viewed as a pattern of activity in time as opposed to a structure. The work of Elman et al. (1996) explores the connectionist perspective on development, which, in their hands, includes a strong component of nonlinear dynamics. This book provides a promising synthesis of the two types of models and is especially attractive to the theorist interested in the neurophysiological bases of behavior. They take a strongly biological approach, and their descriptions and discussions of recent advances in genetics and the neurosciences are directly applicable to many of the debates that we have touched on in this chapter. Most importantly, it is clear that instead of talking about attractors in the previous examples, we could be talking about the development of neural networks. An attractor could be defined as a stable mode of operation of a neural network or of a group of networks. In any case, dynamic models are compatible with neural systems, and the synthesis of the two suggests many promising avenues for research on the development of fluent and disfluent speech.

In summary, it is essential for those who wish to understand stuttering to move beyond the old debates about the "cause" of stuttering. We must place the investigation of stuttering squarely within the general study of the development of cognition and action. Complex human behaviors unfold over time. There is a common set of factors that impact speech motor processes; however, the importance of these factors varies across individuals and within individuals over time. An individual diagnosed as stuttering may produce a part-word repetition when he is 5 years of age and later, when he is 50 years of age. Despite the superficial similarity that our classification of stuttering behaviors suggests, the underlying dynamics of these productions in the same individual may be quite distinctive at age 5 and 50 years. Although stuttering unfolds in a unique way in each person, there are a limited number of factors that have been demonstrated to systematically impact speech motor performance or fluency. Our goal is to understand the dynamic interplay of these factors as the developing brain seeks the stable, adaptive modes of interaction among neural networks that generate the fluent speech most of us take for granted.

ACKNOWLEDGMENT

Preparation of this chapter was supported by NIH Grant DC00559 from the National Institute on Deafness and Other Communication Disorders.

REFERENCES

Armson, J., & Kalinowski, J. (1994). Interpreting results of the fluent speech paradigm in stuttering research: Difficulties in separating cause from effect. *Journal of Speech and Hearing Research, 37*, 69–82.

Bernstein Ratner, N.. (1997). Stuttering: A psycholinguistic perspective. In R. F. Curlee & G. M. Siegel (Eds.), *Nature and Treatment of Stuttering: New Directions* (2nd ed., pp. 99–127). Needham Heights, MD: Allyn & Bacon.

Bassingthwaighte, J. B., Liebovitch, L. S., & West, B. J. (1994). *Fractal physiology.* New York: Oxford University Press.

Conture, E. G. (1990). *Stuttering* (2nd ed.) Englewood Cliffs, NJ: Prentice-Hall.

Decker, R., & Decker, B. (1989). *Volcanoes* (Rev. ed.). New York: Freeman.

Decker, R. W., & Decker, B. B. (1991). *Mountains of fire.* New York: Cambridge University Press.

Denny, M., & Smith, A. (1992). Gradations in a pattern of neuromuscular activity associated with stuttering. *Journal of Speech and Hearing Research, 35*, 1216–1229.

Elman, J. L., Bates, E. A., Johnson, M. H., Karmiloff-Smith, A., Parisi, D., & Plunkett, K. (1996). *Rethinking innateness: A connectionist perspective on development.* Cambridge, MA: MIT Press.

Felsenfeld, S. (1997). Epidemiology and genetics of stuttering. In R. F. Curlee & G. M. Siegel (Eds.), *Nature and treatment of stuttering: New directions* (2nd ed., pp. 3-23). Needham Heights, MD: Allyn & Bacon.

Fox, P. T., Ingham, R. J., Ingham, J. C., Hirsch, T. B., Downs, J. H., Martin, C., Jerabek, P., Glass, T., & Lancaster, J. L. (1996). A PET study of the neural systems of stuttering. *Nature, 382*, 158–162.

Harrington, J. (1988). Stuttering, delayed auditory feedback, and linguistic rhythm. *Journal of Speech and Hearing Research, 31*, 36–47.

Hubel, D. H., & Wiesel, T. N. (1970). The period of susceptibility to the physiological effects of unilateral eye closure in kittens. *Journal of Physiology, 206,* 419–436.

Ingham, R. J., Cordes, A. K., Ingham, J. C., & Gow, M. L. (1995). Identifying the onset and offset of stuttering events. *Journal of Speech and Hearing Research, 38,* 315–326.

Johnson, W. (1942). A study of the onset and development of stuttering. *Journal of Speech Disorders, 7,* 251–257.

Karniol, R. (1995). Stuttering, language, and cognition: A review and a model of stuttering as suprasegmental sentence plan alignment (SPA). *Psychological Bulletin, 117,* 104–124.

Kelly, E. M., & Conture, E. G. (1992). Speaking rates, response time latencies, and interrupting behaviors of young stutterers, nonstutterers, and their mothers. *Journal of Speech and Hearing Research, 35,* 1256–1257.

Kelly, E. M., Smith, A., & Goffman, L. (1995). Orofacial muscle activity of children who stutter. *Journal of Speech and Hearing Research, 38,* 1025–1036.

Levelt, W. J. M. (1989). *Speaking: From intention to articulation.* Cambridge, MA: MIT Press.

Mackey, M. C., & Milton, J. G. (1987). Dynamical diseases. In S. H. Koslow, A. J. Mandell, & M. F. Shlesinger (Eds.), *Perspectives in biological dynamics and theoretical medicine* (pp. 16–32). New York: The New York Academy of Sciences.

Madore, B. F., & Freedman, W. L. (1987). Self-organizing structures. *American Scientist, 75,* 252–259.

McGuire, B., Kilburn, C., & Murray, J. (Eds.). (1995). *Monitoring active volcanoes: Strategies, procedures and techniques.* London: UCL Press Limited.

Perkins, W. H. (1997). Historical Analysis of why science has not solved stuttering. In R. F. Curlee & G. M. Siegel (Eds.), *Nature and treatment of stuttering: New directions* (2nd ed., pp. 218–238). Needham Heights, MD: Allyn & Bacon.

Peters, H. F. M. & Hulstijn, W. (1984). Stuttering and anxiety. *Journal of Fluency Disorders, 9,* 67–84.

Peters, H. F. M., Hulstijn, W., & Starkweather, C. W. (Eds.). (1991). Speech motor control and stuttering. *Proceedings of the 2nd International Conference on Speech Motor Control and Stuttering.* Amsterdam: Elsevier Science Publishers.

Riley, G., & Riley, J. (1979). A component model for diagnosing and treating children who stutter. *Journal of Fluency Disorders, 4,* 279–293.

Shatz, C. J. (1992, September). The developing brain. *Scientific American,* 61–67.

Shatz, C. J. (1990). Impulse activity and the patterning of connections during CNS development. *Neuron, 5,* 745–756.

Smith, A. (1990a). Factors in the etiology of stuttering. *American Speech-Language-Hearing Association Reports, Research Needs in Stuttering: Roadblocks and Future Directions, 18,* 39–47.

Smith, A. (1990b). Toward a comprehensive theory of stuttering: A commentary. *Journal of Speech and Hearing Disorders, 55,* 398–401.

Smith, A., Goffman, L., & Stark, R. (1995) Speech motor development. *Seminars in Speech and Language, 16,* 87–99.

Smith, A., & Kelly, E. (1997). Stuttering: A dynamic, multifactorial model. In R. F. Curlee & G. M. Siegel (Eds.), *Nature and treatment of stuttering: New directions* (2nd ed., pp. 204–217). Needham Heights, MD: Allyn & Bacon.

Smith, A., Luschei, E., Denny, M., Wood, J., Hirano, M., & Badylak, S. (1993). Spectral analysis of activity of laryngeal and orofacial muscles in stutterers. *Journal of Neurology, Neurosurgery, and Psychiatry, 56,* 1303–1311.

Smith, A., & Weber, C. M. (1988). The need for an integrated perspective on stuttering. *ASHA, 30,* 30–32.

Starkweather, C. W., Gottwald, R. S., & Halfond, M. (1990). *Stuttering prevention: A clinical method.* Englewood Cliffs, NJ: Prentice-Hall.

Thelen, E., & Smith, L. B. (1994). *A dynamic systems approach to the development of cognition and action.* Cambridge, MA: MIT Press.

Van Riper, C. (1982). *The nature of stuttering* (2nd ed.). Englewood Cliffs, NJ: Prentice-Hall.

Wall, M. J., & Myers, F. L. (1995). Theories of stuttering and therapeutic implications. In *Clinical management of childhood stuttering* (2nd ed.). Austin, TX: Pro-ed.

Weber, C. M., & Smith, A. (1990). Autonomic correlates of stuttering and speech assessed in a range of experimental tasks. *Journal of Speech and Hearing Research, 33,* 690–706.

Wu, J. C., Maguire, G., Riley, G., Fallon, J., LaCasse, L., Chin, S., Klein, E., Tang, C., Cadwell, S., & Lottenberg, S. (1995). A positron emission tomography [18F] deoxyglucose study of developmental stuttering. *Neuroreport, 6,* 501–505.

Xerri, C., Stern, J. M., & Merzenich, M. M. (1994). Alterations of the cortical representation of the rat ventrum induced by nursing behavior. *Journal of Neuroscience, 14*(3), 1710–1721.

Yairi, E. (1997). Disfluency characteristics of childhood stuttering. In R. F. Curlee & G. M. Siegel (Eds.), *Nature and treatment of stuttering: New directions* (2nd ed., pp. 49–78). Needham Heights, MD: Allyn & Bacon.

Zimmermann, G. N. (1980). Stuttering: A disorder of movement. *Journal of Speech and Hearing Research, 23,* 122–136.

Zimmermann, G. N., Smith, A., & Hanley, J. M. (1981). Stuttering: In need of a unifying conceptual framework. *Journal of Speech and Hearing Research, 24,* 25–31.

4 Epidemiologic Factors and Stuttering research

Ehud Yairi
University of Illinois

WHERE DO VARIABLE FINDINGS IN STUTTERING RESEARCH COME FROM?

For a long period, stuttering research has focused on developing and refining various ways of measuring speech, as well as on the physiologic, affective, and cognitive responses of people who stutter. These measurement methods have been applied primarily in research comparing people who stutter with those do not stutter. Frequent ambiguities and inconsistencies in the resultant data have been blamed, variously, on insensitive measures, imprecise technology, observer variability, or even bias. Relatively less thought and effort have been invested in investigating the possibility that the cause of much of the ambiguous contradictory data lies not with the observers or measures employed, but with the heterogeneity of those being observed. All too often, basic facts about differences within the population of people who stutter or their families have been ignored in the current body of research, sometimes in very significant ways. Several attempts to subtype stuttering through developmentally oriented classification schemes or using other bases, such as symptomatology (see review by Yairi, 1990), have not been submitted to thorough research or have failed to receive sufficient scientific support. This being the case, it is not surprising that subtyping or subgrouping systems have enjoyed little recognition in either the research or clinical domains. In spite of a notable recent attempt to identify subgroups (Schwartz & Conture, 1988), by-and-large, stuttering has continued to be dealt with in our laboratories, and treated in our clinics as a unitary disorder, a "pathognomonic monolith," as it was labeled by St. Onge (1963).

Such observations have led me to conclude that one of the top priorities in our work is to increase and improve the epidemiologic data regarding stuttering, because this information can augment the knowledge base from which improved theories, research, and treatment strategies, as well as policies, can be developed. It has been generally accepted in medicine and other areas of health that sound research in, and understanding of, any disorder must begin with, and continuously consider, the disorder's epidemiology. Certainly, epidemiology is the key to advancing toward differentiation. Several research directions in stuttering, including the role of the home environment and genetics in the development and maintenance of stuttering, phonological factors in stuttering, and treatment efficacy, have been especially affected by insufficient consideration of epidemiological factors. Although my colleagues and I have addressed this problem in previous publications

(Yairi, 1990, 1993, 1997; Yairi, Ambrose, & Cox, 1996), I would like to refocus our attention to the issue in a more concentrated fashion because so much of the information has direct clinical relevance.

GENETIC FACTORS IN STUTTERING

A well-known population characteristic of stuttering is that it runs in families, apparently reflecting a strong genetic component. Data from several of our studies (Ambrose, Yairi, & Cox, 1993; Yairi & Ambrose, 1992b) show that about 68% of children who stutter have stuttering relatives in their extended family. Approximately 39% have a relative who stutterers in their immediate family and about 27 % have a stuttering parent, most often the father. Such basic facts have been overlooked in many, including the most influential, studies that address the nature and treatment of stuttering.

Parents of People Who Stutter

Research on *parental attitude* provides an excellent example of research that has not integrated epidemiological findings with other research questions. It would appear reasonable to assume that the home environment of the 40% of stuttering children who have parents with a stuttering history, or who have current experience of stuttering within the immediate family, stands a good chance to be somewhat, if not considerably, different from that of those children without such history. It would appear particularly logical to assume that fathers and mothers who themselves stuttered hold different attitudes toward speech and stuttering, as well as a number of other important aspects of childrearing, than those with no personal history of the disorder. Nothing, however, along this line of reasoning is reflected in either the Iowa Studies (e.g., Johnson, et al., 1959) on the onset of stuttering, the British studies (Andrews & Harris, 1964) that focused on families of children who stutter, or many other investigations that dealt with the home environment of people who stutter (see review by Yairi, 1997). In all of these, parents with stuttering histories were not segregated in the research designs. Thus, it is possible that trends found to be statistically insignificant for the entire group would emerge more decisively in one of the subgroups of parents.

A similar situation is found in research on *parent personality*. Virtually all investigators have overlooked the fact that an appreciable subgroup of parents was likely to have possessed the same pathology, stuttering, that their children had. Whereas that pathology served as the sole basis for separating study children into two groups, no such separation was deemed necessary for subgroups of parents who were, in fact, the subjects directly under investigation. In other words, although the basic motivation of these studies was to test the assumption that stuttering in children is a symptom of a deep personality maladjustment, and that such maladjustment was caused by the parents' own personality problems, the presence of the same symptoms in certain percentages of the parents should logically have ruled them out of the study or, at least, grouped them separately. Neither of the two large investigations by Johnson et al. (1959) and by Andrews and Harris (1964) considered this factor in their parent personality studies.

Past research on the home environment of stuttering children has also identified *parents' intellectual function* as a factor that possibly contributes to the disorder. Johnson et al. (1959) found that parents of stuttering children, as a group, had fewer years of formal education than parents of normally fluent children. Andrews and Harris (1964) reported that mothers of stuttering children tended to have lower intellectual capacity than mothers of normally fluent controls. It has been reported, however, that people who stutter, as a group, tend to have lower IQ scores and may have lower occupational aspiration than nonstutterers (Andrews & Harris, 1964; Schindler, 1955). These differences between stutterers and the general population may reflect some of the underlying variations contributing to susceptibility to stuttering. For example, stuttering may be only one manifestation of more general deficits in verbal cognition and/or processing. Therefore, studies on parents' intellectual function should be careful to differentiate between parents with stuttering history and those without such history. Because parents of children who stutter are at higher risk to stutter than parents of normally fluent children, and presumably also at higher risk of exhibiting lower intelligence, they might have weighted down the mean scores of the entire group. Such differences may not exist between parents of stutterers who do not stutter themselves and parents of normally fluent children. Again, neither Johnson et al. (1959) nor Andrews and Harris (1964) were keen on making the necessary distinction among subgroups of parents of children who stutter, (nor among parents of control subjects), thus complicating interpretation of their results.

The same reasoning, particularly in regard to the factors of personality and intelligence, may have further implications for research and findings concerning *socioeconomic status*, as well as *social lifestyle*. Although past investigators reported inconsistent findings, more reliable research that applied updated statistical information on national socioeconomic distribution to a sampling of families of stutterers (Morgenstern, 1956) indicated a tendency for greater concentration of stuttering in lower socioeconomic levels. Others (e.g., Johnson et al., 1959), found that parents of children who stutter tended to lead a more socially isolated lifestyle than parents of normally fluent control children. Although much remains unknown about these group tendencies, it is reasonable to suggest that they could actually be a by-product of a multitude of different factors, such as lower intellectual functioning, personality problems, or the direct negative experiences of those parents with a personal history of stuttering. Inasmuch as stuttering parents indeed might have lower intelligence or education, or still exhibit stuttering, they may have to settle for less favorable income opportunities and may also be less sociable than parents who do not stutter. Such traits or life experiences that are either more prevalent in, or unique to, only one subgroup of parents have generally not been considered in the conduct of stuttering research, or in the interpretations of study results and their clinical implications.

Research into the possible parental role in stuttering should particularly consider the importance of parents' stuttering history when the research targets *parents' speech characteristics*, or the relation between various features of their speech and those of their children. In this type of research, the presence of stuttering history in some parents raises the obvious possibility that past or current stuttering has a direct bearing on the criterion measure employed, be it articulatory rate, frequency of disfluency, and so forth. Nevertheless, past studies of parents' speaking rate (e.g., Meyers & Freeman, 1985; Stephenson-Opsal & Ratner, 1988) or disfluency (Meyers, 1989; Roman, 1972;) did not differentiate parents according to their stuttering history. Thus, the data from such studies may be contaminated by parental behaviors that flow from personal experience with stuttering rather than from other factors.

A final example of an epidemiological factor affecting research on the home environment of children who stutter is the strong *imbalance in parents' gender*, with preference given to the inclusion of mothers of stutterers as subjects. Our data, however, show that among parents of stuttering children, there are many more fathers than mothers with a stuttering history. Nevertheless, quite a few investigations, including the well-known 1964 Andrews and Harris study, were limited to mothers. This trend has continued in recent research. In my opinion, the stronger connection of stuttering to the father in the family should have directed investigators to focus considerably more attention on fathers, especially those with a stuttering history. Fortunately, initial signs of change in this area can be found in the work of Kelly (1994). All in all, it appears that research has been stymied by insensitive sampling of subgroups of parents and by the failure to use genetic background and parental experience with stuttering as an independent variable in stuttering research. [1]

Age, Gender, and Recovery

To overlook the epidemiological complexity of stuttering can also be detrimental to research on *spontaneous recovery*. The more reliable available sources, longitudinal studies, have indicated that the rate of recovery from stuttering is as high as 79% (Andrews & Harris, 1964; Panelli, McFArlane, & Shipley, 1978; Ryan, 1990), and perhaps even higher (Yairi & Ambrose, 1992a, 1996). Age and gender interact with recovery in a rather close fashion. Specifically, much of the recovery occurs by age 5 (Andrews & Harris, 1964; Yairi & Ambrose, 1992a). Some children appear to have an even earlier recovery (Yairi, Ambrose, & Niermann, 1993). Thus, with each successive year, the composition of any sample of stutterers gets increasingly loaded with greater percentages of cases that will eventually become chronic. Simultaneously with aging, there is an increase in the proportion of males whose chance for spontaneous recovery is much lower than that of females (females recover at earlier ages and in larger proportions than males). Consequently, research concerning recovery must begin very soon after onset, before early recovery, particularly in females, alters the subject sample with lower chances for further recovery among the remaining subjects. Studies that overlooked these epidemiologic characteristics and used older children (Dickson, 1971; Johannsen & Schulze, 1995; Ramig, 1993) or adults (Sheehan & Martyn, 1970; Wingate, 1964) employed such a late starting point in terms of the developmental course of stuttering that one can assume with a high degree of certainty that much of the phenomenon under investigation, recovery, was simply bypassed by the investigators. They simply were in no position to observe and report the majority of children who exhibited early recovery. In this respect, Ingham and Cordes' analysis (chap. 15, this volume) of recovery studies overlooks such basic epidemiological factors, and thus errs in its conclusions. Furthermore, their conclusions are weakened by the omission of data on recovery in preschool children reported by Yairi and Ambrose (1992). These data amount to more than 25% of the total sample included in Ingham and Cordes' analysis for this age grouping.[2]

Considerations in Genetic Research

A review of the research concerning *genetic aspects* of stuttering has also revealed weaknesses stemming from inadequate considerations of epidemiological factors. As Yairi, Ambrose, and Cox (1996) noted, most past studies concerned with family incidence and familial aggregation of stuttering used subject samples that greatly overrepresented older children or adults. In the Yale Family Study (Kidd, 1984) that investigated the genetics of stuttering, the sample was limited to adult probands. Present data on recovery, however, would seem to indicate that adults who chronically stutter constitute only 20% of the population of people who have ever stuttered. Thus, this well-known study's conclusions about familial risk for stuttering are applicable only to the minority subgroup of persistent stutterers carrying traits that are associated with or that cause chronicity. Indeed, some of Kidd's main conclusions (e.g., that female probands have more relatives at a higher risk for stuttering than do male probands) do not hold when the population of all stutterers is examined (Ambrose, Yairi, & Cox, 1993). The implications of imprecise genetic data could be far reaching. If genetics is one of the factors that determines spontaneous recovery (Ambrose, Cox, & Yairi, 1997), the genetic transmission of susceptibility to recovery from stuttering simply cannot be evaluated in samples of older children or adults that have already lost all recovered subjects. Studies must include very young children near the onset of stuttering so that families of all children who ever stuttered are tapped before recovery processes weed them out.

The genetic issue is further complicated because, as mentioned earlier, age interacts with sex in spontaneous recovery. There is an increasing body of data that convincingly shows an age-related increase in the sex ratio from 2:1 in children under age 4, to 4:1 or 5:1 in older children and adults (Bloodstein, 1995; Yairi, 1983), primarily due to the higher recovery rate in females (Ambrose et al., 1997; Seider, Gladstone, & Kidd, 1983; Yairi, Ambrose, Paden, & Throneburg, 1996). Inasmuch as the genetic predisposition to stutter appears to be influenced by sex, proband samples that misrepresent the proper male-to-female ratio can be expected to also yield biased data regarding genetic patterns in stuttering. Thus, samples of older stutterers present two sources of bias: They usually consist of disproportionally greater numbers of males, as well as disproportionally greater numbers of subjects with strong tendencies toward chronicity. An important conclusion is that research in genetics of stuttering should strive to focus on samples of young probands before the subject composition is altered under the influence of various factors. Longitudinal studies provide an excellent vehicle for this purpose.

PHONOLOGICAL DISORDERS IN STUTTERING CHILDREN

Another area of growing interest in recent years has been the *relation between stuttering and phonological disorders* in children. Recent studies (Yaruss, LaSalle, & Conture, 1995) have suggested that as many as 40% of young stutterers also exhibit phonological difficulties of clinical significance. Here too, the accuracy of the reported incidence may fall victim to insufficient attention to the epidemiology of stuttering. In such studies, the sex and age factors should receive particularly careful consideration because at young ages, males are more prone to exhibit phonological deficits than females. Inasmuch as even in very young stuttering populations males outnumber females by a factor of 2:1, findings of high percentages of phonological deficits in stuttering children might be, in part, a statistical artifact dictated by the skewed sex ratio.

Clinical Efficacy Research

A more serious problem appears to emerge in the growing body of *clinical efficacy studies* with preschool-age children. All three epidemiologic factors, age, sex, and risk factors (persistence/recovery) exert powerful influences when investigating this population. In such research, time from stuttering onset is particularly critical to control, in view of present data showing that high percentages of children exhibit spontaneous recovery during the first 2 years after onset. It should become clear that, if stuttering children are placed in such clinical research programs soon after they began stuttering, they have a good chance of recovering on their own. The shorter the interval from the time of onset, the better the chance for spontaneous recovery and for the investigator to claim undue credit for the improvement. Yet, in some studies, the possibility of spontaneous recovery is not even mentioned (Onslow & Packman, chap.14, this volume). It is quite clear that control groups receiving no treatment are essential to support the authenticity of therapeutic effects (Curlee & Yairi, 1997).[3]

The sex distribution of the subject samples is another critical factor. Girls are considerably more likely to recover than boys (Ambrose, Cox, & Yairi, 1997). Thus, a sample of stuttering subjects that reflects a higher female-to-male ratio than expected for children who stutter at the particular age, and that also includes very young children, some of them with very brief histories of stuttering (e.g., Fosnot, 1993), could easily yield a high success rate that may not validly reflect therapeutic influence. In the context of clinical efficacy research, it is also essential to recognize that other population subgroups have emerged in stuttering, such as stuttering with comorbid disorders, communication or otherwise (Conture, Louko, & Edwards, 1993). Such subgroups may respond differently to treatment.

SUMMARY

In summary, the conception of stuttering as a unitary disorder that affects a uniform population should be discarded in our research and its clinical implications. Attention to the issues raised in this chapter can reduce many potential sources of error in our information about the disorder.

ACKNOWLEDGMENTS

Preparation of this chapter was supported by Grant # R01 DC 00459 from the National Institutes of Health, National Institute On Deafness and Other Communication Disorders, Principal Investigator: Ehud Yairi.

REFERENCES

Ambrose, N., Cox, N., & Yairi, E. (1997). Genetic bases of persistence and recovery in stuttering. *Journal of Speech and Hearing Research, 40,* 567–580 .

Ambrose, N.,Yairi, E., & Cox, N. (1993). Early childhood stuttering: Genetic aspects. *Journal of Speech and Hearing Research,36,* 701–706.

Andrews, G., & Harris, M. (1964). *The syndrome of stuttering.* London: Heinemann.

Bloodstein, O. (1995). *A handbook on stuttering.* (5th ed.). Chicago: Easter Seal.

Blood, G., & Seider, R. (1981). The concomitant problems of young stutteres. *The Journal of Speech and Hearing Disorders, 46,* 31–33.

Conture, E., Louko, L., & Edwards, M. (1993). Simultaneously treating stuttering and disordered phonology in children: Experimental treatment, preliminary findings. *American Journal of Speech-Language Pathology, 2,* 72–81.

Curlee, R., & Yairi, E. (1997). Early intervention with early childhood stuttering: A critical examination of the data. *American Journal of Speech-Language Pathology, 6,* 8–18.

Dickson, S. (1971). Incipient stuttering and spontaneous remission of stuttered speech. *Journal of Communication Disorders, 4,* 99–110.

Fosnot, S. (1993). Research design for examining treatment efficacy in fluency disorders. *Journal of Fluency Disorders, 18,* 221–252.

Ingham, R., & Cordes, A. (1998). On watching a discipline shoot itself in the foot: Some observations on current trends in stuttering treatment research. In N. Ratner and C. Healey (Eds.), *Stuttering research and treatment: Bridging the gap,* (pp. 213–232). Mahwah, NJ: Lawrence Erlbaum Associates..

Johnson, W. & Associates (1959). *The onset of stuttering.* Minneapolis: University of Minnesota Press.

Johannsen, H., & Schulze, H. (1995). A five year longitudinal study of stuttering in childhood underway. In C. W. Starkweather & H. F. M. Peters (Eds.) *Proceedings of the 1st World Congress on Fluency Disorders, Vol. II,* pp.158–158). Nijmegen: University Press, the Netherlands.

Kelly, E. (1994). Speech rates and turn-taking behaviors of children who stutter and their fathers. *Journal of Speech and Hearing Research, 37,* 1284–1294.

Kidd, K. (1984). Stuttering as a genetic disorder. In R. Curlee, & W. Perkins (Eds.), *Nature and treatment of stuttering: New directions* (pp.149–169). Boston: Allyn & Bacon.

Locke, J. (1993). *The child's path to spoken language .* Cambridge, MA: Harvard University Press.

Meyers, S. (1989). Nonfluencies of preschool stutterers and conversational partners: Observing reciprocal relationships. *Journal of Speech and Hearing Disorders, 54,* 106–112.

Meyers, S., & Freeman, F. (1985). Mother and child speech rates as a variable in stuttering and disfluency. *Journal of Speech and Hearing Research, 28,* 436–444.

Morgenstern, J. (1956). Socio-economic factors in stuttering. *Journal of Speech and Hearing Disorders, 21,* 25–33.

Panelli, C., McFarlane, S., & Shipley, K. (1978). Implications of evaluating and interviewing with incipient stutterers. *Journal of Fluency Disorders, 3,* 41–50.

Onslow, M., & Packman, A. (1998). The Lidcombe program of early stuttering intervention. In N. Ratner & C. Healey (Eds.), *Stuttering treatment and research: Bridging the gap* (pp. 195–212). Mahwah, NJ: Lawrence Erlbaum Associates.

Ramig, P. (1993). High reported spontaneous recovery rates: Fact or fiction? *Language, Speech, and Hearing Services in Schools, 24,* 156–160.

Roman, G. (1972). *An investigation of the disfluent speech behavior of parents of stuttering and nonstuttering children.* Unpublished Master's. thesis, Texas Tech University, Lubbock

Ryan, B. (1990). Developmental stuttering. a longitudinal study, report. Paper presented at the convention of the American Speech-Language-Hearing Association, Seattle. Abstract published in *ASHA, 32*, 144.

Schindler, M. (1955). A study of educational adjustments of stuttering and nonstuttering children. In W. Johnson & R. Leuteneger (Eds.), *Stuttering in children and adults* (p. 348–357). Minneapolis: University of Minnesota Press.

Schwartz, H., & Conture, E. (1988). Subgrouping young stutterers: Preliminary behavioral observations. *Journal of Speech and Hearing Research, 31*, 62–71.

Seider, R., Gladstien, K., & Kidd, K. (1983). Recovery and persistence of stuttering among relatives of stutterers. *Journal of Speech and Hearing Disorders, 48*, 402–409.

Sheehan, J., & Martyn, M. (1970). Stuttering and its disappearance. *Journal of Speech and Hearing Research, 13*, 279–289.

St. Onge, K. (1963). The stuttering syndrome. *Journal of Speech and Hearing Research, 6*, 195–197.

Starkweather, C., Gottwald, S., & Halfond, M. (1990). *Stuttering prevention.* Englewood Cliffs, NJ: Prentice Hall.

Stephenson-Opsal, D., & Ratner, N. (1988). Maternal speech rate modification and childhood stuttering. *Journal of Fluency Disorders, 13*, 49–56.

Wingate, M. (1964). Recovery from stuttering. *Journal of Speech and Hearing Disorders, 29*, 312–321.

Yairi, E. (1983). The onset of stuttering in two- and three-year-old children. *Journal of Speech and Hearing Disorders, 48*, 171–177.

Yairi, E. (1990). Subtyping child stutterers for research purposes. *ASHA Reports, 18*, 50–57

Yairi, E. (1993). Epidemiology and other considerations in treatment efficacy research with preschool-age children who stutter. *Journal of Fluency Disorders, 18*, 197–220.

Yairi, E. (1997). Home environments and Parent-Child Interaction in Childhood Stuttering. In R. Curlee and G. Seigel (eds.), *Nature and Treatment of Stuttering* (p. 24–48). Needham Heights, MA: Allyn and Bacon.

Yairi, E., & Ambrose, N. (1992a). A longitudinal study of stuttering in children: A preliminary report. *Journal of Speech and Hearing Research, 35*, 755–760.

Yairi, E., & Ambrose, N. (1992b). Onset of stuttering in preschool children: Selected factors. *Journal of Speech and Hearing Research, 35*, 782–788.

Yairi, E., & Ambrose, N. (1996). Erratum. *Journal of Speech and hearing Research, 39*, 826.

Yairi, E., Ambrose, N. & Cox, N. (1996). Genetics of stuttering: A critical review. *Journal of Speech and Hearing Research, 39*, 771–784.

Yairi, E., Ambrose, N., & Niermann, R. (1993). The early months of stuttering: A developmental study. *Journal of Speech and Hearing Research, 36*, 521–528.

Yairi, E., Ambrose, N., Paden, E., & Throneburg, R. (1996). Predictive factors of persistence and recovery: Pathways of childhood stuttering. *Journal of Communication Disorders, 29*, 53–77.

Yaruss, S., LaSalle, L. & Conture, E. (1995). 100 children who stutter: Revisiting their clinical records. *Asha, 37*, 93.

FOOTNOTES

[1]An interesting discussion regarding the effects of genetic history on the environment in which parents and children interact may be found in Locke (1993).

[2]Ingham and Cordes (chap. 15, this volume) excluded the data because of a minor coding error in the Yairi and Ambrose published data. However, both a private communication and a formal erratum published in the *Journal of Speech and Hearing Research* (Yairi & Ambrose, 1996, pp 826) confirmed that this error did not alter the findings of 89% spontaneous recovery.

[3]I do not agree with Ingham and Cordes' statement (chap. 15, this volume) that the 1992 article by Yairi and Ambrose concluded that treatment was ineffective. No such conclusion was or ever has been made by Yairi and Ambrose in any of their publications. The presence of unassisted recovery does not prove that treatment is ineffective, but rather that the cause of improvement cannot be assumed to be due solely to treatment when spontaneous recovery is not taken into account. In my opinion, we need better controlled research for treatment efficacy.

5 Bridging the Gap Between the Science and Clinical Practice

Barry Guitar
University of Vermont

Psychologists have said that "Psychotherapy is an undefined technique, applied to unspecified problems, with unpredictable outcome. For this technique, we recommend rigorous training." (Raimy, 1950, p.93). We might say, in a cynical moment, "Stuttering therapy is an obscure blend of techniques, applied to a baffling problem, with frequent failure. Only specialists should be allowed to do this." This comment, however facetious, reminds us that a gap often exists between what we do in the clinic and what we know scientifically about what we do (for example, which strategies are effective, why are they effective, and how much long-term change takes place). Sometimes the gap is a mile wide, sometimes only a few slim inches, depending on whether we are treating a client by clinical intuition or by a more standardized use of proven techniques.

On one side of the gap stands science: prestigious, elegant, and often difficult. On the other side is practice: rewarding, individualistic, full of unknowns, and also difficult. As we try to bridge this gap, we believe that a critical mass of research should focus on clinically relevant topics, but we also know that much of the research has focused on what appear to be clinically irrelevant topics (such as models of language production or muscle reflexes) that may also be vital to clinical progress because of unexpected, serendipitous clinical benefits. We urge researchers in our field to throw the full force of their scientific expertise at our most pressing clinical problems, but we also know that such research may be messy, frustrating, and anything but elegant because so many of the seemingly relevant variables are so hard to measure. We urge that research attitudes be brought into clinical practice and we urge that all clinicians use the scientific method in assessing and improving their practice to help us grow as a profession. But we know realistically that some clinicians will be more likely than others to adopt the scientific method, depending on their training, work environment, and temperament. How do we bring these two domains of science and practice together? How have we done it best in the past?

Two Models

With these issues separating science and clinical practice in mind, I'd like to examine two approaches for bridging the gap. The first is for two or more individuals with divergent strengths working together to bring science into the clinic. Some members of a team may be more adept at managing the fine details of science and others may be more temperamentally suited to the interpersonal aspects of clinical work. Many two-member teams such as Curlee and Perkins (1968, 1969, 1973), Martin and

Haroldson (1969, 1971, 1977, 1979), Ingham and Andrews (1971, 1973), Riley and Riley (1980, 1984, 1986), and Ryan and Van Kirk Ryan (1974) fit this description. The association between these individuals may begin in graduate school, in a research setting, or in a clinic. In some lucky pairings, the joint work continues for many years, but for others, diverging interests or philosophical and temperament differences drive them apart.

The second approach occurs when one individual has both talents: when a single person can wear two hats—of science and of clinical practice. This has been called the scientist practitioner model, elaborated by Barlow, Hayes, and Nelson (1984) in their book, *The Scientist Practitioner*. It has been essentially the clinician–researcher model that has been advocated by many (e.g., Costello, 1979; Ringel, 1972) in our profession as an ideal for training programs and a necessity for sustaining progress in our field. It is suggested that with the proper training, clinician–scientists will use the latest research in their practices, evaluate the results of their treatments, and publish data on the effectiveness of their approaches.

We then might ask: How do these approaches—clinician and scientist or clinician–scientist—compare at bridging the gap between science and practice? What are their strengths and their weaknesses?

The model of the clinician and the scientist as different people working together has the strength of joining different talents and interests to work on a single problem. Two minds may be better than one, especially if they are divergent but complementary talents. In some cases, however, this may not work so well. Imagine a situation in which a clinician develops a treatment for stuttering and then asks a scientist to help her figure out why it works. The scientist may become so impressed with the treatment effect that she develops a theory to explain it and parlays the treatment into a commercial enterprise, leaving the clinician without credit or compensation. In other cases, the researcher's desire for rigor becomes a search for methodological purity and results in an endless string of papers about measurement issues when possibly more critical issues, such as what treatment variables are effective, remain unaddressed.

Clinician–scientists are less likely to be led into this latter temptation, however, because they have extensive clinical experiences to guide them in selecting clinically significant problems—those that can make a difference in therapy. The clinician–scientists' own clinical work informs them about what constitutes clinically significant change. They can use their own observations of their clients in their daily practice to develop hypotheses about important treatment variables.

Clinicians and scientists working together have an advantage over the lone clinician–scientist in another area, however. This concerns the danger that all scientists face when working alone: They can see what they want to see; they can be unconsciously biased to confirm their hypotheses; they can be blinded by their theories. Imagine a clinician–scientist who believes in a theory of stuttering as a hypertonic avoidance behavior and who uses desensitization as his primary therapy. In his clinical research, he may see what he thinks is significant change in stuttering as a result of desensitization, but another, more neutral, observer might see a host of other variables (that would support other theories) affecting outcome. Being blinded by his "pet" theory, this clinician–scientist may observe only the variables that fit the theory and ignore those that don't; then dubious "facts" become recorded in the literature. In the presence of another scientist who was neutral to the theory, more objective observations might have been made, and a deeper understanding of desensitization might have been reached.

Theory blindness (being unable to see research results clearly because one is so attached to a theory) is not limited to lone clinician–scientists; pairs and teams of scientists and clinicians can be afflicted with the disorder, too. But the best examples seem to come from individuals working by themselves. Charles Darwin, for example, wrote "All observation must be for or against some view [theory] if it is to be of any service" and then proceeded to support his theory of evolution with a factual error in categorizing the lineage of the mammal group *Macrauchenia* (Gould, 1996). In the years before Darwin's theory blinded him into making this error, his fact-collecting expedition aboard the *Beagle* may have been so fertile precisely because he was atheoretical at this time in his life: Darwin was just getting beyond the creationist view that pervaded his studies for the ministry, but had not yet developed his evolutionist view that was to be germinated by the specimens he collected on his voyage. Someone has compared this openmindedness (this atheoretical outlook that Darwin had at this time) to looking at a constellation in the night sky but keeping one's eyes open for shooting stars anywhere in the heavens.

Another example of the danger that accompanies too close attachment to a theory was described recently by a friend in Australia (Peter Neilson) who had been studying how the alpha and gamma motoneurons control the sensitivity of the muscle spindle. For his doctoral study—his first solo research—he proposed an experiment that would support the then-current theory that gamma motoneuron activity controls muscle spindle sensitivity. The experiment failed to support his hypothesis and my friend went into a nonproductive funk he now thinks of as "theory withdrawal." As months went by, he began to realize that his failed experiment suggested a new way of understanding the abnormal muscle tone in cerebral palsy. His interest perked up, he became productive again (e.g., Neilson, 1972a, 1972b, 1972c), and he now believes that real scientific progress comes when you demonstrate that your theory is wrong.

It is, of course, also possible to make scientific progress without a theory to prove wrong. Many findings arise in the absence of a theory, such as the discovery of the effects of delayed auditory feedback. Bernard Lee (1951) and John Black (1951) independently stumbled onto this phenomenon when they were tape recording their own speech while they listened themselves through headphones. They found that if they heard their own voice with a slight delay through the headphones as they talked, repetitive stutterlike behaviors occurred. They and other scientists then explored delayed auditory feedback (DAF) in depth and developed theories about stuttering as a problem of auditory feedback. In another instance of scientific serendipity, Israel Goldiamond (1965) discovered a clinical use of DAF quite by accident, without a theory to guide him. When Goldiamond tried DAF as a punishment for stuttering, he found that stutterers outwitted its punishing effects by talking very slowly and fluently. Impressed with its fluency-producing effects, Goldiamond then developed a DAF-based programmed fluency-shaping approach to stuttering that became the model for dozens of treatment programs over the next 30 years and spawned numerous theoretical explanations of their results.

Thus atheoretical, serendipitous results may lead to solid scientific advances and may stimulate their own theories in the course of time. In *Physics Today*, Amikam Aharoni made a strong argument for such atheoretical research, suggesting that "once an experiment is checked for accuracy and systematic errors, the data should be published, even if there is no theory. Experience shows that if the experiment is good, the theory will come later" (Aharoni, 1995, p.33). But it may be that the attitudes and conditions that favor atheoretical research are more likely to occur in the case of the single clinician–scientist rather than in a team of scientists and practitioners. A team may be assembled to approach a particular problem and may be funded by agencies that require theory-driven proposals (e.g., Costello Ingham & Riley, 1997). Clinician–scientists, working alone, may have more opportunities to explore interesting phenomena in their treatment rooms and "play" in their clinical laboratories, activities that may be fertile for discoveries.

Yet another issue in bridging the gap between science and treatment is the potential conflict between the welfare of the client and the requirements of research. This conflict may occur with either the clinician and scientist or the clinician–scientist model, but may be most easily handled when the scientist and clinician are different people. When one and the same person is the clinician and the scientist, clients may not fully trust the clinician's dedication to their best interest. During my dissertation studies on the effects of EMG biofeedback, for example, my stringent criterion for a stable baseline almost drove away some of my subjects. They couldn't understand why they had to undergo so many sessions without treatment if my aim was to help them become more fluent. In other studies, I have seen reversal of treatment in an ABAB design give clients reason to doubt that their best interests are at heart. Sometimes, I think that I can finesse this problem by telling clients that I want to make sure the treatment they are receiving is effective. But this is unconvincing if I am so obsessed with research protocols that the client's welfare is a secondary consideration.

The issue of client welfare has recently surfaced in discussions of research on very young children just beginning to stutter (Bernstein Ratner, 1997; Curlee & Yairi, 1997; Zebrowski, 1997). Should treatment be withheld so that the effect of spontaneous remission can be studied? Should treatment be given when the likelihood of recovery without treatment is high? Arguments for client welfare can be made on both sides of this debate.

When the clinician and researcher are different people, the clients may observe that the clinician negotiates with the scientist to protect them in a way that does not compromise the research and they are likely to cooperate fully in treatment studies. For example, in the treatment research of Ryan and Van Kirk Ryan (1983), Bruce Ryan and Richard Martin designed the studies and ensured the welfare of the research while Barbara Van Kirk worked on the details of treatment and ensured the welfare of clients. Ryan and Van Kirk Ryan have continued to work in this way in more recent treatment studies as well (Ryan, personal communication, October 23,1996). How do we encourage this cooperation more? How do we prepare future clinicians and researchers to emulate it?

Training

I have presented arguments suggesting that both the clinician and scientist model and the clinician–scientist model have advantages. Thus, they should both be encouraged. But readers may wonder if the best solution to the problem isn't to train all our students to become clinician–scientists, making them capable of functioning either alone as clinician–scientists or on a team of clinicians and scientists. As appealing as this may sound, research suggests that this may not be a viable option: Science and clinical practice may attract opposite personality types and the clinician–scientist model may fit very few students. Zachar and Leong's (1992) study of psychology graduate students indicated that personality variables such as "objectivism," "subjectivism," "social," and "investigative" predicted student vocational interest in science or clinical practice in opposite directions. That is, psychology graduate students who hoped to become scientists scored high on objectivism and investigative variables, but low on subjectivism and social variables. Students who hoped to become clinicians scored very much in the opposite direction. When the authors administered their Scientist–Practitioner Inventory (Leong & Zachar, 1991), about 38% of these students could be labeled by their scores as practitioners (clinicians), 38% of the students could be labeled as scientists, and only about 12% of the students could be labeled as scientist–practitioners (the remaining 12% were neither and could perhaps be administrators). The authors urged graduate schools in psychology to accept the possibility that there is a limit to what education can do to change personality and that many clinical psychologists will not become scientist–practitioners, nor will they even develop scientific conceptual understanding.

If these findings can be replicated and extended to our field, efforts to train all students to become clinician–scientists may be disappointing. We might be wiser to accept the likelihood that some students' interests and temperaments suit them to be strictly scientists, others strictly clinicians, and only a small number to be clinician–scientists. The training of clinicians may not be a difficult issue for the field: Many readers probably accept the current wisdom that even those students who will be strictly clinicians must be trained to be consumers of research and must have a solid grounding in normal development of communication and in speech, language, and hearing sciences. The training of clinician–scientists may be an issue we have thought less about.

What training makes a good clinical researcher? It may, in part, be training in science. Consider the background of an early clinician–scientist, Sigmund Freud. Freud started out as a physiologist, studying eels' testicles and the effect of cocaine on the human eye. This training in careful observation steadied Freud's nerves when he responded to the amorous advances of his patient, Anna O, by developing a hypothesis about transference and the unconscious, thus giving birth to psychoanalytic theory. Another example of the benefit of scientific training for clinician–scientists is the psychologist Carl Rogers, who was steeped in agricultural statistics growing up on his father's scientifically run farm, and later studied agronomy at the University of Wisconsin. This background in "split-plot design" and other earthy elements of agronomy prepared Rogers to carry out his research on the effects of psychotherapy.

In our own field, Charles Van Riper is an example of a clinical scientist who was trained in engineering, Old English scholarship, and experimental psychology; this background in research prepared him to record and report on 20 years of varying treatment protocols and assessing treatment outcomes (Van Riper, 1958). Using a tighter standard of clinical research with a less encompassing reach, Dick Martin (e.g., Martin, Kuhl, & Haroldson, 1972) compiled a record of rigorous experimentation, using single-subject design to study the effects of a variety of treatment variables on stuttering. Martin began as a clinician in the schools of South Dakota, but soon realized that his therapy was ineffective and determined to increase his effectiveness as well as his ability to measure it by taking a doctoral program rich with offerings in experimental psychology.

A broad education, especially one involving linguistics, cognition, and physiological psychology, is likely to create better clinician–scientists. Consider the first speech-language pathologist, Lee Edward Travis, who, trained in several areas of speech, psychology, and medicine, was able to pioneer a host of research and treatment domains in stuttering. We would be wise to guide our students to become more interdisciplinary in their training. Note the richness of such interdisciplinary interactions in such centers as Nijmegen, Sydney, and Haskins Laboratories: Stuttering specialists should be expanding their areas of focus and their research teams to include many other disciplines.

If we take as our educational mission the training of clinicians to develop a scientific attitude toward clinical practice and the training of clinician–scientists to use the scientific method in the laboratory at first and then in the clinic, what shall be their tasks as they advance our profession in to the next decades? Some of the major challenges that need to be undertaken are those relating to effective diagnostic and treatment techniques for stuttering. We must first develop some notions of what clients' complaints are. Frequency of stuttering? Duration of stuttering? Overall severity? Feelings that accompany the moment of stuttering? Attitudes about being someone who stutters? Communicative effectiveness? Are the complaints different for different ages? Different individuals? We must try to address these complaints. What tools can evaluate them? What techniques can change them? How can we validly and reliably can we measure changes? What are "good enough" changes, so we don't have to expect perfection, especially if our clients don't?

These research questions require the help of clinician–scientists or scientists working with clinicians rather than individuals who are clinicians only, simply because clinician–scientists are more likely to use "disconfirmatory strategies" (Faust, 1986) to try to disprove hypotheses and would thereby be more objective. A good example is in the reporting of outcome data on treatment approaches. Clinicians, because of their understandable desire for their clients to succeed, often report high success rates for their treatment, but when results are closely examined, it is clear that some measurement methodologies are biased in favor of good results. For example, long-term outcome may be assessed by telephoning clients who expect assessment phone calls from persons identifying themselves as associated with the program; because of the strong cues present in such an arrangement, clients are often able to speak more fluently in this situation than in others. A disconfirmatory strategy would seek to gather long-term outcome data in the most conservative way; that is, the clinician–scientist would want to make the assessment as rigorous as possible so that the speech sample was genuinely representative of the client's speech in a variety of real-world situations.

CONCLUSION

I have suggested that there is a large and understandable gap between science and clinical practice. The gap may be narrowed in the future by training our students to be scientists, clinicians, or clinician–scientists; some will fit more easily into one role than in another and there is no reason why we must make them all the same. By temperament and training, some of our students, following a research path, will seek to uncover the verities of stuttering, to develop better diagnostic tools, and to understand the mechanisms of treatment; others, pursuing clinical endeavors, will seek to help as many stutterers as possible by devising new diagnostic tools and new treatments and by refining old ones. We must foster both. Clinicians should be encouraged to disseminate their methods as widely as possible, through presentations and publications. The problem is not that unexamined treatments are being recommended, but that there are not enough opportunities for clinicians to fully describe their treatments in print so that clinician–scientists can examine them. Treatments need to be shared because the creative clinicians who can lift us out of our therapy ruts with innovations and individualized variations of treatment are not necessarily those best suited to the task of measuring their effectiveness. Rather than denigrating clinicians for publishing descriptions of treatment without effectiveness data, clinician–scientists and scientists on teams with clinicians should educate clinicians about how to fully and effectively describe their procedures, and the scientists and clinician–scientists should examine both new and old diagnostic tools and treatment methods, attempting to disconfirm their effectiveness and, in the process, uncovering elements of truth.

REFERENCES

Bernstein Ratner, N. (1997). Leaving Las Vegas: Clinical odds and individual outcomes. *American Journal of Speech-Language Pathology, 6,* 29–33.

Black, J. W. (1951). The effect of delayed sidetone upon vocal rate and intensity. *Journal of Speech and Hearing Disorders, 16,* 56–60.

Curlee, R., & Perkins, W. (1968). The effect of punishment of expectancy to stutter on the frequencies of subsequent expectancies and stuttering. *Jounal of Speech and Hearing Research, 11,* 789–795.

Curlee, R., & Perkins, W. (1969). Conversational rate control therapy for stuttering. *Journal of Speech and Hearing Disorders, 34,* 245–250.

Curlee, R., & Perkins, W. (1973). Effectiveness of a DAF conditioning program for adolescent and adult stutters. *Behavioral Research and Therapy, 11,* 395–401.

Curlee, R., & Yairi, E. (1997). Early intervention with early childhood stuttering: A critical examination of the data. *American Journal of Speech-Language Pathology, 6*, 8–18.

Costello, J. M. (1979). Clinicians and researchers: A necessary dichotomy? *Journal of the National Student Speech and Hearing Association, 7,* 6–26.

Goldiamond, I. (1965). Stuttering and fluency as manipulatable operant response classes. In L. Krasner & L. Ullman (Eds.), *Research in behavior modification: New developments and implications* (pp.106–156). New York: Hold, Rinehart & Winston.

Gould, S. J. (1996). Why Darwin? *The New York Review of Books, 43,* 10–14.

Lee, B. S. (1951). Artificial stutter. *Journal of Speech and Hearing Disorders, 16,* 53–55.

Martin, R., Kuhl, P., & Haroldson, S. (1972). An experimental treatment with two preschool stuttering children. *Journal of Speech and Hearing Research, 15,* 743–752.

Neilson, P. D. (1972a). Speed of response or bandwidth of voluntary system controlling elbow position in intact man. *Medical and Biological Engineering, 10,* 450–459.

Neilson, P. D. (1972b). Frequency response characteristics of the tonic stretch reflexes of biceps brachii muscle in intact man. *Medical and Biological Engineering, 10,* 460–472.

Neilson, P. D. (1972c). Voluntary and reflex control of the biceps brachii muscle in spastic-athetotic patients. *Journal of Neurological and Neurosurgical Psychiatry, 35,* 589–598.

Raimy, V. C. (Ed.). (1950). *Training in clinical psychology (Boulder Conference).* New York: Prentice-Hall.

Riley, G. & Riley, J. (1980). Motor and linguistic variables among children who stutter: A factor analysis. *Journal of Speech and Hearing Disorders, 37,* 504–514.

Riley, G. & Riley, J. (1984). A component model for traeting stuttering in children. In Peins, M. (ed.), *Contemporary Approaches in Stuttering Therapy.* Boston: Little, Brown.

Riley, G. & Riley, J. (1986). Oral motor discoordination among children who stutter. *Journal of Fluency Disorders,* 11, 335–344.

Ringel, R. L. (1972). The clinician and the researcher: An artificial dichotomy. *Asha, 28,* 351–353.

Ryan, B., & Van Kirk, B. (1974). The establishment, transfer, and maintenance of fluent speech in 50 stutterers using delayed auditory feedback and operant procedures. *Jounal of Speech and Hearing Disorders, 39,* 3–10.

Ryan, B., & Van Kirk, B. (1983). Programmed stuttering therapy for children: Comparisons of four establishment programs. *Journal of Fluency Disorders, 8,* 291–321.

Van Riper, C. (1958). Experiments in stuttering therapy. In J. Eisenson (Ed.), *Stuttering: A Symposium* (pp.275–390). New York: Harper & Row.

Zachar, P., & Leong, F. (1992). A problem of personality: Scientist and practicioner differences in psychology. *Journal of Personality, 60,* 665–677.

Zebrowski, P. (1997). Assisting young children who stutter and their families: Defining the role of the speech-language pathologist. *American Journal of Speech-Language Pathology, 6,* 19–28.

6 A Conceptual Framework for Investigating the Neurobiology of Stuttering

Christy L. Ludlow
Voice and Speech Section, National Institute on Deafness and Other Communication Disorders, National Institutes of Health

Stuttering has eluded understanding since antiquity (Travis, 1978). Recently, two new advances are promising: Several investigative teams have embarked on linkage analysis to determine if a specific region of the genome is associated with chronic developmental stuttering; and functional brain imaging is being used to describe brain activation abnormalities during disfluent speech (Barinaga, 1995; Fox et al., 1996; Wu, et al., 1995). Despite procedural differences among investigators using functional brain imaging, the results thus far confirm previous research (Moore & Haynes, 1980; Wells & Moore, 1990; Wood, Stump, McKennhan, Sheldon, & Proctor, 1980), which suggested a reduction in left hemisphere dominance during stuttering (Braun et al., 1997; Fox et al., 1995; Wu et al., 1995). These studies are difficult to interpret, however. On the one hand, they may represent brain organization changes as a result of persons struggling with a lifelong chronic speech impairment. On the other hand, they may suggest that persons who develop chronic adult stuttering are those who initially had a different brain organization for speech.

The purpose of this chapter is to identify some of the opportunities and obstacles to understanding the neurobiology of the epigenesis of stuttering, that is, the brain organization differences that may have led to the emergence of stuttering. It also demonstrates why it is important to develop a neurobiological model of the epigenesis of stuttering. The type of model employed has a direct bearing on the expectation of who might be affected when embarking on linkage analysis to identify a genomic locus associated with the emergence of stuttering. A better understanding of the neurobiology of developmental stuttering will provide a conceptual framework from which to formulate treatment.

CHARACTERIZATION OF STUTTERING

A major roadblock to determining the pathogenesis of stuttering is deciding who has the disorder and to what degree (Ludlow, 1990). The types of symptoms that should be included as stuttering have been disputed. Some symptoms are designated as primary and others as secondary, based on their expected time of appearance during the development of chronic stuttering (Van Riper, 1973). More recently, however, both secondary and core symptoms of stuttering have been found in young children who stutter (Conture & Kelly, 1991; Yairi, Ambrose, & Niermann, 1993; Yairi, Ambrose, Paden, & Throneburg, 1996). Some investigators report that the types and frequency of disfluencies, rather than disfluency durations, can differentiate children at risk for a chronic speech disorder from those undergoing normal developmental speech dysfluency (Throneburg & Yairi, 1994), although the same authors later suggested a cautious interpretation of such findings (Yairi et al., 1996). The World Health Organization definition (World Health Organization, 1977) includes only repetitions of sounds and syllables and sound prolongations (Wingate, 1976) in the definition of stuttering. However, persons who stutter often have additional speech characteristics such as speech blocks, associated movements (eye blinks, grimaces) and use other speech behaviors such as reiterations, intrusions, or circumlocutions to avoid disfluency.

The following conceptual framework regarding the neurobiology of the development of stuttering suggests that the type and frequency of symptoms may not be the best way to define the disorder. If stuttering is a behavioral syndrome resulting from the interaction of several factors involved in the development of an individual's speech expression skills, then individual variation in stuttering symptoms would be expected. Idiosyncratic differences in how a child adapts to speech difficulties during the emergence of speech and language function would be expected. It may be impossible to determine which of the manifest speech behaviors are the result of the child's difficulties in producing fluent speech or are the child's attempts to overcome these difficulties. With a view that stuttering is an emergent property of an unstable and vulnerable speech production system, it would not be warranted to try and separate "core" stuttering symptoms from other symptoms deemed "secondary" (Ludlow, 1990). In fact, the symptoms of stuttering may only be an indirect reflection of the brain mechanisms for speech and language production that render the affected individual less efficient in speech production. Symptom frequency and type result when the less efficient cerebral system for speech and language production becomes evident in behavior, although the brain function abnormality for speech expression may be constantly present (Braun et al., 1997). Some adults who rarely produce sound repetitions or prolongations report internalized stuttering and must be constantly vigilant to avoid disfluency (Bloodstein, 1995). Given these observations, stuttering may be an inconsistent expression of an unstable speech and language production system. The challenge then is to determine the characteristics of the unstable neurobiological system, rather than to focus on symptom occurrence.

Stuttering Involves the Interface Between Speech and Language

Stuttering symptoms become most prominent when the speaker needs to use speech to express new information to others. This is one of the reasons that disfluency is so difficult to study in the laboratory in contrast with other speech disorders such as phonological disorders and dysarthria. In these other disorders, subjects' errors when reading or repeating single words or syllables are representative of symptoms during spontaneous speech. Similar approaches cannot be used in stuttering, where symptoms usually occur only when the speaker must use speech to communicate language meaning to others. Speech without communicative intent contains less disfluency; we have observed that even severely affected adults will speak fluently when instructed to speak nonsense or gibberish. Either the lack of language processing or reduced speech production constraints when particular words are not required, may account for the absence of symptoms. Linguistic processing may play a role as longer, more complex sequences are more likely to contain symptoms (Postma, Kolk, & Povel, 1990). Stuttering occurs more frequently when the speaker is required to communicate new information via speech, rather than during singing, acting, or repetition of others. Thus, the interface between language formulation and speech production engenders stuttering symptoms, not either task alone. Any increases in language and speech production processing demands render persons who stutter more prone to symptom production; more complex utterances (Bernstein Ratner & Sih, 1987), less familiar words (Hubbard & Prins, 1994), open class content words (Brown, 1938; Johnson & Brown, 1935), or words containing longer, more complex phonological sequences (Brown, 1945; Silverman, 1972; Soderberg, 1966, 1967; Taylor, 1966). The neurobiology of the development of the speech/language production system in those who stutter renders it more fragile and susceptible to disruption, particularly when the complexity of speech and language processing increases.

The coincidence of stuttering with other speech and language disorders during development has long been debated. Studies of the syntactic and language skills of children who stutter have not had clear-cut results (Andrews et al., 1983; Muma, 1971; Nippold, 1990). Studies by Conture and his colleagues suggest that phonological production deficits and disfluency can occur together in early childhood (Conture, Louko, & Edwards, 1993; Daly, 1994; Louko, 1995; Louko, Edwards, & Conture, 1990; Wolk, Edwards, & Conture, 1993) although phonological errors and stuttering are not related in their locus of occurrence in children affected with both disorders (Throneburg, Yairi, & Paden, 1994). Furthermore, stuttering has long been recognized as closely associated with cluttering which can be characterized as an expressive-receptive phonological disorder (Daly, 1993, 1994; St. Louis, 1992; St. Louis & Hinzman, 1986). These associations suggest that some children have a more fragile speech and language system because of an inefficiency in the integrative brain mechanisms involved in the interface between language encoding and speech production processes. This fragility may underlie the emergence of stuttering symptoms and other speech and language disorders.

Therefore, to understand the neurobiology of the development of stuttering, we must understand the processes involved in developing speech formulation and production skills for language communication. During the developmental period of normal disfluency, increasing cognitive processing demands are required during speech communication. Some children are more susceptible to a period of disfluency during this period of increased processing demands. Most will emerge with a normally functioning system due to improved efficiency as a result of normal mechanisms of developmental neural plasticity and adaptation. Some children do not achieve the establishment of an efficient speech/language production system within the critical period for language development, between birth and puberty. How their neurolinguistic system differs from others may be the foundation of the neurobiology of chronic stuttering. Further information is needed, then, on the processing demands involved in speech development. Standardized speech and language tests measuring the level of speech and language skills that a child has achieved may not be helpful, as it may not be the achievement of particular developmental milestones that is important. Rather, it may be the efficiency or stability of the neural mechanisms involved in developing such behaviors. For example, vocabulary testing only determines what words the child has learned, but it does not provide information on how the child achieved that level of word knowledge or what brain mechanisms were used to produce that knowledge.

Many models of speech production include processes of semantic differentiation, lexical selection, a syntactic framework, phonological rules, and phonetic realization (Dell, Juliano, & Govindjee, 1993; Garrett, 1991; Levelt, 1989, 1992). The processes involved in learning to express language information efficiently through speech during child development may differ somewhat and may include phoneme segmentation, skill in coordinate movement patterning, learning new motor patterns, planning complex utterances, and self-monitoring. In a recent study comparing chronically affected adults who stuttered with control subjects, we found that the adults who stuttered demonstrated less accurate and less efficient speech learning skills for acquiring new novel sound sequences (Ludlow, Siren, & Zikria, 1997). Because these findings indicated that chronically affected adults who stuttered had less efficient speech learning skills, we need to explore whether these skills relate to the development of speech production for language expression. Some skills may be transient, and only employed at a particular stage in speech/language development and may no longer have a role once that stage is completed. One example may be differentiation between the phonemes within a word. As some data suggest, children learn to further spatially differentiate their consonant productions within words as they become more proficient in speech production (Nittrouer, Studdert-Kennedy, & Neely, 1996). If the brain mechanisms involved in such skills are not achieved efficiently during a critical development phase, the resulting speech production system may remain unstable throughout life.

APPROACHES TO DEFINING STUTTERING AS A DISORDER

If symptom characteristics are expected to vary in each individual and might not be a good indication of developmental neurobiological differences, then which parameters should be considered for determining who is affected by a similar epigenesis? In other disorders, two aspects reflect differences in genetic predisposition; the age of onset and the temporal pervasiveness of the disorder. For example, in dopa-responsive dystonia, preadulthood onset is part of the syndrome identification for those with mutations in the GTP cyclohydrolase I gene (GCH1) (Furukawa et al., 1996; Nygaard, 1995). Similarly, in idiopathic torsion dystonia, preadult onset is used for the identification of patients with the dystonia I gene (DYT1) locus (Bressman et al., 1994; Kramer et al., 1994). Certainly, acquired stuttering in adulthood following brain injury has different characteristics from developmental stuttering (Ludlow, Rosenberg, Salazar, Grafman, & Smutok, 1987);

however, it is not known whether onset at different times during childhood might indicate different mechanisms involved in the epigenesis. The emergence of stuttering during the normal period of developmental disfluency (between 2 and 5 years of age) when fluent speech is becoming established may depend on different factors from stuttering emerging later in childhood (between 6 and 8 years of age), when associated with important life events such as prolonged illness, death in the family, a move, or a divorce. Others have suggested that recovery from developmental stuttering, which occurs in the majority of affected cases, may be due to a genetic factor rather than stuttering occurrence being a genetic factor (Yairi, Ambrose & Cox, 1996). This latter view suggests that developmental stuttering is part of a normal continuum of a temporary instability in the speech/language expression system during the period of rapid speech and language development. In fact, the variation in the duration of the persistence of stuttering symptoms may reflect the normal range in speech developmental neurobiology.

The critical age hypothesis concerning the optimal period for language development, proposes that, following puberty, the brain becomes less plastic making later language acquisition less efficient in most individuals (Lenneberg, 1968). Children isolated from language input early in life are often reduced in their language skills for life, as evidenced by "wolf" children and the sad case of Genie (Fromkin, Krasher, Curtiss, Rigler, & Rigler, 1974). An optimal period has also been demonstrated for phonological development; after age 7, learning a speech sound system is less efficient (Asher & Garcia, 1969; Locke, 1992) and after 15 years of age, the ability to acquire native speech sound production skills in a foreign language is limited (Flege, Munro, & MacKay, 1995). Given the changing plasticity of the speech and language system during particular periods in development, one approach to categorizing stuttering might be a staging approach based on the language age of symptom onset and the duration of symptom persistence. The emergence of chronic stuttering may depend on limits in the developmental plasticity of the neurobiological substrates involved in fluent and efficient speech/language expression. Perhaps the longer the disorder persists during the critical period for speech and language expression, the more resistant the neurobiological substrates underlying speech expression are to the emergence of a fluent and efficient speech production system.

A staging system for determining the degree of stuttering severity across individuals might be as follows.

Stage 1. Recovery from stuttering in less than 6 months.

Stage 2. Recovery from stuttering between 6 months and 1 year with complete recovery prior to 8 years of age.

Stage 3. Stuttering past 8 years of age with complete recovery by puberty.

Stage 4. Stuttering continuing into adolescence with complete recovery by 18 years of age.

Stage 5. Stuttering into adulthood with intermittent remission of symptoms.

Stage 6. Chronic adult stuttering affecting speech communication.

Skills such as phonological processing, speech motor learning, and speech auditory self-monitoring may be involved in the emergence of an efficient speech and language production system. These skills need to be evaluated for a relationship with the recovery or persistence of developmental stuttering. For example, impairments in language processing may relate to the persistence of stuttering (Yairi et al., 1996). Such findings provide indications for designing interventions to assist children who stutter with the acquisition of fluent speech production.

A staging approach to severity might help address one of the difficulties that plagues the study of all developmental speech and language disorders when attempting to determine who is affected and who is not. Stuttering is most prevalent during the developmental period of speech/language acquisition (1 to 7 years). Perhaps only subtle residual impairments (such as less efficient speech learning skills) may be present in adults who recovered during childhood. As with specific language impairment (Gilger, 1995), difficulties with studying the genetic aspects of these disorders lie in determining who is affected and who is not, particularly because the symptoms change with development and are part of a continuum of normal development (Felsenfeld, 1996). When studying the genetics of stuttering, this distinction is critical before attempting to develop ascertainment criteria for individuals to be genotyped.

The Many Paths to Epigenesis

Stuttering has been hypothesized as a multifactorial disorder (Smith, 1990, 1992; Smith & Weber, 1988; Zimmerman, Smith, & Hanley, 1981) with symptom occurrence depending on the interactions among several factors both during development and later while speaking. Several factors may lead to an unstable or inefficient neurobiological system during the developmental emergence of an integrated system for language and speech production, such as a lack of cerebral dominance for language and/or a different brain organization underlying speech and language production. Certainly stuttering can be considered a complex trait, as are many developmental disorders, such as specific language impairment, developmental dyslexia, childhood autism, and cluttering (Cox, 1993; Felsenfeld, 1996; Gilger, 1995; Risch & Merikangas, 1993, 1996; Yairi et al., 1996). Some characteristics are common to many of these disorders: they appear at a specific stage in development and interfere with the spontaneous emergence of particular communication skills following an earlier normal developmental course. As Locke (1992) suggested, there is evidence of a positive family history associated with abnormal brain development in dyslexia (Galaburda, Sherman, Rosen, Aboitiz, & Geschwinder, 1985), specific language impairment (Plante, 1991; Plante, Swisher, & Vance, 1989, 1991), and autism (Bauman & Kemper, 1985; Dawson, Finley, Phillips, & Galpert, 1986; Steffeberg et al., 1989). All have a higher concordance in monozygotic than in dyzygotic twins, although the familial patterns are more evident in specific language impairment than in stuttering (Ludlow & Dooman, 1992). In dyslexia and specific language impairment, left–right differences in the size of the temporal plenum are reduced when affected individuals are compared with controls (Galaburda et al., 1985) and similar characteristics are also found in relatives of children with specific language impairment (Plante, 1991). Similarly, in stuttering, one CT study demonstrated a greater incidence of left–right symmetry in language related structures in individuals who stuttered (Strub, Black, & Naeser, 1987).

A predominance of affected males is common to most speech and language disorders, as is differential recovery; females show more recovery than males (Yairi et al., 1996). This difference may be the result of male and female differences in brain organization for speech and language processing. Recent evidence has suggested that males tend to use predominantly a left hemisphere system for phonological processing, whereas females tend to employ bilaterally distributed brain mechanisms for the same tasks (Shaywitz, et al., 1995). Perhaps because males tend to use a left hemisphere system for phonological processing, when these left hemisphere mechanisms are impaired, males may possess less plasticity and may be less able to employ alternative mechanisms in the right hemisphere for recovery (Shaywitz et al., 1995; Shaywitz et al., 1996). Recent PET scan studies have demonstrated that left hemisphere mechanisms for speech and language function differently in adults with chronic stuttering, particularly in the auditory association areas of the left hemisphere (Braun et al., 1997; Fox et al., 1995), the regions showing more left lateralization in males. Research needs to be done on young children near stuttering onset to determine whether functional anomalies in the left hemisphere are related to the onset of stuttering. However, such studies cannot be conducted without the development of valid noninvasive functional imaging techniques for use in young children. The possibility of an interaction between anomalies in left hemisphere development and sex differences in the degree of neuroplasticity of the brain mechanisms utilized during the optimal period for speech and language development needs to be evaluated. Information is needed on developmental changes in brain organization for speech and language processing in affected and unaffected males and females prior to puberty. The developmental processes involved in the emergence of efficient brain mechanisms for speech and language processing are largely unknown.

Two broad etiologic groups of persons affected by stuttering have been proposed (Poulos & Webster, 1991); one group with a genetic predisposition and another who may have experienced brain injury during development. Developmental anomalies could be due either to genetic risk factors or to other factors interfering with neuronal development, such as malnutrition, failure to thrive, trauma, and psychosocial factors. A knowledge of brain development patterns, including cell migration, programmed cell death, neuronal plasticity, and the continued interaction between neural activity and growth of brain structure and function (Purves, 1994) is essential for determining which factors may interfere with the development of an efficiently functioning speech/language production system.

Neurobiology of Development

The emergent processes of cell differentiation and convergence are important in development and may provide the biological bases for the genesis of an integrated system for speech and language functioning. The development of an embryo from a blastula is contingent on cell proliferation, migration, growth, differentiation among cell types, and programmed cell death (apoptosis). Initially, cells proliferate at a rapid rate and have the potential to become any type of cell. Intrinsic factors such as specific patterns of gene expression are regulated by a variety of molecular mechanisms, leading to production of proteins that determine cell fate and function. Cell differentiation creates new structures and is genetically regulated; for example, a progenitor cell is limited to a specific cell type by gene activation (Shostak, 1991a).

Cells may also migrate to new positions where they differentiate into various cell types. The extracellular matrix, composed of a variety of materials, provides some of the directional cues for cell migration. Transforming growth factors (TGF-ß), a superfamily of proteins, play a key role in cell growth and differentiation (Wall & Hogan, 1994). Extrinsic influences also affect how a cell develops and include hormonal modulation and cell-to-cell interactions. An interaction of intrinsic and extrinsic factors determine a cell's ultimate fate (Cypher & Letourneau, 1992; Shostak, 1991b).

Postnatal growth of the brain does not depend on the proliferation of additional neurons (Rakic, 1985); primates are born with at least all the cortical nerve cells that they will have. The neurobiological processes that are ongoing during childhood include the generation of glial cells, axon myelination, and the addition of vasculature and connective tissues. Most dramatic is neural growth to produce the dense matrix of axons, dendrites, and synapses (Purves & Lichtman, 1985a). These processes result in convergent integrated and efficient systems capable of supporting highly complex behavioral skills. Brain development throughout childhood involves the creation of novel interconnections to produce the circuitry supporting increases in knowledge. Such interconnections depend on neural activity for their long term potentiation and establishment. Thus, brain development is a highly interactive process. The plasticity of behavioral development is the result of a continual interplay between cellular growth processes and neural activity. Neuroplasticity during development is essential for the emergence of new behaviors and underlies the potential for recovery from impairment during development, such as speech disfluency.

The development of neural interconnections also involves a selective process. Programmed cell death (or apoptosis) is a normal physiological process that eliminates unwanted, functionally abnormal, or harmful cells (Stellar, 1995). This process occurs during both embryonic and postnatal development and throughout life.

Programmed cell death involves targeting affected cells, loss of cell contact with neighboring cells, gene activation, DNA fragmentation, cell shrinkage and fragmentation (Hengartner & Horvitz, 1994). Cell death and cell survival are controlled by combined intracellular and extracellular signals. Specific genes initiate the cell death sequence, others conduct the actual killing, while yet others serve to prevent cell death. Nerve growth factor is an example of a protein regulating growth during both development and restitution of function following injury (Russell, 1995). Processes of cell growth, determination, and apoptosis continue throughout the life span. The interplay between gene expression and neural activity shapes the outcome of these processes.

Thus, brain development involves at least two processes; the proliferation of new connections between neurons and the selective elimination of others. Both these processes are dependent on neural activity. Either the lack of development of efficient interconnections, the elimination of inefficient ones, or both, could be the basis for the lack of a stable or efficient speech production system in children affected with stuttering.

Behavioral observations suggest that some critical changes occur in the speech/language neurobiological system between the ages of 3 and 8, when individuals experience the greatest risk of a period of instability in speech/language leading to disfluency. Brain organization systems for behavior are now conceived of as interactive modular systems that project via subcortical and cortical neural systems (Goldman-Rakic, 1988).

What are these changes? The competing processes of proliferation of new connections via cell growth and selectivity, shaped by both genetic programming and neural activity, produce modular systems via divergence of cell connections as well as the convergence of cellular connections (Purves, 1988). Cell growth is achieved by constant remodeling of the cytoskeleton or cellular structures; various adhesion proteins and integrins abound in the growth cone membrane to accomplish this process. Cell survival is contingent on axons reaching a particular target. The neurotrophic theory suggests that target cells are the source of certain substances that direct the axon such as nerve growth factor (NGF) (Purves & Lichtman, 1985b). When the axon reaches the target, it differentiates from a growing structure to a secreting structure as a consequence of contact with the target (Vrbova, Gordon, & Jones, 1995). It forms a synapse, thus, altering the cell phenotype. In peripheral nerve development, axon outgrowth and synaptogenesis occur and are followed by elimination of improper or unnecessary connections.

In the development of motor control, NGFs sustain cellular activity following connections made in the periphery. Either NGF or second messenger systems also stimulate further axonal outgrowth and dendritic density outgrowth with peripheral innervation and activity, which are important for the establishment of modular circuits. Several of the facial, some laryngeal, and possibly other vocal tract cortical neurons are thought to have monosynaptic connections to lower motor neurons (Kuypers, 1958). Thus, efficiency of corticocortical and corticobulbar connections is required for the control of rapid and precise movements involved in speech production.

Neurobiological processes that support stable and efficient function may be important for fluent speech production. Certainly cell-to-cell interactions can be the basis for such functions. Neurotransmitters and second messenger neuromodulators can serve as trophic agents involved in the rearrangement of synapses following changes in sensory experience or injury (Russell, 1995). Studies of cells in slices have demonstrated activity-dependent long-term potentiation of synaptic connections between cells (Malenka, 1995). As Hebb (1949) originally proposed, cellular studies now confirm how synaptic connections are altered by frequent simultaneous firing of two convergent neurons, producing adaptation and change. Such neuronal changes may be the basis for the emergence of an efficient and stable motor system during the development of speech skills.

Although we have no knowledge regarding which processes could be affected in the development of stuttering, studies of the neurobiology of brain development have exploded in recent years and have potential for providing significant new insights in the decade ahead. Certainly, increased understanding of the neural organization and development of speech systems and of the factors involved in enhancing neuroplasticity during the emergence of new behaviors will be the basis for improved treatment of stuttering.

THE NEUROBIOLOGY OF SPEECH AND LANGUAGE

Until the last decade, information on speech and on language organization in the brain came from studies of the association between brain lesion locations following stroke or brain injury, and residual speech and language functions. The dichotomy between the findings that anterior left hemisphere brain lesions produce nonfluent Broca's aphasia with impairments in speech fluency and syntactic structure, and that posterior left hemisphere lesions produce fluent Wernicke's aphasia with impairments in word retrieval and comprehension, has long been recognized. The disconnection hypotheses regarding syndromes of aphasia were introduced by Geschwind and included conduction aphasia with damage to the arcuate fasciculus between Broca's and Wernicke's areas; transcortical motor aphasia, a disconnection between the language system and the supplementary motor area resulting in restricted spontaneous speech; and, transcortical sensory aphasia, the isolation of the language areas from interaction with auditory, tactile and visual input modalities (Geschwind, 1964, 1965a, 1965b, 1970a, 1970b, 1971, 1972).

The use of functional imaging, however, has suggested that speech and language processing involves distributed processing among many brain regions, in addition to those identified from brain lesion studies. Speech and language functioning is now regarded as requiring the efficient and stable interaction among many brain mechanisms rather than being the function of a few specific centers (Raichle, 1990).

Many of the early functional brain imaging studies involved single-word processing, comparing the mode of presentation of words with the types of language processing that must be generated. Separate modular systems for accessing words by different stimulus modes, such as auditory versus visual, were demonstrated (Petersen, Fox, Mintaur, & Raichle, 1988, 1989; Petersen, Fox, Snyder, & Raichle, 1990; Posner, Petersen, Fox, & Raichle, 1988). Presentation of written words was found to activate the left mesial striate cortex, thought to be associated with the visual perception aspects of the task. Regardless of whether presentation was visual or auditory, if semantic processing was required, left prefrontal cortical activity was shown. Activation for real words in the left hemisphere was also seen in the prefrontal cortex and was interpreted as involving the semantic decoding aspects of real word recognition.

Two separate pathways for speech output and word generation have been proposed, based on whether the word production could be considered learned or automatic (Raichle, 1994). Learned word production appears to involve the anterior cingulate, left prefrontal and left temporal cortices, whereas automatic word production involves the sylvian-insular cortex bilaterally. These two routes for verbal response selection proposed by Raichle, automatic and nonautomatic, provide a distinction that may relate to the propositional and nonpropositional differences in stuttering frequency during language production. Disfluencies occur less frequently during automatic speech production, such as counting or repeating overlearned sequences. Automatic speech production may involve the sylvian and insular regions in both hemispheres. In contrast, nonautomatic speech production, which more frequently contains disfluencies, involves the left prefrontal cortex, the anterior cingulate cortex, the left temporal cortex, and the right cerebellum. Similarly, two speech production routes were postulated, based on comparisons of patients with conduction and transcortical motor aphasia (McCarthy & Warrington, 1984). The possibility of the differential involvement of these two pathways in the generation of stuttering symptoms needs to be explored (see Fig. 6.1). The nonautomatic speech and language systems have been postulated as being affected in stuttering (Ludlow, 1991).

The PET studies demonstrating these two speech systems employed subtraction paradigms, which are based on the expectation that one task, such as word repetition, is an ingredient of another, such as word generation. Subtraction is based on the assumption that cognitive processing systems are additive; that is,

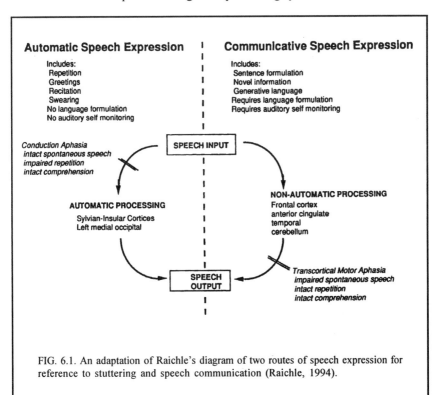

FIG. 6.1. An adaptation of Raichle's diagram of two routes of speech expression for reference to stuttering and speech communication (Raichle, 1994).

brain mechanisms involved in a simple task are components of those involved in a more complex task. It may be fallacious to consider complex tasks as involving the simple addition of two brain mechanisms in an additive fashion rather than involving different brain mechanisms and systems (Frakowiak, 1994).

To avoid the additive task assumption, other researchers have employed correlational and principle components analyses to examine functional imaging data for relationships among metabolic changes in different brain regions across tasks. For example, two automatic speech tasks, audible and silent counting, were contrasted during regional cerebral blood measures (Ryding, Bradvik, & Ingvar, 1987). A factor analysis of the principal components demonstrated two different systems, one associated with audible speech and the other associated with internal speech. The system associated with audible speech involved the right temporal-parietal and left parietal regions, similar to the system involved in automatic speech production (Raichle, 1994). The second system was associated with internal speech and involved the prefrontal regions, mainly in the left hemisphere, with a coupling between the prefrontal and parietal regions. The authors concluded that modular systems between different brain regions in the two hemispheres must interact during both automatic speech production and internal speech.

These functional brain imaging studies have not borne out previously held concepts that Broca's area is specific to speech production. Rather, the left hemisphere frontal regions seem to have a more general role in higher level motor programming rather than a specific role in speech or language processing (Liotti, Gay, & Fox, 1994). Similarly, the supplementary motor area may be involved in higher level motor encoding rather than in language-specific processing (Liotti et al., 1994; Petersen, Fox, Posner, et al., 1988, 1989; Petersen, Fox, Snyder, et al., 1990; Ryding et al., 1987). Perhaps the brain may not have modular systems that segment task performance the way we conceptualize behavioral task entities; the modular organization for speech may be overlaid upon several cognitive processing components and maynot be as distinct as we previously thought.

Few studies have focused on speech production independent from language, a question that would be of importance in determining the neurobiology of stuttering. Several studies have suggested that speech is controlled bilaterally (Ingvar, 1983; Larsen, Skinhoj, & Lassen, 1978; Lassen, Ingvar, & Skinhoj, 1978) and that speech production is rarely disrupted by cortical lesions alone. Mutism (speech loss without impaired language) has been reported following bilateral lesions of the corpus callosum (Plum & Posner, 1980), section of the corpus callosum (Bogen, Fisher, & Vogel, 1965; Sussman, Gur, Gur, & O'Connor, 1983), bilateral lesions of the globus pallidus (Plum & Posner, 1980), bilateral lesions of the cingulate gyrus (Faris, 1969), or bilateral lesions of the dorsomedial or centrolateral thalamus (Krayenbuhl, Wyss, & Yasargil, 1961). Although commissurotomy patients are often initially mute, they usually recover. Recovered speech, however, cannot occur in response to stimuli presented to the right hemisphere, suggesting that speech cannot be produced by the right hemisphere when disconnected from the left hemisphere language areas (Bogen et al., 1965; Gazzaniga, Bogen, & Sperry, 1967; Gazzaniga, Volpe, Smylie, Wilson, & LeDoux, 1979). These results, however, were based on patients with intractable epilepsy, whose brain organization for language and speech may have been abnormal before surgery. In penetrating missile wounds, chronic acquired stuttering persisted for 10 years following injury associated with basal ganglia lesions on either side (Ludlow et al., 1987). Therefore, speech production may involve highly distributed processing in the brain, making the demands for efficient functioning much greater than previously thought. This involvement of distributed processing in speech production may be the reason that acquired stuttering can occur following many different types of brain injury without a particular lesion location (Helm, Butler, & Benson, 1978; Helm, Butler, & Canter, 1980; Rosenbek, Messert, Collins, & Wertz, 1978). Any factor that might interfere with the stability or efficiency in brain functioning for speech and language may be associated with disfluent speech.

THE NEUROBIOLOGY OF STUTTERING

Information elucidating the neurobiology of stuttering in chronically affected adults should expand dramatically within the next few years, as several laboratories have begun to use functional imaging to study stuttering. The first paper appeared in 1995 (Wu et al., 1995) and several groups have already presented early data comparing adults who have stuttered since childhood with fluent speakers during disfluent and fluent speaking tasks. Wu et al. (1995) compared 4 adults who stuttered with unaffected adults on an oral reading task and during choral reading, a fluent speech task using ^{18}F-deoxyglucose positron emission tomography (PET). When the individuals who stuttered were compared with themselves and unaffected controls while fluent and disfluent, decreased glucose uptake was found in the left language areas, the left superior frontal lobe, the right cerebellum, the left deep frontal orbital region and posterior cingulate during stuttering. The only difference between the two groups on the fluent speech tasks was reduced metabolism in the left caudate and the substantia nigra. More recently, Fox et al. (1996) compared adults with chronic stuttering with unaffected adults during oral reading, when stuttering was manifest, and during choral reading when stuttering was absent, using PET to study cerebral blood flow. They found evidence of an aberrant speech/language system in adults with chronic stuttering, associated with heightened activity in the cerebellum and right frontal regions and decreased activity in the left temporal and auditory association areas. These abnormalities were most evident during oral reading with stuttering.

It is impossible to know to what degree these brain activation patterns in the disfluent adults were a result of disfluent speech or due to inherent brain function differences. Sometimes stuttering is associated with extreme effort, which could explain the increased activity in the motor regions in the right and left hemispheres and in the cerebellum. The decreases in the left hemisphere auditory association areas and increases in the frontal speech production system in the left hemisphere were reversed when the adults who stuttered became fluent during choral reading. The reduced activation in the auditory association areas could represent either reduced self-monitoring used as a compensation by chronically affected adults who did not want to listen to their stuttered speech, or an underlying deficit in speech self-monitoring. Certainly the auditory self-monitoring aspect of speech production needs to be investigated more carefully; the profound effects of alterations in time and frequency of speech feedback on stuttering have also been a profound and unexplained aspect of the disorder (Kalinowski, Armson, Roland-Mieszkowski, Stuart, & Gracco, 1993).

More recently, we have demonstrated brain activation differences between adults who stutter and control subjects performing tasks where no stuttering occurred (Braun et al., 1997). Differential involvement of speech and language regions in the two hemispheres for stuttering and compensatory mechanisms were also found through correlational analyses. Activation in the left hemisphere was related to the severity of stuttering, whereas activation in the right hemisphere may have been related to compensatory behaviors associated with fluency in the affected adults.

Other evidence shedding light on the neurobiology of stuttering in chronically affected adults has included the effects of thalamic stimulation on acquired stuttering and the alleviation of stuttering following thalamic surgery in four cases (Andy & Bhatnagar, 1991, 1992; Bhatnagar & Andy, 1989). Acquired stuttering differs in characteristic symptomatology from developmental stuttering (Ludlow et al., 1987) and may be closer to palilalia, a speech rate disturbance sometimes found in Parkinsonism (LaPointe & Horner, 1981). However, the thalamic neurons have receptive fields that are active during speech (McClean, Dostrovsky, Lee, & Tasker, 1990) and thalamic stimulation has been shown to disrupt speech production (Fedio & Van Buren, 1975).

Therefore, the data to date suggest that the total distributed processing network involved in speech/language production is altered in adults who stutter chronically. The hypothesis that one particular brain region is dysfunctional seems less likely.

APPROACHES TO GENETIC ANALYSIS OF STUTTERING

Etiologic theories of stuttering have included a genetic susceptibility for developing stuttering (Andrews et al., 1983; Andrews, Morris-Yates, Howie, & Martin, 1991). The pattern of transmission in families follows an autosomal, sex-modified pattern, which can occur in isolation or in association with other developmental speech and language disorders such as cluttering, articulation, and language delay (Cox, Seider, & Kidd, 1984; Pauls, 1990). A determination of whether stuttering is a specific trait, or whether it lies on a continuum of developmental disturbances in speech and language functioning associated with different degrees of recovery, has great importance regarding the potential for success in identifying risk factors.

The genetic aspects of stuttering have been recognized for some time; however, both epidemiological studies (Cox, Kramer, & Kidd, 1984), and pedigree analyses (Kidd, Heimbuch, & Records, 1981) have not supported a single major locus. A recent study used very young preschool children as probands, and examined additional family members. This study provided evidence for a single gene locus, although a multifactorial/polygenic transmission of susceptibility for stuttering could not be rejected (Ambrose, Yairi, & Cox, 1993). The ratio of males to females is 2:1 in early childhood stuttering and differs from the sex ratio of 4:1 in chronically affected adults, indicating that the females have a higher recovery rate. Although recovery is more frequent in females (Cox & Kidd, 1983), affected adult females sometimes have a high proportion of affected family members (Kidd et al., 1981). Thus, it is thought that the genetic factors may be stronger for females with chronic adult stuttering. However, this difference between males and females may relate also to gender differences in brain organization for language processing: If females can use both the right and left hemispheres for language processing (Shaywitz et al., 1995), they may have a greater likelihood of recovering from stuttering by employing right hemisphere mechanisms for speech and language learning.

Although it has been postulated that stuttering is inherited only as a susceptibility and that environmental factors are associated with the emergence of stuttering, investigators have been unable to identify prenatal, developmental, or medical factors that distinguish individuals who stutter from unaffected family members or control subjects (Cox et al., 1984). A study of monozygotic and dyzygotic twin pairs with at least one twin who stuttered demonstrated a high concordance in monozygotes of 10:12 (83%) and only 2:19 (10.5%) in dyzygotes (Godai, Tatarelli, & Bonanni, 1976). Another study found that concordance was 63% in monozygotes and 19% in fraternal, same-sex twins (Howie, 1981). The fact that monozygotes are not always concordant does indicate that factors other than genetics may have a role in the etiology of stuttering (Cox, 1988).

Stuttering is likely to be a complex trait, presenting some of the inherent pitfalls found when linkage analysis has been applied in other complex behavioral disorders (Risch & Merikangas, 1993, 1996). First, in sporadic cases without familial factors, other developmental and environmental factors may be involved in the development of stuttering symptoms. Sporadic cases are thought to be as high as 50% of cases. Second, a significant proportion of individuals who stutter may have symptoms secondary to birth injury (Poulos & Webster, 1991), which could confound familial analysis if these individuals are not separately identified. Third, only examination results can be used to identify affected individuals because of the inaccuracy of informants' reports of stuttering (Hedges et al., 1995). All members of a family must be carefully examined to identify other factors that might be responsible for the occurrence of stuttering symptoms such as trauma, conversion disorders, mental retardation, or epilepsy (Pauls, 1990). In addition, as Pauls (1990) suggested, "because so many stutterers become fluent speakers later in life, valid and reliable means have to be developed to diagnose stuttering ...."(p.37).

Others have suggested that the genetic component for stuttering could be factor(s) that affect the potential for recovery from stuttering (Yairi et al., 1996). Because the majority of children who are affected recover from childhood disfluency, the genetic risk factor might consist of an inability to recover from disfluency rather than the occurrence of developmental disfluency. However, given the suggestion made earlier that gender differences in brain organization for language may modify recovery from developmental disfluency, the interaction between gender and recovery may alter developmental plasticity.

Interactions among several factors during an individual child's development may influence the ontogeny of an efficient speech/language system. Clinicians frequently report that stuttering often appears following a significant event such as a childhood illness, death of a parent, divorce, or abuse. Perhaps many more children have a genetic risk factor for stuttering than develop the disorder because a disruptive factor does not appear at the time when the child's speech and language development are most vulnerable. Penetrance has been estimated to be as low as 20% by some (Howie, 1981) and between 60% and 80% by others (Cox, 1988; Godai et al., 1976) based on the concordance among monozygotic twins.

In summary, several competing models are viable alternative approaches to be considered for linkage analysis:

> 1. A single genetic trait may render the developing speech and language system vulnerable to disturbances by emotional, maturational, linguistic, cognitive, and gender factors, with recovery being dependent on an interaction of these factors. If this is the case, then linkage analysis should include any family member with a history of developmental stuttering of any duration as affected and only those without any history of disfluency as unaffected.

> 2. All children may be vulnerable to developing disfluency depending on the interaction among emotional, maturational, cognitive, linguistic, and gender factors, with recovery being dependent on a single genetic trait (Yairi et al., 1996). If this is the case, then those with chronic adult stuttering would be those who are affected and those who have had a history of developmental stuttering but have recovered would be unaffected family members.

> 3. A third alternative is that developmental disfluency may be a continuum dependent on the interaction among multiple developmental factors that render the individual child vulnerable to developmental disfluency at a particular time in development (Smith, 1990; Smith & Kelly, 1997; Smith & Weber, 1988). These factors include genetic risk factors, linguistic development, motor skills, environmental demands, gender, and the response of the child and the family to disfluency. If this is the case, then linkage analysis would be difficult because of the multifactorial nature and low penetrance of genetic factors in the disorder.

Determining whether those affected, those recovered, and unaffected family members differ in their speech and language functioning for skills thought to be risk factors for the development of disfluent speech should help in selecting one of these or other models for the epigenesis of stuttering before embarking on linkage analysis. If both those chronically affected with stuttering and those who have recovered have risk factors present, then a specific genetic trait for the occurrence of stuttering would have been altered in all those who have stuttered at some point in their lifetime. If, on the other hand, only those chronically affected with stuttering have risk factors present, and not those who have recovered or have never been affected, then a specific genetic trait interfering with recovery from stuttering would be present only in those with chronic adult stuttering.

Another alternative would be that many members of families with a high rate of stuttering have genetic risk factors present, including those with chronic adult stuttering, those who have recovered from childhood stuttering, as well as family members with only transient normal developmental disfluency. All such persons would have a genetic trait for the susceptibility of stuttering. The occurrence of stuttering, then, would be dependent on interactions of the genetic predisposition with other factors affecting speech and language functioning during development.

When embarking on linkage studies, a decision must be made concerning the model of epigenesis that is being employed. Thus, the conceptual framework for the neurobiology of stuttering is of considerable importance to future endeavors investigating the genomic loci of factors associated with the epigenesis of stuttering.

REFERENCES

Ambrose, N. G., Yairi, E., & Cox, N. (1993). Genetic aspects of early childhood stuttering. *Journal of Speech and Hearing Research, 36,* 701–706.

Andrews, G., Craig, A., Fever, A. -M., Hoddinott, S., Howie, P., & Neilson, M. (1983). Stuttering: A review of research findings and theories circa 1982. *Journal of Speech and Hearing Research, 48,* 226–246.

Andrews, G., Morris-Yates, A., Howie, P., & Martin, N. G. (1991). Genetic factors in stuttering confirmed. *Archives of General Psychiatry, 48,* 1034–1035.

Andy, O. J., & Bhatnagar, S. C. (1991). Thalamic-induced stuttering (surgical observations). *Journal of Speech and Hearing Research, 34,* 796–800.

Andy, O. J., & Bhatnagar, S. C. (1992). Stuttering acquired from subcortical pathologies and its alleviation from thalamic perturbation. *Brain and Language, 42,* 385–401.

Asher, J., & Garcia, R. (1969). The optimal age to learn a foreign language. *Modern Language Journal, 53,* 334–341.

Barinaga, M. (1995). Brain researchers speak a common language [news]. *Science, 270,* 1437–1438.

Bauman, M., & Kemper, T. L. (1985). Histoanatomic observations of the brain in early infantile autism. *Neurology, 35,* 866–674.

Bernstein Ratner, N. & Sih, C. C. (1987). Effects of gradual increases in sentence length and complexity in children's disfluency. *Journal of Speech and Hearing Disorders, 52,* 278–287.

Bhatnagar, S. C., & Andy, O. J. (1989). Alleviation of acquired stuttering with human centremedian thalamic stimulation. *Journal of Neurological and Neurosurgical Psychiatry, 52,* 1182–1184.

Bloodstein, O. (1995). *A handbook of stuttering.* (5th ed.). San Diego, CA: Singular Publishing Group, Inc.

Bogen, J. E., Fisher, E. D., & Vogel, P. J. (1965). Cerebral commissurotomy. A second case report. *Journal of the American Medical Association, 194*: (12), 1328–1329.

Braun, A. R., Varga, M., Stager, S., Schulz, G., Selbie, S., Maisog, J. M., Carson, R. E., & Ludlow, C. L. (1997). Altered patterns of cerebral activity during speech and language production in developmental stuttering: An $H_2^{15}O$ positron emission tomography study. *Brain, 120,* 761–784.

Bressman, S. B., de Leon, D., Kramer, P. L., Ozelius, L. J., Brin, M. F., Greene, P. E., Fahn, S., Breakefield, X. O., & Risch, N. J. (1994). Dystonia in Ashkenazi Jews: Clinical characterization of a founder mutation. *Annals of Neurology, 36,* 771–777.

Brown, S. F. (1938). Stuttering with relation to word accent and word position. *Journal of Abnormal and Social Psychology, 33,* 112–120.

Brown, S. F. (1945). The loci of stutterings in the speech sequence. *Journal of Speech Disorders, 10*, 181–192.

Conture, E., & Kelly, E. (1991). Young stutterers' nonspeech behaviors during stuttering. *Journal of Speech and Hearing Research, 34*, 1041–1056.

Conture, E. G., Louko, L. J., & Edwards, M. L. (1993). Simultaneously treating stuttering and disordered phonology in children: Experimental treatment, preliminary findings. *American Journal of Speech-Language Pathology, 2*, 72–81.

Cox, N. J., & Kidd, K. K. (1983). Can recovery from stuttering be considered a genetically milder subtype of stuttering? *Behavior Genetics, 13*, 129–139.

Cox, N. J., Kramer, P. L., & Kidd, K. K. (1984). Segregation analyses of stuttering. *Genetic Epidemiology, 1*, 245–253.

Cox, N. J., Seider, R. A., & Kidd, K. K. (1984). Some environmental factors and hypotheses for stuttering in families with several stutterers. *Journal of Speech and Hearing Research, 27*, 543–548.

Cox, N. J. (1988). Molecular genetics: The key to the puzzle of stuttering? *ASHA Journal, 30*, 36–40.

Cox, N. J. (1993). Stuttering: A complex behavioral disorder for our times? *American Journal of Medical Genetics (Neuropsychiatric Genetics), 48*, 177–178.

Cypher, C., & Letourneau, P. C. (1992). Growth cone motility. *Current Opinion in Cell Biology, 4*, 4–7.

Daly, D. A. (1993). Cluttering: Another fluency syndrome. In R. F. Curlee (Ed.) *Stuttering and related disorders of fluency* (pp. 179–204). New York: Thieme Medical Publishers.

Daly, D. A. (1994). Speech cluttering. *Journal of the American Medical Association, 272*, 565.

Dawson, G., Finley, C., Phillips, S., & Galpert, L. (1986). Hemispheric specialization and the language abilities of autistic children. *Child Development, 57*, 1440–1453.

Dell, G. S., Juliano, C., & Govindjee, A. (1993). Structure and content in language production: A theory of frame constraints in phonological speech errors. *Cognitive Science, 17*, 149–195.

Faris, A. A. (1969). Limbic system infarction: A report of two cases. *Neurology, 19*, 91–96.

Fedio, P., & Van Buren, J. M. (1975). Memory and perceptual deficits during electrical stimulation in the left and right thalamus and parietal subcortex. *Brain and Language, 2*, 78–100.

Felsenfeld, S. (1996). Progress and needs in the genetics of stuttering. *Journal of Fluency Disorders, 21*, 77–103.

Flege, J. E., Munro, M. J., & MacKay, I. R. A. (1995). Factors affecting strength of perceived foreign accent in a second language. *Journal of the Acoustical Society of America, 97*, 3125–3134.

Fox, P. T., Ingham, R. J., Costello-Ingham, J., Downs, T., Hirsch, T., & Lancaster, J. L. (1995). Supplementary motor and premotor over activity in stuttering: A PET study of stuttering and induced fluency. *Society for Neuroscience Abstracts, 21*, 2113.

Fox, P. T., Ingham, R. J., Ingham, J. C., Hirsch, T. B., Downs, J. H., Martin, C., Jerabek, P., Glass, T., & Lancaster, J. L. (1996). A PET study of the neural systems of stuttering. *Nature, 382*, 158–162.

Frakowiak, R. S. J. (1994). Functional mapping of verbal memory and language. *Trends in Neuroscience, 17*, 109–115.

Fromkin, V., Krashen, S., Curtiss, S., Rigler, D., & Rigler, M. (1974). The development of language in Genie: A case of language acquisition beyond the "critical period." *Brain and Language, 1*, 81–107.

Furukawa, Y., Shimadzu, M., Rajput, A. H., Shimizu, Y., Tagawa, T., Mori, H., Yokochi, M., Narabayashi, H., Hornykiewicz, O., Mizuno, Y., & Kish, S. J. (1996). GTP-cyclohydrolase I gene mutations in hereditary progressive AMD dopa-responsive dystonia. *Annals of Neurology, 39*, 609–617.

Galaburda, A. M., Sherman, G. F., Rosen, G. D., Aboitiz, F., & Geschwind, N. (1985). Developmental dyslexia: Four consecutive patients with cortical anomalies. *Annals of Neurology, 18*, 222–233.

Garrett, M. (1991). Disorders of lexical selection. In J. M. Levelt (Ed.), *Lexical access in speech production* (pp. 143–180). Cambridge, MA: Basil Blackwell.

Gazzaniga, M. S., Bogen, J. E. & Sperry, R. H. (1967). Dyspraxia following division of the cerebral commissures. *Archives of Neurology, 16*(6), 606–612.

Gazzaniga, M. S., Volpe, B. T., Smylie, C. S., Wilson, D. H., & LeDoux, J. E. (1979). Plasticity in speech organization following commissurotomy. *Brain, 102*(4), 805–815.

Geschwind, N. (1964). Non-aphasic disorders of speech. *International Journal of Neurology, 4*, 207–214.

Geschwind, N. (1965a). Disconnexion syndromes in animals and man. II. *Brain, 88*, 585–644.

Geschwind, N. (1965b). Disconnexion syndromes in animals and man. I. *Brain, 88*, 237–294.

Geschwind, N. (1970a). The clinical syndromes of the cortical connections. *Modern Trends in Neurology, 5*, 29–40.

Geschwind, N. (1970b). The organization of language and the brain. *Science, 170*, 940–944.

Geschwind, N. (1971). Current concepts: aphasia. *New England Journal of Medicine, 284*, 654–656.

Geschwind, N. (1972). Language and the brain. *Scientific American, 226*, 76–83.

Gilger, J. W. (1995). Behavioral genetics: Concepts for research and practice in language development and disorders. *Journal of Speech and Hearing Research, 38*, 1126–1142.

Godai, U., Tatarelli, R., & Bonanni, G. (1976). Stuttering and tics in twins. *Acta Genetica Medicae et Gemellologiae (Roma), 25*, 369–375.

Goldman-Rakic, P. S. (1988). Topography of cognition: Parallel distributed networks in primate association cortex. *Annual Review of Neuroscience, 11*, 137–156.

Hebb, D. O. (1949). *The organization of behavior.* New York: Wiley.

Hedges, D. W., Umar, F., Mellon, C. D., Herrick, L. C., Hanson, M. L., & Wahl, M. J. (1995). Direct comparison of the family history method and the family study method using a large stuttering pedigree. *Journal of Fluency Disorders, 20*, 25–34.

Helm, N. A., Butler, R. B., & Benson, D. F. (1978). Acquired stuttering. *Neurology, 28*, 1159–1165.

Helm, N. A., Butler, R. B., & Canter, G. J. (1980). Neurogenic acquired stuttering. *Journal of Fluency Disorders, 5*, 269–279.

Hengartner, M. O., & Horvitz, H. R. (1994). Programmed cell death in Caenorhabditis elegans. *Current Opinion in Genetics and Development, 4*, 581–586.

Howie, P. M. (1981). Concordance for stuttering in monozygotic and dizygotic twin pairs. *Journal of Speech and Hearing Research, 24*, 317–321.

Hubbard, C. P., & Prins, D. (1994). Word familiarity, syllabic stress pattern, and stuttering. *Journal of Speech and Hearing Research, 37*, 564–571.

Ingvar, D. H. (1983). Serial aspects of language and speech related to prefrontal cortical activity: A selective review. *Human Neurobiology, 2*, 177–189.

Johnson, W., & Brown, S. (1935). Stuttering in relation to various speech sounds. *Quarterly Journal of Speech, 21*, 481–496.

Kalinowski, J., Armson, J., Roland-Mieszkowski, M., Stuart, A., & Gracco, V. L. (1993). Effects of alterations in auditory feedback and speech rate on stuttering frequency. *Language and Speech, 36*, 1–16.

Kidd, K. K., Heimbuch, R. C., & Records, M. A. (1981). Vertical transmission of susceptibility to stuttering with sex-modified expression. *Proceedings of the National Academy of Sciences, USA, 78*, 606–610.

Kramer, P. L., Heiman, G. A., Gasser, T., Ozelius, L. J., de Leon, D., Brin, M. F., Burke, R. E., Hewett, J., Hunt, A. L., Moskowitz, C., Nygaard, T., Wilhelmsen, K., Fahn, S., Breakefield, X., Risch, N., & Bressman, S. (1994). The DYT1 gene on 9q34 is responsible for most cases of early limb-onset idiopathic torsion dystonia in non-Jews. *American Journal of Human Genetics, 55*, 468–475.

Krayenbuhl, H., Wyss, O. A. M., & Yasargil, M. G. (1961). Bilateral thalamotomy and pallidotomy as treatment for bilateral Parkinsonism. *Journal of Neurosurgery, 18*, 429–444.

Kuypers, H. G. J. M. (1958). Cortico-bulbar connexions to the pons and lower brainstem in man: An anatomical study. *Brain, 81*, 364–388.

LaPointe, L. L., & Horner, J. (1981). Palilalia: A descriptive study of pathological reiterative utterances. *Journal of Speech and Hearing Disorders, 46*, 34–38.

Larsen, B., Skinhoj, E., & Lassen, N. A. (1978). Variations in regional cortical blood flow in the right and left hemispheres during automatic speech. *Brain, 101*, 193–209.

Lassen, N. A., Ingvar, D. H., & Skinhoj, E. (1978). Brain function and blood flow. *Scientific American, 239*(4), 62–71.

Lenneberg, E. H. (1968). *Biological foundations of language.* New York: Wiley.

Levelt, W. J. M. (1989). *Speaking: From intention to articulation.* Cambridge, MA: MIT Press.

Levelt, W. J. M. (1992). Accessing words in speech production: Stages, processes and representations. *Cognition, 42,* 1–22.

Liotti, M., Gay, C. T., & Fox, P. T. (1994). Functional imaging and language: Evidence from positron emission tomography. *Journal of Clinical Neurophysiology, 11,* 175–190.

Locke, J. L. (1992). Thirty years of research on developmental neurolinguistics. *Pediatric. Neurology, 8,* 245–250.

Louko, L. J., Edwards, M. L., & Conture, E. G. (1990). Phonological characteristics of young stutterers and their normally fluent peers: Preliminary observations. *Journal of Fluency Disorders, 15,* 191–210.

Louko, L. J. (1995). Phonological characteristics of young children who stutter. *Topics in Language Disorders, 15,* 48–59.

Ludlow, C. L., Rosenberg, J., Salazar, A., Grafman, J., & Smutok, M. (1987). Site of penetrating brain lesions causing chronic acquired stuttering. *Annals of Neurology, 22,* 60–66.

Ludlow, C. L. (1990). Research procedures for measuring stuttering severity. *ASHA Reports, 18,* 26–31.

Ludlow, C. L. (1991). Measurement of speech motor control processes in stuttering. In H. F. M. Peters, W. Hulstijn, & C. W. Starkweather (Eds.), *Speech motor control and stuttering* (pp. 479–491). Amsterdam: Elsevier.

Ludlow, C. L., & Dooman, A. G. (1992). Genetic aspects of idiopathic speech and language disorders. *Otolaryngologic Clinics of North America, 25,* 979–994.

Ludlow, C. L., Siren, K. A., & Zikria, M. (1997). Speech production learning in adults with chronic developmental stuttering. In H. Peters, W. Hulstijn, & P. van Lieshout (Eds.) *Proceedings of the 3rd International Nijmegen Conference on Speech Motor Production and Fluency Disorders* (pp.221–230). Nijmegen, The Netherlands: University of Nijmegen.

Malenka, R. C. (1995). LTP and LTD: Dynamic and interactive processes of synaptic plasticity. *The Neuroscientist, 1,* 35–41.

McCarthy, R., & Warrington, E. K. (1984). A two-route model of speech production: Evidence from aphasia. *Brain, 107,* 463–485.

McClean, M. D., Dostrovsky, J. O., Lee, L., & Tasker, R. R. (1990). Somatosensory neurons in human thalamus respond to speech-induced orofacial movements. *Brain Research, 513,* 343–347.

Moore, W. H., & Haynes, W. O. (1980). Alpha hemisphere asymmetry and stuttering: Some support for a segmentation dysfunction hypothesis. *Journal of Speech and Hearing Research, 23,* 229–247.

Muma, J. R. (1971). Syntax of preschool fluent and disfluent speech: A transformational analysis. *Journal of Speech and Hearing Research, 14,* 428–441.

Nippold, M. A. (1990). Concomitant speech and language disorders in stuttering children: A critique of the literature. *Journal of Speech and Hearing Disorders, 55,* 51–60.

Nittrouer, S., Studdert-Kennedy, M., & Neely, S. T. (1996). How children learn to organize their speech gestures: Further evidence from fricative-vowel syllables. *Journal of Speech and Hearing Research, 39,* 379–389.

Nygaard, T. G. (1995). Dopa-responsive dystonia. *Current Opinions in Neurology, 8,* 310–313.

Pauls, D. L. (1990). A review of the evidence for genetic factors in stuttering. *ASHA Reports, 18,* 34–38.

Petersen, S. E., Fox, P. T., Posner, M. I., Mintun, M. A., & Raichle, M. E. (1988). Positron emission tomographic studies of the cortical anatomy of single-word processing. *Nature, 331,* 585–589.

Petersen, S. E., Fox, P. T., Posner, M. I., Mintun, M. A., & Raichle, M. E. (1989). Positron emission tomographic studies of the processing of single words. *Journal of Cognitive Neuroscience, 1,* 153–170.

Petersen, S. E., Fox, P. T., Snyder, A. Z., & Raichle, M. E. (1990). Activation of extra striate and frontal cortical areas by visual word and word-like stimuli. *Science, 249,* 1041–1044.

Plante, E., Swisher, L., & Vance, R. (1989). Anatomical correlates of normal and impaired language in a set of dizygotic twins. *Brain and Language, 37,* 643–655.

Plante, E. (1991). MRI findings in the parents and siblings of specifically language-impaired boys. *Brain and Language, 41,* 67–80.

Plante, E., Swisher, L., & Vance, R. (1991). MRI findings in boys with specific language impairment. *Brain and Language, 41*, 52–66.

Plum, F., & Posner, J. B. (1980). *The diagnosis of stupor and coma* (3rd ed.). Philadelphia: Davis.

Posner, M. I., Petersen, S. E., Fox, P. T., & Raichle, M. E. (1988). Localization of cognitive operations in the human brain. *Science, 240*, 1627–1631.

Postma, A., Kolk, H., & Povel, D. -J. (1990). Speech planning and execution in stutterers. *Journal of Fluency Disorders, 15*, 49–59.

Poulos, M. G., & Webster, W. G. (1991). Family history as a basis for subgrouping people who stutter. *Journal of Speech and Hearing Research, 34*, 5–10.

Purves, D. (1988). *Brain and body: A trophic theory of neural connections.* Cambridge, MA: Harvard University Press.

Purves, D. (1994). *Neural activity and the growth of the brain.* Cambridge, England: Cambridge University Press.

Purves, D., & Lichtman, J. W. (1985a). Pattern and positional information. In D. Purves & J. W. Lichtman (Eds.), *Principles of neural development* Sunderland, MA: Sinauer Associates.

Purves, D., & Lichtman, J. W. (1985b). Neuronal health during development. In D. Purves & J. W. Lichtman (Eds.), *Principles of neural development* (pp. 135–143). Sunderland, MA: Sinauer Associates.

Raichle, M. E. (1990). Exploring the mind with dynamic imaging. *Seminars in the Neurosciences, 2*, 307–315.

Raichle, M. E. (1994). Images of the mind: Studies with modern imaging techniques. *Annual Review of Psychology, 45*, 333–356.

Rakic, P. (1985). Limits of neurogenesis in primates. *Science, 227*, 1054–1056.

Risch, N. & Merikangas, K. (1993). Linkage studies of psychiatric disorders. *European Archives of Psychiatry and Clinical Neurosciences, 243*, 143–149.

Risch, N., & Merikangas, K. (1996). The future of genetic studies of complex human diseases. *Science, 273*, 1516–1517.

Rosenbek, J., Messert, B., Collins, M., & Wertz, R. (1978). Stuttering following brain damage. *Brain and Language, 6*, 82–96.

Russell, D. S. (1995). Neurotrophins: Mechanisms of action. *The Neuroscientist, 1*, 3–6.

Ryding, E., Bradvik, B., & Ingvar, D. H. (1987). Changes of regional cerebral blood flow measured simultaneously in the right and left hemisphere during automatic speech and humming. *Brain, 110*, 1345–1358.

Shaywitz, B. A., Shaywitz, S. E., Pugh, K. R., Constable, R. T., Skudlarski, P., Fulbright, R. K., Bronen, R. A., Fletcher, J. M., Shankweiler, D. P., Katz, L., & Gore, J. C. (1995). Sex differences in the functional organization of the brain for language. *Nature, 373*, 607–609.

Shaywitz, B. A., Shaywitz, S. E., Pugh, K. R., Skudlarski, P., Fulbright, R. K., Constable, R. T., Fletcher, J. M., Liberman, A. M., Shankweiler, D. P., Katz, L., Bronen, R. A., Marchione, K. E., Lacadie, C., & Gore, J. C. (1996). The functional organization of the brain for reading and reading disability (dyslexia). *The Neuroscientist, 2*, 245–255.

Shostak, S. (1991a). Embryos and development. In *Embryology: An introduction to developmental biology* (pp. 7–32). New York: HarperCollins.

Shostak, S. (1991b). Pattern formation in the blastula. In *Embryology: An introduction to developmental biology* (pp. 415–447). New York: HarperCollins.

Silverman, F. H. (1972). Disfluency and word length. *Journal of Speech and Hearing Research, 15*, 788–791.

Smith, A. (1990). Toward a comprehensive theory of stuttering: A commentary. *Journal of Speech and Hearing Disorders, 55*, 398–401.

Smith, A. (1992). Commentary on a theory of neuropsycholinguistic function in stuttering. *Journal of Speech and Hearing Research, 35*, 805–809.

Smith, A., & Kelly, E. (1997). Stuttering: A dynamic, multifactorial model. In R. Curlee & G. Siegel (Eds.), *Nature and treatment of stuttering: New directions* (2nd ed., pp. 204–217). San Diego: Singular.

Smith, A., & Weber, C. (1988). The need for an integrated perspective on stuttering. *ASHA Journal, 30*, 30–32.

Soderberg, G. A. (1966). The relations of stuttering to word length and word frequency. *Journal of Speech and Hearing Research, 9*, 584–589.

Soderberg, G. A. (1967). Linguistic factors in stuttering. *Journal of Speech and Hearing Research, 10*, 801–810.

St. Louis, K. O., & Hinzman, A. R. (1986). Studies of cluttering by speech-language pathologists and educators. *Journal of Fluency Disorders, 11*, 131–149.

St. Louis, K. O. (1992). On defining cluttering. In F. L. Myers & K. O. St. Louis (Eds.), *Cluttering: A clinical perspective* (pp. 37–53). Kibworth, Leics, England: Far Communications.

Steffeberg, S., Gillberg, C., Hellgren, L. & et al., (1989). A twin study of autism in Denmark, Finland, Iceland, Norway and Sweden. *Journal of Child Psychology and Psychiatry, 30*, 405–416.

Stellar, H. (1995). Mechanisms and genes of cellular suicide. *Science, 267*, 1445–1462.

Strub, R. L., Black, F. W., & Naeser, M. A. (1987). Anomalous dominance in sibling stutterers: Evidence from CT scan asymmetries, dichotic listening, neuropsychological testing, and handedness. *Brain and Language, 32*, 338–350.

Sussman, N. M., Gur, R. C., Gur, R. E., & O'Connor, M. J. (1983). Mutism as a consequence of callosotomy. *Journal of Neurosurgery, 59*(3), 514–519.

Taylor, I. K. (1966). What words are stuttered? *Psychological Bulletin, 65*, 233–242.

Throneburg, R. N., & Yairi, E. (1994). Temporal dynamics of repetitions during the early stage of childhood stuttering: An acoustic study. *Journal of Speech and Hearing Research, 37*, 1067–1075.

Throneburg, R. N., Yairi, E., & Paden, E. P. (1994). Relation between phonologic difficulty and the occurrence of disfluencies in the early stage of stuttering. *Journal of Speech and Hearing Research, 37*, 504–509.

Travis, L. E. (1978). The cerebral dominance theory of stuttering:1931–1978. *Journal of Speech and Hearing Disorders, 43*, 278–281.

Van Riper, C. (1973). *The treatment of stuttering.* Englewood Cliffs, NJ: Prentice-Hall.

Vrbova, G., Gordon, T., & Jones, R. (1995). Development of motoneurons. In *Nerve-muscle interaction* (2nd ed., p. 30). London: Chapman & Hall.

Wall, N. A., & Hogan, B. L. M. (1994). TGF-b related genes in development. *Current Opinion in Genetics and Development, 4*, 517–522.

Wells, B. G., & Moore, W. H., Jr. (1990). EEG alpha asymmetries in stutterers and non-stutterers: Effects of linguistic variables on hemispheric processing and fluency. *Neuropsychologia, 28*, 1295–1305.

Wingate, M. E. (1976). *Stuttering theory and treatment.* New York: Irvington.

Wolk, L., Edwards, M. L. & Conture, E. G. (1993). Coexistence of stuttering and disorders phonology in young children. *Journal of Speech and Hearing Research, 36*, 906–917.

Wood, F., Stump, D., McKennhan, A., Sheldon, S., & Proctor, J. (1980). Patterns of regional cerebral blood flow during attempted reading aloud by stutterers both on and off haloperidol medication: Evidence for inadequate left frontal activation during stuttering. *Brain and Language, 9*, 141–144.

World Health Organization. (1977). *Manual of the International Statistical Classification of Diseases, Injuries, and Causes of Death* (pp. 202). Geneva: Author.

Wu, J. C., Maguire, G., Riley, G., Fallon, J., LaCasse, L., Chin, S., Klein, E., Tang, C., Cadwell, S., & Lottenberg, S. (1995). A positron emission tomography [18F]deoxyglucose study of developmental stuttering. *Neuroreport, 6*, 501–505.

Yairi, A., Ambrose, N., & Cox, N. (1996). Genetics of stuttering: A critical review. *Journal of Speech and Hearing Research, 39*, 771–784.

Yairi, E., Ambrose, N. G., & Niermann, R. (1993). The early months of stuttering: A developmental study. *Journal of Speech and Hearing Research, 36*, 521–528.

Yairi, E., Ambrose, N. G., Paden, E. P., & Throneburg, R. N. (1996). Predictive factors of persistence and recovery pathways of childhood stuttering. *Journal of Communication Disorders, 29*, 51–77.

Zimmerman, G., Smith, A., & Hanley, J. M. (1981). Stuttering: In need of a unifying conceptual framework. *Journal of Speech and Hearing Research, 46*, 25–31.

7 Stuttering: A Neurophysiological Perspective

Luc F. De Nil
University of Toronto, The Toronto Hospital

THE MULTIDIMENSIONAL NATURE OF STUTTERING

The failure of unidimensional explanations of stuttering has resulted in widespread recognition that stuttering can best be understood within the context of a multidimensional model. Although describing stuttering as a multidimensional disorder allows researchers and clinicians to appreciate the complexity of the speech problem, it does present the challenging task of identifying the different dimensions that are important in characterizing the disorder. One historical approach to this problem has been to define stuttering not as a unitary speech disorder, but to differentiate between different subtypes, each characterized along different dimensions. One such model was proposed by Van Riper (1982), who differentiated between four tracks of stuttering development. In this model, each individual track can be characterized by a more or less distinct pattern of motoric (both speech and nonspeech), emotional, and cognitive variables associated with its onset and development. More recently, Adams (1990) and Starkweather, Gottwald, and Halfond (1990) have proposed the Demands and Capacity (DC) Model to account for the multidimensional nature of stuttering. According to the DC model, stuttering onset and development can best be understood along four dimensions; motoric, linguistic, cognitive, and emotional. Importantly, each of these dimensions can be characterized at the level of either the child or the environment (parents). Furthermore, because every child's history of stuttering development is unique to the family in which the child lives (Starkweather et al., 1990), the relative influence of each of these dimensions on the onset and development of stuttering may differ from child to child. For some children, stuttering development is influenced by variables along all four dimensions. In others, not all four dimensions need to be considered in order to understand the onset of stuttering.

Still another approach to the multidimensional nature of stuttering was proposed by Wall and Myers (1984). These authors differentiated among psycholinguistic factors (i.e., phonology, prosody, syntax, semantics/cognition, propositionality, pragmatics), psychosocial factors (i.e., parents and other significant adults, peers, social load of discourse), and physiological factors (i.e., voice onset and termination time, laryngeal and supralaryngeal tension, sensorimotor coordination, autonomic nervous system, coarticulation, genetics, respiration). Although they acknowledged that these three factors may interact with each other, as indicated in their pictorial model by the overlap between the three components, a number of observations are important for our present purposes. First, the overlap between the three factors is not complete. This suggests that, for instance, the psycholinguistic factor may play a role in the child's stuttering that is independent of either the physiological or the psychosocial factor. A second observation is that the physiological factor includes primarily sensorimotor variables. This latter observation suggests that the psycholinguistic and psychosocial factors may exist, at least in part, autonomously from the physiological factor.

Limiting the influence of physiological variables in speech production in general, and in stuttering specifically, to sensorimotor processes seems to be a rather common assumption, at least implicitly, in the literature. Mental processes, including cognitive processes involved in language formulation and self-perception, often are seen as related to, but fundamentally distinct from these neurophysiological processes. This view is reminiscent of a dualistic view of human nature, as formulated most strongly by Descartes (1985), and more recently by Bruner (1990), Nagel (1974), and Warner (1994), among others. According to this view, a more or less clear separation between mind (cognition) and body (physiology) exists, and the study of neurophysiological processes, no matter how sophisticated, will never be able to provide a complete understanding of human behavior and sensation.

However, others have developed a view in which no clear distinction can be drawn between psychological processes on the one hand, and neurophysiological processes on the other. In the words of Churchland and Sejnowski (1992), it appears highly probable that psychological processes are in fact processes of the physical brain, not "of a nonphysical soul or mind" (p. 1). Similar theses have been proposed and defended by others (Fodor, 1994; Llinás & Churchland, 1996).

Observations of the effects of traumatic brain injury or neurological disease processes on patients' cognitive functions, personality, and social interaction patterns (Damasio, 1994) seem to provide strong support for a neurophysiological perspective and to argue against a more dualistic perspective. Also, recent advances in neuroscience, in particular the growing understanding of the biological bases of many psychiatric and neurological disorders, have provided growing evidence for the inseparability of brain and mind. Such a view, clearly, has implications for how we describe and understand the multidimensional nature of stuttering.

NEUROPHYSIOLOGY AS THE UNIFYING DIMENSION IN STUTTERING

In an influential paper, Zimmermann, Smith, and Hanley (1981) argued that stuttering needs to be studied within the framework of normal neuromotor control processes. According to these authors, understanding the different dimensions of stuttering, whether they reflect psychological, social, or learning influences, needs to include a thorough understanding of the effects of these processes on synaptic inputs to the motoneuron pools. Although their paper clearly assigned a central role to neurophysiology as the unifying conceptual framework, the proposed model seems to leave open the possibility that cognitive and other processes may transcend neural activity. In other words, Zimmermann et al. (1981) did not question the independence of psychological, social, and learning processes from their associated neural processes.

In the present chapter, I suggest a different way of viewing the influence of psychological, social, learning, and sensorimotor variables on stuttering (Fig. 7.1). Fluent and disfluent speech behavior (and, indeed, human behavior in general) can be studied within each of three levels; a processing level (central neural processes), an output level (observable behavior), and a contextual level (environment). According to the model presented here, the behavioral (output) level represents observable manifestations of underlying neurophysiological activity (processing level). Although categorizing this behavior as either cognitive, linguistic, or motor

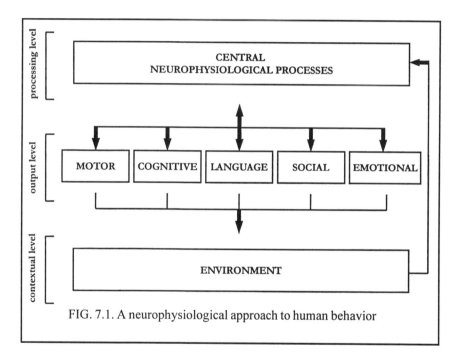

FIG. 7.1. A neurophysiological approach to human behavior

probably appears to be a convenient way of organizing our observations into functional units, this does not automatically imply the existence of categorically distinct underlying neural processes. Indeed, resource sharing appears to be the rule rather than the exception in the brain.

The relationship between the neurophysiological processes at the processing level and the observed behavior at the output level is not unidirectional. In many instances, the behavior manifested at the output level will provide feedback, through various afferent channels, to the central processes. Such afferent signals, in turn, may alter the way these processes function. Examples of this type of feedback include physical alterations to the articulators (e.g., oral anesthetization during a visit to the dentist, bite blocks in speech experiments), auditory or proprioceptive feedback (e.g., perceived slips-of-the-tongue or misarticulations), or observed environmental consequences of one's own behavior.

Similarly, environmental variables (contextual level) generally do not affect an individual's behavior directly. Typically, these variables exert their influence only after being filtered centrally through the neurophysiological processes. Because the manner in which environmental information is processed centrally may differ significantly among individuals, and at different stages during an individual's development, it can be expected that the same environmental stimuli may have very different behavioral consequences in different individuals, or in the same individual at different times. And, indeed, this is often what is observed. Consider, for instance, the different language acquisition curves that a 3-year-old and a 30-year-old likely will show, because of age-related changes in neural plasticity, when immersed in the same foreign language environment. As a second example, one can make the observation that siblings often will develop distinct personalities despite parents' efforts to be consistent in their childrearing practices. In clinical practice, it is also a common observation that individuals who stutter differ greatly in their response to a given stressful event, or to a particular fluency therapy approach.

Within this philosophical and theoretical framework, the question of whether or not an increased understanding of the role of neurophysiological processes in the onset, development, and maintenance of stuttering will have clinical implications clearly is a redundant question. Indeed, neurophysiological processes form the core of all behavior that we observe in people who stutter; not to understand these processes means that we do not fully understand these behaviors. Furthermore, within this model, changing observable behavior, which is at the core of what we do clinically, necessarily involves modifying the way information is processed centrally. As a consequence, working on overt stuttering behavior, without understanding how it affects underlying neurophysiological processes, is like working in the dark. In the worst case, it leads to seemingly inexplicable hit-and-miss clinical results. In the best case, such "blind" intervention raises the issue of interindividual differences in responsiveness to treatment.

Evidence of a Neurophysiological Basis of Stuttering

Although we may not fully understand the neurophysiological factors that are involved in stuttering, several lines of research have provided compelling evidence for a biological basis for stuttering. In the following section, I briefly review the lines of evidence that, in my opinion, most clearly point to a neurophysiological substrate for stuttering.

Genetic Influences. The family and twin studies data available to date provide ample support for the presence of a genetic component in stuttering, without negating the importance of environmental and learning variables. In a recently published paper, Yairi, Ambrose, and Cox (1996a) concluded that the evidence currently available clearly points to "the interaction of one or more genes with environmental variables" (p. 780). A similar conclusion was reached by Felsenfeld (1997). This characterization of stuttering fits well with current models of behavioral genetics, including those developed for other childhood speech and language disorders. What is much less clear at the present time is the nature of the genetically transmitted characteristic. There seems to be rather general agreement among researchers that what is transmitted is not stuttering itself, but some predisposition to fluency breakdown (Peters & Guitar, 1991). Identifying this predisposition probably will have to wait until we have a more thorough understanding of the nature of neural processes that govern speech and language formulation (Bradshaw, 1989; Hellige, 1993). However, the presence of a genetic influence in the onset and development of stuttering leaves little doubt that biological factors are importantly involved in the disorder.

Sex Ratio. Most studies investigating gender differences in stuttering have reported a ratio of approximately 4 affected males to 1 female (Bloodstein, 1995). A number of recent studies, in particular those reported by Yairi and his colleagues (Yairi, 1983; Yairi & Ambrose, 1992a, 1992b), have suggested that this sex difference in stuttering may be less apparent at the time of onset of fluency problems. Regardless, by the age of 6, the widely reported 4:1 ratio seems to be firmly in place. In the past, this difference in incidence between males and females was explained in a number of different ways, including cultural differences in childrearing practices (Johnson, 1955), different societal stress levels on boys and girls (Schuell, 1946, 1947), and biological and genetic differences between the sexes (Geschwind & Galaburda, 1985; Kidd, Kidd, & Records, 1978; MacFarlane, Hanson, Walton, & Mellon, 1991).

Indirect support for a biological and genetic cause for the observed sex ratio comes from the observation of a similar sex ratio (males > females) to that found in stuttering in a number of different disorders for which a neurological basis has been well established. These include dyslexia (Lewis, Hitch, & Walker, 1994), Down syndrome (Mikkelsen, Poulsen, & Nielsen, 1990; Petersen, & Fiez, 1993), congenital deafness (Cremers, Van Rijn, & Huygen, 1994), Tourette syndrome (Popper, 1988; Williams, Pleak, & Hanesian, 1987), and autism (Brown et al. 1982; Levitas et al., 1983). The preponderance of males in each of these disorders strongly suggests that boys are more susceptible biologically to a number of developmental disorders, including stuttering. Furthermore, the apparent universality of the sex ratio in stuttering also argues against a cultural or environmental explanation (Van Riper, 1982). Whether the higher susceptibility among males results in an increased chance to develop stuttering, or a decreased likelihood for early recovery remains to be seen (Yairi, Ambrose, Paden, & Throneburg, 1996b).

One possible explanation for the sex ratio in stuttering may be found in observed differences in language lateralization between males and females. Recent neuroimaging studies have shown increased bilateral speech and language representation in females compared to males. The latter are more likely to have a strong left hemisphere lateralization for speech and language (Shaywitz et al., 1995). Possibly as a result of this difference in lateralization, males are somewhat more likely to develop speech or language difficulties following a left hemisphere stroke (Bradshaw & Nettleton, 1981) and to develop neurogenic stuttering (discussed later; see also Bloodstein, 1995). The bilateral representation of speech and language in females, and their apparent higher resiliency for developing speech and language, suggests that the male to female ratio in stuttering may be linked to sex differences in the lateralization of speech and language functions. As is reviewed in the next section, further support for this hypothesis comes from observations suggesting atypical lateralization of speech and language processes in males who stutter.

Lateralization of Speech and Language Functions in Stuttering. There is strong evidence to support the hypothesis that stuttering is associated with atypical lateralization of speech and language processes, at least in adults. The seminal work done by Moore and his colleagues (for a review, see Moore, 1984), using electrophysiological and behavioral measures of brain lateralization during tasks involving language processing and speech production, consistently showed increased activation in the right hemisphere for individuals who stutter. Boberg, Yeudall, Schopflocher, and Bo Lassen (1983) reported a shift in frontally recorded brain potentials (alpha waves) from right to left hemisphere following intensive stuttering treatment. This observed shift supports the hypothesis that the observed electrophysiological activation is fluency related.

Following initial studies of regional cerebral blood flow distribution by Wood and Stump (1980) and by Pool, Devous, Freeman, Watson, & Finitzo (1991), more recent functional neuroimaging research using positron emission tomography (PET) has largely supported the hypothesis of increased right hemisphere activation in people who stutter. In a comparison of oral reading in stuttering and nonstuttering individuals, Fox et al. (1996) reported extensive hyperactivity of the motor system, characterized by a diffuse overactivity of the cerebral and cerebellar motor systems, right lateralization of cerebral motor systems, and an absence or deactivation of temporal activation in the stuttering speakers. In our research of single-word oral reading, increased right hemisphere activation was not limited to the motor regions of the cortex, but involved primary frontal, premotor, motor, temporoparietal regions, as well as subcortical regions (De Nil, Kroll, Kapur, & Houle, 1998; Kroll, De Nil, Kapur, & Houle, 1997). The distribution of these cortical and subcortical regions, and their hypothesized functional role in language formulation, suggest that the observed increase in right hemisphere activation reflects a fundamental reorganization of processes involved in language and speech, rather than a cognitive attentional process that interferes with normal left hemisphere speech production processes (Webster, 1990). Further evidence that the observed right hemisphere activation in stuttering individuals reflects a basic neural organization pattern was reported by Braun et al. (1997). In their research, they compared stuttering and nonstuttering adult males on a variety of simple oral motor tasks not involving speech. The nonstuttering subjects showed left-lateralized neural activation, whereas the stuttering subjects, again, revealed primarily right lateralization during these nonspeech tasks. Although Braun and his colleagues did not find clear indications of a right hemisphere advantage for speech, the stuttering subjects in their study also failed to show the primarily left hemisphere activation observed in the nonstuttering controls during speech tasks. Increased fluency, resulting from fluency-enhancing conditions such as choral reading (Fox et al., 1996), or intensive fluency treatment (Kroll et al. 1997), results in a more normalized activation pattern in the left cortical motor regions, although stuttering speakers continue to show increased activation in the right hemisphere compared to normally fluent speakers.

The data available to date concerning increased right hemisphere activation in adults who stutter strongly support the hypothesis that their neural processing during language and speech formulation is organized differently from that observed in nonstuttering speakers. It seems unlikely that this right activation reflects a reactive emotional process because avoidance-related anxiety has been shown to produce increased activation in regions of the brain (in particular the temporal pole) not observed in PET studies of stuttering done to date (Reiman, 1990). Nevertheless, a number of fundamental issues still remain to be resolved:

> 1. To date, most lateralization studies have been conducted using adults who stutter. As a result, it is possible that the increased right hemisphere dominance reflects a reactive reorganization that develops after the onset of stuttering. However, this interpretation of the lateralization findings is not supported by research showing that cortical lateralization of function is largely innate; although it may show some changes in gradient as a result of developmental experiences, lateralization does not typically reverse later on in life (Hellige, 1993). However, as long as lateralization data closer to the onset of stuttering are not available, it will be difficult to exclude this explanation for the lateralization findings.

> 2. It is possible that stuttering adults used in such studies are not representative of the total stuttering population, but form a subgroup of those that did not recover or for whom early intervention was not effective. As such, the observed atypical neural processes may reveal more about conditions associated with the likelihood of recovery (or its absence) than about causal factors for the disorder.

The resolution of such issues is not beyond experimental reach given the present sophistication in electrophysiological recording of brain activation patterns in very young children (Molfese & Molfese, 1988). Moreover, although present functional neuroimaging methods pose a number of difficulties that make it extremely difficult to use children as experimental subjects, future technological advances in this area undoubtedly will allow researchers to test and refine their hypotheses in younger subjects (Benson et al., 1996; Chugani, 1996).

ACQUIRED STUTTERING

Although relatively rare, stutteringlike symptoms can occur as a result of a traumatic brain injury or as one of the symptoms of a developing neurological disease. Although the issue of whether the speech disfluencies typically observed in these patients are the same as those seen in developmental stuttering has not been resolved completely (Bloodstein, 1995; Helm-Estabrooks, Yeo, Geschwind, & Freedman, 1986; Moore, 1984), it is clear to anyone who has worked clinically with people with acquired stuttering that it can be extremely difficult sometimes to differentially diagnose between neurogenic and developmental stuttering on the basis of speech observation. Although the debate over whether or not neurogenic stuttering constitutes a different disorder than developmental stuttering probably will go on for a while, the very existence of acquired stuttering provides strong support for the hypothesis that one or more neural systems in the central nervous system play an important role in the generation of fluent speech. The fact that acquired stuttering has been observed following damage to numerous regions of the brain is congruent with the notion that functions in the brain are represented as distributed networks, rather than as anatomically localized cortical or subcortical regions (Bradshaw & Nettleton, 1981; Wise et al., 1991).

RELATED OBSERVATIONS

Although the preponderance of males who stutter, the existence of neurogenic stuttering, and patterns of cortical lateralization seem to provide some of the strongest support for a neurological basis of stuttering, there are a number of additional findings that strengthen this conclusion. People who stutter show a consistent pattern of articulatory discoordination, even during perceptually fluent speech (Caruso, Abbs, & Gracco, 1988; De Nil, 1995; Zimmerman, 1980), they are slower at initiating oral and laryngeal movements (for a review, see Bloodstein, 1995), and they seem to have more difficulty using proprioceptive feedback in oral movements (De Nil & Abbs, 1991). It has been argued that these observed differences may not necessarily result from an underlying neural component, but may reflect a learned task-coping strategy (Bakker & Brutten, 1989) or subtle fluency disruptions in speech that appears perceptually fluent (Armson & Kalinowski, 1994). Although the reported articulatory timing disruptions and decreased proprioceptive accuracy in stuttering individuals is congruent with observed patterns of reduced left hemisphere activation (Bradshaw & Nettleton, 1981), further research is needed to investigate these issues.

The Role of Automaticity in Speech and Stuttering

A central issue in our understanding of the neurophysiology of stuttering is how observed neural patterns result in the speech disfluencies that can be observed at the behavioral level. A concept that may prove to be useful in clarifying this issue is the level of automaticity during execution of motor tasks, including speech and stuttering. For most of us, many everyday tasks, such as walking and speaking, are characterized by a high level of automaticity during routine performance. Still others acquire high levels of automaticity for tasks such as typing, playing a musical instrument, certain sports, and so forth. Most people are barely aware of individual components of these motor tasks as a result of proficiency acquired following years of intentional or unintentional practice. A high level of automaticity present in task performance allows for less focus on the motor execution aspects of the task and more focus on other task-related variables. For instance, a person can watch the traffic or enjoy a beautiful landscape when walking, or can concentrate on formulating the message while talking.

Level of automaticity is not an absolute task characteristic, but represents a dynamic continuum ranging from complete control on the one extreme to almost reflexlike performance on the other (Laberge, 1995). Depending on task requirements and situational circumstances, the degree of automaticity for a given task may vary along this continuum.

For instance, most of us will not be consciously aware of how we walk, but if the terrain suddenly becomes quite rough, we may lower the level of automaticity and increase control over where we put our feet down, or how long our stride will be. Similarly, we usually do not give much attention to our articulatory movements as we speak, but if we trip over a word that is difficult to articulate, or speak in a noisy environment, we may, temporarily, monitor our articulatory movements more closely.

Sometimes, this increased attention and monitoring will allow people to execute the motor task more efficiently, but often this is not the case and the increased control will make task execution less coordinated. Frequently, this decrease in coordination is a direct result of uncertainty about which parameters are to be controlled for efficient task execution. The example of a person walking a beam is a good illustration of this effect. When a relatively wide beam is lying flat on the ground, most individuals with average balancing skills will report little difficulty in walking the beam. As a matter of fact, for most individuals, walking the beam will not be all that much different from walking on the ground. It represents a semiautomatic process that is characterized by high levels of movement coordination and motor fluency. However, as soon as the beam is lifted a few feet off the ground, most individuals will show a marked difference in their walking patterns. All of a sudden, their movements become less coordinated and less fluent than when the beam was lying on the ground. It should be noted that the dimensions of the beam have not changed physically; it has not become narrower or more slippery. In a sense, the only thing that has changed in the situation is the perceived consequences of failure. Under these new circumstances, falling off the beam may no longer be perceived as a trivial event, but as one that has the potential of physical harm. In an attempt to avoid disaster, motor execution in most people will shift from a highly automatic process to one that involves a high degree of volitional control. Unfortunately, this often has a destabilizing effect because walking represents a motor task with many potential control parameters that cannot possibly be controlled individually. The simple act of moving the beam a few feet higher off the ground creates a situation in which it is unclear, at least initially, which subset of all possible control parameters is most important for successful completion of the task. As a result, some of the initial control efforts may be ineffective, leading to somewhat erratic behavior.

Nevertheless, most people, with practice, will learn how to walk the beam more comfortably and with more confidence. Some, such as Olympic gymnasts or acrobats, even obtain an extremely high degree of proficiency in such motor tasks after years of practice. One way to envision what happens during this learning process is to think of the individual as learning, through self-discovery, guidance, or both, which motor parameters are important to control, and the most effective way to control them. Through practice, the individual regains confidence in his or her motor skills and the motor task changes back from a controlled to a semiautomatic task, resulting in greater movement fluency.

Similarly, increased fluency during speech-oriented treatment may result from increased control of effective control parameters (speaking rate, reduced intraoral muscular tension, adequate respiration, etc.). Often, this increased control initially comes at a price in the form of decreased naturalness, as in the case of our beam walker whose movements initially will appear stiff and somewhat awkward. Just as increased practice will result in more natural movements for the gymnast, increased and prolonged speech skill practice by the stuttering individual often will result in more natural speech patterns, although, as with any motor skill, the final level of naturalness that is reached will differ from individual to individual.

Perceived consequences of failure will greatly affect speech, normally a highly automatic cognitive and motor task (Koopmans, Slis, & Rietveld, 1996). Depending on the situation, many of us will feel that there are times when we have to be much more conscious of what we say and how we say it. For example, we may feel that we have to "weigh our words more carefully," or that we have to articulate precisely and clearly. In such cases, we shift our attention more toward particular aspects of the language formulation and speech task at hand; the result is decreased automaticity. Often these situations, which seem to demand increased vigilance and monitoring, and in which the perceived consequence of failure of speech becomes more negative, result in increased disfluencies in people who stutter. In contrast, many people who stutter appear to experience fewer or no disfluencies during relatively highly automated tasks such as singing, counting, or when reciting memorized material (Bloodstein, 1995).

Recent research has started to unravel the neural processes that are involved in attention and automaticity of skill (Laberge, 1995; Raichle et al., 1994). One of the regions that has been observed to play an important role in focusing attention during task performance is the anterior cingulate region (Damasio, 1994; Posner & Petersen, 1990). In our studies of single word reading in stuttering adults (discussed earlier) we have evidence of increased levels of neural activation in the anterior cingulate region in people who stutter compared to nonstuttering individuals. Although the functional significance of this finding is not yet completely clear, one interpretation is that it represents the neural manifestation of increased selective attention, associated with decreased automaticity (Laberge, 1995), resulting in increased disfluency. Interestingly, Raichle et al. (1994), in a recent PET study of nonstuttering individuals, showed that as performance of complex language tasks become more automatic through repeated practice, activation in this medial region of the cortex decreases significantly. Similarly, in people who stutter, the well-documented reading adaptation effect shows a significant drop in stuttering frequency following repeated readings of the same material (Bloodstein, 1995). These observations, taken together, suggest that changes in automaticity may play an important role in stuttering, and that further study of the role of automaticity in fluent and disfluent speech may help to clarify the causal relationship between central neural processing patterns and observed speech disfluencies.

CLINICAL IMPLICATIONS OF A
NEUROPHYSIOLOGICAL VIEW

Within the currently proposed framework, a thorough understanding of neurophysiological processes in language formulation, speech production, and stuttering is of central importance for the development of effective clinical intervention techniques. It suggests that changing observable behavior in a manner that provides long-lasting and predictable results necessitates modifying how information gets processed centrally.

Admittedly, our present knowledge of the relationship between observed neurophysiological variables and the symptomatology of stuttering still lacks specificity. As a result, the extent to which a better understanding of these variables will help clinicians in the assessment and treatment of stuttering has to be somewhat speculative. This section outlines some general directions that would allow us to apply neurophysiological knowledge to clinical intervention in stuttering.

Before I discuss this topic, however, a few additional words need to be said about whether observed neurophysiological differences between stuttering and nonstuttering individuals are innate or acquired. As discussed earlier, it has been argued quite accurately that even when neurophysiological differences can be observed between stuttering and nonstuttering individuals, it cannot be assumed that these differences reflect a basic, innate characteristic that is causally related to stuttering (Armson & Kalinowski, 1994; Bloodstein, 1995). Although a behavior such as stuttering may not manifest itself until later during a child's development, following a period of seemingly normal speech fluency, this does not preclude the influence of innate biological factors. Second, it should be clear that the innate nature of a behavior does not exclude a role for the environment or the learning process, or the influence of experience-based adjustments on the development and manifestation of that behavior (Damasio, 1994). In the final analysis, whether any of the observed neuromotor differences between stuttering and nonstuttering individuals are innate is an empirical question that will only be resolved by further studies, especially those done with children prior to or as close as possible to the onset of stuttering.

However, from a clinical point of view, whether certain observed characteristics are innate or not may not be the most important question to ask at the present time. That is, even if a number of neurophysiological differences between stuttering and nonstuttering individuals can be shown to develop as a result of stuttering, the presence of these differences may still be very important clinically. Such variables may prove to have a central role in the further development and maintenance of stuttering. For instance, a number of studies have shown that stuttering individuals show more pronounced right hemisphere activation during speech and language tasks (see previous discussion). At the present time, one cannot exclude the possibility that this atypical lateralization develops as the result of some compensatory mechanism at some time following the onset of stuttering. Nevertheless, the observation that regions of the brain that appear less efficient at processing time-dependent stimuli (Bradshaw & Nettleton, 1981; Moore, 1984), or that may interfere with normal left hemisphere processing (Webster, 1990), show increased activation in people who stutter may have important implications for the type of activities clinicians use in their fluency intervention. For instance, with some clients, clinicians may find it most effective to use treatment techniques that increase control over the sequential timing of smaller speech units, and that appear to strengthen left hemisphere processing of speech (Kroll, De Nil, Kapur, Houle, 1997). Conversely, with different clients, it may be more effective to exploit the particular strengths of the right hemisphere in focusing on the integrated ("melodic") nature of longer speech segments. The observation of atypical brain lateralization may also have important implications for how clinicians deal with the occurrence of relapse following treatment (Kroll, De Nil, Kapur, Houle, 1997). For instance, is the type and extent of neural reorganization following treatment related to the likelihood of posttreatment relapse or of long-term successful fluency maintenance? If so, can we develop clinically useful indicators of this functional reorganization that may serve as predictors of treatment outcome? And, can we develop effective treatment and/or maintenance techniques that maximize the likelihood of success? The central issue, then, that needs to be addressed deals with the functional link that exists between observed or hypothesized neurophysiological variables (processing level), regardless of whether they are innate or not, and the fluency disruptions and other behaviors observed in the speech of those who stutter (output level). If we understand this relationship, it becomes possible to start answering clinically relevant questions: whether this functional link can be influenced, and how this can best be accomplished.

Typically, it is impossible to directly alter neural structures and systems involved in speech and language behaviors. When such alteration does take place, it is most often a consequence of neurosurgical treatment for some other medical condition. Clearly, it is highly unlikely that neurosurgical intervention, due to its invasive nature, will contribute to the treatment of most communication disorders, including stuttering, in the foreseeable future. However, several attempts have been made to use therapeutic drugs to influence neural processes in individuals who stutter (for recent reviews, see Brady, 1991; Ludlow & Braun, 1993). Although a number of individuals appeared to respond positively to some of these drugs, at least temporarily, it is evident that the effects of such intervention can differ dramatically from individual to individual. The observation of such interindividual variability may not be all that surprising if one keeps in mind that drugs often act on widely distributed neural systems that, in turn, are comprised of many interacting and delicately balanced neuroanatomical and neurochemical subsystems. Not only are the effects of pharmaceutical intervention on these distributed neural systems often not completely understood, but the therapeutic effects are also influenced by the presence of interindividual differences in brain anatomy and physiology.

Recent developments in functional neuroimaging techniques such as positron emission tomography (PET) and functional magnetic resonance imaging (fMRI), have allowed researchers to explore previously elusive cognitive and other neural processes in individuals with and without communication problems (Demonet, Price, Wise, & Frackowiak, 1994; Friston, Frith, Liddle, & Frackowiak, 1991; Grafton et al., 1992; Liotti, Gay, & Fox, 1994). The ability to use functional imaging technology to observe patterns of neural activation and to investigate the effects of drugs on central neurotransmitters will lead to greater sophistication in our understanding of the neurophysiological bases of human behavior in general, and speech and language processes in particular. This, in turn, has the potential to provide us with the tools and knowledge needed to study the effects of drugs that show promise as complements to behavioral therapeutic interventions for disorders of communications, including stuttering.

Fortunately, neuropharmacological agents are not the only means by which clinicians can attempt to modify underlying neurophysiological processes. As shown in our model (Fig. 7.1), these processes are also influenced by sensory feedback generated at the output level (behavior) and by stimuli provided at the contextual level (environment). It is this type of intervention that is most familiar to most clinicians working with clients who stutter. For instance, many clinicians routinely teach stuttering clients to slow their speech rate, or to use gentle voice onsets or soft articulatory contacts during speech. As we have been able to show using PET scanning of stuttering subjects pre and posttherapy (De Nil et al., 1998; Kroll et al., 1997), such behavioral interventions can result in a reorganization of neural processes. In our studies, adults who stutter showed a preponderance of widely distributed right hemisphere activation, including primary and secondary cortical motor regions, pretreatment. Immediately following an intensive behavioral treatment program based on the precision fluency shaping program (Kroll, 1989; Webster, 1980), the stuttering individuals showed increased activation in the cortical motor regions in the left hemisphere. This shift in activation from right to left hemisphere is thought to reflect the greater volitional control over articulatory movements that the adults were using during speech production. Similar results were reported earlier by Boberg et al. (1983) using electrophysiological measures of alpha-wave activity in the brain.

A second observation in the studies by De Nil et al. (1998) and by Kroll et al. (1997) was that behavioral treatment not only affected neural activation in primary motor regions (associated with changes in the control of overt articulatory movements), but also changed the activation patterns observed in the anterior cingulate region. This cortical region is believed to be involved in emotional and cognitive processes related to attention, emotion, and movement (including silent articulatory rehearsal) (Damasio, 1994; Murtha, Chertkow, Bearegard, Dixon, & Evans, 1996; Petersen, Fox, Posner, Mintun, & Raichle, 1989; Posner & Petersen, 1990). Given the nature of the task during which cingulate activation was observed (silent reading), the hypothesized function of this cortical region, and the absence of this increased activation following successful stuttering treatment, De Nil et al. (1998) and Kroll et al. (1997) suggested that the cingulate activation represents cognitive anticipation in stuttering individuals. This observation, if replicable, shows that behavioral change can result in a dramatic functional reorganization of neural processes involved in the control of overt speech behavior, as well as those associated with covert cognitive reactions. Whereas the study by Kroll et al. (1997) focused on one particular type of fluency treatment approach, other researchers have reported reorganization of neural activation patterns associated with choral speech and other fluency enhancing interventions (Fox et al., 1996; Wu et al., 1995). It seems highly likely that other forms of fluency intervention that focus on overt speech motor behavior, covert cognitive processes such as self-perception and attitudes, or psycholinguistic processes will also result in functional neural reorganizations that can be investigated using the appropriate neuroimaging technology.

This type of research has the potential to complement research into treatment effectiveness by providing clues to the questions why certain clinical approaches work, and perhaps more importantly, why they do not work with every individual who stutters. Many techniques currently used in treatment, including speech rate manipulation, gentle voice onset, gentle articulatory contact, language modeling, environmental manipulation, and cognitive restructuring, have been shown to be highly effective for many children and adults who stutter. It is also evident from the data on maintenance and relapse in stuttering treatment that none of these techniques is universally effective with every individual seen in treatment (Boberg, 1981). Although the reasons why certain intervention techniques work well with one individual but not with another are unquestionably complex, a thorough understanding of what does or does not change at the neural processing level will advance our ability to tailor our clinical approaches to individual characteristics of the client with whom we are working. As such, looking at treatment efficacy should include a more thorough analysis of the processes behind the observed (lack of) changes, in addition to a measurement of the outcome of treatment in terms of frequency of disfluency.

Another area in which increased insight into the neurophysiogical processes underlying stuttering will have important implications is prognosis. Few will disagree with the notion that one of the central issues in clinical intervention, especially in working with young children who stutter, is prognosis. It is generally agreed that between 50% and 80% of the children who show early symptoms of beginning stuttering recover, most within the first 24 months after the onset of disfluencies (Yairi, 1997; Yairi & Ambrose, 1992a; Yairi et al., 1996b). At present, there are no well-established predictor variables that allow clinicians to differentiate between children who are and those who are not likely to recover (Starkweather et al., 1990). However, a number of recent studies have suggested that a positive family history of chronic stuttering may indicate a reduced chance of spontaneous recovery in young children (Yairi et al., 1996a, 1996b). As we come to better understand the nature and specific role of the factor(s) that is (are) genetically transmitted, it may be possible to develop more specific criteria and/or tests that will allow clinicians to improve their ability to detect those children that are at greatest risk for developing chronic stuttering. Whether or not the presence of a positive family history also has value in predicting treatment outcome in older children or adults is presently an open question (Janssen, Kraaimaat, & Brutten, 1990).

In conclusion, at the present time, discussion of the implications of neurophysiological research in stuttering often has to be formulated in tentative terms. This, in itself, does not come as a surprise given the state of our current understanding of the central neurophysiogical processes underlying normal speech and language formulation. Indeed, although in the last few decades, tremendous advances have been made in our understanding of brain–behavior interaction (Kandel, Schwartz, & Jessell, 1991), many questions and unknowns still remain. This is especially true for the study of language formulation and speech production. As a result, advancement in the study of the biological basis of stuttering will have to progress hand in hand with growing sophistication in the study of the role that the brain plays in human behavior in general, and speech and language formulation in particular. Nevertheless, there is little doubt in my mind that recent advances in our ability to investigate these processes directly, in particular with respect to functional neuroimaging, and to observe the dynamic nature of these processes as task and contextual variables change, will result in significant progress in our understanding of stuttering and its clinical treatment.

Acknowledgments

The preparation of this manuscript was made possible by a grant from the Natural Sciences and Engineering Council of Canada. I would like to express special thanks to E. Charles Healey, Nan Bernstein Ratner, Christopher Dromey, Sophie Lafaille, and Torrey Loucks for their constructive and insightful comments on previous versions of this chapter.

REFERENCES

Adams, M. R. (1990). The demands and capacities model: I. Theoretical elaborations. *Journal of Fluency Disorders, 15*, 135–141.

Armson, J., & Kalinowski, J. (1994). Interpreting results of the fluent speech paradigm in stuttering research: Difficulties in separating cause from effect. *Journal of Speech and Hearing Research, 37*, 69–82.

Bakker, K., & Brutten, G. J. (1989). A comparative investigation of the laryngeal premotor, adjustment, and reaction times of stutterers and nonstutterers. *Journal of Speech and Hearing Research, 32*, 239–244.

Benson, R. R., Logan, W. J., Cosgrove, A. J., Cole, A. J., Jiang, H., LeSueur, L. L., Buchbinder, B. R., Rosen, B. R., & Caviness, V. S. Jr. (1996). Functional MRI localization of language in a 9-year-old child. *Canadian Journal of Neurological Sciences, 23*, 213–219.

Bloodstein, O. (1993). *Stuttering: The search for a cause and cure.* Boston: Allyn & Bacon.

Bloodstein, O. (1995). *A handbook on stuttering.* Chicago: National Easter Seal Society.

Boberg, E. (Ed.). (1981). *The maintenance of fluency.* New York: Elsevier.

Boberg, E., Yeudall, L. T., Schopflocher, D., & Bo Lassen, P. (1983). The effect of an intensive behavioral program on the distribution of EEG alpha power in stutterers during the processing of verbal and visuospatial information. *Journal of Fluency Disorders, 8*, 245–263.

Bradshaw, J. L. (1989). *Hemispheric specialization and psychological function.* Chichester: Wiley.

Bradshaw, J., & Nettleton, N. (1981). The nature of hemispheric specialization in man. *The Behavioral and Brain Sciences, 4*, 51–91.

Brady, J. P. (1991). The pharmacology of stuttering: A critical review. *American Journal of Psychiatry, 148*(10), 1309–1316.

Braun, A. R., Varga, M., Stager, S., Shultz, G., Selbie, S., Maisog, J. M., Carson, R. E., & Ludlow, C. L. (1997). Altered patterns of cerebral activity during speech and language production in developmental stuttering: An $H_2^{15}O$ positron emmission tomography study. *Brain, 120*, 761–784.

Brown, W. T., Friedman, E., Brooks, J., Wisniewski, K., Raguthu, S., & French, J. (1982). Autism is associated with the fragile X-syndrome. *Journal of Autism and Developmental Disorders, 12*, 303.

Bruner, J. (1990). *Acts of meaning*. Cambridge, MA: Harvard University Press.

Caruso, A. J., Abbs, J. H., & Gracco, V. L. (1988). Kinematic analysis of multiple movement coordination during speech in stutterers. *Brain, 111*, 439–456.

Chertkow, H. (1996). Anticipation causes increased blood-flow to the anterior cingulate cortex. *Human Brain Mapping, 4*, 103–112.

Chugani, H. T. (1996). Functional brain reorganization in children. *Brain and Development, 18*, 347–356.

Churchland, P. S., & Sejnowski, T. J. (1992). *The computational brain*. Cambridge, MA: MIT Press.

Cremers, C. W., Van Rijn, P. M., & Huygen, P. L. (1994). The sex-ratio in childhood deafness, an analysis of the male predominance [review]. *International Journal of Pediatric Otorhinolaryngology, 30*, 105–110.

Curlee, R. F., & Siegel, G. M. (1997). *Nature and treatment of stuttering: New directions* (2nd ed.), (pp.452). Boston: Allyn & Bacon.

Damasio, A. (1994). *Descartes' error: Emotion, reason, and the human brain*. New York: Avon Books.

Demonet, J. F., Price, C., Wise, R., & Frackowiak, R. S. (1994). A PET study of cognitive strategies in normal subjects during language tasks: Influence of phonetic ambiguity and sequence processing on phoneme monitoring. *Brain, 117*, 671–682.

De Nil, L. F. (1995). The influence of phonetic context on temporal sequencing of upper lip, lower lip, and jaw peak velocity and movement onset during bilabial consonants in stuttering and nonstuttering adults. *Journal of Fluency Disorders, 20*, 127–144.

De Nil, L. F., & Abbs, J. H. (1991). Kinesthetic acuity of stutterers and non-stutterers for oral and non-oral movements. *Brain, 114*, 2145–2158.

De Nil, L. F., Kroll, R. M., Kapur, S. & Houle, S. (1998). *A positron emission tomography study of silent and oral single word reading in stuttering and nonstuttering adults*. Manuscript submitted for publication.

Descartes, R. (1985). *The philosophical writing of Descartes*. Cambridge, England: Cambridge University Press.

Felsenfeld, S. (1997). Epidemiology and genetics of stuttering. In R. F. Curlee & G. M. Siegel (Eds.), *Nature and treatment of stuttering: New directions* (2nd. ed., pp. 3–23). Boston: Allyn & Bacon.

Fodor, J. A. (1994). The mind-body problem. In R. Warner & T. Szubka (Eds.), *The mind-body problem* (pp. 24–40). Oxford, England: Basil Blackwell.

Fox, P. T., Ingham, R. J., Ingham, J. C., Hirsch, T. B., Downs, J. H., Martin, C., Jerabek, P., Glass, T., & Lancaster, J. L. (1996). A PET study of the neural systems of stuttering. *Nature, 382*, 158–162.

Friston, K. J., Frith, C. D., Liddle, P. F., & Frackowiak, R. S. (1991). Investigating a network model of word generation with positron emission tomography. *Proceedings of the Royal Society of London - Series B: Biological Sciences, 244*, 2–6.

Geschwind, N., & Galaburda, A. M. (1985). Cerebral lateralization: Biological mechanisms, associations, and pathology. I. A hypothesis and a program for research. *Archives of Neurology, 42*, 429–459.

Grafton, S. T., Mazziotta, J. C., Presty, S., Friston, K. J., Frackowiak, R. S., & Phelps, M. E. (1992). Functional anatomy of human procedural learning determined with regional cerebral blood flow and PET. *Journal of Neuroscience, 12*, 2542–2548.

Hellige, J. B. (1993). *Hemispheric asymmetry: What's right and what's left*. Cambridge, MA: Harvard University Press.

Helm Estabrooks, N., Yeo, R., Geschwind, N., & Freedman, M. (1986). Stuttering: Disappearance and reappearance with acquired brain lesions. *Neurology, 36*, 1109–1112.

Janssen, P., Kraaimaat, F., & Brutten, G. J. (1990). Relationship between stutterers' genetic history and speech-associated variables. *Journal of Fluency Disorders, 15*, 39–48.

Johnson, W. (Ed.). (1955). *Stuttering in children and adults*. Minneapolis: University of Minnesota Press.

Kandel, E. R., Schwartz, J. H., & Jessell, T. M. (1991). *Principles of neural science*. New York: Elsevier.

Kidd, K. K., Kidd, J. R., & Records, M. A. (1978). The possible causes of the sex ratio in stuttering and its implications. *Journal of Fluency Disorders, 3*, 13–23.

Koopmans, M., Slis, I., & Rietveld, T. (1996). The effect of lexical constraints on spontaneous stuttered speech. *Clinical Linguistics and Phonetics, 10*, 207–223.

Kroll, R. M. (1989). Stuttering: Its nature and treatment. *Psychiatry, 3*, 16–28.

Kroll, R. M., De Nil, L. F., Kapur, & S., Houle, S. (1997). A positron emission tomography investigation of post-treatment brain activation in stutterers. In H. F. M. Peters & W. Hulstijn, (Eds.). *Proceedings of the Third International Conference on Speech Motor Production and Fluency Disorders* (pp.307–320). Amsterdam: Elsevier.

Laberge, D. (1995). *Attentional processing: The brain's art of mindfulness.* Cambridge, MA: Harvard University Press.

Levitas, A., Hagerman, R. J., Braden, M., Rimland, B., McBogg, P., & Matus, I. (1983). Autism and the fragile X syndrome. *Journal of Developmental and Behavioral Pediatrics, 4*, 151.

Lewis, C., Hitch, G. J., & Walker, P. (1994). The prevalence of specific arithmetic difficulties and specific reading difficulties in 9- to 10- year-old boys and girls. *Journal of Child Psychology & Psychiatry & Allied Disciplines, 35*, 283–292.

Liotti, M., Gay, C. T., & Fox, P. T. (1994). Functional imaging and language: Evidence from positron emission tomography. *Journal of Clinical Neurophysiology, 11*, 175–190.

Llinás, R., & Churchland, P. S. (Eds.). (1996). *The mind-brain continuum: Sensory processes.* Cambridge, MA: MIT Press.

Ludlow, C. L., & Braun, A. (1993). Research evaluating the use of neuropharmacological agents for treating stuttering: Possibilities and problems. *Journal of Fluency Disorders, 18*, 169–182.

MacFarlane, W. B., Hanson, M., Walton, W., & Mellon, C. D. (1991). Stuttering in five generations of a single family: A preliminary report including evidence supporting a sex-modified mode of transmission. *Journal of Fluency Disorders, 16*, 117–123.

Mikkelsen, M., Poulsen, H., & Nielsen, K. G. (1990). Incidence, survival, and mortality in Down syndrome in Denmark. *American Journal of Medical Genetics, 7*, 75–78.

Molfese, D. L., & Molfese, V. L. (1988). Right-hemisphere responses from preschool children to temporal cues to speech and nonspeech materials: Electrophysiological correlates. *Brain and Language, 33*, 245–259.

Moore, W. H., Jr. (1984). Central nervous system characteristics of stutterers. In R. F. Curlee & W. H. Perkins (Eds.), *Nature and treatment of stuttering: New directions* (pp. 49–71). San Diego, CA: College-Hill.

Murtha, S., Chertkow, H., Beauregard, M., Dixon, R., & Evans, A. (1996). Anticipation causes increased blood flow to the anterior singulate cortex. *Human Brain Mapping, 4*, 103–112.

Nagel, T. (1974). What is it like to be a bat? *Philosophical Review, 83*, 435–450.

Peters, T. J., & Guitar, B. E. (1991). *Stuttering: An integrated approach to its nature and treatment.* Baltimore: Williams & Wilkins.

Petersen, S. E., & Fiez, J. A. (1993). The processing of single words studied with positron emission tomography. *Annual Review of Neuroscience, 16*, 509–530.

Petersen, S. E., Fox, P. T., Posner, M. I., Mintun, M., & Raichle, M. E. (1989). Positron emission tomographic studies of the processing of single words. *Journal of Cognitive Neuroscience, 1*, 153–170.

Pool, K. D., Devous, M. D., Freeman, F. J., Watson, B. C., & Finitzo, T. (1991). Regional cerebral blood flow in developmental stutterers. *Archives of Neurology, 48*, 509–512.

Popper, C. W. (1988). Disorders usually first evident in infancy, childhood, or adolescence. In J. A. Talbott, R. E. Hales, & S. C. Yudofsky (Eds.), *Textbook of psychiatry* (pp. 649–735). Washington: American Psychiatric Press.

Posner, M. I., & Petersen, S. E. (1990). The attention system of the human brain. *Annual Review of Neuroscience, 13*, 25–42.

Raichle, M. E., Fiez, J. A., Videen, T. O., MacLeod, A., K., Pardo, J. V., Fox, P. T., & Petersen, S. E. (1994). Practice-related changes in human brain functional anatomy during nonmotor learning. *Cerebral Cortex, 4*, 8–26.

Reiman, E. (1990). PET, panic disorder, and normal anticipatory anxiety. In J. Ballenger (Ed.), *Neurobiology of panic disorders* (pp. 245–270). New York: Wiley-Liss.

Schuell, H. (1946). Sex differences in relation to stuttering: Part I. *Journal of Speech Disorders, 11*, 277–298.

Schuell, H. (1947). Sex differences in relation to stuttering: Part II. *Journal of Speech Disorders, 12,* 23–28.

Shaywitz, B. A., Shaywitz, S. E., Pugh, K. R., Constable, R. T., Skudlarski, P., Fulbright, R. K., Bronen, R. A., Fletcher, J. M., Shankweiler, D. P., Katz, L., & Gore, J. C. (1995). Sex differences in the functional organization of the brain for language. *Nature, 373,* 607–609.

Starkweather, C. W., Gottwald, S. R., & Halfond, M. M. (1990). *Stuttering prevention: A clinical method.* Englewood Cliffs: Prentice Hall.

Van Riper, C. (1982). *The nature of stuttering (2nd ed.).* Englewood Cliffs: Prentice-Hall.

Wall, M. J., & Myers, F. L. (1984). *Clinical management of childhood stuttering.* Austin, Texas: Pro-Ed, Inc.

Warner, R. (1994). In defense of a dualism. In R. Warner & T. Szubka (Eds.), *The mind-body problem* (pp. 343–354). Oxford, England: Basil Blackwell.

Webster, R. L. (1980). *The precision fluency shaping program: Speech reconstruction for stutterers.* Clinician program guide. Virginia: University Publication.

Webster, W. G. (1990). Motor performance of stutterers: A search for mechanisms. *Journal of Motor Behavior, 22,* 553–571.

Williams, D. T., Pleak, R., & Hanesian, H. (1987). Neuropsychiatric disorders of childhood and adolescence. In J. A. Talbott, R. E. Hales, & S. C. Yudofsky (Eds.), *Textbook of neuropsychiatry* (pp. 365–383). Washington: American Psychiatric Press.

Wise, R., Chollet, F., Hadar, U., Friston, K. J., Hoffner, E., & Frackowiak, R. S. (1991). Distribution of cortical neural networks involved in word comprehension and word retrieval. *Brain, 114,* 1803–1817.

Wood, F., & Stump, D. (1980). Patterns of regional cerebral blood flow during attempted reading aloud by stutterers both on and off haloperidol medication: Evidence for inadequate left frontal activation during stuttering. *Brain and Language, 9,* 141–144.

Wu, J. C., Maguire, G., Riley, G., Fallon, J., LaCasse, L., Chin, S., Klein, E., Tang, C., Cadwell, S., & Lottenberg, S. (1995). A positron emission tomography [18F]deoxyglucose study of developmental stuttering. *Neuroreport, 6,* 501–505.

Yairi, E. (1997). Disfluency characteristics of childhood stuttering. In R. F. Curlee & G. M. Siegel (Eds.), *Nature and treatment of stuttering: New directions* (pp. 49–78). Boston: Allyn & Bacon.

Yairi, E., & Ambrose, N. (1992). A longitudinal study of stuttering in children: A preliminary report. *Journal of Speech and Hearing Research, 35,* 755–760.

Yairi, E., Ambrose, N., & Cox, N. (1996a). Genetics of stuttering: A critical review. *Journal of Speech and Hearing Research, 39*(4), 771–784.

Yairi, E., Ambrose, N., Paden, E., & Throneburg, R. (1996b). Predictive factors of persistence and recovery: Pathways of childhood stuttering. *Journal of Communication Disorders, 29,* 51–77.

Zimmerman, G. (1980). Articulatory dynamics of fluent utterances of stutterers and nonstutterers. *Journal of Speech and Hearing Research, 23,* 95–107.

Zimmermann, G. N., Smith, A., & Hanley, J. M. (1981). Stuttering: In need of a unifying conceptual framework. *Journal of Speech and Hearing Research, 24,* 25–31.

8 Clinician/Researcher: A Way of Thinking

Jeanna Riley
Riley's Speech and Language Institute, Tustin, California

A review of the literature of the late 1960s and early 1970s reveals a preponderance of research conducted on adults who stutter, with very few studies on children who stutter. In such studies, stuttering was also primarily viewed as a unitary disorder; stutterers were compared to controls who did not stutter. Although the homogeneity of the stuttering population seemed implied, the theories that were prevalent at that time did reflect the possibility of varying etiologies. The main theories of stuttering evolved from work done years before; their themes were developmental (Bloodstein & Gantwerk, 1967; Johnson, 1942; Wischner, 1948), intra and interpersonal (Bender, 1942; Coriat, 1943; Douglass & Quarrington, 1952; Glasner & Vermilyea, 1953; Murphy & Fitzsimons, 1960; Sheehan, 1954), and organic (Bryngelson, 1940; Karlin, 1959; Travis, 1931; Weiss, 1950; West 1958). There was evidence to support each of the theories. However, many questions remained. Among the questions that needed to be answered were: (a) are there differences as well as similarities among people who stutter? (b) does severity distinguish subgroups of people who stutter? (c) does the experience of long-term stuttering contribute to population variability, or does variability in the population contribute to pattens of severity and chronicity? and finally, (d) how adequate or likely is a single causation theory of stuttering?

STUTTERING IN CHILDREN: AN OPPORTUNITY TO INVESTIGATE HETEROGENEITY

To obtain accurate answers to some of these questions, it seemed logical to look to children who stuttered, and to examine them as close to the onset of symptoms as possible. In the 1960s and 1970s, there was a paucity of such studies. It was clear that data, even field data, should be gathered in a way that would be useful and replicable in descriptive articles. We began our clinic with the assumption that stuttering children presented with heterogenous factors rather than with a unitary etiology of stuttering; thus, our clients were differentially diagnosed and treated. Observation and testing were done with a minimum of preconceived ideas in order to determine what the child's behavior, especially close to onset, could reveal about stuttering. In particular, we hoped that it would become clearer which behaviors were learned and which ones were part of the child's original system for speech and language. In addition to quantifying the stuttering on the Stuttering Severity Instrument (1972), reactions of the parents and children were obtained on the Stuttering Prediction Instrument (1981), along with extensive testing of speech motor timing and accuracy, as well as language performance.

Speech motor testing referenced the normative data on diadochokinetic rates developed by Fletcher (1972) and Ludwig (1987). The accuracy of syllable production, the presence or absence of airflow breaks, sequencing and rate of speech were also evaluated; these measures led to the development of our Motor Problems Inventory (Riley, 1976) and The Oral Motor Assessment and Treatment: Improving Syllable Production protocol (Riley & Riley, 1985; see Riley & Riley, 1986 for discussion). In the latter study, oral motor assessment was conducted with 200 randomly selected nonstuttering children, ages 4–11, to provide a normative base. The data showed that reduced diadochokinetic rate correlated at $r = .67$ with the total Oral Motor Assessment scale. To assess diadochokinetic rate, the child was required to repeat a syllable or set of syllables 10 times in order to challenge the speech motor system. If the syllables used for testing have low incidence (infrequent in ordinary language), any slowing or breakdown is more likely to indicate motor rather than language processing problems. Reduced rate, when observed, was not randomly distributed during the 10 set repetition; rather, in our data, it was more evident after the first 2.5 s. Beckett (Riley, Riley, & Beckett, 1985) examined 14 syllable sets repeated 10 times by 30 children. He reported that, "Rate... seemed to be affected by breaks in performance after the first 2.5 seconds. Performance seems to break down with continued production." (p. 27).

For stuttering children with slowed diadochokinetic rate, a study of the results of speech motor training as treatment for stuttering was conducted (Riley & Riley, 1991). The theoretical framework underlying Speech Motor Treatment was first elucidated by Stetson (1951). His research in motor phonetics led to a set of principles including the premise that the syllable is the basic unit of speech production, and the notion that abutting speech sounds overlap (are coarticulated). McDonald (1964) synthesized these ideas and made them more accessible to clinicians. Coarticulation was described in more detail by Kent and Minifie (1977), and by Sharf and Ohde (1981) among others. Speech motor training proved to be beneficial for some children in our clinic who stuttered. Stuttering among the subjects was reduced between 37% to 80%, with a mean of 67%, after only speech motor training. We concluded that speech motor treatment does not usually eliminate stuttering; however, it does reduce severity (Riley & Riley, 1995).

Language testing of the children that we evaluated was based on a conversational sample of at least 50 utterances. These utterances were scored for the number of fragmented or incomplete sentences, number of word order errors, instances of word finding problems, overall level of sentence complexity, and the child's ability to formulate a sentence given a key word or two. A rating scale similar to one used by physicians, in which a score of 0 indicated no problem and a score of 4 indicated a severe problem was used to quantify language findings.

Componential Analysis of the Children's Capacities

Several years of collecting such data led us to view stuttering using a componential perspective (Riley & Riley, 1979, 1980, 1984). There seemed to be a good possibility that discrete behavioral components exhibited by children could contribute to the breakdown of their fluency. These components were described by a factor analysis of selected variables on 76 children who stuttered, ages 5–12 (Riley & Riley, 1980). Nineteen variables, including linguistic and motor variables, were included. Four factors accounted for 74.3% of the variance in stuttering behavior. Factors I and III included primarily linguistic variables with loadings of .53 to .84. Factor II included oral and fine motor variables (.38–.53) and was related to the child's age (.74). We concluded that "…these factors seem to be components that can occur singly or in various combinations with a given child. They do not appear to define subgroups that are mutually exclusive." (Riley & Riley, 1980, p. 509). The children we evaluated did not appear to fit into subgroups. We viewed a subgroup as a type of categorical placement that implies that all the children within that subgroup demonstrate the same factors. Conversely, we viewed components as similar to risk factors. A child might have one, two, or more factors, and each factor may be addressed clinically, as needed. When the children who stuttered were compared to each other, we observed that their capacities varied. Individual children did exhibit certain capacity limitations (components). The children in our study averaged 2.4 components, or areas of behavior that could adversely affect fluency. The components found with the greatest frequency were speech motor problems and high self-expectations.

In the process of evaluating the capacities of children who stuttered, it began to appear that some of the children had evidence of language formulation and phonological problems, with or without accompanying speech motor problems; some had problems with their attention span. Most had problems with what we called high self-expectations or self-demands, which we observed as children "being hard on themselves." We attempted to operationally define these observations. As we began to theorize from our clinical data, it seemed that often, the child presented with a vulnerable system for fluency (Riley & Riley, 1988). In our clinical practice, the child's particular vulnerabilities (capacities) were described, then addressed in treatment, before the fluency itself was targeted. The rationale was that putting fluency over a tenuous system created the potential for relapse. Improving the underlying system limitation, whether it was language formulation, speech motor ability, the child's perfectionistic demands, and/or improving the family communication system, resulted in enough improvement of the child's fluency that we were encouraged that this was a helpful direction. However, stuttering was often still present, although at a milder level of severity. That is, the duration of long, hard blocks was less and phonatory arrest or articulatory posturing behaviors often evolved into easier repetitions.

Capacities and Demands Analysis: A Case Example

The following vignette illustrates our approach to evaluation and treatment:

> Kenny, a 4-year-old boy, was brought to the clinic by his parents. His stuttering had begun 18 months before and had progressed to a moderately severe level. His receptive and expressive language skills were well above average. He spoke at a rapid rate as measured by the Oral Motor Assessment scale. He tried to produce long, complicated sentences. He had high demands on himself. He was perfectionistic about some things, including his speech. Perfectionism was measured on the High Self-Expectations Rating Chart (Riley & Riley, 1984), using the 0–4 scale

derived from scores from the Burks Behavior Rating scale (excessive suffering, excessive anxiety, excessive self-blame, poor ego strength), and was also based on parent's report of the child's perfectionism, and clinician's judgment of child's perfectionism, including low frustration threshold.

Increasing Capacity and Decreasing Demands. A demands profile was used with the parents to encourage positive listener behavior. This profile was scored on a 10-point scale anchored by the values *usually, sometimes,* and *never.* The behaviors we discussed with parents were use of relaxed face, use of short sentences, insertion of pauses in speech to the child, reacting to the content of the child's speech rather than to its form (including encouragement of child talk, use of one question at a time, and talk about people, objects, and events meaningful to the child), provision of a variety of stimulating language experiences, and reading to the child in relaxed manner, followed by discussion of the reading. Along with these behaviors, parents were encouraged to react to the child's feelings (Kelly, 1994).

After hour-long sessions that included Speech Motor Training with the child over about 12 weeks, the family conversations were much more relaxed, with more time for turn taking, more pauses between turns, and fewer direct corrections or demands of the child. The child's perfectionism component was treated by; clarifying the problem, including teaching the child to identify when he was beginning to become frustrated, providing other options for him to choose, helping him to cognitively reframe unrealistic demands on himself, and teaching the child to recognize others who are not "perfect," and to recognize that it is "okay not to be perfect" (see Riley & Riley, 1984).

During this process, the frequency and severity of Kenny's stuttering were reduced 50%. The remaining stuttering was targeted by teaching the use of "easy" speech versus "hard" speech. Kenny achieved a score in the subclinical range on the SSI by the end of treatment. The total time of treatment was 40 hours, with only 8 hours required in the direct modification of the stuttering. A one year follow-up revealed only occasional easy repetitions. He was not bothered by his speech, nor were his listeners. This case is an example of assessment and treatment of the child's reduced capacities for fluency (components), which in this case were problems with speech motor accuracy and the demands of high self-expectations, a disruptive communication environment, and time pressure from the parents. After treating the components, or the multiple risk factors that were present in this child's case, the stuttering was reduced. Further treatment of the stuttering resulted in fluency that was maintained.

The "capacities and demands" characterization of stuttering by Adams (1990) and by Starkweather and Gottwald (1990) provides a helpful framework with which to view stuttering; this perspective permits us to recognize the heterogeneity among people who stutter. Smith (1990; see also this volume) also suggested that a different way of thinking about stuttering is needed. Smith (1990) proposed that views of stuttering that posit a primary cause be set aside and replaced with a multiple risk model. This model would seem to be similar to the concept of components that can occur in various combinations in a given child. In one of Yairi, Ambrose, Paden, and Throneburg's (1996) latest articles examining factors that appear to be related to persistent stuttering, they reported that some capacity limitations of children who stutter predict that they will not spontaneously recover or outgrow the condition; these capacities include expressive and receptive language skills, phonological ability, and nonverbal intelligence (as measured by Leiter scores). Thus, these types of components may be useful in predicting chronicity of dysfluency, as well as in treating stuttering.

Despite such evidence of multiple risk factors in stuttering, the National Institute of Neurological and Communicative Disorders and Stroke (1979) described stuttering in the following way: "After a decade of intensive research, we believe that stuttering consists of a core of respiratory/laryngeal/articulatory spasm or incoordination that is resistant to therapy, associated with learned secondary behaviors that are relatively easily extinguished" (p. 226). During each decade, similar observations have been made by a variety of researchers.

THE GAP BETWEEN RESEARCHER AND CLINICIAN ROLES

Many researchers have now arrived at the realization that research with children can provide data "closer to the source" of stuttering. Replacing a prior lack of interest in studying children who stutter, momentum has begun to build as researchers from many different centers (such as Prins & Ingham, Yairi, Ryan, Conture, Onslow, and others) have begun to examine very early characteristics of stuttering. However, at the same time that renewed interest in childhood stuttering has appeared, many clinicians, in my personal experience, have reported apprehension in treating children who stutter, stating a fear that the stuttering can be made worse by direct treatment. In an attempt to make treatment innocuous, clinicians often employ play techniques, sometimes without tracking changes in the stuttering behaviors. Many clinicians seem to be waiting for the researcher to establish what is "safe" to do with the child. The researcher, in turn, may be critical of clinicians who do not employ their findings; however, reported methods of obtaining fluency in a laboratory setting do not necessarily maintain over time in the field. When clinicians are able to effectively use some of the methods from data-based research with the child or adult, and fluency is experienced, confidence begins to increase.

Historically, maintenance of fluency has always been a difficult issue. In use of a particular approach, the clinician (and client) expressed disappointment if the achieved fluency did not maintain. Occasionally, researchers appeared to become dogmatic and insisted that research had provided a mechanism for the achievement of fluency. Treatment teaches the person who stutters what to do. Maintenance requires client usage of techniques; if he or she chooses not to use them, that is a personal choice. All of us in the area of treatment have experienced the guilt and depression that the person who stutters, child or adult, experiences about not being fluent when he or she thinks they could if they so chose.

The price that persons who stuttered might have to pay to be fluent, such as consciously monitoring their speech, was often more than they wished. At this point, the gap between researcher and clinician may widen further. From the perspective of some researchers, once a mode of achieving fluency has been accomplished, it is just a matter of putting it into effect; from the point of view of the clinician, sometimes there seems to have been something left out of the equation, because fluency is often achieved but not maintained. Both want the person who stutters to achieve fluency; like many of the researchers, clinicians know that frequency and severity of stuttering is important, but there also needs to be a feeling of internal control.

Bridging the Gap

Perhaps what was left out of the equation was the person who stutters. As Ed Conture noted at the 1995 ASHA Convention, the person who stutters has valuable information for us; it would be beneficial to listen. What does the person who stutters keep telling us as researchers and clinicians? We hear that the stutterer wants to be fluent, but not necessarily stutterfree if the price is exorbitant; they want to be freer from fear and anxiety and the control that these emotions exert over their lives. Persons who stutter want to experience a feeling of assurance that they aren't going to drop into an endless block again without a way out of it. We need to listen to them. Then, perhaps, any fluency achievements could be better maintained.

We developed a *Subjective Scale of Stuttering* (SSS, 1993) to provide a systematic method for the person who stutters to contribute information to the therapy process. It provides a way for both the person who stutters and the clinician to measure and track changes. I use this scale in conjunction with scales developed by others to gain information about attitudes and perceptions of the person who stutters. The SSS also improves and clarifies communication between the person who stutters and the clinician. In my clinical practice, it provides an opportunity to compare my evaluation of stuttering severity to my clients'. SSS items are scored on a 1–9 range (with 1 representing a positive response and 9 a negative one) by the person who stutters. I have found it useful to rate answers to the following questions:

> •How much time during conversation do you think about stuttering while talking to a close friend, parents, stranger, authority figure, when you speak on the telephone?
> •How would you score your fluency today?
> •How often do you change words when you think you may get stuck on a word?
> •To what extent do you feel internally hurried during conversation?
> •How much energy do you expend on how you speak rather than what you say?
> •What percent of the time do you spend "deciding" what you will say?

•How often do you refrain from a conversation because of a fear of stuttering?

•What was the range of fluency you experienced during the past week?

After time has been spent in therapy, I ask,

•How fluent are you now compared to when you entered therapy?

•During how much conversational time are you concentrating on the content now, compared to when you entered therapy?

•How often do you change words now compared to when you entered therapy?

If the person who stutters has been in a fluency shaping program, the following questions are asked:

•How natural sounding would you rate your speech now?

•How natural sounding would you rate the speech on these recorded samples?

For this question, an audiotape is played of three speakers: a person who has been through a fluency shaping program, a disfluent normal speaker, and a person with mild stuttering. For the researcher, the information is useful in terms of determining the degree of naturalness that a person who stutters perceives in these three presentations. It provides important information to the clinician regarding the outcomes of therapy. For example, when the researcher is asking the person who stutters to rate his or her naturalness, how does the person view naturalness? If the person on the tape who has been through the fluency shaping program is evaluated negatively by the person who stutters, it is unlikely that he or she will maintain their own unnatural sounding speech posttreatment. Therefore, the person may be stutterfree in the lab, yet unwilling to sound "unnatural" in other settings. This provides important information about whether or not the person who stutters will continue to use fluency shaping tools. If he or she doesn't think naturalness is being achieved, it is unlikely that the fluency shaping tools will continue to be utilized.

This same information should be asked of the clinician. Do the client and the clinician choose normal disfluencies or mild stuttering as sounding natural? If so, then perhaps stutterfree speech isn't as important to the client or the clinician as natural sounding speech, even if there are some disfluencies (Franken, Boves, Peters. & Webster, 1992; Franken, van Bezooijen, & Boves, 1997; Kalinowski, Noble, Armson, & Stuart, 1994). This exercise asks the person who stutters how he or she wants to sound. We should not assume that we know the answer to this question without asking.

The scale is currently being used in a large research project. We will compare SSS scores to some standard behavioral measures such as percent stuttered syllables, duration of disfluencies, and physical concomitants on the Stuttering Severity Instrument. For both researcher and clinician, listening to the person who stutters may increase their ability to communicate with each other.

PERSPECTIVES OF RESEARCHERS AND CLINICIANS

How do researchers and clinicians think about stuttering? What are the differences and similarities? What are the opportunities and limitations?

Differences between researcher and clinician are often found in comparing the lab and the field: there are controls in the lab that usually aren't possible in the field, especially in regard to treatment methodology. A current study being conducted by Jan Costello Ingham and Glyn Riley (1996) compares two different methods of treatment with children who stutter and is an excellent example of defining the parameters of treatment and staying within them. A concerted effort is being made to define the targets in a systematic, replicable manner. In order to assess the possible clinician bias issue, each clinician provided both types of treatment in this study. The specific treatment variables were isolated as much as possible in order to determine treatment effectiveness without compromising the outcome by adding additional variables such as parent counseling. Controlled research usually manipulates one variable at a time, and although it is difficult to do this in clinical practice, we can make inroads in this area.

In contrast to the researcher, the focus of the clinician is to help the person who stutters in as many ways as possible in as little time as possible; therefore, more than one variable (e.g., treatment method, counseling, homework, etc.) is usually manipulated simultaneously. Some research tools, such as lengthy baselines and withdrawal from therapy conditions cannot be charged to the client, to public schools or to third-party payers. Treatment research has to seek funding sources willing to finance all the conditions needed to make a scientific determination of treatment effectiveness. Subjects in such research probably have to be paid to come in for measures during the "no therapy" times, such as baselines, withdrawal, and follow-up, all necessary for understanding treatment effects. Additionally, the clinician has to be just as willing to pursue extensive data collection.

Similarities between researchers and clinicians exist as well. Both need to employ critical, investigative thinking and both need to keep a database in a systematic manner. Both need to obtain baseline measurements, if possible, take multiple measures, and establish reliability of measurement. Although a clinician may state that one cannot sterilize and control variables in a clinical setting in the same way one does in the lab, accurate and detailed data can be maintained on client history, evaluation procedures, and treatment applications and effects.

Recognizing Limitations

In order for either researchers or clinicians to move forward in a scientific way, an open mind is needed to take in new information, and/or change a well-grooved perspective, if necessary. Just as astronomers have had to change their theories about the solar system at a very rapid pace as Galileo sends back new data on Jupiter, there is a need to keep our hypotheses as working hypotheses. That is, we need a framework from which to proceed, but we need it made of replaceable parts, rather than constructed of cement. To allow ourselves to become locked into a rigid bias and then become religiously "evangelistic" about our "science" is not science at all, of course. We all have our biases, but acknowledging them may allow us to use them as a boat to move in a given direction while not clinging to them as if they were a life raft. The second law of thermodynamics in classical physics affirms that closed and isolated systems run down. Singer (1990) stated that, "The discipline of scientific investigation requires a person to be aware of what has been learned in the past and yet to regard it as provisional, rather than absolute." (Perhaps) it entails accepting the paradox that we need to know but we can't ever completely know.

As researchers, we have the opportunity to acquire data-based information while at the same time recognizing the limitations of our methodology. Often, we want to generalize to an extent that supersedes our knowledge. How valid is the information the researcher provides the clinician and how far can it be generalized without losing validity in the clinical setting? In order to answer this, the clinician has to be in a constant state of investigative thinking while at the same time following a paradigm, a plan, a direction. At times, it becomes difficult, as a clinician, not to become entrenched in a procedure that is no longer evaluated for its effectiveness and parsimony. It also takes effort to keep up with the state-of-the-art research in many clinic or public school settings, especially when therapeutically effective application of the research to that clinical setting is not easily apparent.

BRIDGING THE GAP

Where do we go from here as clinicians and as researchers? Mutual respect is essential, which means understanding the language of each discipline. We are, after all, the experts in communication, which means being able to listen, process, and dialogue. Perhaps an important bridge is made up of each person's understanding of the other's predicament. The researcher needs to hear the clinician when he or she finds new approaches that seem to be working; in many instances, the clinician is putting energy into solving the puzzle before her or him in a practical, effective way. There may be little time to distill the work into written form, but there needs to be a forum where one can be heard. The Special Interest Division in Fluency can provide that opportunity. The researcher needs to be heard as he or she also continues to try to solve the therapeutic puzzle by limiting the variables and testing the hypotheses. The person who stutters also needs to be heard. Bridging the gap means letting new information inform our own individual biases and remaining open to data that are presented.

An important aspect of our plan for the understanding and treatment of stuttering is to be able to predict and replicate. The accuracy of our theory becomes crucial in achieving this goal. Both Einstein and Hawking (1988) were among the many scientists interested in discovering a grand unifying theory of the universe, something that has the power to explain all of the variables. We in the field of stuttering need to continue to work toward a unifying theory of stuttering that will take into account immense numbers of known variables: variables found in the lab, in the field, and in the person who stutters.

Is the clinician willing to put in the time and have the discipline to conduct single subject designs to add to the database? Is the clinician willing to submit clinical data to scientific scrutiny? Is the clinician willing to keep up with the research instead of becoming locked into a procedure because it is simple or familiar?

Is the researcher willing to listen to the clinician's way of thinking and translate clinical observations into solid research? Is the researcher open to accepting probabilities rather than determining direct cause and effect? A March, 1996 *Los Angeles Times* article by K.C. Cole on research concluded that in many domains of science we are, at best, able to predict the present:

> Galileo got to its target not by predicting the future, but by following well-known patterns to their logical conclusions. Unfortunately, nature has conspired to make even pattern perception unreliable under many common conditions. For example, no amount of understanding of the behavior patterns of atoms allows one to predict just where an atomic particle will be at a certain time. The best you can get is a probability. (p.A5)

There is a need to recognize that we, too, are working with complex systems. Our understanding of stuttering when viewed as a complex system of behavior/ physiology/emotion and social dynamics, certainly argues for caution in interpreting clinical and research results. There may be some basic, underlying principle, that, when described and quantified, could provide a unifying system for stuttering similar to the Periodic Table for chemicals. Perhaps brain imaging techniques, DNA studies, genetics, the effect of various medications on fluency, or better understanding the effects of the mind on the body, will provide the framework on which to build a grand unifying theory — or at least some guiding principles.

An old saying reminds us that "the mind, like a parachute, works better when opened." For clinician and researcher, continuing to explore, analyze, and synthesize should rely on flexible perspectives or ways of thinking; each listening to the other is a way to expand our opportunities for knowledge.

REFERENCES

Adams, M. R. (1990). The demands and capacities model I: Theoretical elaborations. *Journal of Fluency Disorders, 15*, 135–141.

Bender, J. (1942). The stuttering personality. *American Journal of Orthopsychiatry, 10*, 140–146.

Bloodstein, O., & Gantwerk, B. (1967). Grammatical function in relation to stuttering in young children. *Journal of Speech and Hearing Research, 10*, 786–789.

Bryngelson, B. (1940). A study of laterality of stutterers and normal speakers. *Journal of Social Psychology, 11*, 151–155.

Cole, K. C. (1996, March 20). Predicting with caution. *Los Angeles Times*, p.A5.

Coriat, I. H. (1943). The psychoanalytic conception of stammering. *Nervous Child, 2*, 167–171.

Douglass, E., & Quarrington, B. (1952). The differentiation of internalized and exteriorized secondary stuttering. *Journal of Speech and Hearing Disorders, 17*, 377–385.

Fletcher, S. (1972). Time-by-count measurement of diadochokinetic syllable rate. *Journal of Speech and Hearing Research, 15*, 763–769.

Franken, M. C., van Bezooijen, R., & Boves, L. (1997). Stuttering and communicative suitability of speech. *Journal of Speech and Hearing Research, 40*, 83–94.

Franken, M. C., Boves, L., Peters, H. F. M., & Webster, R. L. (1992). Perceptual evaluation of speech before and after fluency shaping stuttering therapy. *Journal of Fluency Disorders, 17*, 223–242.

Glasner, P., & Vermilyea, F. D. (1953). An investigation of the definition and use of the diagnosis, "Primary Stuttering." *Journal of Speech and Hearing Disorders, 18*, 161–167.

Hawking, S. W. (1988). *A brief history of time.* New York: Bantam Books.

Johnson, W. (1942). A study of the onset and development of stuttering. *Journal of Speech Disorders, 7*, 251–257.

Kalinowski, J., Noble, S., Armson, J., & Stuart, A. (1994). Pretreatment and posttreatment speech naturalness ratings of adults with mild and severe stuttering. *American Journal of Speech-Language Pathology, 3*(2), 61–66.

Karlin, I. W. (1959). Stuttering: Basically an organic disorder. *Logos, 2*, 61–63.

Kelly, E. M. (1994). Speech rates and turn taking behaviors of children who stutter and their fathers. *Journal of Speech and Hearing Research, 37*, 1284–1294.

Kelly, E. M. & Conture, E. G. (1992). Speaking rates, response time latencies, and interrupting behaviors of young stutterers, nonstutterers, and their mothers. *Journal of Speech and Hearing Research, 35*, 1256–1267.

Kent, R., & Minifie, F. (1977). Coarticulation in recent speech production models. *Journal of Phonetics, 5*, 115–133.

Ludwig, C. (1987). *An interaction study of phonology and length of utterance in developmental verbal dispraxics and normals in repetition and conversational speech.* Unpublished doctoral dissertation, Southern Illinois University.

McDonald, E. (1964). *Articulation testing and treatment: A sensory-motor approach.* Pittsburgh, PA: Stanwix House.

Murphy, A. T. & Fitzsimons, R. (1960). *Stuttering and personality dynamics.* New York: Ronald Press.

National Institute of Neurological and Communicative Disorders and Stroke. (1979). *Report of the panel on communicative disorders to the advisory neurological and communicative disorders and stroke council* (NIH Publication No. 81-1914). Washington, DC: U.S. Government Printing Office.

Riley, G. (1972). *Stuttering Severity Instrument for Children and Adults.* Austin, TX: ProEd.

Riley, G. (1976). *Motor problems inventory.* Los Angeles: Western Psychological Services.

Riley, G. (1981). *Stuttering Prediction Instrument.* Austin, TX: ProEd.

Riley, G., & Ingham, J. C. (1996). *Predicting treatment outcome in children who stutter.* (Research grant R01 DC01100). Bethesda, MD: National Institute on Deafness and other Communication Disorders.

Riley, G., & Riley, J. (1979). A component model for diagnosing and treating children who stutter. *Journal of Fluency Disorders, 4*, 279–293.

Riley, G., & Riley, J. (1980). Motoric and linguistic variables among children who stutter. *Journal of Speech and Hearing Disorders, 45*, 504–514.

Riley, G., & Riley, J. (1984). A component model for treating stuttering in children. In M. Peins (Ed.) *Contemporary approaches to stuttering therapy* (pp.123–171). Boston: Little, Brown.

Riley, G., & Riley, J. (1986). Oral motor discoordination among children who stutter. *Journal of Fluency Disorders, 11*, 334–335.

Riley, G., & Riley, J. (1988, April). Stuttering: Looking at a vulberable system. *ASHA, 30*, 32–33.

Riley, G., & Riley, J. (1991). Treatment implications of oral motor discoordination. In H. F. M. Peters, W. Hulstijn, & C. W. Starkweather (Eds.), *Speech motor control and stuttering* (pp.471–476). Amsterdam: Elsevier.

Riley, G., Riley, J., & Beckett, R. (1985). *Oral motor assessment and treatment: Improving syllable production.* Austin, TX: ProEd.

Riley, J. (1993, July). *Subjective stuttering scale.* Paper presented at the meeting of the Stuttering Foundation of America, Northwestern University, Evanston, IL.

Riley, J., & Riley, G. (1995). Speech motor improvement program for children who stutter. In C. W. Starkweather & H. F. M. Peters (Eds.), *Stuttering: Proceedings of the First World Congress on Fluency Disorders* (pp. 269–272). New York: Elsevier.

Sharf, D., & Ohde, R. (1981). Physiologic, acoustic and perceptual aspects of coarticulation: Implications for the remediation of articulation disorders. In N. Lass (Ed.), *Speech and language: Advances in basic research and practice* (pp.Vol.5). New York: Academic Press.

Sheehan, J. G. (1954). An integration of psychotherapy and speech therapy through conflict theory of stuttering. *Journal of Speech and Hearing Disorders, 19*, 474–482.

Singer, J. (1990). *Seeing through a visible world.* New York: HarperCollins.

Smith, A. (1990). Factors in the etiology of stuttering. In J. A. Cooper (Ed.), *Research needs in stuttering: Roadblocks and future directions*, ASHA Reports, Number 18 (pp. 39–47). Rockville MD: American Speech-Language-Hearing Association.

Starkweather, C. W., & Gottwald, S. R. (1990). The demands and capacities model II: Clinical applications. *Journal of Fluency Disorders, 15*, 143–157.

Stetson, R. (1951). *Motor phonetics*. Amsterdam: North-Holland.

Travis, L. E. (1931). *Speech pathology*. New York: Appleton-Century-Crofts.

Weiss, D. A. (1950, February). *A basic analysis*. Lecture presented at the New York Society for Speech and Voice Therapy, New York.

West, R. (1958). An agnostic's speculations about stuttering. In J. Eisenson (Ed.), *Stuttering: A symposium*. New York: Harper & Row.

Wischner, G. J. (1948). An experimental approach to stuttering as learned behavior. *American Psychologist, 3*, 278–279.

Yairi, E., Ambrose, N. G., Paden, E. P. , & Throneburg, R. N. (1996). Predictive factors of persistence and recovery: Pathways of childhood stuttering. *Journal of Communication Disorders, 29*, 51–77.

9 Integrating Affective, Behavioral, and Cognitive Factors in Stuttering

Gerald M. Siegel
University of Minnesota

KNOWING OUR ABCS: AN HISTORICAL PERSPECTIVE

If one were familiar only with the work of the pioneers in our field, Travis, Johnson, West, and Van Riper, it would seem curious that Walt Manning and I were asked to consider the integration of affective, behavioral, and cognitive aspects of stuttering — the "ABCs" of stuttering — because in the work of these early writers, the integration would have been assumed from the outset. The apparent split that currently motivates this topic seems to be of recent origin. Although the earlier writers offered very different explanations of the cause and nature of stuttering, they all acknowledged the importance of the ABCs in precipitating and maintaining stuttering, and they incorporated these factors into their programs of therapy.

In this chapter, I don't attempt formal definitions of these terms, but assume they can be understood intuitively by anyone working in stuttering. I begin with an historical overview that mainly allows me to indulge my increasing enjoyment of nostalgia and that attempts to show that, in the beginning, our major thinkers contended with all three variables in their consideration of stuttering. Then I suggest that if a schism exists today, it is likely to be the outgrowth of the behavioral revolution in stuttering that began in the 1960s. And finally, I suggest, in a very modest way, how cognitive and affective aspects can be integrated into a program of research that is primarily behavioral in nature — not as an advertisement for the particular research program, but rather as an exemplar.

Travis

I begin this historical review by considering the contributions of Lee Travis, purportedly "the first individual in the world to be trained by conscious design at the doctoral level for the definite and specific professional objective of working experimentally and clinically with speech and hearing disorders" (Johnson, 1955, p. 7). I think it is fair to say that the first major theory, or, to use Kuhn's (1970) term, the first *paradigm* in the area of stuttering was the Orton–Travis cerebral dominance theory, as elaborated by Travis in his 1931 textbook. [See Perkins's (1996) treatment of this same period for a somewhat different rendering of this early history] Travis believed that stutterers are constitutionally different from normal speakers, and that the cause of the disorder is rooted in the nervous system, even though it might be induced by environmental experiences, such as forcibly having one's handedness changed.

Despite his frankly organic bias, Travis saw no contradiction between a neurological theory of stuttering and a concern for the stutterer's social and emotional adjustment and of course, as we well know, he eventually changed his orientation to a psychoanalytic explanation and treatment of stuttering. It is fascinating to read the brief histories Travis included at the end of his 1931 chapter on stuttering. In every case that he described, he commented on the stutterer's adjustment and personality as well as on developmental, medical, and, of course, handedness history. Furthermore, when discussing management of stuttering, Travis devoted a section in his text to "mental hygiene," a topic that his protege Bryngelson (Bryngelson, 1965; Bryngelson, Chapman, & Hansen, 1950) developed extensively while still maintaining the cerebral dominance theory of stuttering. It is not hard to see why Travis and Bryngelson considered cognitive and affective variables to be important in the treatment of stuttering. To the extent that the underlying neurological cause was resistant to change, clinicians had no alternative except to help the stutterer cope with his handicap, and this necessarily involved cognitive and affective elements. Furthermore, as Bloodstein (1981) noted:

> It is a curious feature of an essentially neurophysiological breakdown theory that it permits considerable emphasis in therapy on the stutterer's attitudes and adjustments. One reason for this is that if stutterers can avoid some of the strong emotional reactions that ordinarily accompany stuttering, they may thereby eliminate a major source of the external pressures presumed to precipitate breakdowns of their vulnerable neuromuscular organization. (p. 345)

Travis recognized the role of emotion and the environment even when he was most doggedly organic in his approach. In a quote that sounds very much like an early version of a "demands-capacities" model, he wrote:

> The fact is inescapable that social situations affect the speech of stutterers. They affect the speech of normal speakers. It happens that the stutterer often does not possess the margin of safety to withstand them. (Travis, 1931, p. 135)

West (1958), too, saw no contradiction in incorporating the psychosocial aspects of this presumably "epileptic" disorder, and some of his recommendations for topics to be included in treatment are surprisingly reminiscent of Wendell Johnson. For example:

> •Stuttering should be explained to the stutterer.
> •The stutterer's attitude toward his listener must be changed.
> •The stutterer's attitude toward himself must be changed.
> •Activities in which he achieves social success should be selected for the stutterer.
> •The stutterer's attitude toward stuttering must be changed (West, 1958, pp. 209–214).

Johnson

In sharp opposition to the organic theories of Travis and West, or the behavioral theories that were to come later, Wendell Johnson's (1942, 1956) diagnosogenic theory is a cognitive theory of stuttering, as are all variants of the "anticipatory-struggle" hypothesis (Bloodstein, 1995, 1997). Johnson differentiated between stuttering behavior and the frame of mind that leads to it, and although Johnson looked to the environment for the origins of stuttering, it was the stutterer's cognitions that most engaged him.

> There are two major aspects of stuttering; there are the movements or activities which the speaker performs in being nonfluent or hesitant, and there are the feelings or attitudes or motivations — and conflicts among them — with which he anticipates, performs, and remembers these activities... To be a stutterer involves more than talking with a certain type or amount of nonfluency. It involves also, and as a rule more importantly, a way of feeling about the nonfluency, or about certain aspects of it, and a way of feeling about its real and imagined consequences. It involves some kind of self-evaluation and a pattern of interpersonal relationships. (pp. 215–216)

In Johnson's treatment of stuttering, feelings, attitudes, and motivations — rather than overt behaviors — distinguish persons who stutter from those who do not. In Johnson's (1956, p. 216–217) formal definition of stuttering as an "anticipatory, apprehensive, hypertonic, avoidance reaction," it is the anticipation and apprehension that are the essence of stuttering, rather than any particular pattern of behaving.

> As we have previously considered, there is much to be said for the proposition that stuttering is basically a perceptual and evaluative problem rather than a motor speech problem. To the degree that this is the case, the stutterer has a need to retrain his habitual ways of perceiving and evaluating his speech behavior. (Johnson, 1956, p. 286)

Although much of Johnson's therapy was designed to retrain the stutterer's habitual ways of perceiving and evaluating speech, Johnson also focused on behavior. He could not ignore the stuttering behaviors that were the manifestations of these perceptual and evaluative tendencies, and so he experimented with alternative ways of stuttering (the Iowa "bounce"), and in so doing, he, too, ultimately integrated affective, cognitive, and behavioral factors.

Van Riper

The last of the pioneers whose work I want to consider is Charles Van Riper. Van Riper was the consummate eclectic, who devoted his energies more to exploring systems of therapy than to advancing any particular theory of stuttering. He wrote of himself:

> In my special field of stuttering I believe that I am viewed as an eclectic. I
> certainly hope that I am. It bothers me greatly, for instance, when people
> write of *vanriperian* stuttering therapy for I've never practiced it. Instead,
> I've used every kind of therapy for stutterers ever mentioned in the
> literature: classical conditioning, operant conditioning, suggestion, semantic
> reorientation, distraction, masking, drugs, many kinds of psychotherapy
> and a host of other approaches to the problem. (1979–1980, p.2)

His eclectic approach to stuttering is lavishly revealed in a report of the
varied stuttering treatments he systematically experimented with between 1936
and 1957 (Van Riper, 1958). In that report, his appreciation of the interplay of
cognitive, affective, and behavioral contributions to stuttering was already evident
in 1936, in the first entry in his therapy log.

> It should be noted that the basic assumptions upon which this rationale
> rested were these: (1) Stuttering consists largely of learned behavior and
> can be modified and reduced through training procedures; (2) Stuttering
> consists largely of avoidance and frustration responses, both of which
> reinforce the stuttering; (3) The stutterer's self-concept can be altered
> so that less stuttering will occur (Van Riper, 1958, pp. 277–278).

Over the 20 year course of this remarkable experimentation with diverse methods
of treatment, there was never a reported period in which affective, cognitive, and
behavioral aspects of stuttering were not incorporated. In the earliest reports, Travis'
influence was clearly visible. The stutterers concentrated on unilateral handedness
activities, to the extent that "one male, an excellent flute and piano player, was shifted
to the trumpet" (Van Riper, 1958 p. 279). Even during this early approach, however, Van
Riper incorporated sessions to clarify goals, to teach the stutterers to resist situational
stresses, and to stutter without avoidance. Throughout the recorded period of
experimentation, stutterers were always invited to express their feelings in more or less
psychotherapeutic contexts, to evaluate their stuttering and their reactions to it, as
well as to work directly on more successful methods of stuttering.

In summary, the pioneers in our field tended to integrate affective, behavioral,
and cognitive approaches regardless of their theoretical orientation. The schism
between behavioral and affective and cognitive variables is a phenomenon, therefore,
of the modern era. It began, I believe, with Israel Goldiamond's entry into the field.

SPLITTING THE ABCS

Goldiamond

In my judgment, the most far-reaching development in stuttering within the last 30
years came not from within the fraternity, but rather through an outsider. Goldiamond,
an experimental psychologist with virtually no history of research in stuttering,
published a major paper on the operant analysis of stuttering in 1965 that sent
ripples throughout our field. In contrast to approaches that aimed to ameliorate
stuttering, Goldiamond raised the prospect of eliminating it entirely. This prospect,
plus the aura of respectability emanating from experimental psychology, made for a
heady combination in a field that has long suffered from Freudian "science envy."
Perhaps most importantly, Goldiamond's work made it possible to study the effects

of very powerful conditioning procedures — including punishment — without the fear that such experimentation would inevitably exacerbate the stuttering or cause symptom substitution. Goldiamond's work led to two lines of further development. One of these, which I won't consider here, exploited Goldiamond's observations concerning the effects of DAF-induced prolongation on stuttering and spawned the fluency shaping procedures so much in evidence in modern therapies for stuttering.

The second development in the aftermath of Goldiamond's publication was the initiation of innumerable conditioning studies in laboratories across the country and abroad into the effects on fluency of various reinforcement procedures. It is this work, with which I'm more closely associated, that, in my mind, led to the temporary fractionation of behavioral from cognitive and affective variables in stuttering research.

There were a number of aspects of Goldiamond's (1965) treatment of stuttering as operant behaviors that discouraged the consideration of affective and cognitive components of the disorder. For one, consistent with general behavior modification approaches, stuttering was considered to be under the control of environmental contingencies, and not internal mental states. In addition, the approach was frankly ahistorical and focused on current controlling variables rather than on accumulated history.

It may be argued, however, that Goldiamond did not ignore affect and cognition, but rather redefined them within his own behavioral framework. Rather than assume that the stutterer's feelings and emotions should occupy a central place in stuttering treatment, Goldiamond treated them as epiphenomena and suggested that if the behavior was first modified in the appropriate direction, the emotional responses would change in their turn.

Although his treatment is typically discussed exclusively in terms of changes in speech patterns, I recently noticed in a section of his chapter that I had only skimmed in the past, that as part of the program, the stutterers were also given private tutorials in the experimental analysis of behavior (Goldiamond, 1965, pp. 153–154). I have not seen any consideration of the contribution of these tutorial sessions to success in achieving fluency, nor any indication of who provided the tutorials, nor what sorts of therapeutic interactions they involved, so there may have been more to the treatment than was formally recorded in the experimental reports.

The Legacy of Behaviorism

I know that my colleague Dick Martin would not have been comfortable with this sort of loosely described tutorial. Martin did consciously attempt to eliminate affective and cognitive variables in his investigations of stuttering. This was not therapy whose heart had been excised; it was experimental research based on a laboratory model that attempted to control all variables except those explicitly under study. In this model, affective and cognitive variables were not dismissed as unimportant, but they were excluded until they can be integrated into formal experimental designs. So far as I know, that integration never took place, in Martin's laboratory or elsewhere. Although there is no assurance that the ABCs would ever have been incorporated into a full-scale behavioral analysis of stuttering, that possibility was pretty much preempted by the general demise of behaviorism in the past 20 years and the increasing emphasis on physiological explorations of stuttering. Certainly Goldiamond made no explicit contribution to this integration, and research in our field soon wandered off into different and multiple directions, with scant attention, however, to continuation of the behavioral revolution. In fact, many modern therapies, with their emphasis on fluency shaping, pay little homage to the learning theory from which this work originally sprung.

In this last section, I suggest that it is possible to work within a behavioral framework and still attend to cognitive and affective variables. I provide an example of how cognitive and affective elements might be incorporated into a behavioral analysis of at least one phenomenon that emerged from the operant research at the University of Minnesota, and that continues to engage my interest — mostly because I don't understand it.

"TIME-OUT"

Of the many response-contingent laboratory methods designed to attenuate stuttering, the "time-out" procedure first introduced by Haroldson, Martin, and Starr (1968) proved to be the most consistently effective (J. Ingham, 1993; Prins & Hubbard, 1988). It was modeled after a practice in psychology. Imagine that you are asked to help someone break a habit such as nail biting. You might have the subject view a favorite television movie and arrange to have the screen go blank each time the subject raises his hand to his mouth. The behavior would occasion a time-out from the positive reinforcement of viewing the movie and would, therefore, be considered a punishment. The expected result would be a reduction in the nail-biting responses.

In the specific case of stuttering, the speaker had to stop speaking for several seconds immediately after each stuttering moment, usually as judged by an experimenter. The rationale in the stuttering research was that the time-out from speaking was regarded by the stutterer as a loss of reinforcement, and therefore as punishing.

Although the technique was quite effective, the explanation has never been entirely convincing to me. Given the amount of energy stutterers expend trying to avoid speech, it seemed hardly plausible that they would consider a momentary pause in speaking to be a loss of positive reinforcement. In addition, some of the accumulated data don't square comfortably with this interpretation. For example, duration of the time-out interval seems to have no effect (James, 1976), but I would have expected a longer interval of silence to be more punishing, if punishment is indeed the underlying process. Furthermore, stutterers differed in how they interpreted the time-out interval (Adams & Popelka, 1971; James & Ingham, 1974), some identifying the interval of forced silence to be punishing but others as a useful period in which to relax, or to recall previously acquired fluency skills. Thus, although the phenomenon is quite robust, the mechanism that accounts for its success is still largely unknown.

The ABCs and Time-Out

I can imagine a number of different reasons why asking stutterers to pause contingent on their stuttering might reduce the behavior, and I have recently begun to explore these possibilities in a series of studies that attempts to examine the effects of time-out in a way that incorporates cognitive and affective elements. One possibility is that Martin and his colleagues were right and the stutterers reacted to the forced interval of silence as a punisher because speaking, even for stutterers, is positively reinforcing. If this is correct, then it should be possible to use time-out from speaking to modify some other aspect of behavior, for example, rate of speech or choice of words. We have begun to test this possibility by adapting a verbal conditioning procedure described by Taffel (1955). Normal speakers are shown a pile of index cards, each with a verb in the middle, and four pronouns printed along the bottom. The speakers are asked to make up sentences for each verb, using any one of the four pronouns. After a baseline period, we introduce a 5 s time-out contingent on the pronoun they preferred during baseline. We reason that if time-out from speaking is punishing, the subjects should begin avoiding their previously preferred pronoun when it is followed by time-out. If time-out is not effective in this situation, we may need to look for another explanation for its effectiveness when applied to stuttering.

Another possible explanation for the effectiveness of time-out suggested by some of the stutterers is that the interval of silence gives them a chance to rehearse previously learned strategies for dealing with stuttering. If that is the case, we should be able to interfere with the effectiveness of time-out by requiring the stutterers to carry out some mundane task such as arithmetic computations during the silent interval, thereby preventing them from rehearsing fluency strategies during the interval.

We can also manipulate the affective quality of the time-out interval by instructing stutterers either that it is a period to help them to "gather their thoughts" (positive affect), or that it is being imposed as a punishment for their stuttering (negative affect).

Still another possibility is that time-out was effective in the stuttering experiments because it was an externally imposed interruption, rather than a loss of the opportunity to talk, or that the time-out is effective only because it highlights a response that the subject wishes to suppress, such as nail biting, and will be ineffective in suppressing a neutral or valued response. This suggests that the effectiveness of the procedure can be made to vary according to which response is selected, and how that response is evaluated by the subject.

These studies are in the early stages of formulation and implementation and I do not know yet what the outcomes will be. What is important for the current discussion is that they are an example of how behavioral experiments can be designed that incorporate cognitive and affective variables. If this particular line of research proves informative, it will expand our understanding of a behavioral variable that has been shown capable of modifying stuttering in a laboratory environment. There are many such mysteries in stuttering, including the effects of rhythm, singing, choral reading, and so forth, and I often feel that as we crack any one of them, we come closer to a fundamental understanding of the nature of the disorder. At the same time, integrating affective, behavioral, and cognitive variables in common designs may bring the behavioral research into a more realistic realm, where, as is true in the stutterer's daily life, these sorts of events cooccur and interact.

The exciting aspect is to find ways to treat all three of these as independent variables that can be studied in an objective and systematic way. That, for me, is the ultimate motivation for learning my ABCs.

REFERENCES

Adams, M. R., & Popelka, G. (1971). The influence of "time-out" on stutterers and their dysfluency. *Behavior Therapy, 2,* 334–339.

Bloodstein, O. (1981). *A handbook on stuttering,* (3rd ed.). Chicago: National Easter Seal Society.

Bloodstein, O. (1995). *A handbook on stuttering,* (5th ed.). San Diego: Singular.

Bloodstein, O. (1997). Stuttering as an anticipatory struggle reaction. In R. F. Curlee & G. M. Siegel (Eds.), *Nature and treatment of stuttering: New directions,* (2nd ed., pp.169–181). Boston: Allyn & Bacon.

Bryngelson, B. (1965). *Personality development through speech.* Minneapolis: Denison.

Bryngelson, B., Chapman, M. E., & Hansen, O. K. (1950). *Know yourself: A workbook for those who stutter.* (Rev. ed.) Minneapolis: Burgess.

Goldiamond, I. (1965). Stuttering and nonfluency as manipulatable response classes. In L. Krasner & L. P. Ullman (Eds.), *Research in behavior modification* (pp.106–156). New York: Holt, Rinehart, & Winston.

Haroldson, S., Martin, R. R., & Starr, C. D. (1968). Time-out as a punishment for stuttering. *Journal of Speech and Hearing Research, 11,* 560–566.

Ingham, J. C. (1993). Current status of stuttering and behavior modification — I: Recent trends in the application of behavior modification in the treatment of children and adults. *Journal of Fluency Disorders, 18,* 27–55.

James, J. E. (1976). The influence of duration on the effects of time-out from speaking. *Journal of Speech and Hearing Research, 19,* 206–215.

James, J. E., & Ingham, R. J. (1974). The influence of stutterers' expectancies of improvement upon response to time-out. *Journal of Speech and Hearing Research, 17,* 86–93.

Johnson, W. (1942). A study of the onset and development of stuttering. *Journal of Speech Disorders, 7,* 251–257.

Johnson, W. (1955). The time, the place, and the problem. In W. Johnson (Ed.), *Stuttering in children and adults* (pp.3–24). Minneapolis: University of Minnesota Press.

Johnson, W. (1956). Stuttering. In W. Johnson, S. J. Brown, J. J. Curtis, C. W. Edney, & J. Keaster (Eds.), *Speech handicapped school children,* (Rev. ed., pp.202–300). New York; Harper & Bros.

Kuhn, T. S. (1970). *The structure of scientific revolutions* (2nd ed.). Chicago: University of Chicago Press.

Perkins, W. (1996). *Stuttering and science.* San Diego: Singular.

Prins, D., & Hubbard, C. P. (1988). Response contingent stimulation and stuttering: Issues and implications. *Journal of Speech and Hearing Research, 31,* 696–709.

Taffel, C. (1955). Anxiety and the conditioning of verbal behavior. *Journal of Abnormal and Social Psychology, 51,* 496–501.

Travis, L. E. (1931). *Speech pathology.* New York: Appleton-Century-Crofts

Van Riper, C. (1958). Experiments in stuttering therapy. In J. Eisenson (Ed.), *Stuttering: A symposium* (pp.275–390). New York: Harper & Row.

Van Riper, C. (1979–1980). Who knows? *Western Michigan University Journal of Speech, Language and Hearing, 16,* 1–2.

West, R. (1958). An agnostic's speculations about stuttering. In J. Eisenson (Ed.), *Stuttering: A symposium* (pp.169–222). New York: Harper & Row.

10 Progress Under the Surface and Over Time

Walter H. Manning
University of Memphis

THE ABCS OF STUTTERING TREATMENT

I must begin by telling you that I am honored to contribute to this volume. But I'm reminded of something one of my clients said a few months ago: "What if I become really fluent and find that I have nothing to say?" So although I am honored to be in this situation, and although I do not stutter much anymore, the question remains… do I have anything to say?

Like Jerry Siegel, I've been asked to discuss the integration of the affective, behavioral, and cognitive features of stuttering during treatment; features that have been called the "ABCs" of treatment. My initial response to this issue of integrating, at the very least, these three levels of treatment is simply to say "Yes, we should definitely do that!" It doesn't sound like rocket science to me.

I don't necessarily believe that clinicians need to pay attention to each of these levels during all treatment. But I do believe that recovery from the problems of stuttering, whether it's assisted or unassisted, includes not only behavioral alterations, but fairly specific affective and cognitive changes.

Stuttering: On the Surface

I'd first like to make a couple of comments about the behavioral features of stuttering. These features are best thought of as the surface or literal features of the syndrome. They are very much like the exterior of the volcanoes that Anne Smith describes elsewhere in this volume. They are the most obvious part of the problem; they are what we see and hear first. These behavioral features are often the primary things, sometimes the only things, that the lay public or inexperienced clinician responds to.

Even if you consider only these surface features, the problem of stuttering can be pretty complex. Something as seemingly simple as obtaining a valid and reliable measure of stuttering events or time intervals can be more than a little tricky.

Certainly there's much still to be learned about the features of stuttering that are on the surface, particularly for young children at the outset of the problem. The work of people like Ehud Yairi and Ed Conture and their legions of doctoral students has provided additional and important facts about the possible varieties of stuttering form types in young children, clustering of stuttering events, and verbal and nonverbal qualities that indicate chronicity. Clearly this information about the surface features of the problem is both fascinating and essential for making accurate diagnostic and treatment decisions.

Stuttering: Below the Surface

But, there are also many critical features of the syndrome that exist under the surface. This is more obviously the case for adolescents and adults, and sometimes for young children.

I'd like to take a moment here to tell you a story about a college student I had the opportunity to work with when I was on the faculty at the University of Nebraska. John was the starting wingback on the University of Nebraska football team. In addition, he was a good student and was at the University on an academic, rather than an athletic scholarship. One day in group treatment, we were discussing how we avoid certain situations and words and he told us a story. When John was in junior high school, the teacher gave a quiz, in one of his classes. After completing the quiz the students handed their papers to the student across the aisle to be graded. When his paper was returned, John found that he had received a grade of 95. The teacher went around the room calling on the students to stand and give their score. John eventually stood and immediately felt that he wouldn't be able to say his grade of 95. He quickly considered saying "85." But that number seemed too daunting also. He thought for a moment, quickly said "75" and took his seat. The teacher recorded a 75 in her grade book and that was the end of it. No one associated the moment or the speaker with stuttering. No stuttering had reached the surface to be identified. But, it was in fact, a profound stuttering event. Important affective and cognitive events took place beneath the surface.

It's obvious to most of us, I think, that we do need to attend to the features of the syndrome that are not so obvious: features that exist beneath the surface. Not to deal with these features, even if they are difficult to measure, is, as Joe Sheehan (1980) argued, unreasonable and even unethical. More recently, some others have also made this point about the features of stuttering that are under the surface.

Ed Conture, in his 1990 text *Stuttering*, when discussing treatment for young children, stated that being able to modify aspects of fluent or stuttering behavior does not mean that we are necessarily changing all or the most critical aspects of the syndrome.

Woody Starkweather, in his 1987 book *Fluency and Stuttering,* said that although we may not yet have the means to apply rigorous scientific study to what we consider to be the essential features of a event, that should not preclude our study of those features. "… [O]ur first duty as scientists is to be true to the validity of the phenomenon being observed. If we lack the means to examine it objectively, we cannot assume or pretend that it doesn't exist" (Starkweather, 1987, p. 122).

I believe that the best clinicians I had during my own time in treatment were the ones who understood what was going on under the surface of the behavior. The ones who understood what might be called, to borrow an old term from psycholinguistics, the "deep structure" of the syndrome. By deep structure I'm talking about the cognitive and affective aspects of stuttering. Even these terms — cognitive and affective — are kind of abstract. Perhaps one way to operationalize these terms is to consider the decision-making process of the speaker who stutters. To what degree does that person limit their options in life — about speech as well as other things? To what degree do they narrow their choices because of the possibility, let alone the reality, of stuttering? How do they think and feel and decide about this ongoing problem? Or, as our colleagues in Great Britain might say it, how does the speaker construe himself?

As I mentioned earlier, I don't think that we necessarily have to spend a lot of time on these features of the deep structure during treatment. I think it is reasonable to suggest that if, as a result of treatment, we can help someone make significant changes in the surface features of the problem — things like the frequency and type of stuttering — some of the cognitive and affective aspects of the problem will change also. But sometimes they don't. Or they don't change much. And even if these cognitive and affective features do change and follow along with changes in the surface features such as the frequency of stuttering, it takes a good while for that to happen — I'm talking years here; maybe as many as 10 or 15!

Three Things to Consider

I'd like to suggest three issues to consider as we deliberate this idea of integrating the affective, cognitive, and behavioral aspects of treatment. These issues may influence how we think about change for people who stutter. They also may suggest some possibilities for future study.

1. Our Sample of Subjects, and Therefore Lots of Our Data, is Probably Biased. What we know about stuttering and people who do it is based on the clients we see in our clinics and laboratories. Even the population of people we see has a wide variety of characteristics. They are more different than they are alike. But more than that, many people who stutter never come through the doors of our centers. A large number of people adjust to the problem without our intervention. They are able to alter their behavior on the surface and their cognitions under the surface in ways we know hardly anything about. I don't think that they necessarily do it as efficiently or as completely as they might with our help. But they do it outside of our understanding. Perhaps they choose to do it that way because the cost of assisted change is not worth their time or money. Or maybe it's the effort they have to put forth. Or maybe it's the realization that consciously choosing treatment would make the problem authentic. But the point is, the examples of clients we see in our centers may represent half, maybe less than half, of the total population of those who stutter. Whatever the percentage, I'd like to suggest that the sample of people we see who stutter is far from representative of all humans who suffer from this problem.

I don't know that there's much we can do about this except appreciate that our data come from such a biased sample. And, of course, it might be worthwhile to begin thinking about how we can find out more about this large group of people who exist outside of treatment.

I think what has happened with at least some of them is that, although the surface features of stuttering may decrease or are hidden, they have managed to alter the affective and cognitive parts of the syndrome so that they can separate the stuttering from the handicap — at least pretty well — at least most of the time. I wish we could get to know more of them, understand how they do it, and maybe help them do it better. I'd like to think that at the very least, even though they may not be stuttering much on the surface, we could make the problem less mysterious for them and help them improve the quality of their lives.

2. Our Window for Viewing Our Clients (and Especially Their Change) is Extremely Narrow. The window is narrow both vertically and horizontally. That is, the time we have to observe change isn't really very long and the depth of the problem, the cognitive and affective features, are sometimes difficult to observe and quantify.

We see clients for a brief time. Three weeks is short, a semester or two is short. Even though during that time we often see some dramatic changes in the surface behaviors, it's a narrow view of change. This is especially true for our students and this contributes to the mystery of the problem. They usually aren't able to see the overall process of change except through the narrow window of one semester. Even a couple of years is short, for there's a lot that continues to change long after formal treatment ends.

Based on my conversations with other people who stutter and who eventually achieved high levels of fluency, and certainly in my own case, I believe significant change continues to occur for 15 to 20 years following treatment. During formal treatment, the frequency of my stuttering and the surface features of my speech began to change. The way I thought about myself and my speech began to change some also; but it was just a start. By far the major changes in the cognitive and affective features of the problem, ways of making decisions and ways of thinking about my speech and myself continued to evolve for many years. Gradually, changes took place in my risk taking, how I responded to failure, the nature of my self-talk in response to demands I placed on myself, and the ways I pushed the envelope of my speech.

The changes that occur and the progress we hope to promote in treatment are hardly ever linear. I don't think there's any question that the behavioral, affective, and cognitive features of the syndrome each change at different rates. So, although sometimes it's true that change and progress can be accurately reflected by the surface features, sometimes it's not. Sometimes, progress under the surface may be inversely related to the frequency of stuttering. Better decisions under the surface can result in increased participation and, of course, increased opportunities for stuttering. Progress can be seen in the form of decreased stuttering, of course, but it is often more accurately reflected by the choices one makes in the social, educational, vocational aspects of their lives. As the speaker makes more open decisions, and, as members of the National Stuttering Project say, begins to "let go" of the often self-imposed limits of not being normally fluent, the handicapping effects of the problem begin to decrease.

So I think that there needs to be a depth to our view of our clients and a breadth to our view of change. We need to attend to issues like the loss of control and helplessness, locus of control, self-efficacy, even the ability to appreciate the humorous aspects of the stuttering experience, as speakers gradually learn to alter automatic, reflexive ways of speaking and making decisions about their lives and their fluency problem. Change is so much more than just the stuff on the surface.

3. Contrasting Treatment Strategies Doesn't Necessarily Tell us What we Should be Learning About the Efficacy of Intervention. By this, I mean that I'm not convinced that investigations comparing the efficacy of particular treatment strategies make a lot of sense. Different treatments tend to focus on somewhat different levels of the syndrome — the behavioral, the cognitive, and the affective features. The results of these studies do tell us something about the relative effectiveness of particular strategies and associated techniques. Generally, we find that any treatment that asks the client to monitor the way he or she speaks, and thinks about the problem, and teaches them to do these things more efficiently, assuming they want to, can result in greater fluency for some clients. These studies also tell us that some people don't do so well in treatment. And finally, they show us that even though many people do well during treatment, they are likely to relapse a little or a lot later on.

Of course, we need such studies and that's why there's been a call for them during the past few years. But to me, doing studies that compare one treatment strategy with another seems a lot like discussing the relative merits of religions or political parties. Or it reminds me of the type of discussion I would hear as a teenager when one of my buddies would argue that the cars made by Ford were better than any other car. "Chevy!" another friend would respond. "FORD!" "CHEVY!." The give-and-take would go on. And then one day, other guys who were hanging around began yelling names like "Toyota," even "Yugo." Today, if they were in this profession with us, those same two guys would be yelling "Stuttering modification!" "Fluency shaping!!" And the same guy who yelled, "Yugo!" might stand up and yell, "Benjamin Bogue's unit method of restoring perfect speech!"

The point is, that sometimes we can take a Ford, a Chevy, or even a Yugo to get to where we want to go. But a more basic issue, I think, is that it depends on where we and our clients are in life and it depends also on *our* needs and *our* style. For the client, it depends on whether she or he is at one of those nodes, those landmark points in life when a person is truly ready for change. Where is the client in the decision-making process and the change process? I'm convinced that if we can get people who are at those points in their lives, the prognosis for success is infinitely better then when they are not.

Another aspect of this discussion on the efficacy of treatment is that some treatment approaches are more congruent with certain clinicians. That is, even if a particular treatment strategy may be shown by some measure to work better than another, this is not going to be the case for all clinicians. The person who is administering the treatment is a critical variable and some clinicians will do much better with a particular strategy than with others. For example, I could do a strict behavioral modification program — one of the many that tends to deal effectively with the surface features of stuttering — and I could do it with some success. Actually, years ago I did. I could believe in the approach and I could make it work. But it's not me. I couldn't do it as well as some of my students. It wouldn't be as genuine or natural for me. It's not my style and I'd soon tire of it. I'd probably move on to selling shoes or vinyl siding and make some real money.

Maybe rather than asking which treatment strategy is best, we should be asking the infinitely more complex question of why a particular strategy or technique might be best for a certain clinician, for a particular client, at a specific time.

I suspect that's what happened to me. I happened to come in contact with Gene Cooper at a time when I was truly ready for change. In addition, Gene believed in what he was doing and his approach was congruent with who he was. I don't think that this means that his interpersonal communications treatment was any better than other approaches. It just means that, for that clinician, for that client, at that time it worked pretty well. Even then, it took a long time after treatment for me to get unhandicapped.

So, maybe one direction we should be going is looking closely at the decision-making process used by expert clinicians (whatever they are). These are issues that I've attempted to address in a recent book titled *Clinical Decision Making in the Assessment and Treatment of Fluency Disorders* (1996). It's difficult, of course, to know exactly who these experts are. Maybe they are the experienced clinicians with many years of success and failures with children and adults who stutter. Maybe they are the clinicians who are old, say over the age of 50. Or maybe, based on the attendance at this conference, they are the clinicians with ponytails!

CONCLUSION

So, lest there be any doubt, I definitely think that we should pay attention to the affective, behavioral, and cognitive aspects of change for those with fluency disorders. I think we have no choice. I believe they are all critical both for the recovery process and especially important for lasting change.

I'd like to conclude by saying one more thing; something I've thought about a lot in preparing this paper, and something I've never written or spoken about before.

I want to tell you how thankful I am that I am able to speak fluently. I hardly ever take my fluency for granted. For many years I had things to say and I refused to try. I refused to even consider making the choice to say them. Perhaps even more basic, I had things to say and I didn't even know it. It's a lot like typing on a computer screen, you don't know what you think until you type it or you say it. And then those ideas lead to new thoughts that you wouldn't have had otherwise.

I am so thankful that I no longer feel handicapped. As I've said, that didn't happen immediately, or for many years following my formal treatment. But that's where I am now. I rarely stutter — maybe 10–15 times a year. When I do, I don't avoid, I'm not likely to panic, and I have confidence that I can repair the fluency break. But the most important part is that the possibility of stuttering rarely enters into my choices, my decision making about what to do or what not to do.

I am thankful that I can pick up a telephone and enjoy the experience. I can say wonderful things and communicate wonderful ideas and feelings to my friends, my family, and my colleagues. I'm thankful that I can spontaneously banter back and forth with people; tell jokes pretty well, be effective in front of a group, and connect with strangers — people I never would have spoken to before, in a shop or on the road.

I'm thankful that I have been able to take my thoughts and turn them into fluent words during good times and bad. I've been able to give eulogies for dear friends, colleagues, and parents. I'd rather not do that sort of thing, but I'm honored and very proud to do it well.

I'm thankful that I can do what I'm doing today, be an active colleague with people I admire, people with whom I share the same boat.

So treatment works. It doesn't necessarily work quickly and it involves so much more than changing only the surface features of the problem. And if the fluency is going to be easy and spontaneous and natural, that change must involve the way we think and feel about ourselves as well as our ability to speak fluently.

If, as clinicians and researchers, we attend to all those levels of the stuttering syndrome, I believe we have a much better chance to make a magnificent difference in the lives of people, people who otherwise would be forced to endure a lifetime of handicap and struggle.

REFERENCES

Conture, E. G. (1990). *Stuttering.* (2nd ed.) Englewood Cliffs,NJ: Prentice-Hall.

Manning, W. H. (1996). *Clinical decision making in the diagnosis and treatment of fluency disorders.* Albany, NY: Delmar

Sheehan, J. G. (1980). Problems in the evaluation of progress and outcome. In W. H. Perkins (Ed.), *Seminars in speech, language, and hearing,*389–401. New York: Thieme-Stratton.

Starkweather, C. W. (1987). *Fluency and stuttering.* Englewood Cliffs, NJ: Prentice-Hall.

11 A Preliminary Look At Shame, Guilt, and Stuttering

Bill Murphy
Purdue University

SOME PERSONAL REFLECTIONS

Beginning to write a chapter is a bit like beginning the journey of therapy with a client. I have a pretty good idea of the end goal and perhaps knowledge of the general stages I may pass through, but the individual steps are hazy.

Let me begin this journey with an introduction, sharing with you a bit about myself, especially my stuttering. I, like most who stutter, experience varying degrees of anxiety about my ability to speak easily. My stuttering has been particularly trying for me this past year since I began taking a medication that affects my speech management skills. Of course, as a therapist and, hopefully, a good problem solver, I've attempted to manage the increase in stuttering in several ways. Temporarily decreasing the amount of medication before a major oral presentation, as well as inserting lots of Sheehan's voluntary stuttering (Sheehan, 1975) into my speech has proven helpful. Of utmost importance is to share this predicament with audiences. When I speak to others about my stuttering, there is a decrease in avoidance and an increase in approach behavior. The result, bolstered by voluntary stuttering, is an increase in fluency, and it is easier to motorically manage any remaining stuttering.

But I believe even more is happening. Empathy is a powerful tool. If I can sense the audience's uneasiness as I stutter and if I can accept this without defensiveness, I have additional management options available. When I bring up my stuttering conversationally, I am sending a message to my audience, and reinforcing one in myself—that stuttering is not a situation that needs to cause me, or you, excessive alarm and embarrassment. In a very real sense, I am normalizing the event of stuttering for myself and the audience. I can present, as an acceptable and minimally distracting behavior, what was once a terrifying event. If I am successful, not only do I lessen my own negative emotions and become a better communicator, but I also increase my enjoyment as a speaker even when I stutter.

Normalizing stuttering is a skill, at least for me, that required diligent practice to acquire. It was not something learned by just practicing how to motorically change stuttering behavior. Neither fluency shaping nor stuttering modification afforded me a complete therapy package to use in my recovery journey. An additional therapy element was needed.

During the past few years, I have talked with a large number of speech language pathologists (SLPs) across the country about the scope of practice used in the treatment of school-age children and adults who stutter. In spite of research suggesting alternative bases for stuttering behaviors, the majority treat stuttering in older children and adults with a one-pronged attack, simply as a speech motor problem. Therapy procedures are focused on attempts to inhibit stuttering behavior and elicit fluent speech. The parents of stuttering children, as well as adult clients, are given similarly limited messages regarding the nuts and bolts of therapy.

Please understand, I do believe we change our stuttering by changing how we talk. My experience as both a speech language pathologist, and as a person who stutters, has taught me that our field already does an excellent job helping stutterers improve the management of our speech motor systems. As an individual challenged by stuttering, I depend on those skills. I could not manage without them. I also have the fundamental belief that if speech motor work is our only approach, we limit the success we will have in helping people to recover from stuttering. If we are to treat the stutterer in a comprehensive and realistic manner, we need to plan for the successful use of speech motor skills, as well as for the inevitable times when, because of stress, fatigue, illness, or whatever, motor techniques will temporarily falter and stuttering moments will break through.

EMOTIONALITY AND STUTTERING

When clients are presented with the singular message that recovery from stuttering is achieved simply by focusing on changing how one talks, progress may repeatedly falter. That message lays the groundwork for failure, not only for the client and parents, but also for the clinician. Chronic stuttering leads to the concomitant development of a host of negative thoughts and feelings that may significantly interfere with the therapeutic process. Changing one's speech is, in and of itself, difficult and complex. It is not always successful in all situations. Speech motor tools are limited in several ways. The tools take a long time to successfully learn. They cannot reasonably be expected to work all of the time. They do not address the social/affective issues that accompany stuttering.

It may shock some when I state that all older children who have been stuttering for awhile experience emotional problems about their stuttering. This should not be a hotly debated point. After all, fluent normally developing children, in general, experience a range of emotional problems (Turecki & Wernich, 1994), just as each and every adult who reads this text has struggled with various emotional conflicts during his or her life. Why is it, therefore, so difficult to believe that a child possessing a disability, such as stuttering, could develop emotional problems and coexisting negative attitudes related to speech?

Emotional problems should not be equated with mental illness. These are two different phenomena. Hopefully, the research of De Nil and Brutten (1991) significantly strengthened the argument that stuttering children evidence negative thoughts and feelings toward the act of speaking. Admittedly, for many, this is not a particularly new concept. Research has investigated the attitudes of people who stutter for at least the past 40 years. (De Nil & Brutten, 1991). We know that both children and adults who stutter tend to have more negative attitudes toward speaking than nonstutterers (Andrews & Cutler, 1974; Brown & Hull, 1942; De Nil & Brutten, 1991; Erickson, 1969; Silverman, 1980). The importance of investigating the relationship of attitudes to the remediation of stuttering behavior has not been ignored. Watson's (1988) summary of this research indicates that attitudes can be prognostic indicators of successful therapy, that stutterers' attitudes can facilitate speech change, and that attitude change can facilitate the maintenance of fluency. There is now considerable evidence that supports the position that negative thoughts and feelings toward stuttering not only increase the disability attached to stuttering, but also hinder the recovery process.

Complete knowledge of the nature of these thoughts and feelings and the role they play is still lacking. Watson (1988), addressing these issues, suggested that studies of attitudes associated with stuttering have provided only incomplete insights for a number of reasons, including lack of distinction between measures of thoughts versus feelings, and general limitations of assessment procedures. The measurement of these attitudinal domains, and their relationship to the treatment of stuttering, is not an easy task. Suggestions that these attitudes are complex multidimensional domains have been made, with a call for further research (Gregory, 1979; Rosenberg & Hovland, 1960; Triandis, 1971).

In this chapter, I concentrate on only two of the many emotions that can be associated with stuttering, and offer a preliminary look at the emotions of shame and guilt. I suggest that shame and a specific type of guilt are primary negative affective states for many stutterers and that they contribute not only to the development of stuttering, but also become a significant hindrance to successful therapy.

The concepts of guilt and, especially, of shame, are not new to the study of stuttering. Sheehan (1970) and Van Riper (1982) contain references to guilt and shame. Bloodstein (1995) suggested that the very core of stuttering is shame.

Shame and Guilt in Stuttering

To my knowledge, there have been no recent investigations into the relationship of shame—or guilt, with which shame is often confused—to stuttering. This is somewhat perplexing, because shame and guilt have generated considerable interest among psychologists during the past 10 years, primarily due to the recent development of new measures for the assessment of such emotions (Tangney, 1996). Although historically there has been significant disagreement as to the nature of shame and guilt and the role they play in behavior, current research has settled much of the early debates.

Because there has been considerable misunderstanding about the nature of shame and guilt, not only with lay persons, but also with psychologists (Tangney, 1996), I provide some background for discussion. Current work (Tangney, 1995a; Tangney, Burggraf & Wagner, 1995) fully supports Lewis' (1971) landmark analysis, indicating that both shame and guilt are negative experiences that involve negative self-evaluation. However, the focus of the negative self-evaluation differs. With shame, the focus is the evaluation of the whole self. If a failure occurs, one's self is labeled as defective or bad. Shame is extremely painful; the person tends to have a sense of worthlessness or powerlessness. Shame focuses on how the so-called defective self is viewed by others and is often accompanied by wanting to run away or hide. Shamed people feel exposed. As we will understand later, shame is highly correlated with avoidance behaviors, personal distress, and nonempathy toward others. Shame can also generate anger toward whoever is thought to be disapproving of the defective self (Tangney, Wagner, Fletcher, & Gramzow, 1992). Shame has also been linked to depression, bipolar illness, and spousal abuse (Goldberg, 1991; Lansky, 1987; Nathanson, 1987). In addition, shame has been described as a key component of substance abuse, eating disorders, and child abuse (Fossum & Mason, 1986) and as a factor in codependency issues (Bradshaw, 1988).

Guilt, on the other hand, although also not an enjoyable emotion, does not seem to be as destructive as shame. Guilt comes from a negative evaluation of a particular behavior. Guilt focuses on the behavior, done or not done. It does not cause concern over one's total being. Rather, focus is on the "bad deed." Guilt is about doing and triggers regret over the person's actions. Guilty feelings focus the individual on reparative action, that is, apologizing or trying to fix the bad deed. Guilt can actually enhance relationships (Baumeister, Stillwell, & Heatherton, 1994). The drive toward reparation suggests guilt may engender feelings of empathy toward others. Guilt, for all its negative press and stereotyping (e.g., "guilt-tripping parents"), has not proven to be generally related to psychological maladjustment (Tangney, 1995b). Exceptions begin to appear when guilt becomes fused with shame (Tangney et al., 1995). This concept is expanded later during discussion of stuttering and specific client–parent–clinician interactions.

The Relationship Between Shame and Stuttering

Examining similarities between stuttering and shame may help to determine whether shame should be considered a meaningful and clinicallly relevant component of stuttering. Such examination shows that this speech disorder and affective state share many phenomena.

Stuttering, Shame, and Avoidance Behavior. Lewis (1971) found that shame is not only a painful emotion, but that it is generally accompanied by a sense of feeling small, powerless; such feelings can lead to a desire to escape, hide, or avoid. Recent studies (Ferguson, Stegge, & Damhuis, 1991; Tangney, 1995) have validated Lewis' conclusions. The affective state of shame motivates an avoidance response probably because it provides a sense of painful exposure to either a real or imagined audience. The shamed person does not want to reveal the negative part of the self. Barrett, Zahn-Waxler, and Cole (1993) also found avoidance patterns of behavior as early markers of shame proneness in toddlers.

In describing stuttering, avoidance behavior is near the top of the descriptor list. Historically, avoidance has almost been synonymous with stuttering, not just as a characteristic of speaker behavior, but also as a causative component of the disorder itself (Johnson, 1956), as well as a rationale for developmental changes (Bloodstein, 1958). Clinically, within a short period of work with stutterers, one easily observes a host of sound, word, or situational avoidances. Of course, it is possible that stutterers engage in avoidance behavior only out of fear or anxiety. However, given the definition and description of shame, it is likely that this affective state contributes to and is part of the stuttering behavior for many individuals.

Stuttering, Shame and Anxiety, Social Uneasiness. A study exploring shame proneness and psychological symptoms (Tangney et al., 1995) determined that there are high correlations between shame and social anxiety, self-consciousness, and fear of negative evaluation. Given the nature of shame and the fear of discovery, these findings should not be surprising. In stuttering, a core emotion frequently described in the literature is anxiety (Weber & Smith, 1990). As Bloodstein (1995) clearly pointed out, anxiety is difficult to measure consistently because of its many definitions. Thus, it is not surprising that we have conflicting studies supporting either the presence or absence of anxiety in stuttering. On the other hand, in the clinic, parents often speak of their child's stuttering in relationship to anxiety. Seldom does a session go by without the adult stutterer describing anxiety about the speaking situation and/or stuttering. It is probably true that stutterers, on the whole, have more social phobia than normal speakers toward conversation (Bloodstein, 1995). Whatever the nature of this anxiety—fear of not being understood or negative listener judgement—speech and social anxiety are part of many stutterer's lives. Given the strong relationship between anxiety and shame, it is probable that shame is also apart of their lives.

Stuttering, Shame, and Other-Oriented Empathy. Empathy can be defined as the vicarious sharing of another person's emotional experience, and requires specific skills (Feshback, 1975). To experience empathy, one must be able to sense the other's perspective and accurately assess the other person's emotions.

Research is now investigating distinctions between other-oriented empathy and a self-oriented personal distress response (Batson, 1990; Batson & Coke, 1981). An empathic individual experiencing an other-oriented response can accurately experience the feelings of another person vicariously and remain focused on the needs of the other person. "Other-oriented empathy heightens one's understanding of another person's experiences, enhances other-directed feelings of sympathy and concern, and leads one to extend aid or comfort in the best interest of the other" (Tangney, 1995c, p.130).

Conversely, self-oriented personal distress focuses on the needs and feelings of the self, not on the feelings of the other. Studies by Feshback and Lipian (1987), and Tangney (1991, 1995c) support the idea that feelings of shame are negatively related to other-oriented empathy and positively related to self-oriented personal distress. Shame is never enjoyable, eliciting painful emotions that force a focus on oneself and lead away from the feelings of others.

To my knowledge, there is no research measuring the empathy of individuals who stutter. Reviewing my own experiences as a stutterer, prior to extensive self-therapy and 25 years of clinical work assisting clients' management of stuttering, I suggest the presence of a tendency for many of us to neglect our listeners and focus only on our own emotional state related to stuttering. Clients entering therapy, and many who have frequented clinicians' offices for years, cannot overcome their own emotional pain. May I suggest they are experiencing shame?

Suggesting to clients the importance of considering how the listener may perceive their stuttering is painful and not an easily accepted task. Encouraging stutterers to talk about their speech in a socially appropriate manner, openly acknowledging stuttering, as well as acquiring other means to put listeners at ease, is often met with resistance. People who stutter may be so absorbed in their own shame, in their own self-oriented personal distress, that other-oriented empathy is difficult and hinders therapy progress.

Stuttering, Shame, and Anger. Lewis (1971) was one of the first to observe a correlation between shame and anger. Lewis suggested that when experiencing shame, due to its characteristics, hostility is first directed toward the self. But because shame also creates the imagery of disappointment in the behaviors of others, these feelings of anger are eventually redirected toward others. This other-directed anger acts as a defense to help the shamed individual regain a sense of control. Similar studies have found a shame–anger link in young adults (Tangney, 1995c; Tagney et al., 1992) and in children as young as fifth grade (Tangney, et.al., 1990).

The prevalence of anger as a phenomenon of stuttering may not be clear at first glance. Inappropriate expression of anger would probably not be common to all stutterers. There is, however, enough tantalizing clinical experience to further investigate. Anyone subscribing to the various "E-mail" news groups, for example, Stutt-l, Stut-hlp, realizes it is not uncommon to hear stutterers expressing anger toward their listeners. Some anger, of course, is justifiable. People who stutter are often treated unfairly by those around them.

Yet, often when individuals who stutter explain their anger in a situation, the situation does not clearly warrant the hostile response. Perhaps the experience was while ordering fast food. Admittedly the stutterer might have had significant disfluencies when conversing with the food server, who in turn exhibits uneasiness (e.g., looking down or away, or attempting to finish the stutterer's sentence) However, in this situation, inappropriate anger may be attributed to negative assumptions such as, "How dare that person make fun of me, or finish my sentences!" The stutterer, experiencing shame, focuses inward on the perceived judgement toward him or her, which elicits anger as a defensive maneuver.

Stuttering, Shame, and Long-Term Therapy Success. Retention of clinically provided speech management skills in daily life has always been a problem. Data exist to support the notion that the more stutterers associate negative thoughts and feelings with speaking, the less chance there is for long-term therapeutic success (Guitar, 1976; Guitar & Bass, 1978). Shame, as an affective experience, can contribute to this phenomenon, especially if therapeutic programs only attempt to make the stutterer fluent, without developing a tolerance to disfluency or reduction of other negative attitudes.

If shame about stuttering exists, and desensitization or other shame-reducing techniques are not successful, or are absent from the therapy paradigm, the negative emotions resulting from the belief that one is a defective speaker will only promote attempts to hide speech differences. Clients will have difficulty tolerating less than perfect speech outside of the safe clinic setting. Any degree of perceived speech differences, for example, slowness, sound lengthening, and so forth, can trigger painful shame, thus inhibiting implementation of management techniques even though the speech may be judged "better" by listeners.

Stuttering, Shame, and Guilt. No attempt has been made as yet to link guilt or shame with stuttering. As stated earlier, guilt is now believed to be different from shame, having other implications for motivation and behavior in interpersonal relationships. However, there is an exception. Guilt becomes maladaptive if fused with shame and it is this component that triggers feelings of failure, ultimately leading to a sense of defectiveness (Tangney et al., 1995). If a person does something wrong or fails with a task, this has the potential to create feelings of guilt. If guilty, attempts would be made to correct the failure, through an apology or by repeating the task successfully (Tangney et al., 1995). But, if an apology cannot be offered or if multiple failures continue, the sense of self-defectiveness may occur. The result is shame-fused guilt, guilt with an overlay of shame, offering little opportunity for redemption.

Does Therapy Create Shame and Guilt? Stuttering and, especially, stuttering therapy may offer circumstances for development of shame-fused guilt. It is unfortunate but true that most older children who stutter chronically do not succeed in managing their speech all of the time. Of course, there is no doubt that changing speech motor patterns does decrease their stuttering significantly (Coppola & Yairi, 1982; Riley & Riley, 1984; Wall, 1982), but for many older children, this occurs only on a temporary basis. Children may find this type of fluency management, away from the clinic and in real life situations, difficult and unreliable. It is a skill that requires diligent speech monitoring, immediate stuttering identification, and swift speech motor changes. Successful self-management of chronic stuttering is a complex, highly cognitive task, and failure is a common occurrence in the lives of our child clients (Bloodstein, 1995). If the SLPs only goal and message to the child is to speak fluently—to stop stuttering—success will not be immediately forthcoming. In fact, significant harm may occur if the child has difficulty with self-management. These older children are the first to recognize the return of stuttering. When their only clinical goal is fluency, with no tolerance and plan for stuttering instances, the odds of developing guilt increase.

The situation can be compounded when parents enter the therapy paradigm and are indoctrinated with similar information. Parents often watch therapy in a controlled environment where fluency is more easily attained. Quite logically, parents can readily accept this quick fluency and expect the child to be capable of easily extending this into daily living situations. When SLPs and parents accept this unrealistic belief system, a conspiracy of fluency is formed. This conspiracy ultimately states that children can and should be expected to easily establish and maintain fluency.

Fallacious expectation sets up unattainable fluency goals with no provisions for failure. It is easy to see how this approach can result in the introduction of shame-fused guilt, which worsens if the parents, either by encouragement or self-selection, become surrogate therapists. Many parents accept the tasks, which they believe to be either explicitly or implicitly assigned, of correcting, stopping, signaling, practicing, encouraging, and exhorting their child to work harder, do better, and maintain more fluency. When parents are channeled into this role, they relinquish the more appropriate role as guiders and cheerleaders. Rather, they become members of what could be described as the stuttering police. This intervention paradigm may create shame-infused guilt in children.

When therapy focuses only on speech motor changes, only the first half of the puzzle of stuttering—a single prong—is addressed. As stated earlier, limiting or reversing the development of stuttering is more complex. Of course, we as SLPs do not want to neglect speech management work; we are quite skilled at this task. But, we must be cognizant of the role that emotions, including the possibility of shame, play in the development and maintenance of stuttering. We must begin to develop a model of therapy that prevents or reduces negative emotional overlays, including shame. This is the second prong, and another piece of the puzzle. The bottom line, the reward if we succeed, is that those children who continue to stutter but have fewer emotional complications will eventually, as they mature emotionally and cognitively, have the best success in managing stuttering behavior, and the maximum degree of recovery.

These assumptions require a holistic therapy paradigm that addresses the entire individual. A complete therapy program would, therefore, include methods to prevent and/or reduce the exacerbation of stuttering behavior, and provide a model to describe the origins and acquisition of negative emotions, including shame, as a part of the development of stuttering.

How Shame Develops. Most emotions, particularly shame, originate in the child's environment (Abell & Gecas, 1997; Harper & Hoopes, 1990; Kaufman, 1985; Tangney, 1995b), and are themselves defined by significant people in our social milieu. Parents, classmates, teachers, and other significant people in the child's life may trigger emotions related to stuttering by verbal and nonverbal communication. Teasing by school friends is typical and triggers shame. Parents may exacerbate shame when they avoid ever talking about stuttering with the child. This "conspiracy of silence," which Sheehan described (Sheehan, 1970), may suggest to the child that stuttering is something that is too awful to be discussed.

Shame is a feeling state that needs to be hidden (Bradshaw, 1988). People do not typically want to reveal this emotion and the reasons behind it. When stuttering becomes linked to shame it, too, has to be hidden. Once shame is present, it becomes internalized (Kaufman, 1985). The emotions are self-perpetuating, regenerated repeatedly by the child, even if the external stimulus (a parent inappropriately reminding a child to "use your techniques," or a classmate laughing) is no longer present.

Using this model, it is currently unknown whether shame precedes anxiety and other negative emotions or visa versa. But these feeling states are negative and demoralizing; they do nothing to enhance the life of our clients. Shame, and other negative emotions, potentially place demands on the speech motor system, possibly exacerbating the development of stuttering and interfering with the recovery process at all ages.

Stuttering in many children thus becomes, at least in part, an intertwining of speech motor behavior (probably from physiological origins, Smith, 1990), negative attitudes, and uncomfortable emotions (Peters & Guitar, 1991). The child begins to feel bad when the stuttering behavior occurs, casting these emotions into negative thoughts about the ability to speak, and reacting to this sequence of events by trying to, once again, physically change speech patterns. These speech changes are not consistently successful, leading to more speech tension and fragmentation. At some point, the speech failures and negative emotions become attached to the child's concept of self. The self acquires the identity of failure, at least in relationship to speaking skills. Shame and other emotions then compound the cycle of events. Because secrecy is the bedfellow of shame, and stuttering becomes linked to these emotions, stuttering behavior itself becomes something that must be hidden. Shame conspires to drive stuttering underground. Stuttering becomes something furtive, a secret to keep (Sheehan, 1975). In the continuing futile attempt to keep the secret, many children develop elaborate avoidance behaviors.

Therapy Approaches to Shame

There is need for therapy to help children, their families, and adult clients to normalize both stuttering and failure. I concentrate in this part of the discussion on the treatment of children, but many of the same concepts, with the appropriate cognitive changes, should apply in the treatment of stuttering adults.

Working With the Child. Because guilt and shame are highly interlinked, interactions relating to speech or stuttering that might lead the child to believe that he or she is at fault or negligent for not being able to eliminate stuttering. Children thought to be in danger of becoming chronic stutterers should be told directly, in a variety of ways and at a cognitive level appropriate for the child, that stuttering is not his or her fault. Therapy distinctions can be made between attaining complete fluency versus the perception of talking as fun, easy, and smooth. Children need to know that fluency breakdowns can happen through no fault of their own. Parents, teachers, SLPs, and other significant people may help by acknowledging that the child is loved and respected regardless of the presence of fluency or stuttering. Children may also be helped if they can understand that stuttering is only a small part of who they are, perhaps a disability, a challenge, but not a handicap.

Traditional stuttering desensitization techniques can be used both to prevent and reduce negative feelings toward stuttering. Pseudostuttering (Dell, 1979), voluntary stuttering (Sheehan, 1975) may be anxiety and shame reducing. If teasing or other forms of ridicule are experienced by the child, direct intervention can be initiated as soon as possible, using a variety of experiential activities to teach problem solving and assertiveness training. The goals of these activities are three-fold: to reduce the shaming effects of the experience, to reduce the possibility of future teasing, and to teach the child to act in an empowering manner if future ridicule is encountered. Throughout this process, stuttering becomes a topic that can be referred to and discussed easily, without discomfort or embarrassment.

Shame reduction/prevention activities should continue as the child grows. Children need assistance to develop empathy and the understanding that listeners may not understand stuttering, that others can become uncomfortable and respond in what may seem hurtful ways. Children can be taught empathy and methods to diffuse these types of speaker–listener quandary. Self-disclosure stuttering strategies can be designed to help the child voluntarily self-disclose in socially appropriate, casual, and emotionally "unloaded" ways. Children can be given examples of what they might conversationally say on days when stuttering is more troublesome than usual, and they can rehearse these casual comments in the therapy session. Class reports can be written on stuttering and articles on stuttering can be published in the school newspaper. Older children working in groups can be encouraged to develop presentations on stuttering for younger children. Older children can also be given the opportunity to develop peer support groups.

Children who stutter need to know that stuttering does not have to be a secret. Attempts to keep stuttering a secret are seldom successful and generally contribute to shameful feelings. When stuttering is left in the open, it becomes a "discussible" topic and there is little room for shame or other negative emotions. Attitudes are positive and the child has self-permission and energy to learn how to smoothly manage speech patterns.

Working With the Parents. Earlier I spoke of what parents should not do. Parents were cast as partners in a conspiracy of fluency and described as member of the stuttering police, but they are not villains. They are not necessarily at fault. What parent does not wish to help his or her child? Rather, it is the SLP who must reexamine with families the roles parents can best play, and it is up to professionals to be explicit with parents about the potential pitfalls of engaging in behavior that may suggest to children that stuttering must be avoided always, at all costs, and that incidents of stuttering must be looked upon as speech management failure.

Parents make good partners in therapy. Parents are important and will exert more influence than SLPs ever can. Ultimately, parents set the tone for how their children respond to most interactions, good or bad. Incorporating parents into the therapy paradigm is a necessity. Of most importance is the parents' ability to help the child put stuttering into perspective and to develop self-esteem. SLPs can assist in these tasks by helping parents develop specific skills. These include educating parents about stuttering, giving them models for educating others, being an advocate for their child, learning to normalize stuttering behavior, and developing the child's self-concept.

Parents can be educated about openness and acceptance of the whole child, including the stuttering. As the child ages, he or she can become skilled in using speech management techniques to modify stuttering or elicit fluency, but parents need to know this can be hard work. Children may want time-out from speech management and the safest place to relax and let down one's guard is at home. Parents should not have to spend time constantly monitoring the child's fluency and indirectly correcting or trying to control his or her speech. Certainly there is a time and a place for practice that has been agreed to by the SLP, the parents, and the child. But that time and place should not comprise the bulk of the parent–child relationship. For the remaining 23 plus hours each day, parents can accept their children as they are: fluent, disfluent, messy, neat, energetic, relaxed, noisy, or quiet. Help parents place fluency and stuttering in the same accepting framework they apply when appreciating their child and expressing love and admiration for the whole, unique individual.

In summary, chronic stuttering in late childhood is difficult to modify and may require much time, energy, and many experiences of failure before a child can begin to achieve consistent, successful self-management. Originating and developing within this time period are negative emotions such as shame, anxiety, and anger, which become associated with stuttering. If these emotions are allowed to develop, they can and often do not only exacerbate stuttering behavior but also play a detrimental role in the child's acquisition and use of speech management skills. SLPs and parents may stop this destructive process by normalizing stuttering, through a program that combines teaching speech motor management and shame reduction.

CONCLUDING THOUGHTS

There appears to be a logical relationship between characteristics associated with shame, shame-fused guilt, and stuttering phenomena. However, the role of shame and guilt in stuttering has not been extensively evaluated; more research is needed. Unfortunately, the empirical study of shame and guilt is not easy, with many problems of measurement. The direct assessment of these internal affective emotions is difficult, if not impossible (Tangney, 1996). One difficulty is that shame and guilt do not possess easily definable, codable facial expressions that occur in other emotions, such as anger or happiness (Izard, 1977). Additionally, most laypeople are confused about the differences between shame and guilt (Tangney, 1996). A recent publication (Tangney, 1996) addressed these and other problems pertaining to conceptual and methodological issues in the assessment of shame and guilt. Anyone interested in pursuing links between shame, guilt, and stuttering should find this article invaluable. The article provides an historical perspective about the assessment of these emotions and gives considerable detail evaluating the relative strengths and weaknesses of the most common current measures.

Among the questions we need answers to are the following: Does shame or shame-fused guilt affect the development of stuttering? At what age or period of psychosocial development do these emotions appear in relationship to stuttering? What is the relationship of shame and shame-fused guilt to other known negative emotions, for example, anxiety, common to stuttering? Do some people who stutter possess a personality that is at risk for shame or guilt proneness Are particular family interaction styles more shame or guilt producing in regard to the development of stuttering? Does the presence of these emotions complicate the treatment of stuttering and, if so, in what ways? How can we expand current treatment paradigms or develop new methodology to treat shame, shame-fused guilt, and stuttering? When we better understand the answers to these questions, we will have made great strides in the effective treatment of stuttering.

ACKNOWLEDGMENTS

As someone who is learning disabled and experiences difficulty with reading and writing, I wish to thank my wife Marybeth Jansky, colleague Hope Gulker, and editors Nan Bernstein Ratner and E. Charles Healey for their encouragement and comments.

REFERENCES

Abell, E., & Gecas, V. (1997). Guilt, shame, and family socialization. *Journal of Family Issues, 18*, 99–123.

Andrews, G., & Cutler, J. (1974). Stuttering therapy: The relation between changes in symptom level and attitudes. *Journal of Speech and Hearing Disorders, 39*, 312–319.

Atkins, C. P. (1988). Perceptions of speakers with minimal eye contact: Implications for stutterers. *Journal of Fluency Disorders, 13*, 429–436.

Barrett, K. C., Zahn-Waxler, C., & Cole, P. M. (1993). Avoiders versus amenders: Implications for investigation of guilt and shame during toddlerhood? *Cognition and Emotion, 7*, 481–505.

Batson, C. D. (1990). How social an animal? The human capacity for caring. *American Psychologist, 45*, 336–346.

Batson, C. D., & Coke, J. S. (1981). Empathy: A source of altruistic motivation for helping? In J. P. Rushton & R. M. Somentino (Eds.), *Altruism and helping behavior: Social, personality, and developmental perspectives* (pp. 167–187). Hillsdale, NJ: Lawrence Erlbaum Associates.

Baumeister, R. F., Stillwell, A. M., & Heatherton, T. F. (1994). Guilt: An interpersonal approach. *Psychological Bulletin, 115*, 243–267.

Bloodstein, O., Stuttering as an anticipatory struggle reaction. In Eiseneson, J. (ed.), Stuttering: A Symposium. New York: Harper & Row (1958).

Bloodstein, O. (1995). *A handbook on stuttering.* San Diego, CA: Singular.

Bradshaw, J. (1988). *Healing the shame that binds you.* Deerfield Beach, FL: Health Communications.

Brown, S. F., & Hull, H. C. (1942). A study of some social attitudes of a group of 59 stutterers. *Journal of Speech Disorders, 7*, 153–159.

Coppola, V. A., & Yairi, E. (1982). Rhythmic speech training with preschool stuttering children: An experimental study. *Journal of Fluency Disorders, 7*, 447–457.

Costello, J. (1983). Current behavioral treatments for children. In D. Prins & R. Ingham (Eds.), *Treatment of stuttering in early childhood.* San Diego: College-Hill Press.

Dell, C. (1979). *Treating the school age stutterer: A guide for clinicians.* Memphis, TN: Speech Foundation of America.

De Nil, L. F., & Brutten, G. J. (1991). Speech-associated attitudes of stuttering and nonstuttering children. *Journal of Speech and Hearing Research, 34*, 60–66.

Erickson, R. L. (1969). Assessing communication attitudes among stutterers. *Journal of Speech and Hearing Research, 12*, 711–724.

Ferguson, T. J., Stegge, H., & Damhuis, I. (1991). Children's understanding of guilt and shame. *Child Development, 62*, 827–839.

Feshback, N. D. (1975). Empathy in children: Some theoretical and empirical considerations. *Counseling Psychologist, 5*, 25–30.

Feshback, N. D., & Lipian, M. (1987). *The empathy scale for adults.* Los Angeles: University of California at Los Angeles.

Fossum, M. A., & Mason, M. J. (1986). *Facing shame: Families in recovery.* New York: Norton.

Goldberg, C. (1991). *Understanding shame.* Northvale, NJ: Aronson.

Gregory, H. (1979). *Controversies about stuttering therapy.* Baltimore: University Park Press.

Guitar, B. (1976). Pretreatment factors associated with the outcome of stuttering therapy. *Journal of Speech and Hearing Research, 19*, 590–600.

Guitar, B., & Bass, C. (1978). Stuttering therapy: The relationship between attitude change and long term outcome. *Journal of Speech and Hearing Disorders, 43*, 392–400.

Harper, J., & Hoopes, M. (1990). *Uncovering shame.* New York, NY: Norton .

Izard, C. (1977). *Human emotions.* New York: Plenum.

Johnson, W., et al., Speech handicapped school children. rev. ed. New York: Harper & Bros. (1956).

Kaufman, G. (1980). *Shame.* Rochester, VT: Schenkman.

Kaufman, G. (1985). *Shame: The power of caring.* Rochester, VT: Schenkman.

Lansky, M. (1987). Shame and domestic violence. In D. L. Nathanson (Ed.), *The many faces of shame* (pp. 335–362). New York: Guilford.

Lewis, H. B. (1971). *Shame and guilt in neurosis.* New York: International University Press.

Lewis, H. B. (1987). *The role of shame in symptom formation.* Hillsdale, NJ: Lawrence Erlbaum Associates.

McLelland, J., & Cooper, E. (1978). Fluency-related behaviors and attitudes of 178 young stutterers. *Journal of Fluency Disorders, 3,* 253–263.

Nathanson, D. L. (1987). A timetable for shame. In D. L. Nathanson (Ed.), *The many faces of shame* (pp. 1–63). New York: Guilford.

Peters, T., & Guitar, B. (1991). *Stuttering: An integrated approach to its nature and treatment.* Baltimore, MD: Williams & Williams.

Riley, G., & Riley, J. (1984). A component model for treating stuttering in children. In M. Peins (Ed.), *Contemporary approaches in stuttering therapy* (pp. 123–171). Boston: Little Brown.

Rosenberg, M., & Hovland, C. (1960). Cognitive, affective and behavioral components of attitude. In M. Rosenberg, C. Hovland, W. McGuire, K. Abelson, & J. Brehm (Eds.), *Attitude organization and change* (pp. 1–14). New Haven, CT: Yale University Press.

Sheehan, J. (1970). *Stuttering: Research and therapy.* New York: Harper & Row.

Sheehan, J. (1975). Conflict theory and avoidance-reduction therapy. In J. Eisenson (Ed.), *Stuttering: A second symposium* (pp. 97–198). New York: Harper & Row.

Silverman, E. M. (1980). Communication attitudes of women who stutter. *Journal of Speech and Hearing Disorders, 45,* 533–539.

Smith, A. (1990). Factors in the etiology of stuttering. *ASHA Reports, 18,* 39–47.

Tangney, J. P. (1991). Moral affect: The good, the bad, and the ugly. *Journal of Personality and Social Psychology, 61,* 598–607.

Tangney, J. P. (1995a). Shame and guilt in interpersonal relationships. In J. P. Tangney, & K. W. Fisher, (Eds.), *Self-conscious emotions: The psychology of shame, guilt, embarrassment, and pride* (p. 130). New York: Guilford.

Tangney, J. P. (1995b). Recent advances in the empirical study of shame and guilt. *American Behavioral Scientist, 38,* 1132–1145.

Tangney, J. P. (1995c). Shame and guilt in interpersonal relationships. In J.P. Tangney, & K.W. Fisher, (Eds.), *Self-conscious emotions: Shame, guilt, embarrassment, and pride* (pp. 114–139). New York: Guilford.

Tangney, J. P. (1996). Conceptual and methodological issues in the assessment of shame and guilt. *Behavioral Research & Therapy, 34,* 741–754.

Tangney, J. P., Burggraf, S. A., & Wagner, P. E. (1995). Shame-proneness, guilt-proneness, and psychological symptoms. In J. P. Tangney & K. W. Fisher (Eds.), *Self-conscious emotions: Shame, guilt, embarrassment, and pride* (pp. 343–367). New York: Guilford.

Tangney, J. P., Wagner, P. E., Burggraff, S. A., Gramzow, R., & Fletcher, C. (1990). The Test of Self-Conscious Affect for Children (TOSCA-C). Fairfax, VA: George Mason University.

Tangney, J. P., Wagner, P. E., Fletcher, C., & Gramzow, R. (1992). Shamed into anger? The relationship of shame and guilt to anger and self-reported aggression. *Journal of Personality and Social Psychology, 62,* 669–675.

Triadis, H. (1971). *Attitude and attitude change.* New York: Wiley.

Turecki, S., & Wernick, S. (1994). *The emotional problems of normal children.* New York, NY: Bantam.

Van Riper, C. (1982). *The nature of stuttering.* Englewood Cliffs, NJ: Prentice-Hall.

Wall, M. (1982). Language-based therapies for the young child stutterer. *Journal of Childhood Communication Disorders, 6,* 40–49.

Wall, M. J., & Myers, F. L. (1984). *Clinical management of childhood stuttering.* Baltimore, MD: University Park Press.

Watson, J. (1988). A comparison of stutterers' and nonstutterers' affective, cognitive, and behavioral self-reports. *Journal of Speech and Hearing Research, 31,* 377–385.

Weber, C. M., & Smith, A. (1990) Autonomic correlates of stuttering and speech assessed in a range of experimental tasks. *Journal of Speech and Hearing Research, 33,* 690–706.

12 Evaluation of Child Factors Related to Early Stuttering: A Descriptive Study

Diane Hill
Northwestern University

A review of the literature concerning the etiology of stuttering reveals the widely held view that stuttering develops and is maintained due to a complex, ever-changing interaction of constitutional and environmental factors (Conture, 1990; Fosnot, 1993; Gregory, 1986; Gregory & Hill, 1980, 1993; Hanley, 1985; Peters & Guitar, 1991; Riley & Riley, 1979; Starkweather, Gottwald, & Halfond, 1990; Wall & Myers, 1995). Since the early 1970s a framework for differential evaluation and treatment of stuttering has evolved at Northwestern University. My colleagues and I have adapted a decision tree originally proposed by Gregory and Campbell (1988), and shown in Fig. 12.1. This process was guided by the overarching notion that optimally effective treatment should be grounded in knowledge of both client variables and environmental factors and the ways in which they may interact. Gregory (1973) and Gregory and Hill (1980) presented a model for differential evaluation including both case history and clinical evaluation components supported by a review of research findings and collective clinical experience. Further development and refinement of this assessment protocol has been influenced by an ongoing review of research findings focused on linguistic and motoric skills of children and adults who stutter; environmental factors shown to influence stuttering; and continuing broad clinical experience attending to communicative, attitudinal, and behavioral factors in treating individuals who stutter (Gregory, Hill, & Campbell, 1995; Gregory & Hill, 1993). Many contributors to the field have reinforced the need for broad ranging evaluation procedures (Conture, 1990; Hanley, 1985; Peters & Guitar, 1991; Starkweather et al., 1990; Wall & Myers, 1995). Research studies and clinical reports reveal that individuals who stutter do not form a homogeneous group (Riley & Riley, 1979, 1983). Individuals clearly present differing profiles of factors. Some factors appear to indicate greater risk for stuttering, whereas others appear related to the likelihood of recovery from stuttering. Ultimately, all factors need to be considered when making decisions about clinical management.

In view of Gottwald's discussion of environmental factors (this volume), this chapter deals primarily with child-specific factors related to the development of stuttering. The following review of relevant research findings is intended to provide a rationale for differential evaluation and treatment procedures of young children presenting stuttering patterns. In addition to child factors dealt with more extensively in the literature such as speech and language performance and family history of stuttering, discussion also focuses on several child factors not discussed extensively elsewhere, namely social, emotional, and behavioral characteristics and experience of life stress. These factors have been highlighted as important by many contributors (Bloodstein, 1995; Peters & Guitar, 1991; Wall & Myers, 1995; Williams, 1985; Wyatt, 1969), yet, many have not been studied systematically. Inclusion of a descriptive study of 2-year-old children seen for differential evaluation and highlights the nature of selected child factors observed near the onset of stuttering including pattern of emergence of stuttering, stuttering characteristics, speech-language skills, and child behavioral variables. Decision making regarding selection of treatment strategies and treatment outcome is discussed.

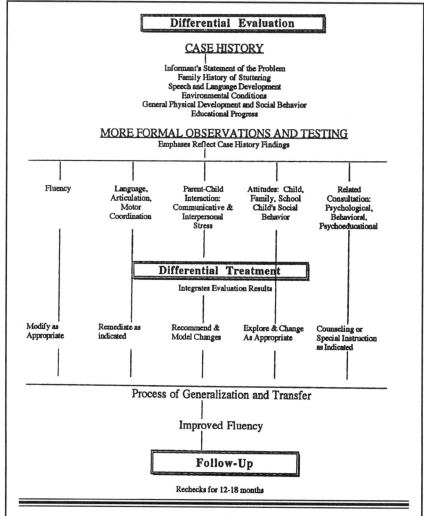

FIG. 12.1. Decision tree for differential evaluation and treatment. From *Decision Making in Speech Language Pathology*, edited by D. E. Yoder and R. D. Kent, 1988, Philadelphia, PA: Decker.

CHILD FACTORS RELATED TO STUTTERING

Case History

A number of specialists strongly favor seeing children very close to the beginning of stuttering. Researchers (Fosnot, 1993; Riley, this publication; Yairi, 1993) point out the importance of eliciting information from parents about children beginning to stutter within the first few months following onset, closely controlling age range and duration of disorder in selecting subject groups for study, and following them longitudinally to determine patterns of recovery and persistence of stuttering. Clinicians (Curlee, 1993; Gregory & Hill, 1993; Peters and Guitar, 1991; Starkweather & Gottwald, 1995) stress the importance of early identification of stuttering in order to provide appropriate feedback to educate parents about their role in supporting fluency development, as well as to recommend appropriate prevention and intervention strategies. Ideally, clinicians should respond to parents' concerns about stuttering as close to onset as possible, first spending ample time in an initial interview to gather information critical for making decisions about a course of action. Typically, a complete case history is then developed by gathering and integrating information from a client questionnaire and from an interview. There are a number of important areas related to the epidemiology of stuttering that may be assessed only through discussion with parents. These include the family history of stuttering, parental description of the developmental stuttering pattern (age of onset, relationship of onset to stage of speech-language development or other child related factors, or environmental factors) and judgments of severity (frequency, associated behaviors, and the level of the child's awareness of the problem). Consequently, clinicians need to focus their line of questioning on the areas most critical to the identification of variables indicating risk for continued stuttering.

Statement of the Problem. In eliciting a statement of the problem, parents should be encouraged to offer as full a description as possible of the aspects of their child's speech that concerns them, indicating when they first observed stuttering behavior and what has prompted them to seek help at the current time. General thinking within the field has been that the longer stuttering persists, the less likely spontaneous recovery becomes. In a longitudinal study of preschool children close to onset, Yairi, Ambrose, Paden, and Throneburg (1996) reported that the average time between parents first noticing a problem and seeking help is approximately 8 months for the group of children showing persistent stuttering and somewhat shorter (2 to 5 months) for their recovered groups. Therefore, recovery may be supported by parents following through on their concern and seeking professional advice early.

Most contributors recommended evaluation when parents express concern about beginning stuttering (Peters & Guitar, 1991; Starkweather, 1987). Although stuttering severity and the presence of associated behaviors have importance for determining the presence of beginning stuttering, other factors, including family history, and speech and language concerns have been shown to be even greater risk factors for persistence of stuttering (Yairi et al., 1996). These are some of the key criteria used by Gregory and Hill (1980, 1993) in responding differentially client by client in providing recommendations for evaluation. A screening evaluation is suggested when parents report primarily a pattern of normal disfluency, no concerns about speech and language or other aspects of development, no family history, and a short-lived concern about disfluency (less than 6 months). The rationale for a screening is to provide the opportunity for prevention through early professional input; whether concern is warranted, education about normal fluency development and characteristics of stuttering, as well as specific recommendations for intervention as needed. An in-depth evaluation is recommended when the parent describes stuttering behavior, reports a family history of stuttering, or concerns about speech-language or overall development. Persistence of high frequency, more typical patterns of disfluency for longer than 6 months may also indicate the need for a comprehensive evaluation in view of the possible reactions of others to speech differences (Adams, 1980) and the potential relationship to other speech-language factors.

Family History of Stuttering. It is well known that stuttering tends to run in families. Based on findings reported by Andrews (1984), Kidd (1984), and Yairi et al. (1996), familial incidence and prevalence of stuttering, the gender of the family member, and the degree of relationship of the family members who stutter to the child all have significance in predicting risk for stuttering. Although Kidd's (1984) study indicated the highest risk for stuttering was found for male relatives of females who stuttered, Ambrose, Yairi and Cox (1993) found the highest risk for male relatives of stuttering males. In a recent report of a longitudinal study, Yairi et al. (1996) found that not only the incidence of stuttering but also its persistence tended to run in families. Studies such as these provide a clear rationale for clinicians to explore family stuttering patterns in developing a case history.

Additional information about family members may be useful as well, such as the extent to which family members who recovered display delayed speech and language development (Homzie, Lindsay, Simpson, & Hasenstab, 1988); and whether family members exhibited speech-language or related problems that required treatment. Late talking and articulation difficulty emerged as significant characteristics of the children with persistent stuttering in Kidd's (1984) comprehensive study. What is not known is the underlying mechanism by which genetic factors contribute to the etiology of stuttering: 1) Do genetic factors increase susceptibility for stuttering? 2) Are familial patterns of behavior instrumental in reinforcing stuttering through critical attitudes, unique ways of attempting to modify stuttering behavior, or family anxiety about persistent stuttering? or 3) Are there more complex environmental patterns specific to families with a history of stuttering? Kidd (1984) suggested that observed patterns of stuttering were best explained by interaction between environmental factors and a combination of several genes, although at this time, specific genes have not been identified.

Age of Child. It is also well known that there is a high rate of spontaneous recovery from periods of stuttering during the preschool years (Andrews, 1984; Yairi et al., 1996). Andrews' (1984) prospective longitudinal study that included children with histories of early, less-severe stuttering indicated that 79% recovered from stuttering by age 16. Later reports of longitudinal studies (Yairi et al., 1996) indicated that two thirds of the subjects recovered. As clinicians make decisions about evaluation and treatment, knowledge of this fact of lessening of risk with increasing age should not override the equally well-established fact that the 25–30 % of the estimated persistent stuttering problems began between the ages of 2 and 4 and that early intervention may produce the greatest treatment efficacy.

Gender. Review of several reports indicates a relatively small male to female ratio of 2:1 (Glasner & Rosenthal, 1957; Yairi & Ambrose, 1992b) for children who are seen close to onset of stuttering with an increase to 4:1 or 5:1 by school age (Bloodstein, 1995). Females appear to recover from stuttering at a much higher rate than do males (Seider, Gladstein, & Kidd, 1983). For females who do not recover, there may be a large amount of genetic loading or a greater number of complicating factors presented. Therefore, persistent stuttering in older preschool girls may indicate less likelihood of recovery and more concern about the need for treatment. Some authorities have reached the judgment that recovery is supported by earlier developing metalinguistic skills in girls (Starkweather et al., 1990) whereas Andrews (1984) pointed to a lower incidence of articulation and language problems in girls. Yairi et al. (1996) suggested that the highest risk of chronicity is for male relatives of males who stutter.

Pattern of Development. Historically, development of stuttering problems was typically reported to be a gradual process, with easier, more variable forms of stuttering followed by increasing fragmentation and tension (Prins, 1983; Van Riper, 1973). Williams (1985) reported that easy repetitions with no accompanying tension are usually the first symptom, that usually the problem develops gradually rather than suddenly, and that a 5 to 6 month interval exists between parents' first notice of disfluencies and the decision to seek help. More recent reports (Yairi, Ambrose, & Nierman, 1993; Yairi et al., 1996) suggest that a significant number of preschool children experience a sudden onset of moderate to severe stuttering. In these cases, a full range of more severe types of disfluencies characteristic of the "core features" of stuttering (Peters & Guitar, 1991; Van Riper, 1971; Yairi & Ambrose, 1992), including repetitions of parts of words, prolongations, and blocks, may be observed at onset. In addition, parents often report observation of secondary characteristics, including audible and visible signs of tension and struggle at or near onset, not unlike those seen in older clients with long-standing stuttering problems (Conture & Kelly, 1992; Schwartz & Conture, 1988; Yairi, 1983).

The sudden onset of stuttering may relate to a series of life events (Wyatt, 1969) or to a traumatic experience (Starkweather, 1987). Although it is not known if the pattern of development, sudden or gradual, bears any significance as a diagnostic indicator, it is understandable that the emotional reactions of both parents and children may be greater when the onset is sudden, and that this may contribute in some way to persistence of stuttering. On the other hand, parents whose children develop stuttering more gradually and exhibit less severe forms may not seek help as early, believing that the problem will resolve.

Frequency and Characteristics of Stuttering. The characteristics and patterns of disfluency observed by parents are of key importance, first, in determining the need for evaluation and later, in making decisions about treatment. The objective of an initial interview is to determine, from the parents' description, whether the child is demonstrating disfluencies characteristic of normal speakers or more characteristic of stuttering (Adams, 1980; Conture, 1990; Curlee, 1980, 1993; Gregory & Hill, 1993). Generally, sound and syllable repetitions (particularly if changes in rate, rhythm, or increased effort are observed), as well as prolonging or blocking of sounds, indicate cause for concern. Stuttering throughout utterances, rather than on just utterance-initial words, and an increase in stuttering frequency (Zebrowski, 1991) may indicate that stuttering is becoming more chronic. It is also important to gain impressions of the child's awareness of speech difficulty. Although growing awareness of speech difficulty has been judged to be a hallmark of more advanced stuttering in older children (Bloodstein, 1995), indications of some level of awareness reflected in the occurrence of associated behaviors (Conture & Kelly, 1991; Schwartz & Conture, 1988) and judgments about speech patterns (Ambrose & Yairi, 1994) have been documented in young children close to stuttering onset. Differing levels of awareness may vary from subconscious perceptions of changes or difficulties to more highly conscious self-awareness and affective reactions (Bloodstein, 1987). The development of more severe types of disfluency, such as prolongations and blocks, may reflect a perception of repetitious speech disruption with subsequent attempts by the child to stabilize his speech mechanism (Conture, 1990). Self-awareness of disruptive speech patterns may be reflected by changes in communicative behavior, such as reducing complexity of language usage, substituting words, abandoning utterances, or limiting talking overall. Clinicians should be alert to indications of awareness, as treatment procedures should deal appropriately with the child's level of awareness of speech difficulty.

Speech and Language Development. Stuttering is often first observed during a period of rapid development of speech and language skills. Clinicians should determine the status of communication skills near the onset of stuttering and form hypotheses about the potential role of speech-language factors in the development and/or maintenance or stuttering. Clinicians should gain a clear understanding of how parents view their child's communicative skill, ease of communication flow, intelligibility, and overall enjoyment of talking at home and in other social settings (Hill, 1995). Williams (1985) reported that stuttering usually begins after a child has been talking normally for 1 or 2 years. However, for some children, stuttering emerges concurrent with presentence development. Delayed speech and language development in one or more areas (see Nippold, 1990, for review; Kline & Starkweather, 1979; Wall, 1980) or gaps in performance among domains of language usage (Hall, Yamashita, & Aram, 1993) may compromise fluency and accompany the development of stuttering. In some cases, treatment for speech or language disorders may contribute to beginning stuttering (Hall, 1977; Lee, 1974; Merits-Patterson & Reed, 1981). Stuttering that develops later, after sentence usage stabilizes, may reflect difficulty coordinating linguistic processes in meeting the demands of ongoing discourse (Scott, Healey, & Norris, 1995; see Weiss, 1995 for review). Yairi et al., (1996) reported findings of lower performance on language measures for young children who persisted in stuttering. These findings provide a clear basis for including speech-language assessment in evaluation of children who stutter.

Health and Developmental Issues. Episodic or persistent health issues may contribute to increased stuttering. Fosnot (1993) reported a high incidence (80 %) of recurring middle ear infections in a population of preschool children seen for stuttering treatment and followed longitudinally for 5 years. We have treated one preschool child for whom patterns of increased disfluency frequently cooccurred with recurrent ear infections. We have seen other children who experienced increased disfluency during episodes of allergic reaction or asthma.

Social and Behavioral Factors. Much of the research regarding psychosocial factors related to stuttering [what Wall & Myers (1995) referred to as "dynamic process of interaction" between the child and his or her environment] focused ⌐n identification of patterns of parent behavior for groups of children who stutter and their nonstuttering counterparts. Studies have primarily investigated parental attitudes and behaviors in consideration of potential interpersonal and communicative stresses placed on a child, including parental rate of speech, parental communication style, parents' reactions to children's speech behaviors, and specific situations in the environment that disrupt or promote fluency. Conversely, little research has focused on the role of children's social or behavioral skills and the relationship they may have to stuttering.

Figure 12.2 provides an overview of both child and environmental factors with the potential to contribute to stuttering (communicative stress, interpersonal stress, and life situations imposing stress); however, further discussion focuses on child factors.

These include variables related to speech and language skills and style of communication; frustration tolerance; and behavioral characteristics related to ability to adapt to situations (e.g., difficulty with transitions or discomfort in new situations), personality characteristics (e.g., sensitivity, fearfulness) and state of being (e.g., fatigue, illness, excitement, activity level). Through discussion with parents in development of a case history, clinicians may gain impressions of significant child factors and how they may interact with environmental variables to contribute to the development and maintenance of stuttering. These impressions then provide a basis for further observation during assessment and ongoing treatment.

Research has not focused on patterns of social-emotional behavior or personality traits of young preschool children beginning to stutter. Yet, parents often report certain common traits that characterize this group of children, such as sensitivity, high drive to communicate, sense of urgency about communication, and difficult behaviours to manage. Such behavioral characteristics have been studied to some extent in school-age children who stutter. Riley and Riley (1983) assessed behaviors related to attitudes, emotions, and attention in children with chronic stuttering, although they did not present their protocol for assessment in detail. They found a pattern of high self-expectations for performance. Rustin and Purser (1991) used a detailed parent interview including questions about the child is developmental, behavioral, social, and affective characteristics and family patterns. They presented descriptive results of a study of 209 children and identified two

POTENTIAL FLUENCY DISRUPTING FACTORS FOR CHILDREN

Child Related Factors

Speech and language skills/style
Language formulation difficulty
Word finding difficulty
Articulation difficulty and/or reduced intelligibility
Gaps in receptive/ expressive skill
Awareness of speech difficulty
Acute auditory awareness
High drive to communicate

Low tolerance for frustration
Gaining listener attention
Ugency about communication
Waiting for a response to requests
Failing to meet own expectations
Attempting difficult tasks
Not having own way

Behavioral characteristics
Difficulty making transitions
Uncomfortable in new situations
Risk taking and impulsive
Active
Attention seeking
Sensitive
Perceptive/observant
Fearful/insecure
Fatigue
Excitement
Ilness /allergies

Environmentally Related Factors

Communicative Stress
Rapidly paced conversation
Frequent questioning
Others dominate conversation
Overlapping conversation
Verbal interruption
Competition for talking time
Correction of speech patterns

Interpersonal stress
Hectic or inconsistent family routine
Inconsistent discipline/conflict
Unrealistic demands on the child
Faced paced life style/many activities
Competing/compared with siblings
Lack of time with parents

Life situations imposing stress
Conflict in the family
Holidays /special occasions
Unexpected events
Being put on stage
Changes in routine, caregiver, school
Parents' schedule/return to work
Large groups of people
Change in family/new sibling
Illness, death or divorce in family
Traumatic experiences

FIG. 12.2.   Overview of potential fluency disrupting factors for children.

possible subgroups of children characterized by the following patterns of temperament and emotional behavior; shy, withdrawn, and socially isolated; and outgoing, adventurous, likely to act out and require discipline. However, the variability in characteristics measured, instruments used, and detail of results presented makes it difficult to interpret and compare the significance of these findings in terms of indications of increased susceptibility for stuttering.

Oyler and Ramig (1995) reported findings of a study of vulnerability in 25 schoolage stuttering children and nonstuttering matched peers based on a parent perception scale. On this semantic differential task, parents were asked to respond on a 5-point rating scale to the rating that best described the personal characteristics of their child compared to other children the same age. The scale included 21 items regarding a wide range of behavior, for example, the child's level of sensitivity, activity, impulsivity, and reactivity to changes in the environment. The results indicated that the children who stuttered were significantly more sensitive than their age-matched peers. Oyler defined sensitivity as emotional susceptibility and reactivity and susceptibility to noise, stress, time pressure, and physical pain. Other significant findings revealed positive family history of stuttering in 65 % of the children who stuttered as well as a high incidence of learning problems. We do not know if indications of vulnerability preceded or were a result of long-standing stuttering problems.

In our clinic, we gain impressions of personality traits and behavioral characteristics by using a two-part informal parent rating scale. On the case history questionnaire, parents are asked to check any and all the items that best describe their child from the following list of descriptors; outgoing, shy, anxious, easy going, aggressive, stubborn, independent, dependent, talkative, reserved, imaginative, cooperative, competitive, sensitive, opinionated, resentful, easily frustrated, and cautious. In addition, during a more complete diagnostic interview, the parents are asked, "Tell me how you would describe your child to a good friend who had never met him or her?" Following this more open-ended description, parents rate children on an informal semantic differential using parameters such as outgoing or inhibited, noisy or quiet, even tempered or strong willed, needy or self-reliant. Both parents' judgments are elicited.

Response to Life Events. In Peters and Guitar's (1991) discussion of developmental factors, they commented that the conditions in the child's life near the onset of stuttering are typically not dramatic, the child is not usually under great stress, nor has he experienced a traumatic event. Van Riper (1973) also indicated that stuttering seems to begin within the context of rather usual patterns of communicating and living. These views may be colored by notions about what constitutes stress for children or how they may be affected by life stress. Life events typically experienced by children may impose stress in either a specific or a cumulative sense. Although no systematic study of the relationship of life events to stuttering has been reported, there is mention in the literature of the possibility that the onset of stuttering may occur at a time of transition or upheaval in a child's life (Starkweather, 1987; Wyatt, 1969). Johnson and Associates (1959) asked parents about 16 life situations that may have occurred near the onset of their child's stuttering and the four most frequently reported included; changes in the child's physical environment, a childhood illness, child became aware of the mother's pregnancy, and the arrival of a new baby. Peters and Guitar (1991) listed 10 life events often reported near the onset of stuttering; a move, parents' separation or divorce, death in the family, family member hospitalized, child hospitalized, parent loses job, new baby in home, another person comes to live, parents away frequently or on extended trip, and changes in routine, excitement or anxiety related to special occasions or visits. Williams (1985) also mentioned extreme changes in disciplinary practices and the child being lost in the stream of family activities as other possibly significant life changes. He indicated the importance of identifying "conditions that exist for a child which for him create confusion, sadness, tenseness and anxiety which can contribute to the disintegration of fluency" (p.13). Yairi and Ambrose (1992) examined the relationship between onset of stuttering and physical and emotional stress through questionnaire items and found that 43 % had histories indicating stress.

The Holmes Social Readjustment Scale for Children. The Holmes Social Readjustment Scale (Holmes & Masuda, 1974; Table 12.1) provides a useful structure to help parents and clinicians identify specific life changes that may affect children. Further, it is possible to quantify the cumulative effect of these changes, requiring social readjustment, within a 3-month period close to the onset of stuttering. Numerical values are given for each of 43 life changes included on the scale. Total point scores can be judged on a continuum; 150 points is considered an average stress rating, 150 to 300 indicates above-average stress, and scores over 300 suggest heavy stress. Under conditions of heavy stress, the authors suggested that many children stand a strong chance of experiencing a change in health or behavior.

Fluency. The main goals of fluency assessment are to determine the presence and extent of the problem and to make decisions about need for treatment. Gathering sufficient sized speech samples, in a variety of speaking situations in clinic and extraclinical situations, with a variety of people including parents, family members, and clinician over time will help confirm judgments about stuttering severity and the need for treatment (Costello, 1993; Curlee, 1993; Gordon & Luper, 1992a,1992b; Onslow, 1992; Peters & Guitar, 1991; Zebrowski, 1994). Measures of frequency of stuttering type disfluencies as well as of the form of the behaviors (duration and accompanying characteristics) all have importance in determining severity (Johnson, Darley, & Spriestersbach, 1978: Riley, 1981; Wingate, 1964). Schwartz and Conture (1988) concluded that a proportion of prolongations, over 25 % of the total disfluencies produced, is an indication of the need for treatment. It is also critical to gain impressions of a child's attitudes about communication and to include indications of awareness and overt reactions to stuttering. These signs may include reactions to difficult speaking tasks, comments about having difficulty speaking, increased stuttering, or change in communicative style in responses to reactions of listeners such as verbal interruption or teasing, and secondary behaviors related to stuttering including increased audible and visible tension and struggle (Cooper & Cooper, 1985; Riley, 1981). Clinicians should elicit information from parents about signs of awareness of stuttering, as noted earlier, and should observe the child closely during the assessment to confirm the parents' impressions.

TABLE 12.1

Holmes Social Readjustment Rating Scale for Children

Parent dies	100	Changes responsibilities/ home	29
Parents divorce	73	Older sibling leaves home	29
Parents separate	65	Trouble with grandparents	29
Parent travels (job)	63	Outstanding personal achievement	28
Death of close family member	63	Move to another city	26
Personal illness/injury	53	Move to another part of town	26
Parent remarries	50	Receives or looses a pet	25
Parent fired from job	47	Changes personal habits	24
Parents reconcile	45	Trouble with teacher	24
Mother goes to work	45	Changes in hours with sitter/daycare	20
Changes in health/ family mem.	44	Move to a new house	20
Mother becomes pregnant	40	Change to a new school	20
School difficulties	39	Change in play habits	19
Birth of a sibling	39	Vacation with family	19
School readjustment	39	Changes friends	18
Change in financial support	38	Attends summer camp	17
Close friend/ illness or injury	37	Changes sleeping habits	16
Starts new activity	36	Change in # of family get-togethers	15
Change in # fights/siblings	35	Changes eating habits	15
Threatened by violence/school	31	Changes amount of TV viewing	13
Theft of personal possessions	30	Birthday Party	12
		Punished for not telling the truth	11

Note: A score of 150 points = average stress; 150–300 points = above average stress; 300+ = heavy stress (strong chance of change in health or behavior). From "Life Change and Illness and Susceptibility," by T. Holmes and M. Masuda, 1974, as cited in *Stressful Life Events.*

Speech and Language Assessment. The need for comprehensive speech and language testing has been underscored as an essential part of evaluations for children who stutter (Conture, 1990; Fosnot, 1993; Gregory & Hill, 1980, 1993; Riley & Riley, 1980; Wall & Myers, 1995). A significant number of children who stutter demonstrate reduced speech and language performance. Concomitant speech and language problems in populations of school-age children who stutter have been reported (Blood & Seider, 1981; Riley & Riley, 1983; St. Louis, Murray, & Ashworth, 1992) (see Nippold, 1990, for review). There is a significant incidence of phonological disorders in groups of children who stutter (Louko, Edwards, & Conture, 1993; Yaruss, LaSalle, & Conture, 1995) (see Louko, 1995, and Nippold, 1990, for a review). Less clear is the relationship of other language skills with stuttering including syntax (Bernstein Ratner, 1995; Bernstein Ratner & Sih, 1987), word finding ability (Adams, 1980; Conture & Caruso, 1987; Gregory & Hill, 1980; Starkweather, 1987; Telser, 1971), or pragmatic skills (Scott, Healey, & Norris, 1995; Weiss, 1995; Weiss & Zebrowski, 1991). Yairi et al. (1996) found reduced expressive language skill to be a contributing factor to persistence of stuttering. Language task effects have been explored and found to have potential importance in understanding factors that disrupt fluency. Fluency breakdown with increasing language complexity has been demonstrated in normal speakers as well as in children who stutter (Bernstein Ratner & Sih, 1987; DeJoy & Gregory, 1975; Gaines, Runyan, & Myers, 1991; Gordon, 1991).

Clinical practice varies with regard to the domains of speech-language assessed and the test instruments included in fluency evaluation protocols. Some fluency assessment protocols include screening of articulation, language, and voice, with additional formal testing completed as needed (Costello, 1993; Curlee, 1993; Peters & Guitar, 1991). Others (Starkweather et al., 1990) include some routine language testing such as MLU and vocabulary measures, with additional standardized tests included as needed, wheras some advocate a wider range skills assessment, including more extensive use of standardized tests in a range of language and speech areas in order to establish a profile of skills (Conture, 1990; Fosnot, 1993; Gregory & Hill, 1993; Myers & Woodford, 1992; Riley & Riley, 1983). Hill (1995) and Wall and Myers (1995) advocated applying language analysis systems across the domains of syntax, semantics, and pragmatics for all children in order to assess interrelationships between language and fluency.

Several issues germane to selection of measures for children who stutter seem worthy of comment. If word finding difficulty seems to be a factor related to stuttering, it appears best to include routine testing both in naming and discourse contexts (German & Simon, 1991; Gregory, & Hill, 1980, 1993). Because there are no standardized tests of word finding for preschool children, informal procedures must suffice (see Hill, 1995, for a review). Although MLU is limited as an adequate measure of expressive language development, particularly for the speech of older preschool children, it appears to remain the procedure of choice (Conture, 1990; Kloth, Janssem, Kraaimaat, & Brutten, 1995; Yairi et al., 1996). However, without a more comprehensive language analysis, clinicians may miss the opportunity to identify language concerns (Miller, 1981) and to gain insight into the possible relationship of linguistic factors and stuttering (Hill, 1995). We see great benefit in obtaining verbatim transcripts of spontaneous speech samples and in completing a measure such as Developmental Sentence Analysis (DSS, Lee, 1974) or Systematic Analysis of Language Transcripts (SALT, Miller & Chapman, 1986), as an important part of differential evaluation (Campbell & Hill, 1987; Gregory & Hill, 1993). It is also important to know how children who stutter use language in social contexts with regard to conversational and narrative skills (Hill, 1995; Prutting & Kirchner, 1983; Weiss, 1995).

Verbatim transcripts, although more time consuming than on-line sampling, can provide the basis for several analyses of speech and language behaviors such as comprehensive fluency assessment; evaluation of a wide range of language skills within discourse and narrative contexts; phonetic transcription for speech analysis; and interpretation of data relating stuttering to levels of language usage, varying interpersonal patterns, and linguistic demands imposed across speaking situations.

A DESCRIPTIVE STUDY OF TWO-YEAR-OLD CHILDREN

The subjects of this descriptive study include eight 2-year-old children seen from 1994 to 1996 for evaluation near the onset of stuttering and subsequent treatment at the Northwestern University Speech and Language Clinic. The purpose of this study was to compare detailed assessment data for this group of very young children with research findings in the literature regarding child factors judged to be of potential importance in the development and maintenance of stuttering. The study also focused on gathering data regarding behavioral characteristics and life event stress levels of young children near the onset of stuttering. A final goal of this review was to evaluate treatment outcome with consideration to the treatment strategy selected, the intensity of treatment provided, and selected child factors needing attention during the treatment process.

Case History Information

Age of Onset and Age at Evaluation. The children studied ranged in age from 27 months to 35 months in age at the time of evaluation with a mean age of 31 months. The mean age of onset reported by the parents was 25.25 months (range 18–30 mos.), which was considerably younger than the onset age reported by Yairi et al. (1996). The range of time that had elapsed between first notice of stuttering and evaluation was 1 to 11 months, with a mean of 5.25 months, consistent with William's findings (1985), and closer to the recovered groups (2–5 months), and somewhat shorter than the persistent group (8.58 months) reported by Yairi et al. (1996).

Gender. The group included 5 boys and 3 girls (ratio 1.6:1), agreeing with reports of Yairi and Ambrose (1992) that the ratio of males to females in the early preschool years is 2:1 or smaller. Although girls have been reported to demonstrate an earlier onset of stuttering by as much as 6 months (Seider et al., 1983; Yairi & Ambrose, 1992), this small group of girls was later to develop stuttering (x=27.3 mos.) than the boys (x=24 mos.). This finding may have been influenced by the fact that two of the girls were somewhat later to develop language than the boys. Further, the two children reported to be the earliest to begin stuttering, both at 18 months of age, were boys.

Family History of Stuttering. Three girls and one boy, 50 % of the group, presented with a positive family history of stuttering [somewhat less than the two thirds identified by Yairi, et al., 1993]. The two girls with somewhat later developing speech and language both had first degree relatives who stuttered. One girl, subject 2, had two immediate family members with a history of stuttering: a father who rarely stuttered except under great stress, and a 9-year-old sister who had been treated at Northwestern between the ages of 3 and 4 with fluency maintained for 5 years post. The other girl, subject 7, had a father who stuttered. He had received treatment at Northwestern 5 years earlier, and reported mild episodic stuttering and word finding difficulty. The third girl, subject 4, had a paternal uncle who stuttered. The one boy, subject 1, had a father who stuttered but who had received treatment for stuttering at Northwestern 7 years earlier, and demonstrated mild occasional stuttering. According to Yairi et al. (1996), males who have male persistent stuttering relatives have the greatest risk for chronic stuttering. Of this group, subject 1 had the greatest risk for persistence of stuttering.

  Speech, Language, and Overall Development. There was a strong pattern of early communication development in this group. Six children were described as early in their speech language development (with words emerging at 9–10 months, word combinations by 12–15 months, and conversing by 14–18 months), and two were described as average (words at 12 months, word combinations at 18–21 months, and conversing by 24 to 30 months. Both of the later children were girls. During intake interviews, only the mother of subject 7 expressed concern about any aspect of communication, noting her daughter's reduced intelligibility However, at the time of the more comprehensive diagnostic interview, several parents noted significant concerns. The father of subject 7, who still stuttered mildly, believed that his daughter showed difficulty finding words (similar to his current difficulty). The parents of subject 8 commented on their son's difficulty organizing his extensive narratives and dealing appropriately with conversational turns. All 8 children were reported to be somewhat early in achieving motor developmental milestones such as sitting alone and crawling. Only two of the children (subjects 5 and 8) were completely toilet trained at the time stuttering was first observed.

  Health and Medical. All 8 children were reported to be generally healthy both by the parents and in letters from their pediatricians. Three of the 8 children (subjects 5, 6, and 8) had experienced frequent ear infections and subject 8 had a myringotomy and insertion of PE tubes. Two others (subjects 1 and 4) had reported allergies. None of the parents viewed these health issues as contributing to the development or maintenance of stuttering.

  Characteristics of Early Stuttering and Pattern of Development. In contrast to earlier reports about the typically gradual nature of stuttering development, 63 % of the children demonstrated a sudden onset of stuttering (one day to one week), greater than the 44 % reported by Yairi and Ambrose (1992b). One parent reported her child to be "one day fluent and the next [with] blocking and facial tension." At the time of evaluation, 4 of the children showed only repetitious type stuttering and four showed prolongations and/ or blocking in addition to sound and syllable repetitions. Seventy-five % of the group demonstrated secondary physical characteristics accompanying instances of stuttering. Audible features reported by parents included an increased rate of speaking, inability "to get sounds out," increased vocal loudness, "shouting out words," and pitch rise accompanying prolongations. Visible behaviors observed included eye blinking, facial tension, labial and lingual tension, shoulders drooping, covering mouth, and looks of frustration. One child abandoned utterances during stuttering and another shut down verbally the day after the initial episode of severe stuttering. None of these eight 2-year-old children had commented on their speech difficulty.

Child Factors Judged to Precipitate Stuttering. During the diagnostic interview, parents were asked to consider specific factors that might have had the tendency to precipitate stuttering. Excitement was named as a child behavior contributing to stuttering by 6 of the 8 parents, consistent with observations by Adams (1992). For example, the parents of subject 3 reported an increase of stuttering during roughhousing with the father, an activity the child eagerly anticipated. Fatigue was also frequently identified as a fluency disrupting influence for 6 children. For 5 children, increased speaking rate was judged to contribute to increased disfluency. Verbal competition was identified by two parents. Increased activity level, being upset, attempting to gain listener attention, and difficulty finding words were judged by two parents as child factors related to periods of disfluency.

Parent Rating of Child Behavior. Parent ratings of characteristics of child behavior are summarized in Table 12.2. With regard to language style, 5 of the children were described as very verbal and having acute auditory awareness (highly aware of noises outside a room, sensitive to loud noises, commenting on speech differences in others, repeating back complex sentences overheard from another room). In terms of frustration level, 3 were described as easily frustrated. Four were rated as demanding of attention, frequently interrupting, and needing to have their own way. In reporting behavioral characteristics, 6 of the children were described as sensitive generally, being especially reactive to what others say and do. Three were characterized as excitable, risk taking, or physically active. Parents indicated that 3 of the children had difficulty separating from them. Two were described as insecure and two as fearful. One child was rated as showing tactile defensiveness. These behavioral characteristics are often encountered during the intervention process and require careful problem solving both in therapy sessions and in working with parents to reduce potential barriers to a successful treatment outcome.

Life Events Occurring Near Stuttering Onset. At the time of evaluation, parents were asked to circle those life events listed on the Holmes Social Readjustment Rating Scale for Children (Holmes & Masuda, 1974) that had occurred within the 3-month period prior to onset of stuttering. The assigned point values for each event identified were totaled. Overall scores ranged from 146 to 334, as indicated in Table 12.2, with a mean of 208.87. Only one child had a score indicating below average stress (under 150 points). Six had scores in the 150–300 point range, indicating above average stress. Only one of the 8 children (subject 2, score 334) received a score indicative of heavy stress, thought to indicate a strong chance of a change in health or behavior according to the authors of the scale. In terms of total scores, overall life event stress did not appear to be exceptionally high for this group of children. Diagnostic data are summarized in Table 12.3.

TABLE 12.2

Parents' Rating of Personality/Behavioral Characteristics

Child Behavior	Frequency/Occurrence
Difficult to manage	6/8
Sensitive to what others say	6/8
Very verbal	5/8
Acute auditory awareness	5/8
Getting own way	4/8
Demanding of attention	4/8
Frequently interrupting	4/8
Easily frustrated	3/8
Excitable	3/8
Risk taking	3/8
Separation anxiety	3/8
Physically active	3/8
Insecure	2/8
Fearful	2/8
Tactile defensiveness	1/8

All 8 children had recently experienced changes in personal habits typical for children age 2 to 3 (increased responsibility for self-care; feeding, dressing, bathing, toilet training) and some children exhibited resistance to such changes. Six of 8 had experienced a change in sleeping habits (move from crib to bed, hours of sleep, difficulty with sleep routines). Five children had siblings born in close proximity to the onset of stuttering and 3 (subjects 1, 2, and 3) were showing extreme reactions (aggressive behavior, acting out, commenting "take the baby back to the hospital," greatly disrupted sleep patterns). Half of the children had had a change in caregiver other than parents and for 2 of them, the transition was described as "traumatic." Four of the children had also begun school or attendance in a new class. Parents of 4 of the children had begun new jobs, had had changes in work schedule, or had begun work-related travel (rated in the top four most stressful events by the scale). Two children had experienced either loss of a close

TABLE 12.3
Summary of Case History Information

Subj.	Sex	Age/onset	Age/eval	Family History	Sp/lang Devel.	Onset	Stuttering Behavior	Associated Behavior	Precipitating Factors	Personality/Behavioral Characteristics	Life Event Scale
1	M	26	27	Father	Early	Sudden	Sound/syllable repetitions	Struggle/eye blinking/facial tension; shouts out words.	Fatigue, ↑speaking rate excitement; getting attention	Dependent; cautious; meticulous; acute auditory awareness	199
2	F	25	27	Father, sister	Average	Sudden	Sound/syllable repetitions			Independent; stubborn; controlling; acute auditory awareness	334
3	M	18	27		Early	Gradual Cyclic	Sound/syllable repetitions; prolongations	Audible tension/ pitch rise; shoulders droop	Excitement; fatigue	Independent; talkative; active; easily frustrated; shy at first; challenges rules; acute auditory awareness	213
4	M	18	29		Early	Gradual	Sound/syllable repetitions		Fatigue; excitement	Dependent; talkative; sensitive; tactile defensiveness; acute auditory awareness; separation anxiety	183
5	M	28	32		Early	Sudden	Syllable repetitions	Struggle/eye blinking; ↑ vocal loudness; frustration	↑speaking rate	Outgoing; talkative; active; sensitive; easily frustrated; separation anxiety	204
6	F	27	32	Uncle	Early	Sudden Cyclic	Blocking ; prolongations	Facial tension; ↓ speaking next day	Excitement; fatigue; ↑speaking rate verb competit	Independent; outgoing; talkative; strong willed; acute perception of environment	146
7	F	30	35	Father	Average	Sudden Cyclic	Sound/syllable repetitions; prolongations	Facial tension/ eyeblinking, covered mouth, abandoned talk; crying	Fatigue; upset, excitement; ↑ speaking rate; word finding	Independent; anxious; sensitive; active; stubborn; easily frustrated	205
8	M	30	35		Early	Gradual	Syllable repetitions, prolongations	Pitch rise on prolongations; frustration	↑speaking rate ↑activity; fatigue; excitement, verb competit.	Outgoing; very talkative; shy in new situations; sensitive; easily frustrated; acute auditory awareness; attentive to detail	187

family member or a personal illness or injury. The frequency of life events experienced by this group of children as identified by their parents is summarized in Table 12.4. Parents often commented on the instructive nature of completing this rating scale, as it sensitized them to the number of changes their children had experienced in a relatively short time span.

TABLE 12.4
Potential Child Stress Factors Related to Life Events

Life Event Change	Frequency of Occurrence
Change in personal habits	8/8
Change in sleeping habits	6/8
Birth of a sibling	5/8
Change in caregiver	4/8
Begin new activity/school	4/8
Mother begins work/changes schedule	2/8
Father changes job/begins travel	2/8
Death of close family member	1/8

These changes, although stressful, were no more numerous or severe than would be expected for any group of children in this age range. However, Oyler and Ramig (1995) found that school-age children who stutter are judged by their parents to be more vulnerable to stress than age-matched peers; it is conceivable that preschool children who begin to stutter may also be highly vulnerable to stress. It may take a smaller accumulation of stressful events to reach a significant threshold for young preschool children who begin to stutter, particularly when they are in a period of rapid change in neuromotor, linguistic, cognitive, and social-emotional growth, although this hypothesis is not easily testable. However, there is clinical value to assessment of life event stress. In my experience, monitoring a child's reactions to life changes and helping them develop skills to support more adaptable responses is often a support to developing fluency enhancing skills.

Formal Observations and Assessment

Fluency Assessment. The results of fluency assessment were based on Systematic Disfluency Analysis (SDA,Campbell & Hill, 1987;1993) of verbatim transcripts of 200 syllable samples of spontaneous speech in four to five speaking contexts varying in conversational and linguistic demand. Results of SDA from three speaking situations including parent–child play interaction, relaxed play with the clinician and pressured play with the clinician, elicited within one session, are included and summarized in Table 12.5. The frequency of less typical or stuttering type disfluencies ranged from 1.5% to 24%; more typical fluency disruption ranged from 3.5% to 17%; and total fluency disruption from 8% to 35%. Within this group of children, severity of stuttering ranged from borderline to severe: one child demonstrated borderline stuttering severity, 2 showed borderline to mild, 1 mild to moderate, 2 demonstrated consistent moderate stuttering, and 2 were severe in all ratings.

Patterns of variability in frequency and severity of stuttering have been shown to vary across settings (Gordon & Luper, 1992b; Yaruss, Logan, & Conture, 1993) as well as speaking situations within the same assessment session in preschool children (Yaruss & Hill, 1995). Half of the subjects showed relatively consistent patterns of frequency and severity of stuttering across the three samples. However, 50% demonstrated variation in two severity rating levels across situations, for example, borderline to moderate, mild to severe, and borderline to mild. This finding suggests the importance of including a number of different speaking contexts in assessment protocols. Consider the data for subject 4. If fluency had been assessed only in a relaxed play interaction, judgments about stuttering severity and need for treatment would have been far different and inaccurate.

Speech and Language Assessment. Speech and language assessment included standardized comprehensive tests of expressive and receptive skills as well as tests of receptive vocabulary and word-finding skills. Articulation tests and phonological analyses were completed as needed beyond phonetic transcription of segments of the verbatim transcripts utilized for SDA. Selected test results are reported in Table 12.5.

On the Peabody Picture Vocabulary Test-Revised (PPVT- R, Dunn & Dunn, 1990) all children exhibited within normal limits performance (5 scored above the 85th percentile and only one at the 25th percentile, a child whose poor attending behavior precluded reaching ceiling). All children also demonstrated age-appropriate development of syntax as measured by Developmental Sentence Scoring Analysis (DSS, Lee, 1974). However, 2 children (subjects 5 and 7, both with well-developed receptive vocabulary) demonstrated relatively long word latencies (3–11 seconds) in naming pictured items on the Northwestern Word Latency Test, an informal test of confrontation naming (Rutherford & Telser, 1967; Telser, 1971). They also demonstrated behaviors characteristic of word-finding difficulty in discourse contexts (misnamings, overuse of indefinite pronouns and nonspecific words, frequent revisions, use of descriptions and explanations in place of specific words and frequent interjections, and repetitions of function words (German, 1987; German & Simon, 1991). One child, subject 8, demonstrated possible pragmatic concerns in the areas of conversational and narrative performance. In contrast to his superior performance on tests of language skills, this child demonstrated significant organizational difficulty during narrative expression. Only one of the eight children, subject 7, demonstrated any articulation errors. In her case, articulatory substitutions and distortions were judged to be developmental, and phonological processes were age appropriate. However, increased rate of speech had a significant negative impact on intelligibility.

Results of speech and language assessment revealed that only about one third demonstrated concomitant expressive language concerns, and that these concerns were not evidenced on routine standardized speech and language tests. Difficulties in lexical access and integration of language processes at the level of pragmatic performance were judged to be possible factors contributing to the maintenance of stuttering. For subjects 5, 7, and 8, support for ongoing development of expressive language development was provided in early stages of treatment, and once fluency was stabilized, additional treatment was provided that focused primarily on improving specific language skills. For subject 7, concerns about speech intelligibility resolved as rate of speech modulated during the course of fluency treatment.

Related Areas. None of the 8 children was referred for consultations to professionals because of concerns about development in related areas such as psychology, occupational or physical therapy, or vision. However, it was recommended that the 2 children demonstrating separation anxiety (subjects 5 and 7) be supported in working through this developmental issue during treatment, monitoring the need for referral to the consultant psychologist. Further, because subject 5 also demonstrated delayed fine motor and difficulty attending to tasks, it was recommended that development of these skills be closely monitored and supported during ongoing treatment.

Recommendations for Treatment

Treatment data are displayed in Table 12.5. Generally, for children who demonstrate borderline stuttering severity without complicating speech and language factors, we recommend prescriptive parent counseling (PPC, Gregory & Hill, 1993). This short-term intervention program, involving both the parents and child, offers a middle ground between a "wait and see" monitoring approach recommended by both Conture (1990) and Curlee (1993) and a more intensive direct treatment program. Biweekly sessions over a 2 month period focus primarily on educating parents about fluency development and stuttering, helping them identify potential fluency disrupting factors, and teaching them to model speech and interactive behaviors conducive to fluency development. These behaviors include modeling an easy approach to speech initiation with smooth transitions throughout utterances spoken at a somewhat slower than normal rate; encouraging turn taking and listening first during semistructured play, later in structured conversation, and eventually encouraging turn taking in home interactions; providing ample time for the child to speak in unhurried, uninterrupted situations; providing one-on-one time with the child each day, and modifying other communicative behaviors as indicated; and balancing questions and comments, and reducing demands for speech performance. If at the end of the four-session program the child's fluency is within normal range, a follow-up plan is initiated for monthly rechecks for 3 to 6 months. In cases where parents have not yet mastered the skills described previously, the program is extended for an additional month or 2 to allow for further parent counseling and monitoring of the child. On occasion, PPC is provided as interim treatment when there are no openings in a more comprehensive treatment program for children who clearly demonstrate stuttering problems.

Prescriptive parent counseling-plus (PPC+) is a variation of PPC with weekly teatment sessions provided and more direct focus on encouraging development of the child's fluency skills. Typically, the decision to use this intervention strategy follows observation and reassessment of the child and parent–child interaction during a PPC program. However, on occasion, PPC+ is recommended as an initial strategy following evaluation for children who demonstrate behavioral characteristics of concern or parents who express great anxiety.

The preschool fluency development group (PDG) program (Gregory and Hill, 1980, 1984, 1993) is a comprehensive treatment program for children who show at least mild stuttering or borderline stuttering with complicating speech or language factors. Sessions are twice weekly with one session devoted to individual treatment and one divided between group and individual treatment. Weekly parent group sessions provide the basis for parent education, training, and problem solving. The parents are trained to model the communicative and interactive behaviors discussed in the description of the PPC intervention program. Parent observation of group and individual sessions reinforces understanding of the nature of the child's problems and the treatment process. For children, the focus is primarily on developing fluency skills. Modeling of easy, relaxed speech is the primary method of instruction with opportunities provided for rehearsal of fluency enhancing skills along a hierarchy of increasing length and complexity of utterances with systematic inclusion of a variety of situational variables (location, persons present, physical activity, topic) included over time to encourage generalization of easy speech. This treatment strategy is centered primarily on a "speak more fluently" approach, although for some children, "stutter more easily" experience is needed.

Treatment Decision Making Based on Results of Evaluation

The stuttering intervention strategies employed varied for the 8 children in relationship to child factors identified during evaluation. Because differential evaluation is viewed as an ongoing process taking place throughout differential treatment, in some cases, more direct intervention was recommended as treatment progressed.

Subject 6, who demonstrated borderline stuttering, was enrolled in PPC. Her parents learned to manage fluency disrupting sessions, and the child developed skills in managing conversational interchange and verbal competition in six sessions over a four-month period. Two of the younger children (subjects 1 and 3), just over 2 years of age, were initially enrolled in PPC due to unavailability of openings in the more comprehensive treatment program. Severity of stuttering, associated behavior, parental anxiety, and predictive factors of persistence (family history for subject 1 and the somewhat long period of stuttering for subject 2) all pointed to the need for more intensive treatment. However, in both cases following short-term PPC, significant changes in fluency were observed. For subject 1, stuttering severity

TABLE 12.5
Summary of Assessment and Treatment Data

Subject: 1 — Systematic Disfluency Analysis

		Dx	Dx	Dx	Post	Post	Post	Tx Strategy	# of Sessions
PPVT-R:	Situation	PCI	P	PP	PCI	P	PP	PPC Shyness/ turn taking sibling jealousy	4 Tx sessions 2 months
48th %ile	Frequency Analysis								
DSS:	More Typical %	17%	11%	16%	3.5%	6.0%	6.0%		
90th %ile	Less Typical %	12%	24%	17%	2.5%	1.5%	2.5%		
Word finding	Total %	29%	35%	32%	6.0%	7.5%	8.5%	PPC+	16 Tx sessions
	Severity Analysis								4 months
Pragmatics:	More Typical Score	122	89	106	31	43	51		
	Less Typical Score	259	463	279	54	20	50		
	Total Score	381	552	385	85	63	101	Follow up	4 recheck
Phonological:	Severity Rating	Sev	Sev	Sev	Bord	Bord	Bord		4 months
	Comments:								Dismiss

Subject: 2 — Systematic Disfluency Analysis

		Dx	Dx	Dx	Post	Post	Post	Tx Strategy	# of Sessions
PPVT-R:	Situation	PCI	P	PP	PCI	P	PP	PPC + Contol issues; resistant; life events stressful	8 Tx sessions 2 months
63rd %ile	Frequency Analysis								
DSS:	More Typical %	7.5%	7.0%	7.0%		5.0%	6.5%		
25th %ile	Less Typical %	8.5%	7.0%	5.5%		3.5%	5.5%		
Word finding:	Total %	16.%	14.0%	12.5%		8.5%	11.5%		
	Severity Analysis							PDG More positve response; fluency skills dev	26 Tx sessions 4 months
Pragmatics:	More Typical Score	46	48	59		54	55		
	Less Typical Score	132	96	83		51	74		
	Total Score	178	144	142		105	129		
Phonological:	Severity Rating	Mod	Mild	Mild		Bord	Mild		
	Comments:								Cont. Tx

Subject: 3 — Systematic Disfluency Analysis

		Dx	Dx	Dx	Post	Post	Post	Tx Strategy	# of Sessions
PPVT-R:	Situation	PCI	P	PP	PCI	P	PP	PPC Vulnerable to activity level; dev coop/turn taking	8 Tx sessions 4 months
≤25%ile	Frequency Analysis								
DSS:	More Typical %	10%	15%	16%		4.5%	5.5%		
75%ile	Less Typical %	9%	7%	12%		1.0%	2.0%		
Word finding	Total %	19%	22%	28%		5.5%	7.5%		
	Severity Analysis								
Pragmatics:	More Typical Score	78	106	60		23	43	Follow up	4 recheck
	Less Typical Score	148	134	146		12	24		4 months
	Total Score	226	240	206		35	67		
Phonological:	Severity Rating	Mod	Mod	Mod		Norm	Bord		
	Comments:								Dismiss

Subject: 4 — Systematic Disfluency Analysis

		Dx	Dx	Dx	Post	Post	Post	Tx Strategy	# of Sessions
PPVT-R:	Situation	PCI	P	PP	PCI	P	PP	PPC Severe separation anxiety	8 Tx sessions 4 months
95th%ile	Frequency Analysis								
DSS:	More Typical %	7.2%	3.5%	7.5%	4.5%	5.0%	7.0%		
90th%ile	Less Typical %	5.6%	5.6%	12.7%	3.0%	0.0%	1.5%		
Word finding	Total %	12.8%	9.3 %	20..2%	7.5%	5.0%	8.5%	PPC+ Refer for counsel.	16 Tx sessions 4 months
	Severity Analysis							PDG	28 Tx sessions
Pragmatics:	More Typical Score	36	45	84	26	25	36		4 months
	Less Typical Score	139	44	155	47	0	21		
	Total Score	175	89	239	73	25	57	Followup	4 recheck
Phonological:	Severity Rating	Mod	Bord	Mod	Bord	Norm	Norm		4 months
	Comments:								Dismiss

Subject: 5	Systematic Disfluency Analysis © 1987, 1994 June Haerle Campbell, Diane G. Hill. All rights reserved							Tx Strategy	# of Sessions
PPVT-R:		Dx	Dx	Dx	Post	Post	Post	PDG	28 Tx
89th%ile	Situation	PCI	P	PP	PCI	P	PP	Attention	sessions
DSS:	Frequency Analysis							issues	4 months
90th%ile	More Typical %	11%	6%	6%		6.5%	6.5%	Separatio	
Word finding:	Less Typical %	15%	13%	9%		2.0%	0.0%	issues	
Significant	Total %	26%	19%	15%		8.5%	6.5%		
	Severity Analysis							Lang. Tx	30 Tx
Pragmatics:	More Typical Score	51	53	22		49	53	Word	sessions
	Less Typical Score	363	444	90		52	0	finding	4 months
	Total Score	414	497	112		101	53		Recheck
Phonological:	Severity Rating	Sev	Sev	Mild		Bord	Norm		fluency
	Comments: During Dx, shut down verbally in PP								
									Dismiss

Subject: 6	Systematic Disfluency Analysis © 1987, 1994 June Haerle Campbell, Diane G. Hill. All rights reserved							Tx Strategy	# of Sessions
PPVT-R:		Dx	Dx	Dx	Post	Post	Post	PPC	6 Tx
95th%ile	Situation	PCI	P	PP	PCI	P	PP	Urgency	sessions
DSS:	Frequency Analysis							to speak	4 months
75th%ile	More Typical %	9.5%	7.5%	10%	.5%	2.0%	3%	Verbal	
Word finding:	Less Typical %	1.0%	2.0%	4%	.5%	0.0%	2%	compet.	
	Total %	10.5%	9.5	14%	1.0%	2.0%	5%		
	Severity Analysis							Follow up	3 recheck
Pragmatics:	More Typical Score	60	48	51	4	16	12		sessions
	Less Typical Score	23	32	54	9	0	23		6 months
	Total Score	83	80	105	13	16	35		
Phonological:	Severity Rating	Bord	Bord	Bord	Norm	Norm	Norm		
	Comments: During Dx, reluctant to talk and avoided eye contact in PP								Dismiss

Subject: 7	Systematic Disfluency Analysis © 1987, 1994 June Haerle Campbell, Diane G. Hill. All rights reserved							Tx Strategy	# of Sessions
PPVT-R:		Dx	Dx	Dx	Post	Post	Post	PDG	39 Tx
92nd%ile	Situation	PCI	P	PP	PCI	P	PP	Separation	sessions
DSS:	Frequency Analysis							anxiety;	
50-75th%ile	More Typical %	3.5%	6%			7.5%	9.5%	cooperation	
Word finding:	Less Typical %	4.5%	6%			0.0%	1.5%		
Significant	Total %	8.0%	12%			7.5%	11.0%		
	Severity Analysis							Sp/lang	16 Tx
Pragmatics:	More Typical Score	21	40			43	55	Tx	sessions
	Less Typical Score	93	93			0	18	Word	
	Total Score	114	133			43	73	finding +	fluency
Phonological:	Severity Rating	Mild	Mild			Norm	Bord	monitor	rechecks
Significant	Comments:							fluency	
									Dismiss

Subject: 8	Systematic Disfluency Analysis © 1987, 1994 June Haerle Campbell, Diane G. Hill. All rights reserved							Tx Strategy	# of Sessions
PPVT-R:		Dx	Dx	Dx	Post	Post	Post	PDG	29 Tx
89 th%ile	Situation	PCI	P	PP	PCI	P	PP	Turn	sessions
DSS:	Frequency Analysis							taking	4 months
90th%ile	More Typical %	7.5%	10.0%	10.0%		1.5%	4%		
Word finding:	Less Typical %	1.5%	2.5%	3.0%		1.0%	0%	Lang. Tx	29 Tx
	Total %	8.5%	12.5%	13.0%		3.5%	4%	Pragmatic	sessions
	Severity Analysis							skills +	4 months
Pragmatics:	More Typical Score	40	78	78		10	20	monitor	
Significant	Less Typical Score	28	57	53		14	0	fluency	
Turns/ Organiz	Total Score	68	135	131		24	20		
Phonological:	Severity Rating	Bord	Mild	Mild		Norm	Norm		Dismiss
	Comments:								

Note. Key to situation codes — *P* = play; *PP* = play with pressure; *PCI* = parent–child interaction. Key to stuttering severity rating — *norm* = normal (0–57); *Bord* = borderline (58–107); *mild* = (108–174); *mod* = moderate (175–285); *sev* = severe (286–800); *v sev* = very severe (≥801). Key for treatment strategy — *PPC* = Prescriptive Parent Counseling; *PPC+* = PPC + additional sessions; *PDG* = Preschool Disfluency Group.

reduced from severe to mild after the first four sessions over a 2-month period. For subject 1, given his risk factors (father who stuttered, persistence of tension and struggle associated with sound and syllable repetitions), treatment progressed to PPC+ (once per week) with more specific focus encouraging the child to experience easy, relaxed speech. After 16 additional treatment sessions, fluency within an essentially normal range had stabilized. For subject 3 because mild stuttering persisted, continuation of PPC for another 2 months was recommended. At the end of that period of eight treatment sessions, normal to borderline fluency had stabilized. The treatment outcome for these children suggests that severity of stuttering may be less important than other factors in selecting a treatment strategy.

Subjects 2 and 4 both demonstrated significant stuttering and other behavioral issues. For subject 2, although she had a family history of stuttering, the heavy stress rating received on the Holmes Scale, her young age, and difficulty adjusting to a new sibling, it was judged that PDG might be too intense and PPC+ was initiated instead. However, we found that neither the child nor environmental factors were amenable to change in the short-term PPC+, and more consistent and direct treatment in PDG was employed. To date, a total of 32 sessions have been provided. Although some changes have been recognized after 6 months of treatment, stuttering continues to cycle from mild to moderate levels. In view of continued intense reactions to new experiences and unresolved sibling jealousy, consultation with the clinical psychologist was initiated.

Subject 4 was initially unable to adapt to the treatment routine and much work was done on building a positive client–clinician relationship and encouraging separation. It was soon apparent that involvement of a consultant psychologist was needed to further support resolution of separation anxiety and control issues. Progress was slow but steady and focused heavily on expression of feelings and on building healthy attitudes as well as fluency skills. Of the entire group, his treatment took the greatest number of sessions (60) and the longest time period to complete (16 months).

The final group of children, subjects 5, 7, and 8, who demonstrated accompanying expressive language difficulty with stuttering ranging from mild to severe ratings, were enrolled in PDG. Initial treatment focused primarily on developing fluency skills, which were well established within two to three 10-week periods of enrollment in the program with 28–39 (average of 32) sessions provided. As shown in Table 12.5, in all three cases, continued language treatment addressed unresolved expressive language concerns and monitored continued fluency development.

Treatment Outcome

Significant changes in fluency were observed following treatment for all children. At the beginning of treatment, disfluency levels for more typical disfluency ranged from 3.5 % to 17 % with a mean of 11.4 %; less typical (stutteringlike) disfluency from 1–24 % with a mean of 7.8 %; and total disfluency from 8–35 % with a mean of 17.5 %. The number of treatment sessions for children enrolled in PPC alone averaged seven; children in PDG ranged from 28–39 sessions with a mean of 32; and children receiving a progression of treatment from more conservative initial PPC treatment to more intensive PPC+ or PDG ranged from 20–60 sessions with a mean of 37 sessions. The mean number of treatment sessions for the entire group was 32 sessions. At the end of treatment (see post-SDA measures in Table 12.5), disfluency levels for more typical disfluency ranged from .5 to 9.5 % with a mean of 4.88 %, less typical disfluency from 0–3 % with a mean of 1.23 %, and total disfluency ranged from 1–11 % with a mean of 6.17 %. Only one child, subject 4, showed a frequency of stutteringlike disfluency at or above the well-accepted 3 % threshold of concern in one speaking situation. Both the clinician and parent judged that the easy syllable repetitions that remained were not often observed and were not of concern. Subject 2 was excluded from the end of treatment data summary

Follow-up programs are judged to be an essential part of the treatment process for stuttering problems. Decisions about dismissal were based on completion of four rechecks conducted over at least a 4-month period during which two to thee fluency samples were elicited and analyzed. For all children, with the exception of subject 2 who was in continuing treatment, rechecks, including fluency sampling and parent discussion, confirmed stability of fluency within a normal to borderline range. Continued periodic rechecks are needed for several years postdismissal to provide more meaningful results with regard to treatment efficacy and recovery from stuttering.

CONCLUSIONS

Results of this descriptive study underscore the importance of performing differential evaluation of fluency disorders in children. Profiles of child factors differed with regard to the nature of the stuttering problem presented, family history of stuttering, communicative skills, behavioral characteristics, and life events experienced. Although there was variability in patterns of child factors presented, the incidence of family history of stuttering and concomitant speech and language problems presented with considerable frequency. Only one child of the 8 children had experienced a series of life events near the time of onset of stuttering that equated to a heavy stress rating, confirming the notion that children who begin to stutter do not do so in response to unusual stress. However, it was noted that many parents reported strong reactions in their children to specific life events, possibly indicating increased vulnerability to stress. The majority of children were characterized as sensitive, very verbal, having acute auditory awareness, and somewhat difficult to manage. For a subgroup of children, social-emotional factors such as separation anxiety, fearfulness, and tactile defensiveness presented major concerns and required careful attention in the development and modification of treatment approaches. In two cases, support from a related professional was needed to help resolve these issues that were judged to interfere with the treatment process. Another subgroup of 3 children demonstrated subtle, yet significant, expressive language difficulty. Although results of evaluation of parent–child interaction and other environmental influences were not reported in this study, they were fully considered throughout the evaluation and treatment process.

Ongoing research efforts should continue to focus on increasing understanding of the contributions of child variables to the development of stuttering. Attention should be given to the development of more standard assessment protocols, resulting in more uniform classification and diagnosis of young children who stutter, and allowing comparison of populations across clinics. Research should continue to focus on the possible cause-and-effect relationships between significant child variables and stuttering. Working to identify subgroups may prove to be more fruitful than studying group differences. For example, in some studies, subject populations with a large age range may have obscured important findings. Continued longitudinal studies offer great promise in helping to refine understanding about recovery from stuttering and variables related to persistence of stuttering. Thus far, there has been limited study of social-emotional factors in young children who stutter. Even as future research continues to refine the understanding of the nature of stuttering, and to provide implications for evaluation and treatment, clinicians must still assess children one by one and ask questions about the potential relationship of significant diagnostic findings to stuttering for each individual child. Dialogue should continue between those more focused on research and those more focused on clinical practice in pursuit of the common goal of improved early intervention and effective treatment of children who stutter.

REFERENCES

Adams, M. (1980). The young stutterer: Diagnosis, treatment and assessment of progress. *Seminars in Speech, Language and Hearing, 1,* 289–299.

Adams, M. (1992). Childhood stuttering under positive conditions. *American Journal of Speech-Language Pathology, 1*(3), 5–6.

Ambrose, N., & Yairi, E. (1994). The role of repetition units in the differential evaluation of early childhood incipient stuttering. *American Journal of Speech Language Pathology, 4,* 82–88.

Ambrose, N., Yairi, E., & Cox, N. (1993). Genetic aspects of early childhood stuttering. *Journal of Speech and Hearing Research, 36,* 701–706.

Andrews, G. (1984). Epidemiology of stuttering. In R. Curlee & W. Perkins (Eds.), *Nature and treatment of stuttering: New directions* (pp. 1–12). San Diego, CA: College Hill Press, Inc.

Bernstein Ratner, N. (1995b). Language complexity and stuttering in children. *Topics in Language Disorders, 15* (3), 32–47.

Bernstein Ratner, N. & Sih, C. (1987). Effects of gradual increases in sentence length and complexity on children's disfluency. *Journal of Speech and Hearing Research, 52,* 278–287.

Blood, G., & Seider, R. (1981). The concomitant problems of young stutterers. *Journal of Speech and Hearing Disorder, 46,* 31–33.

Bloodstein, O. (1995). *A handbook of stuttering, (5th ed.).* San Diego, CA: Singular.

Campbell, J. H., & Hill, D. (1987, November). *Systematic disfluency analysis.* Miniseminar presented at the annual convention of the American Speech, Language-Hearing Association, New Orleans, LA.

Campbell, J. H., & Hill, D. (1993, November). *Application of a weighted scoring system to systematic disfluency analysis.* Poster session presented at the annual convention of the American Speech-Language-Hearing Association, Anaheim, CA.

Conture, E. G. (1990). *Stuttering, (2nd ed.).* Englewood Cliffs, NJ: Prentice-Hall.

Conture, E. G., & Caruso, A. (1987). Assessment and diagnosis of childhood disfluency. In L. Rustin, D. D. Rowley, & H. Puser (Eds.), *Progress in the treatment of fluency disorders* (pp. 84–104). London: Taylor and Francis.

Conture, E. G., & Kelly, E. (1991). Young stutterers' nonspeech behaviors during stuttering. *Journal of Speech and Hearing Research, 43,* 1041–1056.

Conture, E. G., Louko, L., & Edwards, M. L. (1993). Simultaneously treating stuttering and disordered phonology in children: Experimental treatment, preliminary findings. *American Journal of Speech-Language Pathology, 2*(3), 72–81.

Cooper, E. B., & Cooper, C. S. (1985). *Cooper personalized fluency control therapy handbook (Revised ed.)*. Allen, TX: DLM Teaching Resources.

Costello, J. (1993). Behavioral treatment for stuttering children. In R. Curlee (Ed.), *Stuttering and related disorders of fluency* (pp. 68–100). New York: Thieme-Stratton.

Curlee, R. (1980). A case selection strategy for young disfluent children. *Seminars in Speech, Language and Hearing, 1,* 277–287.

Curlee, R. (1993). Identification and management of beginning stuttering. In R. Curlee (Ed.), *Stuttering and related disorders* (pp. 1–22). New York: Thieme-Stratton.

DeJoy, D., & Gregory, H. (1985). The relationship between age and frequency of disfluencies in preschool children. *Journal of Fluency Disorders, 10,* 107–122.

Dunn, L., & Dunn, L. (1990). *Peabody picture vocabulary test (Rev. ed.)*. Circle Pines, MN: American Guidance Service.

Fosnot, S. (1993). Research design for examining treatment efficacy in fluency disorders. *Journal of Fluency Disorders, 18,* 221–251.

Gaines, N., Runyan, C., & Myers, S. (1991). A comparison of young stutterers' fluent versus stuttered utterances on measures of length and complexity. *Journal of Speech and Hearing Research, 34,* 37–42.

German, D. J. (1987). Spontaneous language profiles of children with word-finding problems. *Language, Speech and Hearing Services in the Schools, 18,* 217–230.

German, D. J., & Simon, E. (1991). Analysis of children's word-finding skills in discourse. *Journal of Speech and Hearing Research, 34,* 309–316.

Gordon, P. (1991). Language task effects: A comparison of stuttering and nonstuttering children. *Journal of Fluency Disorders, 16,* 275–287.

Glasner, P., & Rosenthal, D. (1957). Parental diagnosis of stuttering in young children. *Journal of Speech and Hearing Disorders, 22,* 288–295.

Gordon, P. (1991). Language task effects: A comparison of stuttering and nonstuttering children. *Journal of Fluency Disorders, 16,* 275–287.

Gordon, P., & Luper, H. (1992a). The early identification of beginning stuttering I: Protocols. *American Journal of Speech-Language Pathology, 1*(3), 43–53.

Gordon, P., & Luper, H. (1992b). The early identification of beginning stuttering II: Problems. *American Journal of Speech-Language Pathology, 1*(4), 49–55.

Gregory, H. (1973). *Stuttering: Differential evaluation and therapy*. Indianapolis: Bobbs-Merrill.

Gregory, H. (1986). *Stuttering: Differential evaluation and therapy*. Austin, Texas: Pro-Ed.

Gregory, H., & Campbell, J. (1988). Stuttering in the school-age child. In D. E. Yoder & R. D. Kent (Eds.), *Decision making in speech language pathology* (pp. 162–163). Philadelphia, PA: Decker.

Gregory, H., Campbell, J., & Hill, D. (1995). Differential evaluation-differential therapy for stuttering children. *First World Congress on Fluency Disorders Proceedings, 1,* 287–290.

Gregory, H., & Hill, D. (1980). Stuttering therapy for children. In W. Perkins (Ed.), *Strategies in stuttering therapy* (pp. 351–363). New York: Thieme-Stratton.

Gregory, H., & Hill, D. (1984). Stuttering therapy for children. In W. Perkins (Ed.), *Stuttering disorders* (pp. 77–93). New York: Thieme-Stratton.

Gregory, H., & Hill, D. (1993). Differential evaluation-differential therapy for stuttering children. In R. Curlee (Ed.), *Stuttering and related disorders of fluency* (pp. 23–44). New York: Thieme-Stratton.

Hall, N., Yamashita, T., & Aram, D. (1993). Relationship between language and fluency in children with developmental language disorders. *Journal of Speech and Hearing Research, 36,* 568–579.

Hall, P. (1977). The occurence of disfluencies in language disordered school-aged children. *Journal of Speech and Hearing Disorders, 42,* 361–370.

Hanley, J. M. (1985). Speech motor processes and stuttering in children: A theoretical and clinical perspective. In J. Gruss (Ed.), *Stuttering therapy: Prevention and intervention with children* (Publication No. 20, pp. 39–66). Memphis, TN: Stuttering Foundation of America.

Hill, D. (1995). Assessing language in children who stutter. *Topics in Language Disorders, 15*

(3), 60–79.

Holmes, T., & Masuda, M. (1974). Life change and illness and susceptibility. In B. Dohrenwood & B. S. Dohrenwend (Eds.), *Stressful life events.* New York: Wiley.

Homzie, M., Lindsay, J., Simpson, J., & Hasenstab, S. (1988). Concomitant speech, language and learning problems in adult stutterers and members of their families. *Journal of Fluency Disorders, 13,* 261–277.

Johnson, W., & Associates. (1959). *The onset of stuttering.* Minneapolis:The University of Minnesota Press.

Johnson, W., Darley, F., & Spriestersbach, D. (1978). *Diagnostic methods in speech pathology.* New York: Haper and Row.

Kidd, K. (1984). Stuttering as a genetic disorder. In R. Curlee & W. Perkins (Eds.), *Nature and treatment of stuttering: New directions* (pp. 149–169). San Diego, CA: College Hill Press.

Kline, M. L., & Starkweather, C. W. (1979). Receptive and expressive language performance in young stutterers [Abstract]. *Asha, 21,* 797.

Kloth, S. A. M., Janssen, P., Kraaimaat, F. W., & Brutten, G. J. (1995). Speech-motor and linguistic skills of young stutterers prior to onset. *Journal of Fluency Disorders, 20,* 157–170.

Lee, L. (1974). *Developmental sentence analysis.* Evanston, IL: Northwestern University Press.

Louko, L (1995). Phonological characteristics of young children who stutter. *Topics in Language Disorders, 15* (3), 48–59.

Louko, L., Edwards, M., & Conture, E. (1990). Phonological characteristics of young stutterers and their normally fluent peers: Preliminary observations. *Journal of Fluency Disorders, 15,* 191–210.

Merits-Patterson, R., & Reed, C. (1981). Disfluencies in the speech of language-delayed children. *Journal of Speech and Hearing Research, 24,* 55–58.

Miller, J. F. (1981). *Assessing language production in children: Experimental procedures.* Austin, TX: Pro-Ed.

Miller, J. F., & Chapman, R. (1986). *Systematic analysis of language transcripts.* Madison, WI: University of Wisconsin Language Analysis Laboratory.

Myers, S. C., & Woodford, L. (1992). *The fluency development system for young children ages 2–9 years.* Buffalo, NY: United Educational Services.

Nippold, M. (1990). Concomitant speech and language disorders in stuttering children. *Journal of Speech and Hearing Disorders, 55,* 51–60.

Onslow, M. (1992). Identification of early stutterings: Issues and suggested strategies. *American Journal of Speech-Language Pathology: A Journal of Clinical Practice, 1*(4), 21–27.

Oyler, E., & Ramig, P. (1995, December). *Vulnerability in stuttering children.* Mini Seminar presented at the annual convention of the American Speech Language Hearing Convention, Orlando, FL.

Peters, T., & Guitar, B. (1991). *Stuttering: An integrated approach to its nature and treatment.* Baltimore, MD: Williams & Wilkins.

Prins, D. (1983). Continuity, fragmentation and tension: Hypotheses applied to evaluation and intervention with preschool disfluent children. In D. Prins & R. Ingham (Eds.), *Treatment of stuttering in early childhood: Methods and issues* (pp. 21–42). San Diego, CA: College-Hill Press.

Prutting, C., & Kirchner, D. (1983). Applied pragmatics. In C. Prutting & T. Gallagher (Eds.), *Pragmatic assessment and intervention issues in language.* San Diego, CA: College Hill Press.

Riley, G. (1981). *Stuttering prediction instrument for young children.* Tigard, OR: C. C. Publications.

Riley, G., & Riley, J. (1979). A component model for diagnosing and treating children who stutter. *Journal of Fluency Disorders, 4,* 279–293.

Riley, G., & Riley, J. (1980). Motor and linguistic variables among children who stutter: A factor analysis. *Journal of Speech and Hearing Disorders, 45,* 504–514.

Riley, G., & Riley, J. (1983). Evaluation as a basis for intervention. In D. Prins & R. Ingham (Eds.), *Treatment of stuttering in early childhood: Methods and issues* (pp. 43–67). San Diego, CA: Singular.

Rustin, L., & Purser, H. (1991). Child development, families, and the problems of stuttering. In L. Rustin (Ed.), *Parents, families and the stuttering child* (pp. 1–39). Leicester, England: Far Communications.

Rutherford, D., & Telser, E. (1967, November). *Word-finding abilities of kindergarten and first-grade children.* Paper presented at the annual convention of the American Speech-Language-Hearing Association, Chicago, IL.

Schwartz, H., & Conture, E. (1988). Subgrouping young stutterers: Preliminary behavioral observations. *Journal of Speech and Hearing Research, 31,* 62–71.

Scott, L., Healey, E. C., & Norris, J. (1995). A comparison between children who stutter and their normally fluent peers on a story retelling task. *Journal of Fluency Disorders, 20,* 279–292.

Seider, R., Gladstien, K., & Kidd, K. (1983). Recovery and persistence of stuttering among relatives of stutterers. *Journal of Speech and Hearing Disorders, 48,* 402–409.

St. Louis, K., Murray, C., & Achworth, M. (1991). Coexisting communication disorders in a random sample of school-aged stutters. *Journal of Fluency Disorders, 16,* 13–23.

Starkweather, C. W. (1987). *Fluency and stuttering.* Englewood Cliffs, NJ: Prentice-Hall.

Starkweather, C. W., & Gottwald, S. R. (1995). Fluency intervention for preschoolers and their families in the public schools. *American Journal of Speech-Language Pathology, 26,* 117–124.

Starkweather, C. W., Gottwald, S. R., & Halfond, M. M. (1990). *Stuttering prevention: A clinical method.* Englewood Cliffs, NJ: Prentice-Hall.

Stein, N. (1988). The development of children's storytelling skills. In M. Franklin & S. Barton (Eds.). *Childhood language: A reader.* New York, NY: Oxford University Press.

Telser, E. (1971). *An assessment of word-finding skills in stuttering and non-stuttering children.* Unpublished doctoral dissertation, Northwestern University.

Van Riper, C. (1971). *The nature of stuttering.* Englewood Cliffs, NJ: Prentice-Hall.

Van Riper, C. (1973). *The treatment of stuttering.* Englewood Cliffs, NJ: Prentice-Hall.

Wall, M. (1980). A comparison of syntax in young stutteres and nonstutteres. *Journal of Fluency Disorders, 5,* 321–326.

Wall, M., & Myers, F. (1995). *Clinical management of childhood stuttering* (2nd ed.). Austin, TX: Pro-Ed.

Weiss, A. (1995). Conversational demands and their effects on fluency and stuttering. *Topics in Language Disorders, 15* (3), 18–31.

Weiss, A., & Zebrowski, P. (1991). Patterns of assertiveness and responsiveness in parental interactions with stuttering and fluent children. *Journal of Fluency Disorders, 16,* 125–143.

Williams, D. (1985). Emotional and environmental problems in stuttering. In J. Gruss (Ed.), *Stuttering therapy: Prevention and intervention with children.* (Publication No. 20). Memphis, TN: Stuttering Foundation of America.

Wingate, M. (1964). A standard definition of stuttering. *Journal of Speech and Hearing Disorders, 29,* 484–489.

Wyatt, G. (1969). *Learning and communication disorders in children.* New York: The Free Press.

Yairi, E. (1983). The onset of stuttering in two-year-old children: A preliminary report. *Journal of Speech and Hearing Disorders, 48,* 171–177.

Yairi, E. (1993). Epidemiologic and other considerations in treatment efficacy research with preschool age children who stutter. *Journal of Fluency Disorders, 18,* 197–219.

Yairi, E., & Ambrose, N. (1992). Onset of stuttering in preschool children: Selected factors. *Journal of Speech and Hearing Research, 35,* 782–788.

Yairi, E., Ambrose, N., & Nierman, R. (1993). The early months of stuttering: A developmental study. *Journal of Speech and Hearing Research, 36,* 521–528.

Yairi, E., Ambrose, N., Paden, E., & Throneburg, R. (1996). Predictive factors of persistence and recovery: Pathways of childhood stuttering. *Journal of Communication Disorders, 29,* 51–77.

Yaruss, J. S. & La Salle, L. R., & Conture, E. G. (1995). 100 children who stutter: Revisiting their clinical records. *Asha, 37,* 93.

Yaruss, J. S. & Conture, E. G. (1996). Stuttering and phonological disorders in children: Examination of the Covert Repair Hypothesis. *Journal of Speech and Hearing Research,*

39, 349–364.

Yaruss, J. S., & Hill, D. (1995, December). *Young children's speech fluency in different speaking situations.* Poster session presented at the annual convention of the American Speech-Language Hearing Association, Orlando, FL.

Yaruss, J. S., Logan, K., & Conture, E. G. (1993, November). *Differences between clinic and home measurement of stuttering.* Paper presented at the annual convention of the American Speech-Language-Hearing Association, Anaheim, CA.

Zebrowski, P. (1991). Duration of the speech disfluencies of beginning stutterers. *Journal of Speech and Hearing Research, 34,* 483–491.

Zebrowski, P. (1994). Stuttering. In J. Tomblin, H. Morris, & D. Spriestersbach (Eds.), *Diagnosis in speech-language pathology* (pp. 215–245). San Diego, CA: Singular.

13 Family Communication Patterns and Stuttering Development: An Analysis of the Research Literature

Sheryl Ridener Gottwald
New England Center For Speech-Language Services
Bedford, New Hampshire
and
The University of New Hampshire
Durham, New Hampshire

There appears to be widespread agreement about the benefits of early intervention for young children who stutter (Gregory & Hill, 1980; Lincoln, Onslow, & Reid, 1997; Starkweather & Gottwald, 1993). There are still varying opinions, however, about when early intervention should be initiated (Bernstein Ratner, 1997; Cooper & Cooper, 1996; Curlee & Yairi, 1997; Starkweather, 1997) and what the treatment components of an efficient early intervention program should include (Gregory & Hill, 1993; Lincoln & Onslow, 1997; Starkweather, Gottwald, & Halfond, 1990; Zebrowski, 1997). Furthermore, the relationship between family communication patterns, including the speech, language, and interaction patterns of significant people in the child's life, and the development of stuttering continues to be disputed (Starkweather & Gottwald, 1993; Yairi, 1997). Likewise, the benefits of family involvement in early intervention for stuttering are unclear. Some programs describe successful outcomes when family behavior change is a part of the early intervention plan (Adams, 1992; Starkweather, Gottwald, & Halfond, 1990; Zebrowski, Weiss, Savelkoul, & Hammer, 1996). Other early intervention programs have reported successful results when the child's speech behaviors alone are the focus of therapy (Onslow, Andrews, & Lincoln, 1994; Shine, 1984).

Examination of the impact of environmental variables on stuttering development occurs in the context of a long history of research studying the significance of parent input as it relates to child development. The language development literature is replete with studies examining the relationship between speech, language, and interaction patterns of parents and the language development of their children (Bailey & Simeonsson, 1988; Barnes, Gutfreund, Satterley, & Wells, 1983; Fernald, 1989; Moerk, 1974; Nelson, 1993; Yoder, 1986). Specific characteristics of parent input have been related to both language development and language disorders in young children (Fischer, 1987; Newport, Gleitman, & Gleitman, 1977; Rondal, 1978; Rosenberg & Robinson, 1988). For example, parental speech to typically developing young children is marked by higher pitch and exaggerated intonational patterns (Fernald & Kuhl, 1987), articulatory modifications (Bernstein

Ratner, 1987; Sachs, 1977), reduced sentence length (Newport et al. 1977), grammatical and semantic simplification (Snow, 1977), and structured turn taking (Schaffer, 1977). These modifications in parent communication style are considered to have a facilitating effect on language development (Fernald & Kuhl, 1987; Snow, 1977). For example, when an adult responds to an infant's vocalizations as if having a conversation with the infant, the type of sounds produced by the baby at 3 months become more speechlike in response (Bloom, 1988). When mothers interact more frequently and more responsively, the linguistic competencies of young children are enhanced (Spiker, Ferguson, & Brooks-Gunn, 1993).

The speech and interaction patterns of parents communicating with their youngsters with language impairment vary from that used with typical children (Brooks-Gunn & Lewis, 1984; Fraser, 1986; Yoder, 1986). Mothers of children with language impairment have been shown to be more directive and controlling, and to take the initiative in interactive sequences more often than mothers of normally developing children (Buckholt, Rutherford, & Goldberg, 1978). Mothers of children with Down Syndrome, for example, may speak faster to their children (Buckholt et al. 1978), may use shorter sentences (Rondal, 1978), and may talk more often (Buium, Rynders, & Turnure, 1974). Whether these variations in interaction behavior complicate or support development for the child with language disabilities continues to receive scrutiny in the research literature.

Likewise, the relationship between environmental variables, including family speech, language, and interaction behaviors, and the development of stuttering continues to receive critical examination. In a recent review of literature examining parent–child interactions in stuttering development, Yairi (1997) concluded that no significant differences existed in the home environments of children who do and do not stutter. However, research examining the incidence of stuttering in mono- and dizygotic twins supports the conclusion that genetics alone cannot account for the development of stuttering in all children (Ambrose, Cox, & Yairi, 1997). Monozygotic twins had a high but not a 100% concordance for stuttering (Andrews, Morris-Yates, Howie, & Martin, 1991). Such research has implications for the contribution of other variables, including environmental factors, when considering the onset and development of stuttering.

It is not surprising, then, that many speech-language professionals have discovered that environmental modifications for young children who stutter are beneficial (e.g., Kelly & Conture, 1992; Manning, 1996; Starkweather et al., 1990; Wall & Myers, 1995). Treatment progress is often achieved more rapidly and results maintained when the child's speech patterns and communicative environment are modified simultaneously (e.g., Gottwald & Starkweather, 1995; Winslow & Guitar, 1994). Unfortunately, empirical verification of such a model is still weak at best. There has been a significant amount of research examining the relationship between family interactions and children's stuttering; but as Nippold and Rudzinski (1995) suggested in a recent literature review, a clear relationship has not been demonstrated.

Problems With the Available Research

There are numerous factors that have contributed to our lack of knowledge in this realm despite the wealth of research information we have collected since the early 1960s. One of those factors may be directly related to the use of inferential statistics in our study of stuttering development and treatment. Many limitations are placed on interpretation of results when we use the null hypothesis and tests of statistical significance to measure the multiple factors felt to contribute to stuttering development (Attanasio, 1994; Starkweather, 1993). For example, reduction in stuttering as a treatment outcome is relatively easy to quantify in measurable terms. However, such reports of statistical significance in stuttering reduction are not always informative. Some treatment programs designed to reduce stuttering produce speech that is slower, more monotone in quality, and more noticeably different than the speech prior to therapy (Franken, van Bezooijen, & Boves, 1997). Adequate sample sizes, thorough investigation of all of the pertinent variables, rigorous control of intervening variables, and systematic replication are lacking in many of the research efforts to date.

In addition, we are sometimes led down the wrong track when results gleaned from tests of statistical significance are interpreted too broadly or too narrowly, or when insignificant findings are interpreted as if they have meaning. Interpretation of research results in the field of communication disorders is fraught with faulty application of inferential statistics. Attanasio (1994) pointed out that very few studies have truly random sampling, and generalization of results is often applied too liberally. Rejection of the null hypothesis is sometimes incorrectly interpreted as providing support for the alternative hypothesis. On the other hand, if the null hypothesis cannot be rejected, findings are frequently considered to be nonsignificant even if the raw data suggests otherwise. Attanasio (1994) noted that important research information can be easily disregarded when the focus is on statistical significance alone.

For example, one study found that parents asked more questions of their young children who stuttered whereas peer interaction was more negative (e.g., Meyers, 1990). Because stuttering frequency remained the same when the children communicated with their parents and their peers, the author concluded that children's fluency did not seem to be affected by either parent questions or peer negativity. However, there are certainly other ways those results might be interpreted. Perhaps both questions and negativity detrimentally affected the child's fluency; a change in both variables may have been related to decreases in stuttering. Alternative explanations for research findings should be identified as areas for exploration in future research efforts.

In a review of the literature concerning the role of parents' speech behaviors in relation to their children's stuttering, Nippold and Rudzinski (1995) concluded that there was little convincing evidence to prove that parents of children who stutter talk differently to their children than parents of children who do not stutter. These authors also found little objective support for the hypothesis that parent speech behaviors contribute to children's stuttering or that changes in parent behavior increase child fluency development.

However, a careful review of Nippold and Rudzinski's (1995) analysis further demonstrates the pitfalls that may result when utilizing inferential statistics to identify clinical significance. For example, the authors reviewed research reported by Weiss and Zebrowski (1992). One finding of this study was that children stuttered more when using assertive statements than when answering parent questions. Nippold and Rudzinski (1995) then concluded that the children (rather than the parents) "…may contribute to their own stuttering by attempting to produce utterances that challenge their current levels of linguistic competence or speech-motor capacities" (p. 984). What this interpretation did not consider was the role parents may play in structuring conversations for their children to help reduce the linguistic demands that result from language assertiveness. The parent interaction strategy of scaffolding or formatting conversational interchanges, as described by Bruner (1983), was not considered in the Weiss and Zebrowski (1992) study and may have played an important role in the results obtained. In addition, Nippold and Rudzinski (1995) assumed that children answer their parents' questions primarily with short, often single word responses. The Weiss and Zebrowski (1992) study did not provide information about the relationship between parent questions requiring longer responses and the presence of stuttering in children's speech. It is quite possible that the children in the study would have stuttered more when answering questions with responses that were more linguistically complex.

Another example provides support for the contention that important and clinically relevant information may be lost or downplayed in our attempt to focus on statistically significant results. Nippold and Rudzinski (1995) accurately reported Kelly and Conture's (1992) findings that the fathers of boys who stuttered did not differ from the fathers of boys who did not stutter in the fathers' rate of speech, number of interruptions, or response time latency. What Nippold and Rudzinski's (1995) critical review failed to report is that Kelly and Conture (1992) did find a statistically significant difference between the speech behaviors of fathers whose sons had a mild stuttering problem and those fathers whose sons stuttered more severely. Nippold and Rudzinski (1995) summarized this study's results by saying the "…results do not support the view that parents' speech behaviors contribute to children's stuttering" (p. 984). Because there were significant differences between fathers of children who stuttered, it is possible that the speech behaviors of fathers whose children have more advanced stuttering are in some way related to the stuttering problem. It is not clear if the differing speech patterns were a response to the child's stuttering, if they contributed to the development of the problem, if they maintained the problem once it began, or if they were unrelated to the problem. Nippold and Rudzinski (1995) failed to identify these as viable questions stemming from Kelly and Conture's (1992) research findings.

The study of environmental variables related to stuttering development is an immense one. Researchers and clinicians have identified numerous factors that may potentially impact fluency development, including parent speech behaviors, family interaction patterns, family reactions to stuttering, and family lifestyle characteristics. Some of these variables are listed in Table 13.1. In addition to the large number of variables, many are likely to be interrelated as well. It is difficult to extract clinically applicable conclusions from research attempts when the breadth of study is so wide and the number of studies is so limited in any one area.

PARENT SPEECH BEHAVIORS

1. rate of fluent speech
2. pace of conversation
3. kind and number of questions
4. length and complexity of sentences

FAMILY INTERACTION PATTERNS

1. turn-taking
2. quality time for talking
3. topic initiations and changes
4. requests for verbal performance

FAMILY REACTIONS TO STUTTERING

1. negative comments
2. instructions to speak otherwise
3. negative feelings expressed implicitly

FAMILY LIFESTYLE CHARACTERISTICS

1. structured versus unstructured
2. high versus low expectations
3. stable versus unstable
4. clear versus confusing discipline

TABLE 13.1. Some Environmental Factors Which May Impact Fluency Development

As a research community, there is little commonality in the way investigators in the area of stuttering choose and describe subject populations, and collect research data. Some studies have attempted to compare the speech of parents whose children stutter with the speech of parents whose children do not stutter (e.g., Kasprisin-Burelli, Egolf, & Shames, 1972; Kloth, Janssen, Kraaimaat, & Brutten, 1995; Langlois, Hanrahan, & Inouye, 1986). Differences in parent speech behavior, if they exist, are then interpreted to be related to the presence or absence of stuttering. In some studies, for example, variables such as parent speech rate, use of questions and use of interruptions seemed to occur more frequently in the speech of mothers or fathers whose children stuttered. There were many other variables in these studies, such as the match between parent and child interaction styles, that were not controlled for but that may have had as much of an impact on the child's stuttering as the variables under study. Obviously, we need additional research to continue to weed out these insignificant factors.

Research examining the impact of environmental variables on stuttering development has largely been conducted and interpreted in a vacuum. The large body of literature describing parent–child interaction characteristics in other fields (e.g., language disorders, cognitive deficits, developmental delay) is rarely consulted by researchers in stuttering (Bernstein Ratner, 1993). This is true despite the fact that the majority of these studies demonstrate that parents of children with disabilities interact differently with their children than parents of typical children (e.g., Brooks-Gunn & Lewis, 1984; Conti-Ramsden, Hutcheson, & Grove, 1995; Cunningham, Reuler, Blackwell, & Deck, 1981). It is likely that differences in parent speech behaviors seen when parents interact with their young stuttering children mirror those interaction characteristics of parents whose children have a variety of developmental difficulties (Bernstein Ratner, 1993). For example, parents of children with Down Syndrome have been observed to speak more rapidly to their children than do parents of typically developing children (Buckholt et al., 1978). Parent speech rate has been identified as a critical factor in childhood stuttering as well (Gottwald & Starkweather, 1995; Kelly, 1994; Meyers & Freeman, 1985a). The speech and interaction behaviors of parents to their stuttering children are not necessarily unique. Until control groups include more than just fluent children and their parents (i.e., children with other developmental difficulties, including communication problems), we will not know how singular the patterns are that we have extracted.

The literature on child development and parent interaction behavior highlights the importance of considering the child's as well as the parent's contributions to the interaction. Snow and Ferguson (1977) and others (Bruner, 1983; Tomasello, & Farrar, 1986) indicated that early reciprocal interactions between parent and child play a key role in the child's communication development. Interactions that are bidirectional and occur in an evolving way are most facilitating. What appears to be important is not what the parent does or what the child does, but instead, the reactions of each to the other's behavior (Mahoney & Powell, 1988).

Using the sizable literature on language-disordered children and their parents as a reference, it is clear that the relationship between parent speech behavior and child performance is not a linear one. That is, parent interaction behavior most likely does not exist in isolation but in direct response to child behavior. For example, Marfo (1991) found that mothers took more turns and assumed more responsibility for topic control with children who showed less initiative in social interactions. In a study by Whitehurst et al. (1988), parents of late talkers spent more time talking and used more labels than parents of children in the control group. Studies such as these point out the importance of looking at the child's behavior, which may then trigger a modified set of parent interaction behaviors.

Meyers and Freeman (1985b) identified this relationship between child speech behavior and adult interaction variables when they examined interrupting behavior with children who stuttered. These researchers showed that parents and strangers interrupted children who stuttered more often when the child was disfluent. It was the child's stuttering that precipitated the interruption, and not that the parents of children who stutter interrupt more frequently in general.

Another way that the field has attempted to study parent speech behaviors with stuttering children is by examining the efficacy of treatment programs that employ environmental modification as part or all of the intervention plan. When the child's fluency improved, credit was then given in whole or in part to family involvement in the therapy process (e.g., Langlois & Long, 1988; Starkweather et al., 1990). Once again, controlling all of the potentially pertinent factors in order to assess the effects of family involvement is a formidable task. Without control groups to account for each pertinent factor and a large enough sample size, we are not able to confidently sort out the critical variables contributing to successful treatment.

For example, treatment programs describing successful early intervention for children who stutter often fail to consider the high probability that many of those children would have spontaneously recovered without help (Yairi, 1997). Curlee and Yairi (1997) reported that even despite severe stuttering in the first 6 months of onset, as many as 89% of preschoolers who stutter will recover without intervention. Factors that predict which preschoolers will continue to stutter and which will recover, including time spent stuttering, sex of the child, family history of stuttering, and the presence of other developmental problems, are beginning to be identified (Yairi, Ambrose, Paden, & Throneburg, 1996). These factors need to be carefully considered when evaluating the success of any intervention plan, including parent speech and interaction behavior change.

There are many other ways in which we have attempted to examine the relationship between environmental variables and stuttering development, including comparison of the speech of mothers and fathers of children who stutter (e.g., Kelly, 1995; Kelly & Conture, 1992); of parents and peers of children who stutter (Meyers, 1990); of mothers before and after stuttering developed in their children (Kloth et al., 1995); and of parents of children with mild versus severe stuttering problems (Kelly, 1994). Despite the fact that research efforts to date have been quite divergent, making comparisons among studies difficult, some factors have emerged that provide support for including environmental modification in treatment programs for young children who stutter. Two of these factors are discussed in the next part of this chapter.

RELATIONSHIP BETWEEN PARENT SPEECH RATE AND CHILD FLUENCY

Adult speech rate and its relationship to child fluency levels is one variable that has received repeated attention in the research literature to date (Kelly, 1994; Kelly & Conture, 1992; Meyers & Freeman, 1985a). Research comparing the rate with which parents talk to children who do and do not stutter is inconclusive. Meyers and Freeman (1985a) reported that mothers of children who stuttered spoke faster to their children than mothers of children who did not stutter. Conversely, in a study conducted by Kelly and Conture (1992), mothers of children who stuttered did not speak significantly faster than mothers of nonstuttering children. However, mothers of children who stuttered more closely matched their children's speech rates than did the mothers of nonstuttering children. Kelly and Conture (1992) hypothesized that this occurred because of the mother's awareness on some level that the child's speech system was unable to meet the demands of a faster speech model. This possibility emphasizes the importance of the quality of the match between parent models and the child's ability levels rather than of the absolute rate measures of the parents.

By the mid-1980s, the demands and capacities model (Adams, 1990) helped clinicians and researchers view stuttering development not solely as the child's problem or the environment's problem, but as a result of the interaction between the two. At least two research efforts examined relative speech rates, that is the difference between the absolute rate measures for the parent and those for the child. Kelly (1994) examined the relative speech rates of fathers and their sons who stuttered. She found that boys who had higher (more severe) scores on the Stuttering Severity Instrument (SSI, Riley, 1986) also demonstrated more divergent dyadic speech rates when playing with their fathers. That is, boys who stuttered more severely had fathers who talked much more quickly than their sons did. Yaruss and Conture (1995) found the same effects when examining the interaction between children who stuttered and their mothers. Mothers of children with more advanced stuttering spoke much more quickly than did their children. These findings do not necessarily support the notion that parent speech behaviors, such as rate, caused the stuttering problem. But these results do support the transactional nature of interaction. They underline the importance of looking at the relationship between child and parent communication behaviors when examining stuttering development rather than studying either set of behaviors in a static way.

Research thus suggests that parent–child rate differences and child stuttering severity may be related. Several other research attempts have looked at the effect of reducing parent rate on child fluency levels. Stephenson-Opsal and Bernstein Ratner (1988) found that reductions in parental speech rate correlated with reductions in child stuttering for two cases studied longitudinally using single subject design. Two subsequent studies, one conducted by Guitar, Schaefer, Donahue-Kilburg, & Bond (1992) and the second reported by Starkweather and Gottwald (1993), also showed significant positive correlations between reduction in parental speech rate and reduction in child disfluency levels.

Interruptions as a Variable in Fluency

Another interaction variable that has been a focus of a number of research efforts involves conversational turn taking. Clinicians have long felt that having to compete for the conversational floor or having to worry about losing the conversational floor significantly increases speech anxiety for children. This speech anxiety then may demonstrate itself in increased disfluency. Parents have been counseled to modify turn-taking patterns to decrease struggled disfluencies in their children (e.g., Ainsworth & Fraser, 1988; Starkweather & Gottwald, 1990).

Several studies describing the turn-taking behavior of parents and their children who stutter may lend support to this clinical recommendation. As early as

1972, Kasprisin-Burelli, Egolf, and Shames demonstrated that parents of children who stutter interrupted their children more frequently than parents communicating with their children who did not stutter. Mordecai (1979) observed that parents of children who stuttered often asked questions that were followed up immediately with a second question or comment. Before the child could respond to the initial request, the parent took a second turn. Meyers and Freeman (1985b) also found that mothers of stuttering and nonstuttering children tended to interrupt disfluent speech more often than they interrupted the fluent speech of their children. All of the children in this study were more disfluent when interrupted and also when interrupting others.

However, Kelly and Conture (1992) reported conflicting findings. The children in their study were rarely disfluent when they interrupted and mothers were unlikely to interrupt during a child's disfluent episode. These researchers did find a positive relationship between higher SSI scores and longer simultalk durations. That is, mothers who talked for longer periods simultaneously with their children, had children with more advanced stuttering. Thus, it may not be the interruption alone that stresses fluency; rather, it may be the amount of time that there is confusion about whose turn it is that ultimately detracts from fluency.

Several studies have examined the effectiveness of modifying turn taking to increase child fluency levels. Langlois and Long (1988) reported a case study in which reductions in stuttering occurred with a therapy program that included establishing an equal number of parent and child speaking turns. Winslow and Guitar (1994) also reported on a case study that found that when the child's family applied clear turn taking rules, the child demonstrated fewer disfluencies. In both studies, the authors hypothesized that applying turn-taking rules increased conversational structure and predictability; this may have reduced the child's tension level, which then made it easier for the child to speak without stuttering.

VIEWING THE FLUENCY ENVIRONMENT FROM A SYSTEMS PERSPECTIVE

Nippold and Rudzinski (1995) suggested that research to date does not support the notion that parents of children who stutter speak differently, or that parent speech behaviors contribute to children's stuttering. However, the research reviewed here identifies several environmental factors that do appear to be related to fluency development for some children. Individually, these variables are still isolated pieces of information that may function very differently if considered as one part of a system or gestalt. Polkinghorne (1983) suggested that it is often misleading to study a multicomponent process solely by examining its individual parts. It may not be the inherent quality of the single element that carries significance but the relationship of the elements in the whole. We may therefore want to look, not at individual or static segments such as parent speech rate or family turn-taking behavior, but at the relationship of these segments and the interaction of these segments with one another.

A child grows and develops in the context of a family system. Considering the family as a system is helpful in understanding the complex influences of the family on an individual and vice versa (Cornwell & Korteland, 1996). Interactions in the family system are not linear but circular; the behaviors of one member of the family directly affect the responses of each of the other members in a reciprocal and interactive way. Therefore, the family system is constantly evolving; changing the behavior of one member consequently changes the behavior of all members.

In addition, this family system interacts with a number of other environmental systems that impact the development of each individual member. Other systems to consider when examining the development of stuttering might include the preschool, the neighborhood, and the child-care systems, whose interrelationships also affect each individual member. When changing one aspect of the system, one must consider its effects on the other components of the system to ensure effective results that are maintained over time. When considering the development and treatment of childhood stuttering from a family systems perspective, it is critical to address family interaction variables that may be contributing to stuttering, and that modified, could palliate symptoms. For example, if a parent responds immediately when the child stutters, the child may learn to stutter to get the parent's attention more quickly. When the child goes to preschool, he may transfer this learned behavior, and stutter more when attempting to get the teacher's attention. Developing new interaction patterns both at home and at school, so that adult attention is not contingent on stuttering, might help to reduce the "need" to stutter. If one changes interaction patterns at home but not at school, the child's stuttering patterns may not change. One might then assume that environmental modification was ineffective. However, if the problem had been approached from a systems perspective, the treatment paradigm would have included both home and preschool environments. With this broader application, it is more likely that positive changes in fluency would be realized.

When attempting to examine the family as a system, well-defined case studies and qualitative research efforts will allow a more holistic and evolving view of the environment and its relationship to developing fluency. For example, in any individual family, modifying parent rate alone may be insignificant in changing child fluency levels. It may still be true that it is critical for the parents to modify rate when conversing with their child in the car or during other more stressful communication times. Likewise, reductions in parent rate may only prove fruitful if the child's day-care providers also use a slower rate of speech when conversing with the child. A researcher using repeated parent interviews and family observation as part of a qualitative study would be more likely to extract information about the interrelatedness of factors in this area.

DIRECTIONS FOR FUTURE RESEARCH

The information we have collected thus far provides us with a solid foundation on which we can base future research efforts. One focus might be continued examination of the impact of family reactions to their children who stutter (Zebrowski & Schum, 1993). Through family interviews and observation of family systems over time, we may be able to identify why parents of children who stutter may use more negative statements when conversing with their children, as suggested by Kasprisin-Burelli et al. (1972). These researchers found that parents of children who stuttered more often used language with negative implications, such as sarcasm, interruptions, and negative advice when talking to their children than did parents of nonstuttering children. Understanding the impact that such negative comments may have on the development of the stuttering problem may provide useful insights for intervention. Identifying the degree to which family members project their own worries and expectations for the future onto the child who stutters and the effect of that transference on the child's developing fluency skills will help us isolate affective variables that may be critical to address in therapy (Manning, 1996).

Understanding and addressing a family's feelings and attitudes about stuttering development is a first step in helping the family to manage the child's fluency needs more directly and proactively. When this author and a colleague ran a parent group over a 7-year period at Temple University in Philadelphia, the overriding topics of discussion were the strong feelings of fear, frustration, and anger that parents expressed in response to their children's stuttering. When parents are weighted down by a whole host of negative feelings related to their child's stuttering problem, it is easy to understand how they might be inclined to interact more negatively toward the source of their discomfort — the child. Having an opportunity to express and explore those feelings may have allowed parents the freedom to separate their feelings from their behavior, and thus to be able to focus more fully on addressing their children's fluency needs. Future research would help us understand the importance of addressing such parent feelings and the effectiveness of using a group setting to do so.

Not every family is able to make all of the environmental modifications that might be beneficial for the child's fluency development. The stories of two different families provide good examples of each end of the spectrum. One family was committed to working together for the benefit of their 5-year-old from the outset. The parents and the boy's older brothers participated in therapy continuously; as a family unit, they practiced strategies such as using a slowed conversation pace and more structured turn taking. They took an active role in deciding which strategies were realistic ones for them and which were not.

A second family also appeared willing to make changes in their home environment to make it easier for their 5-year-old to speak without struggling. Although they agreed with every clinical recommendation, they came up with few suggestions on their own. Each week they would come back to therapy with reasons why they were unable to accomplish the strategies that were agreed on the week before. In reality, the parents had their own agenda for their child, which was quite different from the clinician's. They wanted their child to be the best athlete in town and the top of his kindergarten class academically. The parents took great pride in teaching him to count higher, to know more facts, and to create better products than his school peers. A considerable amount of time was spent in counseling with this family, but in the end, they made very few environmental changes.

It would be extremely useful to know how to determine which families are more likely to be able to make environmental modifications to support their child's developing fluency. With the second family described earlier, the clinician's time may have been more efficiently utilized by working more intensively with the child to strengthen capacities and asking less of his family in the form of reducing demands. Although a combination of environmental modification and direct treatment is described as an efficient way to manage early stuttering (Starkweather et al., 1990), there is evidence that direct stuttering treatment alone can be effective as well (Lincoln et al., 1997). In the interest of time-efficient intervention, it would be extremely useful to have a method for determining how much and what kind of family involvement would be optimal for any individual family.

As noted previously, narrowing parent and child speech rate differences and increasing turn-taking structure appear to be related to decreases in child stuttering. There is also some indication that when children are more assertive with language, stuttering increases (e.g., Weiss & Zebrowski, 1992). However, many early intervention programs currently recommend following the child's conversational lead (Gottwald & Starkweather, 1995). The rationale for this recommendation rests on the assumption that language and communication pressure might be increased if the child is asked to talk about something he or she is not prepared to discuss. However, recommending a "child lead" model places primary responsibility on the child for structuring conversational interchanges with family members. The demands for assertive language use may be raised when children take the lead in conversations. Understanding the effect of the use of assertive language on developing fluency would directly impact recommendations made to families about preferred interaction styles.

Once an assertive statement has been made by a child, it might be beneficial to examine the ensuing conversational interchange between the child and the adult. The assertive statement itself may not place as much strain on fluency as do the language demands that ensue from discussion of the assertive statement. If the parent scaffolds the conversation, providing structure for the interchange, the language demands on the child will be reduced and fluency may be enhanced. If, on the other hand, the parent remains a passive listener, the linguistic demands of the child's monologue may exceed his capacities, which then may contribute to fluency breakdown. If the parent remains quiet in an attempt to allow the child time to formulate and express his ideas, the responsibility for telling a story rests solely on the child's shoulders. This higher level of linguistic demand could result in considerable stuttering. However, if the parent helps structure the conversation so that the child has a better chance of talking within his linguistic capacity level, fluency breakdown might be less likely. Further research would help us better understand the benefits of scaffolding to reduce the fluency demands that characterize child-initiated interactions. The use of questions by family members also warrants additional attention. Although Weiss and Zebrowski (1992) reported that children's responses to parent questions contained only a small number of disfluencies, they also noted that the question responses were short in length as well. Because utterance length and perhaps the assertive weight of the response may affect fluency, it would be useful to look again at questions that require longer answers and/or content of higher propositional impact. The syntactic demands of question responses, especially for younger children, may also be a factor to consider when examining the impact of questions on fluency. It is likely that having to answer the question, "Why did you beat Billy up at school today?" might result in more stuttering than, "Do you want vanilla or chocolate ice cream for dessert?"

CONCLUSIONS

The relationship among environmental variables, including parent speech and language behaviors, and stuttering development in childhood continues to be a topic of debate. Some of the difficulties encountered when studying the multiple environmental variables that may impact fluency development were identified in this chapter. The use of inferential statistics requires adequate sample sizes, consideration of all of the pertinent and intervening variables, and replication for reliable and valid results. Unfortunately, many of the studies examining the effects of the environment on fluency are lacking in one or more of these areas. In addition, there is little commonality in the way in which researchers have attempted to study this question. The speech patterns of mothers whose children stutter have been compared to the speech patterns of mothers whose children speak normally; to the interactions of fathers of stuttering children; and to their own speech patterns prior to the onset of stuttering in their children. It is extremely difficult to extract commonalities when research efforts are scattered across such a wide spectrum of topics.

Research examining two environmental variables that appear to be related to fluency development and/or stuttering treatment was reviewed. Studies comparing the rate with which parents talk to children who do and do not stutter is inconclusive. However, recent research efforts suggest that stuttering severity may be related to parent–child rate differences rather than to the parents' absolute rate measures alone. In addition, reductions in parent rate have been associated with reductions in child stuttering. Some studies have reported a positive relationship between child stuttering and interruptions by adults. Others have noted a relationship between talking time overlap (when parent and child talked simultaneously) and increased stuttering. Still other researchers have reported increases in fluency when turn taking rules are applied to reduce the threat of interruptions.

Recommendations for a more descriptive approach to data collection in this area were made. Qualitative research efforts should consider the interrelatedness of variables that characterize human behavior. The child's fluency skills develop in the context of an evolving family system that is intimately connected with a variety of other systems (i.e., neighborhood, preschool, child-care settings). A change in one part of the system affects all participants in a reciprocal way. Attempting to treat a child's stuttering problem without considering the systems within which the child communicates may result in less successful and/or perhaps less efficient treatment paradigms.

REFERENCES

Adams, M. R. (1990). The demands and capacities model I: Theoretical elaborations. *Journal of Fluency Disorders, 15,* 135–141.

Adams, M. R. (1992). Childhood stuttering under "positive" conditions. *American Journal of Speech-Language Pathology, 1,* 5–6.

Ainsworth, S., & Fraser, J. (Eds.). (1988). *If your child stutters: A guide for parents* (3rd ed.). Memphis, TN: Speech Foundation of America.

Ambrose, N. G., Cox, N., & Yairi, E. (1997). The genetic basis of persistence and recovery in stuttering. *Journal of Speech-Language-Hearing Research, 40*(3), 567–580.

Andrews, G., Morris-Yates, A., Howie, P., & Martin, N. (1991). Genetic factors in stuttering confirmed. *Archives of General Psychiatry, 48,* 1034–1035.

Attanasio, J. S. (1994). Inferential statistics and treatment efficacy studies in communication disorders. *Journal of Speech and Hearing Research, 37*(4), 755–759.

Bailey, D. B., & Simeonsson, R. J. (1988). *Family assessment in early intervention.* Columbus, OH: Merrill.

Barnes, S., Gutfreund, M., Satterley, D., & Wells, D. (1983). Characteristics of adult speech which predict children's language development. *Journal of Child Language, 10,* 65–84.

Bernstein Ratner, N. (1993). Parents, children and fluency. *Seminars in Speech and Language, 14*(3), 238–250.

Bernstein Ratner, N. (1987). The phonology of parent–child speech. In K. Nelson & A. van Kleeck (Eds.), *Children's Language,* (Vol. 6, pp. 13–24). Hillsdale, NJ: Lawrence Erlbaum Associates.

Bernstein Ratner, N. (1997). Leaving Las Vegas: Clinical odds and individual outcomes. *American Journal of Speech-Language Pathology, 6,* 29–33.

Bloom, K. (1988). Quality of adult vocalizations affects the quality of infant vocalizations. *Journal of Child Language, 15,* 469–480.

Brooks-Gunn, J., & Lewis, M. (1984). Maternal responsivity in interactions with handicapped infants. *Child Development, 55,* 782–793.

Bruner, J. (1983). *Child's talk: Learning to use language.* New York: Norton.

Buckholt, J. A., Rutherford, R. B., & Goldberg, K. E. (1978). Verbal and nonverbal interaction of mothers with their Down's Syndrome and nonretarded infants. *American Journal of Mental Deficiency, 82*(4), 337–343.

Buium, N., Rynders, J., & Turnure, J. (1974). Early maternal linguistic environment of normal and Down's syndrome language-learning children. *American Journal of Mental Deficiency, 79,* 52–58.

Conti-Ramsden, G., Hutcheson, G. D., & Grove, J. (1995). Contingency and breakdown: Children with SLI and their conversations with mothers and fathers. *Journal of Speech and Hearing Research, 38,* 1290–1302.

Cooper, E., & Cooper, C. (1996). Clinician attitudes toward stuttering: Two decades of change. *Journal of Fluency Disorders, 21*(2), 119–136.

Cornwell, J., & Korteland, C. (1996). The family as a system and a context for early intervention. In S. K. Thurman, J. R. Cornwell, & S. R. Gottwald (Eds.), *Contexts of early intervention* (pp. 93–110). Baltimore, MD: Brookes.

Cunningham, C. E., Reuler, E., Blackwell, J., & Deck, J. (1981). Behavioral and linguistic development in the interactions of normal and retarded children with their mothers. *Child Development, 52,* 62–70.

Curlee, R. F., & Yairi, E. (1997). Early intervention with early childhood stuttering: A critical examination of the data. *American Journal of Speech-Language Pathology, 6*(2), 8–18.

Fernald, A. (1989). Intonation and communicative intent in mothers' speech to infants: Is the melody the message? *Child Development, 60,* 1497–1510.

Fernald, A., & Kuhl, P. K. (1987). Acoustic determinants of infant preference for motherese speech. *Infant Behavior and Development, 10,* 279–293.

Fischer, M. (1987). Mother–child interactions in preverbal children with Down syndrome. *Journal of Speech and Hearing Disorders, 52,* 179–190.

Franken, M. C., van Bezooijen, R., & Boves, L. (1997). Stuttering and communicative suitability of speech. *Journal of Speech, Language, and Hearing Research, 40,* 83–94.

Fraser, B. C. (1986). Child impairment and parent/infant communication. *Child: Care, Health, and Development, 12,* 141–150.

Gottwald, S. R., & Starkweather, C. W. (1995). Fluency intervention for preschoolers and their families in the public schools. *Language, Speech and Hearing Services In Schools, 11,* 117–126.

Gregory, H., & Hill, D. (1980). Stuttering therapy for children. *Seminars in Speech, Language, and Hearing, 1,* 351–364.

Gregory, H., & Hill, D. (1993). Differential evaluation - differential therapy for stuttering children. In R. Curlee (Ed.), *Stuttering and related disorders of fluency* (pp. 23–44). New York: Thieme Medical Publishers.

Guitar, B., Schaefer, H. K., Donahue-Kilburg, G., & Bond, L. (1992). Parent verbal interactions and speech rate: A case study in stuttering. *Journal of Speech and Hearing Research, 35,* 742–754.

Kasprisin-Burelli, A., Egolf, D. B., & Shames, G. H. (1972). A comparison of parental verbal behavior with stuttering and nonstuttering children. *Journal of Communication Disorders, 5,* 335–346.

Kelly, E. M. (1994). Speech rates and turn-taking behaviors of children who stutter and their fathers. *Journal of Speech and Hearing Research, 37,* 1284–1294.

Kelly, E. M. (1995). Parents as partners: Including mothers and fathers in the treatment of children who stutter. *Journal of Communication Disorders, 28*(2), 93–106.

Kelly, E. M., & Conture, E. G. (1992). Speaking rates, response time latencies, and interrupting behaviors of young stutterers, nonstutterers, and their mothers. *Journal of Speech and Hearing Research, 35,* 1256–1267.

Kloth, S. A. M., Janssen, P., Kraaimaat, F. W., & Brutten, G. J. (1995). Communicative behavior of mothers of stuttering and nonstuttering children prior to the onset of stuttering. *Journal of Fluency Disorders, 20,* 365–377.

Langlois, A., Hanrahan, L., & Inouye, L. L. (1986). A comparison of interactions between stuttering children, nonstuttering children, and their mothers. *Journal of Fluency Disorders, 11,* 263–273.

Langlois, A., & Long, S. H. (1988). A model for teaching parents to facilitate fluent speech. *Journal of Fluency Disorders, 13,* 163–172.

Lincoln, M. A., & Onslow, M. (1997). Long-term outcome of early intervention for stuttering. *American Journal of Speech-Language Pathology, 6*(1), 51–58.

Lincoln, M., Onslow, M., & Reid, V. (1997). Social validity of the treatment outcomes of an early intervention program for stuttering. *American Journal of Speech-Language Pathology, 6*(2), 77–84.

Mahoney, G., & Powell, A. (1988). Modifying parent–child interaction: Enhancing the development of handicapped children. *Journal of Special Education, 22,* 82–96.

Manning, W. H. (1996). *Clinical decision making in the diagnosis and treatment of fluency disorders.* Albany, NY: Delmar.

Marfo, K. (1991). Maternal directiveness in interactions with mentally handicapped children: An analytical commentary. *Journal of Child Psychology and Psychiatry, 31,* 531–549.

Meyers, S. C. (1990). Verbal behaviors of preschool stutterers and conversational partners: Observing reciprocal relationships. *Journal of Speech and Hearing Disorders, 55,* 706–712.

Meyers, S. C., & Freeman, F. J. (1985a). Are mothers of stutterers different? An investigation of social-communicative interaction. *Journal of Fluency Disorders, 10,* 193–209.

Meyers, S. C., & Freeman, F. J. (1985b). Interruptions as a variable in stuttering and disfluency. *Journal of Speech and Hearing Research, 28,* 436–444.

Moerk, E. (1974). Changes in verbal child–mother interactions with increasing language skills of the child. *Journal of Psycholinguistic Research, 3,* 101–116.

Mordecai, D. R. (1979). An investigation of the communicative styles of mothers and fathers of stuttering versus nonstuttering preschool children. *Dissertation Abstracts International, 40*(10), 4759-B.

Nelson, N. W. (1993). *Childhood language disorders in context: Infancy through adolescence.* New York: Macmillan.

Newport, A., Gleitman, H., & Gleitman, C. (1977). Mother, I'd rather do it myself: Some effects and non-effects of maternal speech style. In C. Snow & C. Ferguson (Eds.), *Talking to children: Language input and acquisition* (pp. 109–147). Cambridge, England: Cambridge University Press.

Nippold, M. A., & Rudzinski, M. (1995). Parents' speech and children's stuttering: A critique of the literature. *Journal of Speech and Hearing Research, 38,* 978–989.

Onslow, M., Andrews, C., & Lincoln, M. (1994). A control/experimental trial of an operant treatment for early stuttering. *Journal of Speech and Hearing Research, 37,* 1244–1259.

Polkinghorne, D. (1983). *Methodology for the human sciences: Systems of inquiry.* Albany: State University of New York Press.

Riley, G. D. (1986). *The stuttering severity instrument.* Tigard, OR: CC Publications.

Rondal, J. (1978). Maternal speech to normal and Down's syndrome children matched for mean utterance length. In C. Meyers (Ed.), *Quality of life in severely and profoundly mentally retarded people: Research foundations for improvement* (pp. 193–265). Washington, DC: American Association on Mental Deficiency.

Rosenberg, S., & Robinson, C. (1988). Interactions of parents with their young handicapped children. In S. Odom & M. Karnes (Eds.), *Early intervention for infants and children with handicaps* (pp. 34–50). Baltimore, MD: Brookes.

Sachs, J. (1977). The adaptive significance of linguistic input to prelinguistic infants. In C. Snow & C. Ferguson (Eds.), *Talking to children: Language input and acquisition* (pp. 51–62). Cambridge, England: Cambridge University Press.

Schaffer, H. (1977). Early interactive development. In H. Schaffer (Ed.), *Studies in mother–infant interaction* (pp. 3–16). New York: Academic Press.

Shine, R. (1984). Assessment and fluency training with the young stutterer. In M. Peins (Ed.), *Contemporary approaches in stuttering therapy.* Boston: Little Brown.

Snow, C. (1977). The development of conversation between mothers and babies. *Journal of Child Language, 4,* 1–22.

Snow, C., & Ferguson, C. (1977). *Talking to children: Language input and acquisition.* Cambridge, England: Cambridge University Press.

Spiker, D., Ferguson, J., & Brooks-Gunn, J. (1993). Enhancing maternal interactive behavior and child social competence in low birth weight, premature infants. *Child Development, 64,* 754–768.

Starkweather, C. W. (1993). Issues in therapy efficacy research. *Journal of Fluency Disorders, 18,* 151–168.

Starkweather, C. W. (1997). Therapy for younger children. In R. Curlee & G. Siegel (Eds.), *Nature and treatment of stuttering: New directions.* Boston: Allyn & Bacon.

Starkweather, C. W., & Gottwald, S. R. (1990). The demands and capacities model II: Clinical implications. *Journal of Fluency Disorders, 15,* 143–157.

Starkweather, C. W., & Gottwald, S. R. (1993). A pilot study of relations among specific measures obtained at intake and discharge in a program of prevention and early intervention for stuttering. *American Journal of Speech-Language Pathology, 2*(1), 51–58.

Starkweather, C. W., Gottwald, S. R., & Halfond, M. M. (1990). *Stuttering prevention: A clinical method.* Englewood Cliffs, NJ: Prentice-Hall.

Stephenson-Opsal, D., & Bernstein Ratner, Nan. (1988). Maternal speech rate modification and childhood stuttering. *Journal of Fluency Disorders, 13*(1), 49–56.

Tomasello, M., & Farrar, M. J. (1986). Joint attention and early language. *Child Development, 57,* 1454–1463.

Wall, M. J., & Myers, F. L. (1995). *Clinical management of childhood stuttering* (2nd ed.). Austin, TX: Pro-Ed.

Weiss, A. L., & Zebrowski, P. M. (1992). Disfluencies in the conversations of young children who stutter: Some answers about questions. *Journal of Speech and Hearing Research, 35,* 1230–1238.

Whitehurst, G. J., Fischel, J. E., Lonigan, C. J., Valdez-Menchaca, M. C., DeBaryshe, B. D., & Caulfield, M. B. (1988). Verbal interaction in families of normal and expressive-language-delayed children. *Developmental Psychology, 24,* 690–699.

Winslow, H., & Guitar, B. (1994). The effects of structured turn-taking on disfluencies: A case study. *Language, Speech and Hearing Services in Schools, 25,* 251–257.

Yairi, E. (1997). Home environments and parent–child interaction in childhood stuttering. In R. Curlee & G. Siegel (Eds.), *Nature and treatment of stuttering: New directions.* Boston: Allyn & Bacon.

Yairi, E., Ambrose, N. G., Paden, E. P., & Throneburg, R. N. (1996). Predictive factors of persistence and recovery: Pathways of childhood stuttering. *Journal of Communication Disorders, 29,* 51–77.

Yaruss, J. S., & Conture, E. G. (1995). Mother and child speaking rates and utterance lengths in adjacent fluent utterances: Preliminary observations. *Journal of Fluency Disorders, 20,* 257–278.

Yoder, P. (1986). Clarifying the relation between degree of infant handicap and maternal responsivity to infant communicative cues: Measurement issues. *Infant Mental Health Journal, 7*(4),281–293.

Zebrowski, P. M. (1997). Assisting young children who stutter and their families: Defining the role of the speech-language pathologist. *American Journal of Speech-Language Pathology, 6,* 19–28.

Zebrowski, P. M., & Schum, R. L. (1993). Counseling parents of children who stutter. *American Journal of Speech-Language Pathology, 2*(2), 65–73.

Zebrowski, P. M., Weiss, A., Savelkoul, E., & Hammer, C. (1996). The effect of maternal rate reduction on the stuttering, speech rates and linguistic productions of children who stutter: Evidence from individual dyads. *Clinical Linguistics and Phonetics, 10*(3), 189–206.

14 The Lidcombe Program of Early Stuttering Intervention

Mark Onslow
Ann Packman
Australian Stuttering Research Centre
The University of Sydney

At present, it seems clear that some children who begin to stutter will recover without formal treatment. The exact portion of a clinical caseload for which this will occur is not known with certainty at present, nor is it known how to predict which children will recover without treatment. Not surprisingly, then, case selection strategies for early intervention are currently a controversial topic (e.g., Bernstein Ratner, 1997; Curlee & Yairi, 1997; Packman & Onslow, in press, Onslow, 1996; Zebrowski, 1997). It seems clear, however, that active treatment for early stuttering is necessary with many children. It also seems clear from clinical reports (Onslow, Andrews, & Lincoln, 1994; Starkweather, Gottwald, & Halfond, 1990; Starkweather & Gottwald, 1993) and laboratory reports (see Onslow, 1996 for a review) that reduction of stuttering to near zero levels is an attainable goal for preschool children, and one that can be achieved in quite few clinician hours. This chapter outlines the Lidcombe Program, which is a treatment for early stuttering that, we claim, warrants consideration as an effective procedure to achieve the goal of rapid elimination of stuttered speech in children for whom that is considered necessary.[1]

THE LIDCOMBE PROGRAM OF EARLY STUTTERING INTERVENTION

Background

The Lidcombe Program was developed at the Stuttering Unit, Bankstown Health Service, Sydney, and at nearby clinics of the University of Sydney. The Stuttering Unit is a specialist, government-funded public clinic that has provided this treatment as one of its basic services for more than 10 years. The clinics at The University of Sydney are teaching clinics for the undergraduate program in speech pathology.[2] The treatment was named after the Sydney suburb of Lidcombe, in which it was developed. More than 1,000 preschool-age children have now participated in the program in our Lidcombe clinics, and our active program of professional development has resulted in the use of the Lidcombe Program throughout Australia in public and private clinics. Our published data, and our clinic files, show that the median time for children treated with this method is 11.5 hour-long weekly clinic visits. That calculation is based on the time taken for children to reduce their stuttering to below 1.0% syllables stuttered (%SS) for three consecutive, weekly, within-clinic speech assessments. When children have reached that below-1.0%SS criterion, and the clinician and parents believe the child's speech to be perceptibly normal, the child is placed in a maintenance program.

We are often asked whether the program was developed with a group of clients that were elite in some way, in the sense that they were success prone and hence not representative of clients who generally present to speech clinics in Australia. Our answer is that our client population was far from elite. Lidcombe is not a high socioeconomic area of Sydney. It is also a multicultural area of Sydney, and it is common for us to use an interpreter during treatment. Clients pay no fee at the Stuttering Unit, and, although a fee is paid at the University clinics, it is modest compared to standard private speech pathology fees in Australia. Further, around half of our cases in the Lidcombe clinics have been treated by speech pathology students under supervision, as part of the clinical training for their professional preparation. Finally, because it is a specialist clinic, the Stuttering Unit receives many referrals of cases from clinics throughout Sydney, and often beyond. Many of these cases are far from success prone. In fact, many are difficult cases who are referred to the Stuttering Unit because an original clinician failed to eliminate stuttering.

Basic Philosophy of the Lidcombe Program

The Lidcombe Program focuses on speech. By making this statement, we do not mean to imply that other aspects of the child and the child's environment are not important in the management of stuttering. Far from this; it is routine in the Lidcombe Program for the clinician to arrange for substantial changes in the child's environment. However, the reason for implementing those changes is not that we believe the environment to be involved in the origin and development of stuttering; The Lidcombe Program alters children's environments so that the program can be presented to children in an optimal fashion. This is an important departure from popular treatment methods to control stuttering that modify aspects of children's environments thought to be involved in causing the condition (see Onslow, 1992, 1996, for reviews). In the Lidcombe Program, the rough and tumble of normal family life is not altered in the interest of creating an optimal living environment for speech. Instead, The Lidcombe Program focuses directly on speech with the intention of equipping the child with sufficient speech skills to cope with the communicative demands of daily living. In short, the Lidcombe Program rests on the premise that stuttering is a speech problem and that children who stutter must learn to manage their faulty speech production system in all life situations.

The Lidcombe Program is consistent with the basic principles of behavior therapy. Parents are taught to present verbal contingencies to their children online in everyday speaking situations. The predominant targets for those parental contingencies are stutterfree speech and stuttering, but we also teach parents to target their children's self-monitoring and self-evaluation. The Lidcombe Program also utilizes the behavior therapy principle of clearly stated goals at the beginning of treatment, and constant reference to those goals during the course of treatment. Those goals always include the elimination of stuttering across all childhood speaking situations for an indefinite period. Objective and subjective stuttering measures are integral to the Lidcombe Program and are always taken into account in clinical decision making. If those measures suggest that stuttering severity is not reducing, then aspects of the program are modified until it does. Children do not enter the maintenance phase, and they do not pass through the maintenance phase, unless clinical speech measures remain below criterion.

Another important behavior therapy principle incorporated within the Lidcombe Program is reliance on empirical clinical research. Existing data provide empirical support for many of the basic components of this treatment. For example, it is known that *response contingent stimulation* reduces stuttering in adults (see Ingham, 1984; Prins & Hubbard, 1988, for a review), and laboratory experiments have suggested that stuttering in 2–5 year-old-children can be eliminated with the presentation of contingent events (Martin, Kuhl, & Haroldson, 1972; Reed & Godden, 1977). Furthermore, the maintenance procedures in the Lidcombe Program, which we will discuss later, are based on research showing the value of that procedure (see Ingham, 1980). Finally, we and our colleagues have published empirical studies of the outcome of the Lidcombe Program, and are continuously attempting to refine the procedure in response to ongoing research. We address these research efforts in the closing sections of our chapter.

Overview of the Lidcombe Program

In the program, parents learn to correct stuttering and to praise stutterfree speech in the child's everyday speaking environment. During this process, parents regularly collect measures of the child's stuttering severity. During weekly visits to the clinic, the speech-language pathologist (SLP) and the parent discuss progress and together make clinical decisions such as how to structure program materials, whether to introduce a new aspect of the program, and so on. We prefer both parents to come to the clinic if possible, but quite often only one parent attends or parents alternate their attendance. During one-hour weekly visits, the parents' speech measures contribute to decisions about clinical management. At each clinic visit, the SLP also collects a measure of percent syllables stuttered (%SS) at the start of the session, using an electronic timing and computing device for this purpose. When clinician and parent measures of stuttering severity have reduced to criteria, the child enters a maintenance phase. Usually those criteria include less than one % syllables stuttered (1%SS). During the maintenance phase, clinic visits are separated by increasing intervals, provided that stuttering severity measures remain at the criterion levels.

The SLP closely monitors all aspects of the intervention, and ensures that, at all times, it is a positive experience for the child. The SLP trains the parent in the clinic and ensures that the child is responding positively before suggesting that the parent work with the child at home. The SLP routinely requires the parent to audiotape what occurs at home and bring the tapes to the clinic to ensure that the clinician's directions are being followed properly. The SLP's intention is to develop a relationship in which the parents, the clinician, and the child work closely together. To us, it is axiomatic that the SLP is an expert with the treatment, but the parent is the expert with the child. In our experience, most families learn to conduct the program without incident, providing that the clinician adopts a problem-solving approach to the program. This is discussed in detail in following sections.

Program Components

There are two components of the program. The first is a core behavioral component and the second is a problem-solving component. These components are complementary, and our experience is that both are essential for the program to succeed.

The Behavioral Component

The behavioral procedures in the program are (a) praise for stutterfree speech and correction of stuttered speech, (b) measurement of stuttering within and beyond the clinic, and (c) programmed maintenance.

Praise for Stutterfree Speech and Correction of Stuttered Speech. Detailed descriptions of these procedures and their administration are available in various sources (Onslow, 1996; Onslow, Andrews, & Lincoln, 1994; Onslow, Costa, & Rue, 1990). The responses to stutterfree speech are praise and, to a lesser extent, tangible reinforcers. Tangible reinforcers include stickers or stamps and various games comprising things that fit together. For example, components of a train set or pieces of Lego can be used. At the start of treatment, the clinician ascertains the range of utterance lengths that the child is likely to be able to say without stuttering. There is much variation in the day-to-day and situation-to-situation severity of early stuttering. Nonetheless, in some cases that, overall, are quite mild, it is clear to the clinician that the child is capable of producing one or several entire utterances without stuttering. In this case, the clinician would recommend that parents offer praise for stutterfree speech only when children complete a certain number of stutterfree utterances. On the other hand, in more severe cases, the treatment would focus initially on shorter stutterfree segments, because that is all the child is capable of. On many occasions with severely stuttering preschool children, the treatment focuses initially on single-word utterances, particularly if the child is aware of the stuttering, or is distressed by it, or is avoiding speech because of stuttering.

Praise for stutterfree speech is modified according to the child's age and cognitive development. Some examples of parental reinforcement of stutterfree speech are, "good talking!" or "no bumpy words there." In so doing, we find it critical to communicate in a manner appropriate to the child. Most children will respond best to terms such as bumpy or "stuck" words.

The techniques for correcting stuttered speech in the Lidcombe program are indeed verbal contingencies, and they originated in the operant laboratory research mentioned previously. However, it is important to note that although the potential value of these techniques was discovered in research laboratories, those laboratory findings were adapted for use in the speech clinic. In other words, it is the concept of controlling stuttering with verbal contingencies, not the specific laboratory procedures, that underpins the Lidcombe Program. As the Lidcombe clinicians have adapted those laboratory findings for clinical purposes over the years, a number of distinct techniques have emerged that are appropriate for families. The correction used in treating a specific child is carefully selected with that child and family in mind, because what works best for one child and family will not be optimal for another. However, a clinician is likely to teach a family to use two or three of the following techniques to be used in combination to reduce a child's stuttering frequency to zero or near zero levels.

1. The parent gives a correct version of the child's stuttered speech segment. This form of correction requires no response from the child, and resembles the normal parental behavior of repeating a child's grammatically incorrect utterance in a correct form (Bohannon & Stanowicz, 1988).

2. The parent notes in passing that a stuttered speech segment has occurred, by saying something like, "That was a bit bumpy" in a matter-of-fact way, and then proceeding with the conversation. Again, no response is required of the child and the interaction is barely altered. However, quite often, a child will respond by repeating the speech segment without stuttering. A variant of this is for the parent to comment in a supportive fashion that the utterance was difficult for the child. For example, a parent might say, "That was hard to say, but you got there."

3. The parent provides a nonspecific, delayed verbal request for a correction of the stuttered segment. If an utterance contains stuttering, the parent may then ask for a stuttered word to be repeated without stuttering. For example, if a child said, "Can I have a d-d-d-drink to take to John's house?" the parent might ask, "Can you say 'drink'?" If the child repeats drink without stuttering, the parent might then say, "That was smooth. Do you want juice or water?" This technique gives the child the option of correcting the stuttered segment. The technique also has the advantage that the utterance is not interrupted by the parent, and the correction can occur with only a short stop in the conversational exchange.

4. The parent provides a nonspecific but immediate cue for the child to correct the stuttered speech segment. This can occur verbally or nonverbally. For example, stuttering might occur when a child is asking, "D-D-Do you want...?" and the parent might elicit a correction by immediately saying "Do I want...?" Parents often learn to provide a range of nonverbal, often subtle, cues to children that can be used alone or in combination with nonspecific verbal cues for correction. For example, we often see parents touching their children supportively or merely raising an eyebrow as a cue for correction.

5. The parent provides a specific, immediate verbal request for a correction of the stuttered segment. It is important that the child always retain the option to decline a second attempt at the sentence. Consequently, many parents find it useful to say something like, "Can you fix that bumpy word?" rather than merely request a correction.

6. The parent praises a stutterfree speech segment that immediately follows a stuttered speech segment. This is a useful technique if the child has a long and effortful episode of stuttering. Instead of saying anything about the stuttering, it is a supportive message to the child if the parent simply ignores it and, if a segment of stutterfree speech follows immediately, offers praise for that. Fundamentally, this is praise for stutterfree speech, but if managed correctly, it also constitutes a contingency for stuttered speech.

7. The parent overcorrects a stuttered speech segment. When the child successfully corrects a stuttered segment, it can sometimes be beneficial for the parent to request several more repetitions. The benefit of this procedure is that the child's experience of the correction is mostly stutter-free speech. It can also assist the child to obtain a "feel" for stutterfree speech and to associate the intervention with feelings of success.

In short, predominantly verbal contingencies for stutterfree and stuttered speech are introduced into children's daily lives. However, we are careful to teach our students that, although the procedure is conceptually simple, its implementation must be flexible. This is not a rigid procedure where stuttering inevitably invokes the same response. In our experience, if the treatment is administered rigidly, it will fail. There are as many ways of implementing the Lidcombe Program as there are families with stuttering children, and for each family, an appropriate implementation must be established.

One of the most fundamental tasks for the clinician is careful monitoring of the procedure to prevent any negative reaction by the child. One way to minimize the possibility of any such reaction is to insist that parents maintain a ratio of 5:10 occasions of praise for each correction of stuttered speech. Beyond the prevention of negative reactions to the program, our clinical experiences and various sources of qualitative evidence (e.g., Onslow & Harrison, 1996) suggest that it is essential that children enjoy the treatment, even to the extent that they will seek out verbal input from their parents about their speech.

At the beginning of the treatment, parents administer praise and correction in formal "sessions." These occur every day, if appropriate, and they may last from 5 to 20 minutes. The child and the parent sit together in a quiet place in the home, and the parent structures the interaction. Depending on stuttering severity and cognitive and linguistic development, the child may name picture cards, talk about a picture book, or discuss the day's activities. At a later stage in treatment, the parent praises stutterfree speech and corrects stuttering online during everyday speaking situations. This on-line procedure ensures that treatment takes place in the child's customary speaking environments. We believe that this is one reason why published results of the Lidcombe Program have been favorable. If a child stutters while shopping with a parent, in the car on the way to preschool, and at dinner time, then that is where therapy occurs. There is no formal generalization phase; rather, generalization is intrinsic to the program's procedures.

At some stage in treatment, sometimes within the first few weeks, children begin to monitor their speech and correct themselves. For example, the child may say, "whoops, that was a bumpy word!" or, "hey Mom, I said that with no bumps!" This is considered an important milestone in treatment and children are praised for doing it. At some time during the treatment, when it is clear that the child is capable of stutterfree speech, parents are encouraged to occasionally prompt the child to produce it. For example, the parent might say to the child "Let's see if you can have no bumpy words during dinner." At a later stage, the parents are instructed to prompt the child to monitor and self-correct.

Regular Speech Measures Within and Beyond the Clinic. Three clinical measures of stuttering are used in the Lidcombe Program. These are a 10-point severity rating (SR) scale, stutters per minute of speaking time (SMST), and percent syllables stuttered (%SS). The former two are made by parents in the child's everyday environment, and the third is made by the SLP online in the clinic, either while talking to the child or observing the child conversing with parents.

The 10-point severity rating (SR) scale is based on how parents judge their child's stuttering severity in different everyday speaking situations, such as during meals, talking to a grandparent on the phone, at bedtime and bathtime, and so on. At the start of the treatment, parents select seven speaking situations that occur regularly for the child in the family's life. Each day, parents select one of those speaking situations and attend to the child speaking in that situation for 5 or 10 minutes, at the end of which time they record a score. The score 1 on the scale means "no stuttering" and a score of 10 means "extremely severe stuttering." This procedure is quick, cheap, convenient, and covert, and allows rapid sampling of the child's speech as stuttering severity varies from day-to-day and situation-to-situation (Onslow, 1996; Onslow, Andrews, & Costa, 1990). We are always amazed by how effectively parents use this scale to communicate to us the day-to-day patterns in their children's stuttering (Onslow, Andrews et al., 1990). In the early stages of treatment, parents tape record the child talking in some of the situations mentioned earlier and bring the recordings to the clinic. The parent and the clinician listen to the tapes together and assign a SR score. If the ratings do not agree, the clinician and the parent discuss them until they reach consensus. Once the clinician is confident that the parent's SRs are valid and reliable, they are recorded in the child's clinic file at each weekly clinic visit. As with other aspects of the Lidcombe Program, the severity rating procedure needs to be used flexibly. For example, it may be better in some cases to have parents assign a severity score to the child's speech for an entire day, rather than for 5 or 10-minute periods as described earlier.

Parents also learn to make SMST measures beyond the clinic to supplement daily SRs. This procedure is based on counts of stuttering. The parent makes a tape recording of the child and later uses a cumulative stopwatch to measure the child's total speaking time while simultaneously counting the numbers of stutters. An SMST measure is obtained by dividing cumulative speaking time by the number of stutters. At the start of each weekly visit to the clinic, the SLP and/or the parent converses with the child while the SLP makes a %SS measure, using a button-press counting and timing device. The clinician records online whether or not each syllable spoken was stuttered by pressing one or another button on the counter timer. The device automatically calculates %SS and syllables spoken per minute (SPM).[3] This measure is made before the start of each weekly clinic visit.

The stuttering measures made by parents and the SLP across speaking situations during treatment are an important feature of the Lidcombe Program, and serve many functions. Most importantly, they provide information about the effects of treatment on stuttering beyond the clinic. This not only brings overall accountability to the treatment, but also provides tangible indications of when the treatment is not working effectively. Normally, after 4 weeks, some effects of the treatment are apparent in a graph of a child's speech measures. If this effect is not apparent, then it is a sign to the clinician that the treatment is impaired in some way and that some problem solving is needed. Speech measures also guide clinical decision making during the program. For example, many children's speech measures reveal a cyclical pattern of severity; in this case, a record of that pattern helps the clinician and parents plan adjustments to the treatment that are responsive to those patterns. Graphed clinical speech measures may also allow the effects of newly introduced strategies to be assessed. For example, shortly after the introduction of online praise and correction, the child may respond immediately with stuttering reductions in all speaking situations. Another fundamental use of speech measures during the Lidcombe Program is to specify treatment targets. We believe that this is of particular value during the period of maintenance; with criteria for satisfactory speech performance indicated plainly in speech measures, parents are able to determine any departure from those targets in the posttreatment period, and respond appropriately. In addition to arresting any potential posttreatment relapses, such measures empower parents in the long-term care of their child's speech during the maintenance program.

Programmed Maintenance. When near zero stuttering has been achieved in everyday speaking situations, the child enters the maintenance phase of the program. During this phase, parents continue to monitor their children's speech in everyday situations and to correct stuttering as necessary. However, the child attends the clinic less and less frequently during this period, as long as the low level of stuttering is maintained. For example, the clinician and the parent may decide at each visit to the clinic that the child's within-clinic %SS score must be less than or equal to 1.0, all SMST scores beyond the clinic for the previous week must be less than 1.0, and average daily parent SRs for the previous week must be less than 2.0. The maintenance visits might be scheduled for 2 weeks, 2 weeks, 4 weeks, 4 weeks, 8 weeks, 8 weeks, 16 weeks, and then 32 weeks, although, again, flexibility is important in designing a maintenance schedule apppropriate to the needs of each child and family. This procedure is based on Ingham's (1980) notion of maintenance as a client response. In Ingham's maintenance procedure, when a client maintains target performance, a longer period occurs until the next maintenance assessment, and when a client fails to meet target performance, there is a return to the start of the sequence of clinic visits. Ingham (1980) showed this procedure to be a useful adjunct to a maintenance program with adult clients, and we have found it to be so with that age group. However, our experience shows that such an "all or none" approach is not in the best interests of our preschool clients and their families, and we have introduced some flexibility into the procedure. For example, if a child fails to meet maintenance criteria at any visit, we normally permit another attempt in the following week. In the event that criteria are not met at that subsequent visit, we do not necessarily restart the entire schedule. More often than not, we return the family to a point several steps prior to where the problem occurred in the schedule.

We have several reasons for imposing this maintenance procedure. First, Ingham showed it to increase the durability of treatment effects with adults and we suspect that it has a similar effect with our very young clients. However, at present, we have no empirical evidence that this is the case. Nonetheless, if for no other reason, we feel that the procedure has merit because it puts in place a long-term mechanism for detecting any signs of posttreatment relapse. Further, we feel that a systematic maintenance program facilitates the achievement of the final goal of the Lidcombe Program, which is to have parents assume long-term responsibility for the maintenance of their children's stutterfree speech. During the maintenance program, parents systematically monitor for any signs of posttreatment regression by measuring their child's speech performance. In the event of any such signs, our parents know to reintroduce the treatment procedures that they have learned. They also know when it is time to contact their clinician to discuss any problems.

Problem Solving Component

The Lidcombe Program requires long-term behavioral and cognitive changes in a family. Parents must change their behavior to provide an environment that contains prompts for stutterfree speech, rewards for stutterfree speech, correction of stuttering, and prompts and rewards for self-evaluation, self-monitoring, generalization, and maintenance. The child must make the behavior change of eliminating stuttering permanently. Those behavioral changes are accompanied by long-term cognitive changes in parents, who must provide a supportive, caring environment for the elimination of stuttering. The cognitive change required of the child is attention to the task of eliminating stuttering. We administer the treatment from within a counseling relationship because the major part of facilitating long-term change, in any client who receives any health care, is identifying and overcoming obstacles to that change; in other words, problem solving. It is the problem solving that differs so much from family to family. We have encountered as many problems in implementing the Lidcombe Program as we have had cases to manage. A problem free administration of this treatment is a rarity and problems can only be identified and redressed when the program is conducted within a relationship in which regular contact occurs between clinician, parent/s, and child.

To us, it is axiomatic that, although the treatment is conceptually simple, it is complicated in its execution. To illustrate this point, below is an excerpt from our list of skills that parents are required to master in the Lidcombe Program. This list pertains only to providing correction and praise; we have equally comprehensive lists of requisite parent skills for collecting clinical measures and for conducting their child's maintenance program.

During each of the daily sessions, parents need to do the following:

1. Direct and maintain the attention and compliance of the child.
2. Conduct a suitable speech-eliciting activity.
3. Prompt the child to produce stutterfree speech.
4. Elicit conversational responses and respond to what the child says.
5. Monitor for moments of stuttering and for periods of stutterfree speech.
6. Correctly identify stuttered and stutterfree speech segments.
7. Present praise and correction accurately and immediately, but not urgently or judgmentally.
8. Prompt and praise self-monitoring and self-evaluation responses.
9. Maintain a supportive attitude.
10. Select an appropriate duration of stutterfree speech to elicit at that session.
11. Make online judgments of when to persist with having a child correct a stuttered utterance, and when to abandon the attempt.
12. Make online judgements of when to correct and when to ignore a stutter.
13. Watch for aspects of the procedure that the child does not appear to enjoy.
14. Be ready to immediately use various techniques for assisting the child to correct a stuttered utterance.
15. Have the child overcorrect if appropriate.
16. Judge what is an appropriate ratio between praise and correction, then establish and maintain that ratio, and vary it as required.
17. Administer a tangible reward system if required.

When parents reach the stage of the program where "on-line" correction and praise of stuttering occurs, they must learn to:

18. Maintain an appropriate rate of praise and correction.
19. Monitor the child everyday for stuttering and for stutterfree speech.
20. Prompt and reward generalization and maintenance.
21. Ensure that praise and correction are spread consistently over the time that they spend with the child, rather than being concentrated during a short period.
22. Judiciously identify speaking situations in which correction and praise are appropriate and situations in which it is not.
23. Detect when it is advisable to stop the correction and offer only praise for a period.
24. Identify when the child is about to enter a particularly troublesome situation, and provide support and encouragement at that time.
25. Correct stuttering without disturbing the child's overall communication.
26. Ensure that the child's long-term attention to the task is maintained.
27. Continually fuel and reinforce the child's drive and motivation to stop stuttering.

To date, our clinical impression is that deficits in parental skill in any of these areas will impair the effectiveness of the Lidcombe Program. For example, the program is unlikely to be a supportive and positive experience if the parent is tense when correcting stuttering (7). And the program will not work if a parent consistently praises a child for speech that contains stuttering and fails to identify stutterings online (6). The program is also unlikely to succeed if parents provide short, concentrated periods of praise and correction rather than a consistent, extended effort (21). And if parents impede a child's capacity to communicate freely (25), the compliance of that child is not likely to be forthcoming.

One reason we are so rigorous about parent training is that this treatment contains material that could impact negatively on small children. Children stutter many times each day. A child can experience significant distress if parents, with the best of intentions and without awareness of what they are doing, suddenly withdraw unconditional love and approval and replace it with unremitting demands for perfect speech. This is why the Lidcombe Program can only be administered by means of weekly meetings with the family who administers the treatment, so that a close working relationship can be established. Only with such a relationship can the child's living environment be explored and can the clinician eliminate the possibility of significant distress to a child. Such a relationship is essential for parents to receive the requisite guidance in administering the program accurately and supportively, and only with such a relationship can it be guaranteed that long-term change will occur within the family.

OUTCOME EVALUATION OF THE LIDCOMBE PROGRAM

We have published two medium-term outcome studies of the Lidcombe Program (Onslow et al., 1994; Onslow, Costa et al., 1990) and one long-term outcome study (Lincoln & Onslow, 1997), which incorporate many of the attributes of acceptable stuttering treatment research (Bloodstein, 1987). These include substantial samples of everyday speech gathered frequently over a long period; demonstration of carryover to speaking situations beyond the clinic; objective measures of stuttering rate that are shown to be reliable; demonstration of effectiveness on a group of subjects; long-term follow-up investigations; and demonstration that posttreatment stutterfree speech is not achieved at the expense of natural sounding speech.

The Onslow, Costa et al. (1990) study was a preliminary investigation of 4 children who received the Lidcombe Program. The children's speech was measured in three speaking situations: within the clinic, beyond the clinic at home, and beyond the clinic away from home. Occasional covert assessments were conducted. The children's speech was taperecorded and assessed blind for %SS scores by an independent clinician whose data were shown to be reliable. The children were assessed in each speaking situation on three occasions over a 2-month pretreatment period and on six occasions over a 9-month posttreatment period. Subjects in the Onslow, et al. (1994) study were 12 cases of early stuttering, with a mean age of 47 months at the start of treatment, and with a mean interval from reported onset to the start of treatment of 16 months. Assessments were similar to the preliminary study except that 7 assessments occurred over a 12-month posttreatment period, all

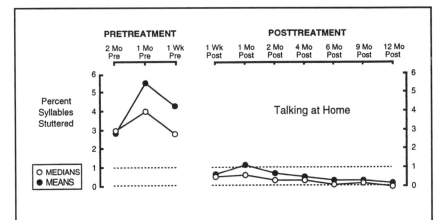

NOTE: "Mo" = "Months," "Wk" = "Week," "Pre" = "Pretreatment," "Post" = "Posttreatment"

FIG 14.1. Some results from "A Control/Experiment Trial of an OPerant Treatment for Early Stuttering," by Onslow, Andrews, and Lincoln (1994) *Journal of Speech and Hearing Research, 37*, p.1251. These results are the mean and median percent syllables stuttered (%SS) for a group of 12 children before and up to 12 months after treatment with the Lidcombe program. These results are for the children while they were talking with the family at home, but we also presented similar results for them talking in other everyday situations. Adapted with permission of the American Speech-Hearing Association.

NOTE. "Mo" = "Months," "Wk" = "Week," "Pre" = "Pretreatment," "Post" = "Posttreatment"

assessments were beyond the clinic, and one of those speaking situations was covertly assessed. This study also incorporated a control group of children who did not receive the treatment.

The overall findings from these two studies are extremely encouraging. The children's stuttering rates in everyday speaking situations showed a sharp discontinuity at the first posttreatment assessment, remaining low for the entire posttreatment interval. The posttreatment data for the Onslow et al. (1994) study are the more impressive, with the children generally stuttering below 1.0 %SS up to and at the 12-month posttreatment assessment. Further, there were no signs of any posttreatment relapse in the latter study, but in the former study, 2 subjects had a single assessment occasion that showed elevated %SS scores. We suspect that the better results from the more recent study occurred because we had become more proficient at administering this treatment. Some of the data from the Onslow et al. (1994) study are presented in Fig. 14.1. These data accord with the clinical data contained in the files of children who are treated by the Lidcombe clinicians.

We were unable to sustain the control group in the Onslow et al. (1994) study. From the outset of that study, the control group was problematic because it consisted of parents who came to the Lidcombe clinics for consultations, concerned about their children's stuttering. Although they agreed to participate in the control group, it was clear that their concerns remained, and many of these parents subsequently chose to withdraw from the study. It soon became obvious that the children in the experimental group were rapidly improving and the remaining control children were not, and consequently, we felt ethically obliged to abandon the control group. Only 2 control children remained as such, the apparent reason being that clear improvements in their children's speech began to occur within 3 months of the start of the study.

Subsequently, a long-term outcome study (Lincoln & Onslow, 1997) followed up 43 children who received the Lidcombe Program, collecting %SS scores each year in various beyond-clinic speaking situations. One group of children ($n = 9$) had participated in the studies described earlier, and consequently pretreatment speech data were available. A second group of children ($n = 34$) also received the Lidcombe Program, but pretreatment data were not available. However, these were clinical cases diagnosed as stuttering and treated in the Lidcombe clinics. Data from this study show that, for a period of up to 7 years posttreatment, the children's stuttering rates remained generally below 1.0%SS. Not one case of relapse, nor any case of clinically significant regression in posttreatment data trends, was detected in the 43 cases studied. At the time of writing, several years after the data collection of the study, no case of relapse among these subjects has come to our attention. Data for one of the children in this study are presented in Fig. 14.2.

Because of the limitations of measures of stuttering based on syllable and stuttering counts and/or on parental reports, the first author and colleagues reported a study of the social validity of the outcome data for the Lidcombe Program (Lincoln, Onslow, & Reed, 1997). The first part of this study involved a group of children treated with the Lidcombe Program and a group of nonstuttering control children matched for age and sex. We collected speech samples from both groups, and had speech-language pathologists, who were experienced in the treatment of early stuttering, measure %SS from those speech samples. We found that the %SS scores assigned to each group were similar. In the second part of this report, we played speech samples of treated children and control children to experienced clinicians and unsophisticated listeners, and asked them to indicate whether each child was "stuttering" or "not stuttering." Our results showed that 60% of unsophisticated listeners judged pretreatment samples of the children to be stuttering, but only 3% judged posttreatment samples to be stuttering. We concluded our article by arguing that the outcome data for the Lidcombe Program are socially valid.

Limitations of the Outcome Data for the Lidcombe Program

As with any research, there are limitations to our outcome studies of the Lidcombe Program. One limitation at present is that the evidence for its effectiveness does not come from a true experimental design. Although our data are extensive, and we have collected objective measures repeatedly over long periods and in everyday childhood speaking situations, those data amount to pretreatment and posttreatment observations. Although those data seem to show unambiguously that the children were stuttering for long periods before the treatment and had near zero stuttering for long periods after the treatment, a control group would "shore up" our case.

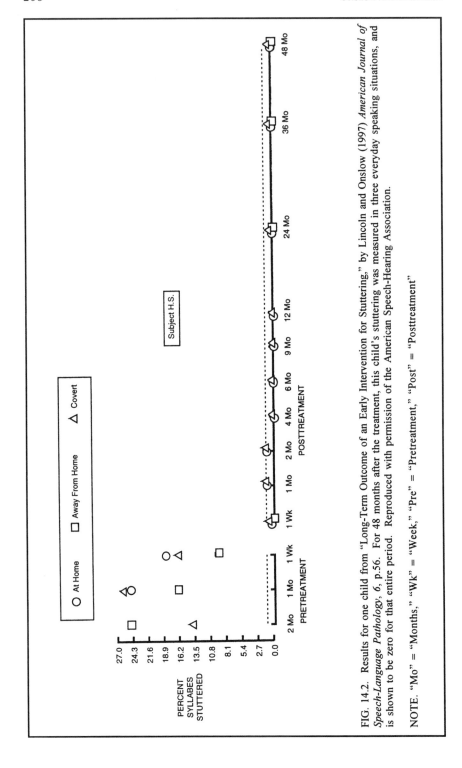

FIG. 14.2. Results for one child from "Long-Term Outcome of an Early Intervention for Stuttering," by Lincoln and Onslow (1997) *American Journal of Speech-Language Pathology, 6,* p.56. For 48 months after the treatment, this child's stuttering was measured in three everyday speaking situations, and is shown to be zero for that entire period. Reproduced with permission of the American Speech-Hearing Association.

NOTE. "Mo" = "Months," "Wk" = "Week," "Pre" = "Pretreatment," "Post" = "Posttreatment"

Our failure to sustain a control group is certainly not for want of trying; as we described previously, the design of the Onslow et al. (1994) study incorporated a control group. However, when the experimental treatment was found to be so effective, we considered it ethically impossible to continue with that experimental method. At present, we are using a control group in an experiment that does not involve the study of control subjects for long periods. We are seeking to establish evidence that the introduction of the Lidcombe Program to experimental subjects produces an immediate reduction in stuttering when compared to a control group.

Another threat to interpretation of our results is the accepted information that some children will recover from stuttering without formal treatment at a speech clinic. Consequently, it is conceivable that, for some of the children in the Onslow et al. (1994) study, spontaneous recovery produced the observed effects. However, we submit that there is a compelling case that it was the treatment that produced near zero stuttering in the children studied. First, the data trends in the Onslow et al. reports generally showed an abrupt discontinuity between pretreatment and posttreatment stuttering rates (see Fig. 14.1), which suggests the presence of a treatment effect. Second, there have been estimates that the majority of spontaneous recoveries occur within 12–18 months after onset (e.g., Andrews, 1984; Yairi, Ambrose, Paden, & Throneburg, 1996). This weakens recovery as an explanation for the reported effects in Onslow, et al. (1994), because the 12 children in the study had a mean history of 16 months from reported onset of stuttering to the start of treatment (range 7–24 months). Finally, a study of the effects of the Lidcombe Program on school-age children (Lincoln, Onslow, Wilson, & Lewis, 1996) used similar outcome methodology to the Onslow et al. study and produced similar results. The chances of spontaneous recovery in that age group were quite small, and hence, that study provides an independent source of evidence that the treatment is capable of controlling stuttering in early childhood.

We believe that the studies reviewed in this chapter have made a strong case for the efficacy of the Lidcombe Program. There are grounds to believe that it is a treatment that gives preschool children near zero stuttering levels for long periods, in exchange for a handful of health care hours. The clinical experiences of our colleagues and ourselves with children and their parents sustain our belief that this is so. Yet, given that, we need to recognize that the treatment is a package. As has been stated many times in discussion sections of outcome studies about this treatment, much work remains to disentangle the variables that contribute to that package. Certainly, a major component consists of parents providing online praise and correction for stuttering, and the laboratory literature on the effects of response contingent stimulation on stuttering sustains a good argument that such parental activity is the functionally effective part of the package. On the other hand, stuttering is known to be reactive to assessment, and the treatment involves regular speech assessments. This may have contributed to outcome.

One of the most interesting potential explanations for the apparent efficacy of the Lidcombe Program is that it invokes environmental changes. There has been a long history of belief that stressors in children's environment are involved in the cause and perpetuation of the condition (see Bloodstein, 1987, for a review).

Consequently, the removal of those stressors to create an optimal speech environment, in which stuttering cannot flourish, is a popular treatment goal (see Bloodstein, 1987; Onslow, 1996, for reviews). A recent count (J. Ingham, 1995) showed that 37 such potential environmental stressors have been suggested, and Bloodstein's (1997) recent iteration of the tension and fragmentation hypothesis reaffirms that the number may be limitless. As we stated previously, the Lidcombe Program does change children's environments, and those changes are likely to include positive attitudes to children's speech, more time spent with children, and so on, similar to the kinds of changes that are thought by many to be the basis of an effective treatment for early stuttering.

Our judgment is to doubt that the effectiveness of the Lidcombe Program is due to the removal of environmental stressors from children's lives, because there are insufficient empirical grounds to support such a premise (see Nippold & Rudzinski, 1995; Onslow, 1992, 1996 for reviews). Nonetheless, it is a possibility that must be excluded as part of the development of this treatment. Indeed, its future would be greatly influenced by findings attributing its effects to communicative and lifestyle changes within families. Consequently, there is currently a study in progress that addresses this issue. We and our colleagues are also currently involved in a series of studies to determine the roles of parental praise and correction and clinical measurement procedures in the treatment. We are also exploring the relative effectiveness of different service delivery options, and we are exploring the upper limits of the age range for which such a treatment is effective. After 8 years of researching, we find ourselves enthusiastic about the value of this treatment and we feel empowered to relieve the distress that early stuttering can cause in families. We look forward to the next 8 years, and perhaps after those we will have answers to remaining questions, and perhaps those answers will maintain our optimism.

REFERENCES

Andrews, G. (1984). Epidemiology of stuttering. In R. F. Curlee & W. H. Perkins (Eds.), *Nature and treatment of stuttering: New directions* (pp. 1–12). San Diego: College-Hill Press.

Bernstein Ratner, N. (1997). Leaving Las Vegas: Clinical odds and individual outcomes. *American Journal of Speech-Language-Pathology, 6*, 29–33.

Bloodstein, O. (1987). *A handbook on stuttering* (4th ed.). Chicago: National Easter Seal Society.

Bloodstein, O. (1997). Stuttering as an anticipatory struggle reaction. In R. F. Curlee & G. M. Siegel (Eds.), *Nature and treatment of stuttering: New directions* (2nd. ed.). Boston, MA: Allyn & Bacon.

Bohannon, J. N., & Stanowicz, L. (1988). Adult responses to children's errors: The issue of negative evidence. *Developmental Psychology, 24*, 684–689.

Curlee, R. F., & Yairi, E. (1997). Early intervention with early childhood stuttering: A critical examination of the data. *American Journal of Speech-Language Pathology, 6*, 8–18.

Ingham, J. C. (1995). Therapy of the stuttering child. In G. Blanken, J. Dittman, H. Grimm, J. C. Marshall, & C.-W. Wallesch (Eds.), *Linguistic disorders and pathologies* (pp. 885–893). Berlin: DeGruyter.

Ingham, R. J. (1980). Modification of maintenance and generalization during stuttering treatment. *Journal of Speech and Hearing Research, 23*, 732–745.

Ingham, R. J. (1984). *Stuttering and behavior therapy: Current status and experimental foundations.* San Diego: College-Hill Press.

Lincoln, M., & Onslow, M. (1997). Long-term outcome of an early intervention for stuttering. *American Journal of Speech-Language Pathology, 6,* 51–58.

Lincoln, M., Onslow, M., & Reed, V. (1997). Social validity of an early intervention for stuttering: The Lidcombe Program. *American Journal of Speech-Language Pathology, 6,* 77–84.

Lincoln, M., Onslow, M., Wilson, L., & Lewis, C. (1996). A clinical trial of an operant treatment for school-age stuttering children. *American Journal of Speech-Language Pathology, 5,* 73–85.

Martin, R. R., Kuhl, P., & Haroldson, S. (1972). An experimental treatment with two preschool stuttering children. *Journal of Speech and Hearing Research, 15,* 743–752.

Nippold, M. A., & Rudzinski, M. (1995). Parents' speech and children's stuttering: A critique of the literature. *Journal of Speech and Hearing Research, 38*(5), 978–989.

Onslow, M. (1992). Choosing a treatment procedure for early stuttering: Issues and future directions. *Journal of Speech and Hearing Research, 35,* 983–993.

Onslow, M. (1996). *Behavioral managment of stuttering.* San Diego: Singular.

Onslow, M., Andrews, C., & Costa, L. (1990). Parental severity scaling of early stuttered speech: Four case studies. *Australian Journal of Human Communication Disorders, 18,* 47–61.

Onslow, M., Andrews, C., & Lincoln, M. (1994). A control/experimental trial of an operant treatment for early stuttering. *Journal of Speech and Hearing Research, 37,* 1244–1259.

Onslow, M., Costa, L., & Rue, S. (1990). Direct early intervention with stuttering: Some preliminary data. *Journal of Speech and Hearing Disorders, 55,* 405–416.

Onslow, M., & Harrison, E. (Producers). (1996). Parents talk about the Lidcombe Programme. [Video] CPS Television, Faculty of Health Sciences, The University of Sydney.

Packman, A., & Lincoln, M. (1996). Early stuttering and the V model. *Australian Journal of Human Communication Disorders, 24,* 45–54.

Packman, A., & Onslow, M. (in press). Treatment of early stuttering: What is the take home message. *American Journal of Speech Language Pathology.*

Prins, D., & Hubbard, C. P. (1988). Response contingent stimuli and stuttering: Issues and implications. *Journal of Speech and Hearing Research, 31,* 696–709.

Reed, C. G., & Godden, A. L. (1977). An experimental treatment using verbal punishment with two preschool stutterers. *Journal of Fluency Disorders, 2,* 225–233.

Starkweather, C. W., & Gottwald, S. R. (1993). A pilot study of relations among specific measures obtained at intake and discharge in a program of prevention and early intervention for stuttering. *American Journal of Speech-Language Pathology, 2,* 51–58.

Starkweather, C. W., Gottwald, S. R., & Halfond, M. M. (1990). *Stuttering prevention: A clinical method.* Englewood Cliffs, NJ: Prentice-Hall.

Yairi, E., Ambrose, N. G., Paden, E. P., & Throneburg, R. N. (1996). Predictive factors of persistence and recovery: Pathways of childhood stuttering. *Journal of Communication Disorders, 29,* 51–77.

Zebrowski, P. M. (1997). Assisting young children who stutter and their families: Defining the role of the speech-language pathologist. *American Journal of Speech-Language Pathology, 6,* 19–28.

FOOTNOTES

[1]Packman and Lincoln (1996) discussed factors that we consider in determining whether a child who has begun to stutter should receive formal treatment.

[2]In Australia, the entry level qualification for the speech pathology profession is a 4-year undergraduate degreee.

[3]We routinely use SPM measures for older children and adults, but we generally find that they are of limited clinical value with preschool children. One reason for this is the absence of any usable speech rate norms for preschoolers and the absence of standard procedures for collecting the measure.

15 On Watching a Discipline Shoot Itself in the Foot: Some Observations on Current Trends in Stuttering Treatment Research

Roger J. Ingham
University of California, Santa Barbara

Anne K. Cordes
The University of Georgia

Participants in this part of the program were asked to discuss either meaningful research paradigms for, or the obstacles to, relevant stuttering treatment research. We chose to focus on the "obstacles" part of this request, a decision aided by the realization that the 1996 Special Interest Division conference might be the perfect place for such a discussion. This chapter, therefore, addresses two issues that we believe represent major problems with current treatment recommendations and treatment research for stuttering. More importantly, this chapter suggests that we, as a discipline, are capable of better performance on our clients' behalf than the Special Interest Division's Guidelines for Practice in Stuttering Treatment would have us believe.

OBSTACLE ONE: REJECTION OF DATA-BASED OUTCOME EVALUATION

One of the major current trends in stuttering treatment research appears to be a growing indifference, or even hostility, toward the importance of therapy outcome evaluation and toward the use of speech production data as a means of evaluating therapies. Signs of this obstacle have existed for some time (Ingham, 1993), but they are especially clear in this Special Interest Division's Guidelines for Practice in Stuttering Treatment (ASHA, 1995). The first page of those Guidelines includes the following statements:

> It should be noted that the Steering Committee felt that the state of knowledge in several key areas — specifically treatment efficacy and the measurement of stuttering — was not developed well enough to allow the promulgation of "standards." It was decided to provide less prescriptive "guidelines."

> Another issue concerned the base of knowledge used to determine whether
> a goal is desirable or a practice appropriate to achieve a goal. The Steering
> Committee felt that *a set of guidelines that was based entirely on empirical*
> *evidence would be too restrictive. Some treatment practices may be quite*
> *useful even though their efficacy has not been determined empirically. The*
> *committee felt that both common practice and published data should be*
> *considered.* (ASHA, 1995, p. 26; emphasis added)

The fact that this Division's "guidelines for practice" would refuse to set standards for the meaningful measurement of stuttering and for the meaningful evaluation of treatment outcomes is truly astounding. These Guidelines essentially encourage clinicians to use procedures for which there is absolutely no documented evidence of efficacy or utility (discussed later).[1] Even more serious is the statement that treatments should not necessarily be selected on the basis of empirical evidence for their efficacy, because requiring evidence of efficacy "would be too restrictive." This Special Interest Division's Guidelines, in other words, claim that it would be too restrictive to select treatments based on evidence that they do or do not work. This statement is tantamount to saying that our Division regards evidence of treatment efficacy as only partially relevant when prescribing therapy, that we officially sanction the use of unproven therapy procedures, and that we will tolerate something that could easily be perceived as quackery. In fact, if this discipline actually did want to shoot itself in the foot, then it could not have done so more effectively than with a public statement dismissing the importance of treatment efficacy data.

As a general starting point for an attempt to avoid professional suicide, we propose the following series of thoughts. First, we believe that most therapists and researchers would agree that the purpose of therapy is to remove, or at least reduce, the client's point of complaint (Baer, 1988, 1990). Secondly, we believe that most would agree that the thing most stuttering clients complain about is, basically, that they stutter, and that the primary purpose of stuttering treatment should be to produce a clinically meaningful improvement in speech fluency.[2]

There are other points about which we believe most clinicians and researchers will agree, including some facts that have been repeatedly and thoroughly documented in our literature: (a) Stuttering in children and adults may show dramatic levels of variability over time, often sufficient to confound changes attributed to treatment; (b) measures of speech performance in clinic conditions may have neither relevance nor resemblance to measures of speech performance in nonclinic conditions; and (c) claims of changes in stuttering should not be confounded by measurement error, reductions (or even nonnormal increases) in speech rate, or unusual speech quality. Despite the fact that the Division's Guidelines refused to make any statement about how to evaluate stuttering treatments, there is also an existing and widely acknowledged 3-factor model of treatment efficacy evaluation for stuttering. This model can be conceptualized as relating to the three points listed above:

1. Because stuttering may show dramatic levels of variability over time, repeated evaluation of speech performance is necessary before, during, and for a clinically meaningful period of time after treatment has ceased;

2. Because measures of speech performance in clinic conditions may have neither relevance nor resemblance to measures of speech performance in nonclinic conditions, repeated evaluation of speech performance is necessary within and beyond clinic conditions; and

3. In order to prevent claims of changes in stuttering being confounded by measurement error, changes in speech rate, or unusual speech quality, reliable and independent measures of stuttering, speech rate, and speech quality must be made during spontaneous speech (see Bloodstein, 1995; Curlee, 1993).

We would like to believe that readers will continue to agree with our reasoning, but at this point, we are aware that we and the Special Interest Division may be diverging. We fail to see how an improvement in a client's speech can be considered meaningful unless it can be reliably and empirically documented, using at least the bare minimum evaluation model just outlined, and unless it is demonstrably satisfactory to that client and to other significant people such as a young client's parents or third-party payers. The Special Interest Division's Guidelines, however, stated clearly that they believe "some treatment practices may be quite useful even though their efficacy has not been determined empirically" (ASHA, 1995, p. 26). It also appears, judging by much of the current literature, that our discipline is ready to accept treatment recommendations that not only do not satisfy a basic outcome-evaluation model such as this, but that quite simply have no data whatsoever to support them. Any number of recent stuttering treatment reports might have been used to make this argument, but the April, 1995, issue of *Language, Speech and Hearing Services in Schools* (Fosnot, 1995) provides one particularly stark example. The seven articles in this issue were designed to discuss treatment options and provide suggestions, but not one of them provided information documenting that the described therapy procedure had ever produced clinically meaningful benefits. To the contrary, many recommended the use of procedures that had previously been demonstrated to be ineffective. These articles also either failed to cite other clinical research that documented effective treatments, or misrepresented that research if it was cited. The most disturbing aspect of these articles, however, may be that they all fit the official Guidelines of this Special Interest Division.[3]

The first article in this collection (Rustin & Cook, 1995) described a program for preschoolers, another for 7–14 year olds, and another for 15–18 year olds. The preschoolers' program involved altering patterns of interaction between the child and parent, plus modifying speech rate and semantic complexity within a nondirective play therapy context advocated by Andronico and Blake (1971). None of these procedures has been shown to be effective in treatment. The parent-based procedures are essentially identical to those advocated by Shames and colleagues in the early 1970s, procedures that were never shown to produce clinically important treatment effects (see Ingham, 1984, chap. 9; Nippold & Rudzinski, 1995). Andronico and Blake provided nothing more than clinical impressions to justify their play therapy, and Rustin and Cook followed suit by offering no data to justify the use of their program. This is also true for the 7–14 year olds' program, which employed social and relaxation skills training for the parents and their child in an intensive setting. Rustin and Cook provided no research justification for this program, despite the fact that numerous studies have shown that relaxation training produces no beneficial effects on stuttering (Ingham, 1984). Finally, the older age children are taught "fluency control" in a 2-week intensive program that also used relaxation and social skills training, a program that was also presented without any reference to data testifying to its efficacy.

Similar criticisms apply to most of the other articles in this publication. The articles by Ramig and Bennett (1995), Healey and Scott (1995), and Daly, Simon, and Burnett-Stolnack (1995) are all distinguished by a complete absence of treatment data that would justify their recommended treatments. Ramig and Bennett described seven principles for working with 7–12 year olds, using a variant of prolonged speech or stuttering modification as a basic procedure. No criteria were supplied for training clinicians or for determining whether the treatment was working. It was claimed that the principles "have been successful for the majority of school-age children the authors and their colleagues have treated" (p. 148), but the only justification provided for this claim was a reference to some "unpublished raw data" (Bennett, Reveles, & Ramig, 1993; Ramig & Bennett, 1995, p. 149). Healey and Scott (1995) outlined a three-phase program, using either fluency shaping or stuttering modification, for elementary school-age children who stutter. The procedures were based on those described by Runyan and Runyan (1986, 1993) and on Goebel's (1989) Cafet program, but Runyan and Runyan have yet to report any beyond-clinic data from their program, and not one peer-reviewed evaluation of Goebel's Cafet program has ever been published. Healey and Scott (1995) supplemented their program with transfer and maintenance procedures, and they advocated repeated within- and beyond-clinic speech performance assessments, but they provided absolutely no assessment data to justify this program or to support their claim that "20% of the children who had completed... our treatment program showed steady reductions in the frequency and duration of their stuttering as well secondary behaviors" (p. 153). Daly et al. (1995) similarly described "cognitive and self-instructional strategies" to aid the maintenance of gains from treatments for adolescents who stutter. It was claimed that the authors' "findings are in accord with those of Meichenbaum and Cameron (1974), who maintain that teaching and reinforcing positive self talk behaviors leads to greater treatment efficacy, more generalization, and longer persistence of treatment effects" (Daly et al., 1995, p. 166). If that was true, then surely it is reasonable to ask why these researchers have not provided any data, nor even a reference to data, that would justify such a claim.

The last three LSHSS articles do purport to provide data in support of their recommendations. Bernstein Ratner (1995) discussed procedures for children who, in addition to stuttering, also have language and/or phonological impairments. She offered literally no data to show that any current behavioral treatment would be ineffective with such children. Instead, she simply asserted that such children should be treated by blending therapy for stuttering with therapy for phonological impairment or by treating both disorders discretely. This conclusion is innocuous in itself, as it simply covers the two logical possibilities, but Bernstein Ratner also essentially recommends a therapy procedure described by Conture, Louko, and Edwards (1993). Her justification for this program was that it was based on the assumption that "overt attention to the child's speech may impose counterproductive stress on the child's system" (Bernstein Ratner, 1995, p. 184). This is little more than one of those Johnsonian chestnuts, recycled for the 1990s, that somehow seem to be repeatedly asserted despite no supportive evidence (see Nippold & Rudzinski, 1995). In addition, the reported effects of Conture et al.'s (1990) treatment for stuttering in children provide very little reason to recommend this treatment. Conture et al. (1993) treated 4 children with phonologic disorders and stuttering, and 4 who stuttered but did not have a phonologic disorder, all age 4 to 7 years. Only within-clinic data are reported, and these show that after a year of "45-minute weekly treatment sessions," the mean reduction in stuttering frequency, from a pre- to posttreatment assessment, was only 14.25%. No child in their study reduced stuttering by more than 55%, and 3 of the 8 actually showed an increase in stuttering frequency [data that Enderby & Emerson (1995, p. 51) misinterpreted as showing that "both groups showed considerable improvement"]. Absent any other data, it seems reasonable to suggest that these changes probably amounted to little more than the routine variability discussed earlier as a threat to treatment evaluation. Furthermore, recommending a therapy based on this evidence is certainly an example of indifference to using solid treatment outcome data as a criterion for selecting therapies.

Gottwald and Starkweather (1995) also describe a therapy program that they claim to support with evaluative data. This program involves procedures for preschoolers and their parents that are designed to reduce demands on the child's capacities for fluent speech. The authors have described this program in various publications, with little information on the method of evaluation used to support the program's claimed results, and the 1995 paper is no exception. Gottwald and Starkweather (1995, p. 119) suggested that the clinician should collect one "sample of the child's speech in as natural a setting as possible," but the data from such samples do not appear to have been made available in any publication. Starkweather, Gottwald, and Halfond (1990) claimed, without data, that their program resulted in maintained normal fluency for all children who finished treatment, and essentially the same dubious claim was made in the 1995 *LSHSS* paper. Of 55 families, 45 were reported to have completed the program. All 45 of these children were reported to be "speaking normally at the time of discharge" (p. 124), and all parents reported maintained fluency in one phone call 2 years later. These two bits of information appear to constitute the complete account of the treatment program's evaluation; no speech performance data are reported.[4]

Finally, Blood (1995b) described a relapse management program, known as Power[2], which is used in conjunction with Shames and Florance's (1980) procedure to treat adolescents who stutter. This article does have the distinction of being the only one that included some form of evaluation data, but the graphs that are provided come close to defying any interpretation, and the data probably have little clinical relevance. Blood reported using Shames and Florance's program to produce

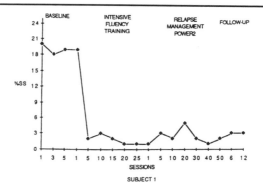

FIG. 15.1.a. Baseline, Intensive Fluency Training, Relapse Management (POWER²), and Follow-Up for Subject 1

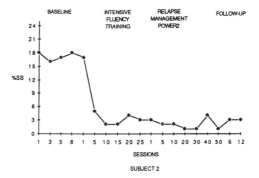

FIG. 15.1.b. Baseline, Intensive Fluency Training, Relapse Management (POWER²), and Follow-Up for Subject 2.

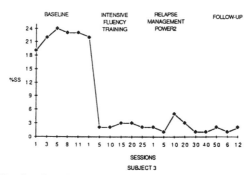

FIG. 15.1.c. Baseline, Intensive Fluency Training, Relapse Management (POWER²), and Follow-Up for Subject 3.

FIG. 15.1. Results from four phases of treatment. From "Power²: Relapse Management with Adolescents who Stutter," by G. W. Blood, 1995, *Language, Speech, and Hearing Services in the Schools, 26,* p.176.

reductions to below 3%SS in 3 adolescent males who stuttered (14, 15, and 15 years). During the maintenance phase, they are introduced to Power[2], a "Relapse Management program" that lasts approximately 50 hours and is designed to improve self-management of speech behavior through cognitive-behavioral strategies. Speech performance was evaluated from repeated 3-min speech samples made at intervals throughout the four phases of the program (Baseline, Intensive Treatment, Relapse Management, and Follow-up), with follow-up assessments obtained at 6 and 12 months after the Relapse Management program had ceased.

As is clear from Fig. 15.1, there was a noticeable and significant drop in stuttering frequency associated with the intensive fluency training. The claim that "Relapse Management" contributed to "further stabilization for the speech changes" (Blood, 1995b, p. 177), however, is simply not supported by these graphs. Indeed, in order to seek an independent interpretation, we presented these figures to a group of 10 graduate students in Communication Sciences and Disorders who had just completed a course in single-subject research methods. Because any phase effects within a single subject study should be logically and perceptually obvious (Herson & Barlow, 1976; Kazdin, 1982), we asked these students to decide what conclusions, if any, they could draw from these figures. Of the 30 possible judgments (3 figures x 10 judges), 15 (50%) were "not sure" what conclusion could be reached about the effects of the Relapse Management procedure.[5] Another 43% of the judgments were judgments that the Relapse Management program caused stuttering to increase, and the remaining 7% concluded that the Relapse Management program produced a reduction in stuttering. No judge made any mention of concluding that stuttering was more or less "stable," or more or less variable, in or after the Relapse Management program Phase. Furthermore, although the reported data might show, at best, that the effects of intervention were sustained within the clinic, Blood provided no beyond-clinic speech data. In short, these data provide no information whatsoever about the effects of Power[2] on stuttering relapse or treatment maintenance — which, of course, was the purpose of the study.

These articles are also frustrating in another, different, respect. In addition to recommending treatments that have been shown in the past to be ineffective, and recommending treatments without empirical support, these articles largely ignored or excluded references to some other therapy approaches that do provide data-based evaluations of treatment with children who stutter. There are a number of treatment studies involving young children who stutter that have demonstrated treatment effectiveness according to outcome evaluations using most of the minimal criteria outlined earlier, and that are widely cited in many contexts (see Table 15.1). Some of the articles in the April, 1995, *LSHSS* do cite some of these studies, but some of the citations are entirely inappropriate and not supported by the studies referenced: Gottwald and Starkweather (1995), for example, cited Onslow, Costa, and Rue (1990) as one of the articles supporting their statement that "the prognosis for fluency restoration is less favorable when the problem becomes encumbered by a history of struggled speech and resultant negative feelings (Gottwald & Starkweather, 1995, p. 117). Onslow et al.'s (1990) article, which described a parent managed operant program, has no bearing on such a claim. Similarly, Bernstein

Ratner (1995, p. 181) stated, "The Stocker Probe (Martin, Parlour, & Haroldson, 1990; Stocker, 1980)... is one option for quickly appraising the degree to which lexical and syntactic formulation demands affect the frequency and quality of stuttering in a child's speech," but Martin et al.'s (1990) study clearly demonstrated that variations in "lexical and syntactic formulation demands" within the Stocker Probe had absolutely no effect on the frequency of stuttering. There is also blatant misattribution, as exemplified by Gottwald and Starkweather's statement that "most treatment programs... begin with single word responses and gradually move to carrier phrase, sentence level, monologue, and conversational speech" (Gottwald & Starkweather, 1995, p. 122) and its accompanying citations to a "workshop" sponsored by one university department and to Shine (1984) and Wall and Myers (1984). Treatment plans based on controlling the length of utterance were devised by Ryan (1974 and earlier) and by Costello (1983 and earlier); references to these original sources would have been an appropriate addition to Gottwald and Starkweather's discussion.

Other recommendations completely ignore relevant, and even contrary, data. Gottwald and Starkweather (1995), for instance, appeared to agree with "several early intervention programs [that] have suggested that parents refrain from making negative comments about fluency such as 'stop stuttering' or 'slow down'.... parents and teachers [should] be encouraged and, if necessary, trained to focus on the content of the child's message and not on the way the message was produced" (p. 121).

There are absolutely no data showing that this recommendation achieves any beneficial effects, whereas there are data from Onslow et al. (1990) and from Reed and Godden (1977), neither of which were cited in this context by Starkweather and Gottwald, that clearly show that parents' contingent comments about stuttering can cause stuttering to decrease. Blood's (1995a, 1995b) articles on Relapse Management made no reference to a large number of studies on the relapse/maintenance issue in stuttering treatment (e.g., Boberg, 1981; Ingham, 1980, 1982) that have provided data evaluating the effects of maintenance programs. Similar oversights characterize Healey, Scott, and Ellis' (1995) article, which studiously ignored a variety of articles that outlined "decision making" procedures in the treatment of school-age children (Blaesing, 1982; Ingham & Costello, 1984; Onslow, 1992; Ryan, 1974). Such examples may seem unimportant or even petty individually, but taken together, they are solid and disturbing evidence that many treatment recommendations are being made in our current literature not only without data but also with complete disregard for previous relevant work.[6]

OBSTACLE TWO: ARGUMENTS THAT TREATMENT IS INEFFECTIVE OR UNNECESSARY

The trend toward reporting and recommending treatments without supportive outcome evaluation data, and of ignoring data-based publications from other sources, may have helped spawn a completely contrary and no less troublesome claim: that stuttering treatment for children may be totally ineffective. This claim represents a second obstacle to effective or meaningful stuttering treatment research: the argument that stuttering treatments for young children might not produce changes exceeding those resulting from "spontaneous recovery." The notion of spontaneous recovery from stuttering is an old one that has been extensively debated (see Ingham, 1984; Martin & Lindamood, 1986; Young, 1975), but it seems to be reviving itself (Yairi, 1993; Yairi & Ambrose, 1992; Yairi & Curlee, 1995). Yairi and Curlee (1995) argued that empirical evidence is lacking not only for the management procedures used with young children who stutter, but also for the generalization and maintenance of any improvements caused by those procedures. This conclusion is clearly similar to the Division's Guidelines: "It should be noted that the Steering Committee felt that the state of knowledge in several key areas — specifically treatment efficacy... — was not developed well enough" (ASHA, 1995, p. 26). Certainly, judging by the quality of many recent treatment reports, this argument may be plausible. However, Yairi and Curlee then proceeded to suggest that the only way to establish such empirical support would be through the use of randomly assigned no-treatment control groups, a stricture on treatment research that may be akin to throwing out the proverbial baby with the bathwater.

Part of Yairi and Curlee's argument was based on the data reproduced in Fig. 15.2 (Yairi & Ambrose, 1992), which compares the rate of recovery in children who received treatment with those who did not receive treatment. These data are from 27 children who were assessed during four visits over a 2-year period, beginning at age 2 to 4 years; 21 were then assessed during a fifth visit 3 to 12 years after the initial visit. There was no significant difference between the "stuttering-like disfluencies" that systematically declined in the children who received treatment ($n = 18$) and in those who did not ($n = 9$); therefore, the conclusion was drawn that children who receive treatment do not improve significantly more than those who do not.[7]

The logic behind this conclusion will create an immediate sense of *déjà vu* among those familiar with the history of treatment research in behavioral therapies. In 1952, Eysenck used the same logic to draw conclusions from a similar comparison of studies that used psychotherapy to treat psychoneuroses and studies that used no treatment. Eysenck concluded that psychotherapy was ineffective because the rate of recovery was similar in the treated and untreated groups of subjects. Unfortunately, it took some years for reviewers of this influential study to realize that many of the individual treatments that Eysenck included in his survey simply did not work: that is, good or effective treatments were combined with ineffective treatments (including psychoanalysis for stuttering; see Bergin, 1971; Hersen & Barlow, 1976). In other words, it was not possible to infer from Eysenck's review that treatment as a whole was no more effective than spontaneous recovery because of the many differences among the treatments that were collapsed to complete his review.

Much the same issue applies to the data presented by Yairi and Ambrose (1992). The treatment described for the 18 children in their study included "a short treatment program of 5 to 12 sessions.... [that] emphasized modeling of slow speech" (1992, p. 757). Clearly, the fidelity or quality with which such treatments are conducted can vary enormously, particularly if they are conducted in a university

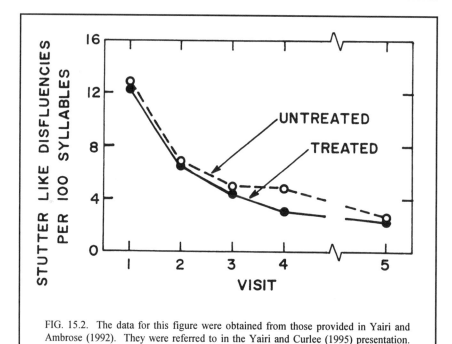

FIG. 15.2. The data for this figure were obtained from those provided in Yairi and Ambrose (1992). They were referred to in the Yairi and Curlee (1995) presentation.

clinic. More importantly, the content of this treatment was not specified: If, for example, "modeling of slow speech" meant teaching the child's parents to speak more slowly, then "there is little objective evidence to demonstrate the effectiveness of these recommendations" (Nippold & Rudzinski, 1995, p. 986). The problem here, in other words, is that Yairi and Curlee used evidence from one particular poorly described and ineffective treatment to suggest that stuttering treatment for children may achieve no more success than would occur via spontaneous recovery, precisely the same error that was incorporated into Eysenck's earlier review.

Despite these problems, however, Yairi and Curlee did raise a legitimate question: Where are the data to show that stuttering therapy is effective in treating young children who stutter? They correctly observed that, in fact, there is no published classically designed group study on the effects of treatment with children. A random-assignment, treatment versus untreated control group design is not the only way to establish treatment efficacy, however; such designs may be inappropriate for some treatment evaluation studies for many reasons. One problem is that withholding treatment may be unethical, an argument that resurfaces routinely about no-treatment control groups. Currently, in fact, the use of placebos or nontreatment controls in therapy research is under severe challenge on both ethical and scientific grounds (see Declaration of Helsinki IV. September, 1989; Lewin, 1995; Rothman & Michels, 1994). Indeed, stuttering treatment studies on children using a nontreatment control group may be unethical if there is evidence that withholding treatment increases the probability that the disorder will persist, and if there is evidence that treatment can reduce their stuttering.

What options are available, then, for determining the efficacy of stuttering treatments? One possibility is to try to compare the outcomes of different stuttering treatment studies with the recovery rates reported among comparable untreated historical controls from longitudinal studies.[8] Such a comparison may also make it possible to test Yairi, Ambrose, Paden, and Throneburg's (1996) recent claim that because the recovery rate among children who have been stuttering for less than 15 months is very high, then "it may be advantageous to defer [their] treatment" (p. 76). In order to complete just such a comparison, we identified 11 studies of children who stuttered that had collected stuttering data, speech rate data, and measurement reliability data, in multiple within- and beyond-clinic assessments, and that had continued to collect data at follow-up assessments in beyond-clinic conditions at least 8 months after treatment ceased (and in most cases, at least 8 months after any formal maintenance program; see Table 15.1). With assistance from some of the authors, those children who were younger than 10 years at the beginning of their treatment were identified (because previous reviews have shown a substantial difference in recovery rates for children after approximately age 9 or 10) and their reported age of stuttering onset was also identified.

Table 15.1 shows that, of the 46 children who received treatment in these studies, 31 (67.4%) could be classified as successfully treated, based on their showing either 90% reductions in stuttering frequency or less than 0.5 stuttered words per minute during the beyond-clinic spontaneous speaking tasks at least 8 months after the end of treatment. In all cases, speech rate data strongly suggested that the effects were not due to reductions in speech rate.[9] Table 15.1 also shows data from historical controls from three studies on ostensibly untreated children, two published and one unpublished: Only 42.8% of the historical controls could be classified as "recovered."[10]

At first glance, then, it appears that stuttering treatments for children do produce effects over and above those obtained without formal treatment: 67% recovered in the treatment studies, and only 43% recovered among the historical controls. However, there are several other factors that should be assessed more carefully, especially because the reported recovery rates are not at all consistent even across these three studies. Ramig's (1993) was conducted on 19 children who were first assessed at 3–8 years. When they were next assessed, 6–8 years later, only 2 of these 19 children had recovered.[11] Panelli et al. (1978), in contrast, reported that 15 children were assessed by three speech-language pathologists at 2–5 years of age and then again on a second occasion at least 5 years later. At the second assessment, 12 of 15, or 80%, had recovered. In the middle, as it were, are J. Ingham and Riley's (1996) data from an ongoing study comparing two treatments for children age 4–9 years. For at least 3 months prior to treatment, and throughout treatment, monthly within- and beyond-clinic recordings (in the home and at another site) were obtained of the child's conversational speech. Recovery occurred without treatment (i.e., before a stable pretreatment baseline could be achieved) in 7 of 15 children, with this recovery confirmed by the parent and by two clinicians.

Group	Age at initial assessment	Age at final assessment	Percent recovered
Preschoolers, Treated (n=22)[a]	2-5 years	3-6 years	81.8%
Preschoolers, Untreated (n=34) [b]	3-5 years	4-14 years	55.9%
School-Age, Treated (n=24)[c]	6-9 years	7-12 years	54.2%
School-Age, Untreated (n=15)[d]	6-9 years	7-16 years	13.3%
Total, Treated			67.4%
Total, Untreated			42.8%

[a] 2 children from Kully & Boberg (1991), 2 from Martin, Kuhl,& Haroldson (1972), 2 from Reed & Godden (1977), 12 from Onslow, Andrews, & Lincoln (1994), 4 from Onslow, Costa, & Rue (1990). Children in Onslow and colleagues' programs may have still been involved in maintenance activities at 9 mos and 12 mos posttreatment, when recordings were made.

[b] 10 children from Ingham & Riley (1996), 15 from Panelli, McFarlane, & Shipley (1978), 9 from Ramig (1993).

[c] 4 children from Kully & Boberg (1991), 7 from Lincoln, Onslow, Lewis, & Wilson (1996), 7 from Ryan (1974), 6 from Ryan & Van Kirk Ryan (1995).

[d] 5 children from Ingham & Riley (1996), 10 from Ramig (1993).

TABLE 15.1. Percentage of children under age 10 from selected data-based treatment reports (see text) who were classified as successfully treated, based on their displaying either a 90% reduction in stuttering frequency (relative to initial assessment) or less than 0.5 stuttered words per minute during recorded beyond-clinic spontaneous speaking tasks at least 8 months after the end of treatment.

One factor that might explain part of the discrepancy across these studies is the age of the children. As shown in Table 15.1, there was a higher rate of recovery among preschoolers in these studies than among school-age children. Yairi et al. (1996) also suggested that the time elapsed between stuttering onset and the onset of treatment may affect treatment outcome: Yairi et al. argued that recovery is more likely among children who have been stuttering for less than 15 months before treatment is initiated than among those who have been stuttering for a longer period. They also argued that unassisted recovery is more probable among young girls who stutter, implying that reports of successful treatment in young children may have been confounded by both age of onset and gender. These predictions can be tested by dividing the children represented in Table 15.1 by gender and by time since stuttering onset (Table 15.2). Children who had been stuttering for less than 15 months certainly did show a much higher rate of recovery without treatment than children who had been stuttering for a longer period of time, suggesting that perhaps recovery may be more probable without treatment during this early phase of stuttering. Such a simplistic conclusion, however, overlooks the fact that the bulk of the treated children were treated only after their frequency of stuttering had stabilized for at least 3 months and so there was no sign that they were likely to recover. By contrast, the trend toward recovery among the younger children who did recover (as in J. Ingham & Riley's data) generally became evident during one 3-month period.

In the absence of a decreasing trend in an individual child's stuttering, it would seem from these data to be rather hazardous to conclude that a child should not receive treatment until stuttering has been present for at least 15 months: Treatment after more than 15 months have elapsed does not appear to have been as effective in these children as treatment initiated sooner. This finding should be taken into account by those who advocate withholding treatment from young children, and it also raises serious questions about the ethics of continuing to withhold treatment in order to preserve the integrity of a longitudinal study of stuttering. Table 15.2 also shows, incidentally, that reports of recovery among young children do not seem to be characterized by a disproportionate number of female cases, and that recovery rates among untreated girls are essentially equivalent to recovery rates among untreated boys.

Initial assessment/ Beginning of treatment	Treated or Untreated	Male or Female	Percent Recovered
		Male	77.8%
	Treated [a]	Female	100.0%
		Combined	85.7%
within 15 mos of stuttering onset			
		Male	73.3%
	Untreated [b]	Female	71.4%
		Combined	72.7%
		Male	57.1%
	Treated [c]	Female	75.0%
		Combined	59.4%
15 mos or more after stuttering onset			
		Male	21.0%
	Untreated [d]	Female	12.5%
		Combined	18.5%

[a] 7/9 boys and 5/5 girls recovered.
[b] 11/15 boys and 5/7 girls recovered.
[c] 16/28 boys and 3/4 girls recovered.
[d] 4/19 boys and 1/8 girls recovered.

TABLE 15.2. Percentage of children represented in Table 15.1 who recovered from stuttering, shown for separately for boys and girls, and for those children whose treatment (or controlled recording/monitoring, for untreated children) started within 15 months of stuttering onset or more than 15 months after stuttering onset.

SUMMARY AND CONCLUSIONS

This chapter presented two related issues that seem to be interfering with the meaningful evaluation of stuttering therapies. First, treatments are being recommended with absolutely no attempt to evaluate their effectiveness within a data-based treatment evaluation framework. Second, a tendency to ignore the data-based studies that are available in our literature is being stretched into the conclusion that young children do not need therapy for their stuttering after all. Our field has developed a rich resource of treatment methods and treatment evaluation procedures. Not only are these being ignored by many recent commentaries on stuttering treatment, but they are being replaced by methods and guidelines that now begin to raise serious doubts about the credibility of therapy practice. At the very least, these are concerns that should be shared by others who believe it is unethical to use unproven therapy practices. The data presented in Tables 15.1 and 15.2 are clearly at odds with any suggestion that treatment effects are no greater than the rate of unassisted recovery. They also convincingly refute the recent suggestion by Kuhr (1994) that operant treatments are ineffective (see also Ryan & Van Kirk Ryan, 1996), a conclusion that may certainly apply not only to those treatments labeled "operant" but also to any treatment for stuttering that has been evaluated within a data-based framework.

Fortunately for our clients and for our discipline, the obstacles raised here are not insurmountable. In fact, one solution to many of the problems discussed in this chapter is as simple as a renewed commitment to critical and thoughtful reading of the research and treatment literature, combined with a renewed commitment to treatment efficacy data as the basis for the decisions we make for and with our clients.

REFERENCES

American Speech-Language-Hearing Association. (1995, March). Guidelines for practice in stuttering treatment. *ASHA, 37* (Suppl. 14), 26–35.

Andronico, M., & Blake, I. (1971). The application of filial therapy to young children with stuttering problems. *Journal of Speech and Hearing Disorders, 36,* 377–381.

Baer, D. M. (1988). If you know why you're changing behavior, you'll know when you've changed it enough. *Behavioral Assessment, 10,* 219–223.

Baer, D. M. (1990). The critical issue in treatment efficacy is knowing why treatment was applied: A student's response to Roger Ingham. In L. B. Olswang, C. K. Thompson, S. F. Warren, & N. Minghetti (Eds.), *Treatment efficacy research in communication disorders* (pp. 31–39). Rockville, MD: American Speech-Language-Hearing Foundation.

Bennett, E. M., Reveles, V. N., & Ramig, P. R. (1993). [Speaking attitudes in children: Summer fluency camp]. Unpublished raw data.

Bergin, A. E. (1971). The evaluation of therapeutic outcomes. In A. E. Bergin & S. L. Garfield (Eds.), *Handbook of psychotherapy and behavior change* (pp. 217–270). New York: Wiley.

Bernstein Ratner, N. (1995). Treating the child who stutters with concomitant language or phonological impairment. *Language, Speech, and Hearing Services in Schools, 26,* 180–186.

Blaesing, L. (1982). A multidisciplinary approach to individualized treatment of stuttering. *Journal of Fluency Disorders, 7,* 203–218.

Blood, G. W. (1995a). A behavioral-cognitive therapy program for adults who stutter: Computers and counseling. *Journal of Communication Disorders, 28,* 165–180.

Blood, G. W. (1995b). Power^2: Relapse management with adolescents who stutter. *Language, Speech, and Hearing Services in Schools, 26*, 169–179.

Bloodstein, O. (1995). *A handbook on stuttering.* San Diego, CA: Singular.

Boberg, E. (1981). Maintenance of fluency: An experimental program. In E. Boberg (Ed.), *Maintenance of fluency* (pp. 71–111). New York: Elsevier.

Conture, E. (1990). *Stuttering* (2nd ed.). Englewood Cliffs, NJ: Prentice-Hall

Conture, E., Louko, L., & Edwards, M. L. (1993). Simultaneously treating stuttering and disordered phonology in children: Experimental therapy, preliminary findings. *American Journal of Speech-Language Pathology, 2*, 72–81.

Conture, E., & Wolk, L. (1990). Stuttering. *Seminars in Speech and Language, 14*, 200–211.

Costello, J. M. (1983). Current behavioral treatments for children. In D. Prins & R. Ingham (Eds.), *Treatment of stuttering in early childhood: Methods and issues* (pp. 69–112). San Diego, CA: College-Hill Press.

Curlee, R. F. (1993). Evaluating treatment efficacy for adults: Assessment of stuttering disability. *Journal of Fluency Disorders, 18*, 319–331

Daly, D. A., Simon, C. A., & Burnett-Stolnack, M. (1995). Helping adolescents who stutter focus on fluency. *Language, Speech, and Hearing Services in Schools, 26*, 162–168.

Declaration of Helsinki IV, World Medical Assiciation, 41st World Medical Assembly, Hong Kong, September, 1989. In G. J. Annas & M. A. Gridin (Eds.). *The Nazi doctors and the Nuremberg Code: Human rights in human experimentation.* (pp. 339–342). New York: Oxford University Press.

Enderby, P., & Emerson, J. (1995). *Does speech and language therapy work?* San Diego, CA: Singular.

Eysenck, H. J. (1952). The effects of psychotherapy: An evaluation. *Journal of Consulting Psychology, 16*, 319–324.

Fosnot, S. M. (Ed.). (1995). Some contemporary approaches in treating fluency disorders in preshool, school-age, and adolescent children [special issue]. *Language, Speech, and Hearing Services in Schools, 26*(2).

Goebel, M. (1989). *Cafet-for-kids.* Annandale, VA: Annandale Fluency Clinic.

Goldiamond, I. (1965). Stuttering and fluency as manipulatable operant response classes. In L. Krasner & L. P. Ullman (Eds.), *Research in behavior modification* (pp. 106–156). New York: Holt, Rinehart, & Winston.

Gottwald, S. R., & Starkweather, C. W. (1995). Fluency intervention for preschoolers and their families in the public schools. *Language, Speech, and Hearing Services in Schools, 26*, 117–126.

Healey, E. C., & Scott, L. A. (1995). Strategies for treating elementary school-age children who stutter: An integrative approach. *Language, Speech, and Hearing Services in Schools, 26*, 151–161.

Healey, E. C., Scott, L. A., & Ellis, G. (1995). Decision making in the treatment of school-age children who stutter. *Journal of Communication Disorders, 28*, 107–124.

Hersen, M., & Barlow, D. H. (1976). *Single case experimental designs: Strategies for studying behavior change.* New York: Pergamon.

Information for authors (1995). *Language, Speech, and Hearing Services in Schools, 26*, 208.

Ingham, J. C., & Riley, G. D. (1996). [Comparison of two treatments for children who stutter]. Unpublished raw data.

Ingham, R. J. (1972). *The development, application, and analysis of a token system for the treatment of adult stutterers.* Unpublished doctoral dissertation, University of New South Wales.

Ingham, R. J. (1980). Modification of maintenance and generalization during stuttering treatment. *Journal of Speech and Hearing Research, 23*, 732–745.

Ingham, R. J. (1981). Evaluation and maintenance in stuttering therapy: A search for ecstasy with nothing but agony. In E. Boberg (Ed.), *Maintenance of fluency* (pp. 179–218). New York: Elsevier.

Ingham, R. J. (1982). The effects of self-evaluation training on maintenance and generalization during stuttering treatment. *Journal of Speech and Hearing Disorders, 47*, 271–280.

Ingham, R. J. (1984). *Stuttering and behavior therapy: Current status and experimental foundations.* San Diego, CA: College-Hill Press.

Ingham, R. J. (1993). Stuttering treatment efficacy: Paradigm dependent or independent? *Journal of Fluency Disorders, 18,* 133–145.

Ingham, R. J., & Costello, J. M. (1984). Stuttering treatment outcome evaluation. In J. M. Costello (Ed.), *Speech disorders in children: Recent advances* (pp. 313–346) San Diego, CA: College-Hill Press.

Kazdin, A. E. (1982). *Single case research designs: Methods for clinical and applied settings.* New York: Oxford University Press.

Kuhr, A. (1994). The rise and fall of operant programs for the treatment of stammering. *Folia Phoniatrica et Logopaedica, 46,* 232–240.

Kully, D., & Boberg, E. (1991). Therapy for school-age children. *Seminars in Speech and Language, 12,* 291–300.

Lewin, D. I. (December, 1995). Are placebo-based trials unethical? *The Journal of NIH Research, 7,* 30–33.

Lincoln, M., Onslow, M., Lewis, C., & Wilson, L. (1996). A clinical trial of an operant treatment for school-age children who stutter. *American Journal of Speech Language Pathology, 5*(2), 73–85.

Martin, R. R., Kuhl, P., & Haroldson, S. (1972). An experimental treatment with two preschool stuttering children. *Journal of Speech and Hearing Research, 15,* 743–752.

Martin, R. R., & Lindamood, L. R. (1986). Stuttering and spontaneous recovery: Implications for the speech-language pathologist. *Language, Speech and Hearing Services in Schools, 17,* 207–218.

Martin, R. R., Parlour, S., & Haroldson, S. (1990). Stuttering and level of linguistic demand: The Stocker Probe. *Journal of Fluency Disorders, 15,* 93–106.

Nippold, M. A., & Rudzinski, M. (1995). Parents' speech and children's stuttering: A critique of the literature. *Journal of Speech and Hearing Research, 38,* 978–989.

Onslow, M. (1992). Identification of early stuttering: Issues and suggested strategies. *American Journal of Speech-Language Pathology, 1,* 21–27.

Onslow, M., Andrews, C., & Lincoln, M. (1994). A control/experimental trial of operant treatment for early stuttering. *Journal of Speech and Hearing Research, 37,* 1244–1259.

Onslow, M., Costa, L., & Rue, S. (1990). Direct early intervention with stuttering: Some preliminary data. *Journal of Speech and Hearing Disorders, 55,* 405–416.

Panelli, C. A., McFarlane, S. C., & Shipley, K. G. (1978). Implications of evaluating and intervening with incipient stutterers. *Journal of Fluency Disorders, 3,* 41–50.

Peters, T. J., & Guitar, B. (1991). *Stuttering. An integrated approach to its nature and treatment.* Baltimore, MD: Williams & Wilkins

Prins, D., & Hubbard, C. P. (1988). Response contingent stimuli and stuttering: Issues and implications. *Journal of Speech and Hearing Research, 31,* 696–709.

Ramig, P. (1993). High reported spontaneous recovery rates: Fact or fiction? *Language, Speech, and Hearing Services in Schools, 24,* 156–160.

Ramig, P. R., & Bennett, E. M. (1995). Working with 7- to 12-year-old children who stutter: Ideas for intervention in the public schools. *Language, Speech, and Hearing Services in Schools, 26,* 138–150.

Reed, C. G., & Godden, A. L. (1977). An experimental treatment using verbal punishment with two preschool stutterers. *Journal of Fluency Disorders, 2,* 225–233.

Rothman, K. J., & Michels, K. B. (1994). The continuing unethical use of placebo controls. *New England Journal of Medicine, 331*(6), 394–398.

Runyan, C. M., & Runyan, S. E. (1986). A fluency rules therapy program for young children in the public schools. *Language, Speech, and Hearing Services in Schools, 17,* 276–284.

Runyan, C. M., & Runyan, S. E. (1993). Therapy for school-age stutterers. An update on the fluency rules program. In R. E. Curlee (Ed.), *Stuttering and related disorders of fluency* (pp. 101–114). New York: Thieme Medical Publishers.

Rustin, L., & Cook, F. (1995). Parental involvement in the treatment of stuttering. *Language, Speech, and Hearing Services in Schools, 26,* 127–137.

Ryan, B. P. (1974). *Programmed therapy for stuttering in children and adults.* Springfield, Il: Thomas.

Ryan, B. P., & Van Kirk Ryan, B. (1995). Programmed stuttering treatment for children: Comparison of two establishment programs through transfer, maintenance, and follow-up. *Journal of Speech and Hearing Research, 38,* 61–75.

Ryan, B. P., & Van Kirk Ryan, B. (1996). Re: Kuhr, A. (1994). The rise and fall of operant programs for the treatment of stammering. *Folia Phoniatrica et Logopaedica, 48,* 309–312.

Shames, G. H., & Florance, C. L. (1980). *Stutter-free speech: A goal for therapy.* Columbus, OH: Merrill.

Shine, R. (1984). Assessment and fluency training with young stutterers. In M. Peins (Ed.), *Contemporary approaches in stuttering therapy* (pp. 173–216). Boston: Little, Brown.

Silverman, F. H. (1996). *Stuttering and other fluency disorders (*2nd ed.*).* Boston, MA: Allyn & Bacon.

Sohn, D. (1996). Publication bias and the evaluation of psychotherapy efficacy in reviews of the research literature. *Clinical Psychology Review, 16,* 147–156.

Starkweather, C. W., & Gottwald, S. R. (1993). A pilot study of relations among specific measures obtained at intake and discharge in a program of prevention and early intervention for stuttering. *American Journal of Speech-Language Pathology, 2,* 51–58.

Starkweather, C. W., Gottwald, S. R., & Halfond, M. M. (1990). *Stuttering prevention.* Englewood Cliffs, NJ: Prentice-Hall.

Stocker, B. (1980). *The Stocker probe technique for diagnosis and treatment of stuttering in young children.* Tulsa, OK: Modern Educational Corporation.

Wall, M., & Myers, F. (1984). *Clinical management of childhood stuttering.* Baltimore, MD: University Park Press.

Yairi, E. (1993). Epidemiological and other considerations in treatment efficacy research with preschool age children who stutter. *Journal of Fluency Disorders, 18,* 197–219.

Yairi, E., & Ambrose, N. (1992). A longitudinal study of stuttering in children: A preliminary report. *Journal of Speech and Hearing Research, 35,* 755–760.

Yairi, E., & Ambrose, N. (1996). Erratum. *Journal of Speech and Hearing Research, 39,* 826.

Yairi, E., Ambrose, N., Paden, E. P., & Throneburg, R. N. (1996). Predictive factors of persistence and recovery: Pathways of childhood stuttering. *Journal of Communication Disorders, 29,* 51–77.

Yairi, E., & Curlee, R. (December, 1995). *Early intervention in childhood stuttering: Myths and facts.* Paper read to the annual convention of the American Speech-Language-Hearing Association, Orlando, FL.

Young, M. A. (1975). Onset, prevalence, and recovery from stuttering. *Journal of Speech and Hearing Disorders, 40,* 49–58.

FOOTNOTES

[1]In addition to the problems discussed later, the Guidelines included the following suggestions, none of which are supported by any published data: Record "anomalies of social interaction such as poor eye contact, generalized low muscle tonus, poor body posture" (ASHA, 1995, p. 29); train "parents in the relaxed production of occasional disfluencies that are normal for their child's age" (p. 33); and recognize that clients can "learn through self-demonstration that speech improves when they 'give permission to stutter' or stutter on purpose" (p. 34).

[2]Some recent writers have begun to argue that the point of complaint for persons who stutter is not necessarily occurrences of stuttering in their speech, a topic that was also discussed at the 1996 Special Interest Division Conference. References are made to not being able to cope with the self-concept of being a person who stutters (Silverman, 1996) or with other aspects of their speech (Conture, 1990). It seems relevant to note here that Ingham (1972) completed a complex treatment study with 98 adults who stuttered, age 18 to 56 years, that gathered data germane to this point. At the beginning of the study, subjects were asked to identify the problem that "they expect to have resolved by their therapy program." All 98 indicated that they wanted to be able to speak without stuttering; 10 of the 98 indicated that removing the fear of speaking was equally important. These data clearly support the contention that stuttering is the principal point of complaint for persons who seek stuttering therapy.

[3]The argument that *LSHSS* is not meant to be a data-based journal, variations of which are often used to defend articles such as those in the April, 1995, issue, assumes that school clinicians are either incapable of understanding treatment efficacy data or are somehow uninterested in whether the treatments they select will be effective with their clients. We do not accept either of these assumptions. In fact, the description of possible manuscript types for LSHSS states that "reports are data-based descriptive or experimental studies.... judged in terms of scientific merit.... that evaluate the appropriateness or effectiveness of a particular assessment or treatment procedure" (Information for Authors, *LSHSS*, 1995, p. 208)). Manuscripts of other types ("articles," in the terminology used by *LSHSS*) can at the very least include reference to data-based publications, if any exist to support the treatments discussed.

[4]Starkweather and Gottwald (1993) also reported intercorrelations among a variety of measures obtained on 14 preschoolers and their parents before and after treatment, including "discontinuous speech time." Starkweather and Gottwald also stated that "families were discharged from treatment if the child's fluency level was considered normal in type and frequency and the parents reported that they were no longer concerned that stuttering would develop" (1993, p. 56), but no actual speech performance data were provided. Even if they had been provided, questions would have to be raised: The discontinuous speech time data, for example, were derived from only 25 utterances within one 15-minute play session. In short, despite the fact that the authors provided numerous published accounts of this treatment procedure, even prior to this article, not one included a data-based evaluation of the treated children's speech performance after treatment either within or outside of the therapy setting.

[5]Presumably these students recognized that it is logically impossible to draw any inferences about the effects of a C phase from within an A–B–C–A treatment design.

[6]One work that is frequently cited among the *LSHSS* articles is Peters and Guitar's (1991) textbook. The most recent reference listed in that text is from 1989, but none of the articles listed in Table 15.1 and published prior to 1989 is included among Peters and Guitar's references. Actually, this text is almost a "textbook illustration" of many of the issues referred to in the present chapter. No information was provided about the evaluation of the therapy procedures that are described in the text, and there was no consideration of methods that clinicians should employ in order to systematically evaluate the effects of stuttering treatment, not even the relatively standard reference to the treatment evaluation criteria that were provided by Bloodstein (e.g., 1995) and cited by other authors (e.g., Conture & Wolk, 1990). The amount of significant information omitted from this text is astonishing: It seems almost inconceivable, for example, that a textbook account of the use of delayed auditory feedback and prolonged speech in stuttering treatment could not refer to Goldiamond's (1965) seminal paper, but Peters and Guitar have succeeded. That such a book should clearly be as widely adopted as this one has been, despite what some might see as its weaknesses or oversights, simply provides more evidence that the issues discussed in the present article should be important current concerns.

The first author also presents two personal experiences that reflect similar issues of a lack of concern for the available literature. One occurred at a recent ASHA conference, where a young researcher reported finding that the frequency of stuttering in children may vary significantly across different speaking situations. That such a presentation would be accepted for an ASHA conference in the mid-1990s, presumably because the conference committee agreed with the researcher that it provided new information, is revealing and troubling. Equally worrying is that, at a major gathering of prominent researchers on stuttering at NIH in 1992, another young researcher described his recent contact, via some colleagues in clinical psychology, with a new therapy technique that might be useful in the treatment of stuttering. The technique that he considered to be new was response-contingent time-out, one of the most extensively researched procedures in the area of stuttering (see Prins & Hubbard, 1988, for one review). If these events are representative, then perhaps the major obstacle to meaningful research on stuttering is the lack of information about the vast stuttering literature that mentors are imparting to current graduate students.

[7]Some interesting issues arise in trying to interpret the data reported by Yairi and Ambrose (1992). In the first place, Table 3 (p. 759) in their article was incorrect and was revised in an Erratum published by Yairi and Ambrose (1996). In the second place, Yairi and Ambrose (1996, p. 826) asserted that "These data do not in any way indicate that treatment is not beneficial nor that it has no effect but that success rates for treated individuals must take spontaneous recovery into account." Yairi and Ambrose (1992, p. 759) also stated that their study "was not designed as a comparative study of treatment versus no treatment." Such statements, however, are rather meaningless. One would have to accept that Yairi and Ambrose had no reason for including subjects who had received treatment, nor for making comparisons between children who received treatment and children who did not (see Table 2 from Yairi and Ambrose, 1992, or see Figure 2 from Yairi and Curlee, 1995). That seems to be even more unacceptable in view of Yairi and Curlee's (1995) claim that these data can be interpreted as evidence that children who received treatment did not improve significantly more than those who did not receive treatment.

[8]Meta-analyses of treatment studies have also become a favored methodology for identifying therapy benefits for many disorders. In the case of stuttering, however, it is far from clear that the results can be trusted (Ingham, 1993), a conclusion that Sohn (1996) also reached with respect to many other disorders.

[9]Arguably, the criterion of successful treatment employed here is not the same as the criterion of recovery in the untreated group. On the one hand, our criterion for successful treatment is probably better described as one that demonstrates a clinically significant treatment effect; a 90% durable reduction in stuttering frequency appears to be a reasonably conservative description of a clinically meaningful change. However, we also acknowledge that in the absence of information about severity, speech quality, or self/parent judgments regarding the presence or absence of a stuttering problem, it is possible that our criterion of recovery would admit subjects with very infrequent but severe stuttering events (see Ingham, 1981). It is also possible that it might exclude some subjects with a low frequency of nonproblematic stuttering. On the other hand, it is also not clear that recovery among the nontreatment group meant a complete absence of stuttering behavior. Panelli et al. (1978), for example, stated that their recovered stutterers were "not exhibiting stuttering behavior during the follow-up examination," but that examination occurred in clinic rather than nonclinic conditions. Reports of treatment-produced recovery have usually relied on far more extensive analyses of speech performance data, especially in beyond-clinic conditions, than is the case in nontreatment recovery studies. In short, it may be inaccurate to equate successful treatment in treated subjects with recovery in untreated subjects because neither successful treatment nor untreated recovery is consistently and clearly defined in terms of the absence of stuttering. Given this shortcoming, however, it still seems reasonable to compare both classes of subjects using our criteria to determine whether treatment does produce beneficial effects and whether they tend to be affected by age since onset of stuttering or gender.

[10]The unpublished data included here were gathered from the extended Baseline Phase of a stuttering treatment research study being conducted by J. Ingham and Riley (1996), and they are presented here for the first time courtesy of those experimenters. There are also other longitudinal studies (see Ingham, 1984; Martin & Lindamood, 1986), but these three were selected because the children's speech was recorded and assessed by qualified clinicians in a manner similar to that used in the treatment studies included in this review. Data provided by Yairi and Ambrose (1992) are not included here because the majority of their subjects did receive treatment (regardless of whether or not it was effective). This was not the case for the three studies chosen for inclusion as nontreatment studies.

[11]It is important to note, with respect to the spontaneous recovery argument, that treatment was recommended for all of these children when they were first assessed, but their parents ignored the recommendation, because either they "could not afford treatment, [or] ...a physician and/or another speech-language pathologist told them that their child would outgrow the problem without treatment" (Ramig, 1993, p. 156).

ACKNOWLEDGMENTS

Preparation of this paper was supported, in part, by Research Grant No. 5 RO1 DC 00060-05 from the National Institute of Deafness and Other Communication Disorders, National Institutes of Health. Special thanks are owed to Peter Ramig, Bruce Ryan, Deborah Kully, Steve McFarlane, Mark Onslow, Michelle Lincoln, and Jan Ingham for providing important additional information about their studies on children who stutter.

Address for all correspondence: Roger J. Ingham, Department of Speech and Hearing Sciences, University of California, Santa Barbara, Santa Barbara, CA, 93106. E-mail: sph1ingh@ucsbuxa.ucsb.edu

16 The Effectiveness of Stuttering Therapy: An Issue for Science?

C. Woodruff Starkweather
Temple University, and
The Birch Tree Foundation

STUTTERING THERAPY AND THE LIMITS OF SCIENTIFIC INQUIRY

Horgan (1996) argues compellingly that we are approaching the limits of science. He notes that many scientific fields have reached the point of "ironic science," where only unanswerable questions remain to be answered. At this terminus, the fertile human imagination continues to pose questions, to speculate about the nature of the universe or of consciousness, for example, but what remains to be known is buried in a heap of unobservable events, or influenced by forces that cannot be measured, or knotted in the paradox of self-reference. Some questions, he also notes, are simply more complex than systematic observation can unravel.

Each of these four criteria for scientifically unanswerable questions — too many unobservable events, unmeasurable influences, the presence of self-reference, and extreme complexity — seem characteristic of stuttering, and in particular, of stuttering therapy. So, it seems that, as scientists, we are responsible for examining the possibility that the question of therapeutic efficacy may not be a question science can answer. This is not to say that the question is unanswerable, only that it might be unanswerable by scientific method.

It is axiomatic in science that not all questions are scientific questions, and that therefore one of the things scientists do is decide whether specific questions are scientific questions or not. This is, in fact, a crucial aspect of scientific inquiry because it helps scientists to be efficient in seeking answers to questions that can be answered scientifically. As scientists, we need to ask ourselves: What is a scientific question and what is not?

Horgan's four criteria were given earlier. Harris (1995) also examines this question and concludes that the following types of questions are not questions for science to answer; questions that cannot be answered by observation, questions that cannot be answered via the scientific method (i.e., hypothesis testing under controlled conditions, based on observation, with conclusions by inference), questions that deal with individual, personal variables, and questions of moral or spiritual issues. In this chapter, I show that the effectiveness of therapy for stuttering is a question that meets all four of Horgan's criteria and the first three of Harris' criteria. There is even an argument to be made on the basis of Harris' fourth criterion, but to do so requires more space than this chapter can provide.

To argue the position that therapeutic effectiveness is not a scientific issue, I first provide a description of the development of stuttering. Smith (this volume) describes the development of stuttering as nonlinear, multifaceted, and dynamic. The descriptions that follow exemplify that position in a general way.

THE DEVELOPMENT OF STUTTERING: FROM SIMPLE TO COMPLEX BEHAVIOR

At its beginning, stuttering is relatively simple. Whole-word or whole-syllable repetitions are the most common behavior in the youngest children (Bloodstein, 1960). Typically, at the beginning, there is little or no evidence of struggle, tension, or forcing, nor any evidence that the child is even reacting to his or her disfluencies. The behavior then begins to become more complex. Sometimes this happens quickly and sometimes slowly. Most commonly, the child is quite young (18 months to 4 years) (Bloodstein, 1987; Starkweather & Givens-Ackerman, 1997) and shows the typical signs of frustration, reacting to these disfluencies much the way any child of this age would react to frustration, by pushing and forcing. This does not work any better for speech than it does for a pull-toy stuck under a chair leg, and harder struggling, the well-documented frustration reaction, develops (Adelman & Maatsch, 1956; Amsel & Roussel, 1952; Amsel & Ward, 1954). Soon, the repetitions occur rapidly, and the repeated elements have been truncated. It is not clear why this truncation occurs. I can imagine both neurological and learning theory explanations. Perhaps the child tries to go faster through the repetition to get it over with. Certainly many adults who stutter report such a motivation.

Parents react now, if not earlier, with a variety of feelings — fear, shame, anger, and guilt have been reported. It has been suggested that children, sensitive to the nonverbal behavior these feelings generate, may acquire these feelings as a result (Starkweather, Gottwald & Halfond, 1990). Many parents, trying not to frighten the child, pretend that nothing is happening, creating a "conspiracy of silence" (Sheehan, 1976), which seems to lead to a deeper shame reaction in the child (see Murphy, this volume). Some parents try to help by giving advice (e.g., "slow down"; "take a deep breath"). This clearly tells the children that something is wrong; they may hear the fear in their parents' voices. However, usually they are unable to slow down, and when they do try taking a breath, it may promote fluency for a while but then stops being effective, sometimes leaving in its wake a far worse breathing anomaly, such as gasping for breath, or a kind of panting behavior. The disorder seems to grow, and this creates more fear, more shame, more struggle, and more frustration.

The Self-Reference Problem and Stuttering

Some very young children learn tricks — jumping up and down, plucking the words from their mouths with their fingers, talking very loudly. When these behaviors have been learned and incorporated into the stuttering behavior, a substantial level of complexity has been reached, with the child reacting to the parents' reactions to the child's reactions. This is what Douglas Hofstadter, in his book *Gödel, Escher, Bach: An Eternal Golden Braid* (Hofstadter, 1979)[1] calls recursion or self-reference, when a process operates on itself. In stuttering, it is the disorder creating the disorder. This process of self-reference, present in stuttering, is one of Horgan's (1996) criteria for variables that are beyond scientific investigation. Self-reference is the soul of paradox, and paradox is something we keep running into in stuttering. We ask clients to stutter on purpose, and most of their stuttering behavior disappears. When we interview clients, we find that their stuttering is most severe in those circumstances where stuttering is least desirable. And similarly, experimental subjects, finding themselves in a circumstance where it is important that they DO stutter, become maddeningly fluent. These ironies and paradoxes stem from the fact that certain behaviors, acquired because they did or might reduce stuttering, become part of the problem, adding layers of recursive, self-referential behavior. One rather bright school child we met had all of his behaviors categorized for us when he came in, with special names for each behavior and contingencies for several different kinds of sounds and circumstances in which to use them. "Did they work?" we asked. "Not much any more," he said thoughtfully. These struggles, which begin in the innocence of trying to talk more quickly than repeating words and syllables will allow, eventually become incorporated into the stuttering, and in this way, the disorder is self-referential — it creates itself.

The implications of this fact for therapy, and consequently for efficacy, are substantial. If people who stutter are struggling not to stutter, and the speech clinician teaches them a way not to stutter, by altering their breathing pattern for example, is this efficacious treatment or an unethical exploitation of the power of suggestion? Should the speech clinician teach ways to stutter more openly, more noticeably? Can we consider treatment that seeks more disfluency, rather than less, as effective? In the case of the covert stutterer, whose fears of revealing his or her stuttering are painful and burdensome, more overt stuttering is a desirable goal, if only in the short term. As these difficult questions are posed, it becomes clearer why Horgan feels that questions concerning variables containing the poison of self-reference are off the list of scientific questions, but it is still not entirely clear if the property of self-reference, present though it may be in stuttering, renders the question of efficacy beyond science. It does seem, however, that without a solution to these fundamentally philosophical questions, it is premature to seek scientific validation of efficacy. We have to decide first what we mean by "effective."

Early Intervention: Breaking the "Braid"

We can prevent the complexity of stuttering from developing, or, if it has developed, we can undo it, untie the knots of frustration and struggle. And the younger the child is, the easier the knots are to untie. In a study of families in the Temple Stuttering Prevention Center, those who had been stuttering the longest took the longest to treat successfully (Starkweather & Gottwald, 1993). The reason for this relationship between time spent stuttering (or age, which is of course related to it) and length of treatment may lie in the concept of a critical period of stuttering chronicity. Andrews and Harris' (1967) data show that of the 43 stuttering children they examined, 93 % of those who persisted in stuttering beyond one year could be predicted from the fact that they were stuttering during a critical period between 5½ and 6½. Neither those who began stuttering earlier and stopped before this critical period, nor those who began after this critical period, persisted in stuttering, with only two exceptions. This, the evidence for a critical period for stuttering chronicity, although only descriptive, is nonetheless compelling. If stuttering treatment is inherently more effective in younger children, or in children who have been stuttering for shorter periods of time, then our assessment of effectiveness, if we can find one, has to be adjusted for age.

We know also from numerous studies on plasticity of development (Brauth, Hall & Dooling, 1991) that very young children are far more amenable to change in their preschool years than they will be in their later school years. The evidence is strong for a loss of plasticity of development for all aspects of human functioning — motor performance, cognitive patterns, emotional functioning, and language. But the evidence is strongest for a critical period for speech and language (Krashen, 1973) than for any other area of human functioning. Is this critical period for speech and language behavior responsible for the tenacity with which stuttering behavior persists? The relative ease with which preschool children are treated, compared to the difficulty of treating the child in school, makes this seem likely.

We know that prevention and early intervention can return the child's behavior to a simple, nonpathological level. We know that early intervention and prevention are not only effective, but far more effective than therapy for school-age children and adults. How do we know this? That is the question that this chapter addresses. How do we know what is effective? And how do we know that early intervention in particular is effective? And how do we know that it is more effective than adult treatment? First, many clinical trials have been reported (Gregory & Hill, 1984; Onslow, this work; Starkweather & Gottwald, 1993; Starkweather et al., 1990). It is interesting, and significant in a general sense, that these high success rates come from a variety of different approaches. Success rate is, however, one of the least meaningful of measures, depending as it does on the definition of stuttering, the definition of success, the skills of the clinicians, and a host of other factors.

A more compelling argument comes from the dramatic suddenness with which the behavior changes when an effective strategy of early intervention has been tried. When a young child is stuttering, and a clinician imposes an effective treatment technique, the child usually stops stuttering soon, or, in some cases, there is a dramatic reduction in stuttering behavior. The suddenness and the timing of the improvement compel the conclusion that an effective treatment has been used for this one child. But the technique that works for one child does not necessarily work for another. If the same technique is used repeatedly with the same result for many children, pretty soon the clinician knows that it works for a lot of children. This is what Sidman (1960) meant by "single-subjects design." He did not intend, as is often averred, that we could generalize from one or a few subjects to the population. It takes many subjects, but run one at a time, to establish the predictability of the event, and to establish it with such confidence that statistics should not be necessary to demonstrate it.

Individualized Therapy and Individual Outcomes.

A problem, however, is that the technique that works so dramatically for one child does not necessarily work dramatically, or at all, for other children. Stuttering is so variable and so highly individualized that, few would disagree, no one method works for all children. That certainly has been our experience. But with careful evaluation of both the child and his or her communicative environment, it is possible to construct individualized therapy plans that have a high probability of rapid success.

When an evaluation indicates that a parent is talking much more rapidly than his or her child, it suggests that the difference in speech rate may be a source of time pressure. The parent can then be trained to talk more slowly, and instructed to do so when talking to the child. Sometimes the child's stuttering disappears the very next day. This does not always happen, of course, but it has happened often enough so that the clinician "knows" (and I use the word advisedly) that for some children, this is an extremely useful technique. With others, it may be another technique — less talking altogether, better sleep habits, a reduction in parental fear, or a different distribution of parental attention — and the child's stuttering may not disappear overnight but in a few weeks or a month. In most cases, too, environmental changes are necessary but not sufficient, and some work has to be done with the child. But it is clear that when we individualize treatment and intervene early, we have a substantially better chance of removing the problem than if we wait and treat them as schoolchildren. Furthermore, the children who are treated during the preschool years do not have to monitor their speech, nor is it necessary to work on their naturalness. And relapse, although possible, is rare.

When sources of environmental demand are removed, they have the effect of simplifying the child's stuttering behavior because a stimulus that evokes a behavior has been removed. The behavior then stops occurring. When the communicative environment remains altered for some time, the child has the opportunity to habituate new patterns of speech behavior. Ultimately, when these new patterns are strengthened through ordinary use, the environmental alterations can be removed, and the child's speech remains simplified with regard to the behavior in question. So, it seems that our knowledge of what is effective with children comes not from group studies of efficacy, but from the accumulated clinical experience of many clinicians working with many individual cases.

We seem to be functioning now as though our knowledge of efficacy is not based on empirical science. Do we do this because it is the right way to get this kind of information or because it is the only way we have?

We know as well as we can know anything in this field that early intervention and prevention are better than waiting. What we need to know better is how to tell, other than by trial and error, which technique is going to work with which children. The trial and error period does not usually take very long, but sometimes it takes too long, and it would be helpful to know what to do with individual children earlier on. Better methods for evaluating the environmental influences on individual children would be a useful line of research.

It would also be useful to know better why these techniques work so well. Nan Bernstein Ratner and her colleagues' research with parental speech rate (e.g., Stephenson-Opsal & Bernstein Ratner, 1988) is an example of useful clinician research. It helps us know a little better why slowing parental speech rate is so effective. It is also quite useful, from a rhetorical perspective, to be able to tell parents that this technique is powerful enough so that even for a group of stuttering children, varying in the nature and complexity of their disorder, there is a statistically significant trend for this technique to produce mean fluency rates that are higher than for children not receiving this kind of input. But we shouldn't take this to mean that such a technique will work for all children. There will be some for whom the reduction in time pressure is not very useful. So this kind of study is useful in several ways, but it is no more useful than any other in telling us what to do with a particular child.

HOW DO WE EVALUATE THE EFFECTIVENESS OF STUTTERING THERAPY?

Ingham (this volume) argues that we need data demonstrating that specific techniques are more successful than placebo controls, or than other techniques with which they are compared. These comparisons would yield results based on statistical evaluation of the differences between groups in the compared conditions. In my opinion, such an approach has three serious shortcomings:

> 1. A clinician choosing a technique for a specific child on the basis of a statistically significant difference between two groups would be committing the fallacy of arguing from the general to the particular. In behavioral therapy, group trends do not guarantee that a technique will be successful with any individual child; they only suggest that the technique is more likely to be successful than another with which it has been compared.

> 2. The comparison would necessarily be based only on observable events, which constitute a small, perhaps even minute, proportion of stuttering events. It would thus be possible that a technique would be shown by the statistical comparison to be "effective," based on observable evidence, when in fact it was ineffective, or even harmful, on the greater part of the disorder. For example, it may be that programs using behavioral contingencies reduce observable disfluency, or even eliminate it, but at the same time create unobservable events that the child uses to suppress the disfluency (for example word changing, reduced talking, obsessive thoughts, etc.) In such a case, what appeared to be efficacious would in fact be deleterious.

> 3. No placebo condition that successfully mimics effective treatment without actually being effective treatment has yet been devised. It is difficult to devise placebos that successfully mimic

treatment conditions even in the case of pharmaceutical research, where specific side effects can sometimes be incorporated into the placebo. But for treatment in which a clinician interacts with a child, it seems impossible. Certainly no one has yet created such a placebo.

Is there a way to design a procedure that will act as an effective placebo for a therapy technique? It seems unlikely. In order to control effectively for the placebo effect, the tendency for individuals to improve because they believe that an effective treatment is being administered to them, the scientist needs to create conditions that closely mimic the conditions of treatment, but without producing the desired effects. This cannot be done in therapy that consists, as ours does, of environmental manipulation, behavioral contingencies, suggestions, training, and information. How can we present something that looks like this but is not? So, Harris' (1995) second criterion for nonscientific questions — those that cannot be answered by the use of scientific method — seems fulfilled.

One of the most striking things about stuttering is its individual variability. Time and time again, this has been the clearest finding (often it is the only finding) in studies comparing stutterers and nonstutterers (Bloodstein, 1972; Janssen, Wieneke, & Vaane, 1983). This variability underscores the importance of creating individually tailored therapy plans based on careful diagnostics. General findings based on group comparisons have substantial value in theory construction, and increase our understanding of the disorder. But for the purpose of determining therapeutic efficacy, they are only minimally useful.

A minority of children seem to begin to stutter as a result of language or articulation therapy. It seems evident that therapy precipitates stuttering from the timing of it and from the pattern of clause types or phonemes on which stuttering occurs. This does not seem to happen because the clinicians are unusually harsh or demanding, although occasionally this may be the case. It seems more likely that the children were somehow at risk to begin with. It would be a great advantage to be able to predict those children for whom articulation or language therapy posed a risk of stuttering development.

Then there are these children that we call "language overstimulation" cases (Amster, 1989). Usually very young and often female, they are born into highly verbal families. It looks as though their language develops far in advance of their motor skill to produce speech sounds. They have long sentences and substantial knowledge of the world but they are still toddling around in diapers and overarticulating speech sounds. One of my most difficult cases was a 15-month-old boy, whose mother was a nonstop talker. He stuttered severely when first seen at 15 months. He was extraordinarily advanced in his language abilities, using long, grammatically complex sentences at this early age. But when he tried to produce these sentences, he would block at the vocal folds, struggle and strain, and finally almost shout the word out. He responded very quickly to environmental changes, including less talking by his parents, and more regular bedtime, but he still presented some abnormality and required some more direct therapy before he was entirely fluent at 3½. He has not stuttered since, and he is now 6.

The individual paths that stuttering takes seem to define the disorder better than generalities or commonalities. Stuttering seems to develop in wholly individual ways. Each child, in the most realistic sense, presents with a unique pattern. For this reason, studies based on group measures are never going to be very helpful in determining what is efficacious. Stuttering itself seems to be such an individual, personal experience, that the evaluation of therapy for it seems to fulfill Harris' (1995) Criterion Number 3 for nonscientific questions.

The use of scientific method to determine the efficacy of stuttering restricts the researcher to variables that are observable. Such a restriction invariably limits the researcher to questions that have empirical answers. There are, of course, observable aspects of this disorder, but do we want to say that efficacious therapies are those that deal only with the observable aspects? If anything, it should be the other way around. My experience has been that when the feelings, thoughts, perceptions, and attitudes are brought up to an increased level of awareness and acceptance, changes in the observable aspects of stuttering follow with little or no additional work. The unobservable events seem more important than the observable ones. So, it seems that the more restricted to observable events a study is, the more likely it will yield trivial information. We have to have a higher standard for efficacy than a restriction to observable events will allow. Thus, the question of treatment efficacy seems to fulfill Harris' first criterion also. The variable in question is not observable.

The Effectiveness of Treatment for Adults

The previous section describes the difficulty posed by the widely variable forms that stuttering takes and how this extreme individuality makes it difficult to find gems of truth in clinical studies based on group comparisons and observations. General statements are particularly difficult to derive with regard to treatment. This does not apply to studies on the nature of stuttering, where it is of considerable value to discover what factors transcend the disorder's variability. Such findings tell us about the physiology of stuttering, about behavioral and linguistic variables, and about stimulus conditions that influence stuttering. An exception should be made also for studies of pharmaceutical agents, which seem to have promise as adjuncts to therapy and where reasonable placebos can be created. As a means for determining the efficacy of other treatments for stuttering, empirical science has a very poor track record, and there is no reason to believe it will improve. We have to use better methods than empirical science has to offer. A consideration of the development of stuttering in later years will make this evident.

The Variability of Stuttering.

As preschool children become school-age children, they acquire other behaviors, thoughts, feelings, mechanisms, and psychological processes that further complicate the disorder. Murphy (this volume) eloquently describes some of these complexities. As the child gets older, a number of heavy duty psychological processes, particularly denial and avoidance, may come into play. Most clinicians have also met adults who are clinically depressed, have attempted suicide, have developed sociopathic tendencies, or who have limited themselves in career or social life, to an extreme degree. When the strategy of avoidance and the mechanism of denial continue to be used into adulthood, they can produce some extraordinarily complex and convoluted phenomena. We have all met the stutterers who began with what seemed like the innocuous avoidance device of changing a word from one that is perceived to be difficult to one that will be easier to say. Sometimes, indeed, the new word is produced more fluently, but alas sometimes it isn't. Gradually, this strategy typically leads to more and more word changing, to changing sentence structure to accommodate a different word, or to changing topics to accommodate a different sentence. Eventually the person is talking in a most roundabout way and is in fact difficult to understand.

Similarly, techniques of struggle and forcing, when carried into adulthood, can, in our experience, lead to extremely tense mouth postures, overly developed muscles of the face, and behaviors that may be cosmetically disfiguring, or even physically painful to perform.

The Impacts of Avoidance and Denial

In addition to its variability, the tendency for avoidance to cover up what might otherwise be overt behavior makes it quite impossible to measure stuttering in any meaningful way. This is such an obvious point, yet it is invariably not considered in studies of the measurement of stuttering. In many clients, the vast majority of stuttering behaviors are reactive and defensive, used by the stutterer to postpone, hide, avoid, or escape from stuttering itself (Van Riper, 1982). Sometimes these behaviors are effective in avoiding the stuttering, but we have no way of knowing whether they have been effective, ineffective, or partially effective. If, in our quest for efficacy, we restrict ourselves to observable events, as empirical approaches would have us do, we will seriously underestimate the severity of both pre and postconditions in these clients. Whether this underestimate will be equal in the two conditions is not certain. So, if we restrict ourselves to observable events, we will develop therapies that do something, but what they do is worth much less than it appears. We have to have a higher standard for efficacy. To the extent that avoidance is a strategy in stuttering, we will measure stuttering inaccurately.

Another important process is denial. Denial, like many other processes, is originally a survival technique. The feelings of embarrassment, humiliation, shame, or fear are intensely unpleasant, and the mind, ever ready to protect the person from such psychological pain, takes the person away from the present reality, tunes him out, and lets him feel ok. It is remarkable that this ubiquitous process has been discussed so little in the stuttering literature. Rollin (1987) describes the many psychological processes involved in disorders of speech and hearing, and discusses denial in connection with all of them except stuttering. In the case of stuttering, his discussion focuses on anxiety. Crowe (1997) thoroughly describes both complete and partial denial, and explicates its presence in any loss of speech, language, or hearing function. Yet, in the chapter in his book devoted to stuttering, denial is not mentioned. Most of the stutterers we have encountered have used denial in one form or another to assuage the pain of stuttering. Jezer (1997) describes how, as a young man, he worked hard to convince himself that his stuttering was not a problem to him. Others we have seen have minimized its importance by telling themselves that it was not as bad as it might have been, by telling themselves that they will deal with it sometime in the vague future, or by reducing their awareness during stuttering episodes, a phenomenon that Van Riper termed "*Le Petit Mort.*"

In my opinion, all stutterers are in a process from the time they begin to stutter. At first, during the toddler stage, the process of dealing with the stuttering may lead them into struggle and forcing, then, in the school-age child, the avoidance strategies of behavioral tricks, and finally, in the young adult, the later forms of denial and avoidance. But at any point, they may begin a process of recovery that leads to more fluent speech. Obviously, in preschool children, this is a strong possibility because the behaviors, thoughts, feelings, and beliefs are not yet strongly established, and the child retains plasticity of speech development. Once they get into school, and the teasing begins, along with the increased awareness of others, the avoidance and denial begin to get more and more powerful, and there are not many processes working toward recovery, although some are always present. But in adulthood, a clearer perception of the world, and of oneself, leads to many beneficial processes. Adults often see the futility of the tricks they learned in school, the pain and abnormality of struggle, and some even learn that avoidance only makes matters worse. Denial is very hard to see, even for adults. The point is that there are processes working for recovery all the time. Clinicians can learn to identify these processes and cooperate with them. Often just getting out of the way so that the process can occur is the best tack to take. Clearly, a therapy that diminishes denial will be highly useful to the client, but how could such a change be measured?

There is no doubt that clinicians are successful with some clients. Unfortunately, nothing works wonderfully well with everyone. But there is good evidence that clinicians are able to recognize what works and what doesn't and are able to determine what works for some and not for others. Useless therapies have come and quickly gone in our field usually with little empirical deconfirmation. Those that are helpful to clients continue to be used, even though no empirical verification exists. We need to establish, at least for the hungry mouths of the managed-care providers, functional ways to demonstrate our efficacy, but clinicians will know that these measurable outcomes mean little in terms of what is really helpful or not helpful for clients. The empirically demonstrated outcomes will always deal with the most trivial aspects of therapy, and the really important outcomes will not be demonstrable except where it counts — to the client and his clinician.

These days, most clinicians combine work on feelings with work on fluency (Starkweather, 1994). And this seems to help, but it still takes too long and has the propensity for relapse. Also, most speech clinicians do not have the skills to work effectively on feelings. It is amazing how many things are helpful for people who stutter that most speech pathologists don't know anything about. We know about the disorder, but we lack many of the most useful tools in dealing with the emotional baggage that stuttering creates. The psychologists, on the other hand, have many tools that are useful in dealing with just this aspect of the disorder, but they really don't know much about stuttering and as a result they don't understand it. Some are willing to learn, and when they do, the results are remarkable, in my limited experience. But many of them have some outworn theory that they apply, and it gets nowhere. Hopefully, specialty training for stuttering therapy will help alleviate this problem.

Anne Wilson Schaef, in her remarkable book *Beyond Therapy, Beyond Science* (1992) showns how science and its rigors have not proved to be adequate to validate, or even describe, the processes of therapy. Schaef began her career, as we all did, with training in scientific method and used it with complete faith as a means for learning about the world, including the world of treatment.

Schaef notes that scientific method is, as she puts it, "nothing but a religious belief system." She goes on to say that "Like any other religious fanatic, a fundamentalist, dogmatic scientist firmly believes that the only true access to truth must come through their procedures and belief system...The process is one of closed-mindedness, ...discounting, righteousness, and superiority." Speech clinicians, in my experience, are also scientists, but of a different sort — they are open minded, willing to explore, understand and accept their own shortcomings, and believe that what they see, hear, and feel are the reality with which they must deal. But they are not dogmatic unless they have been trained to be so by another dogmatist. True scientists, and most clinicians seem to be among them, are willing to consider the possibility that science may not provide the answer to every question.

Of course, one of the reasons we may seem inclined to use scientific method to determine what forms of therapy are efficacious is that we were all trained in the belief that speech pathology is a behavioral science, and that therapy is a form of behavior modification. We would like speech clinicians to consider the possibility that stuttering therapy is not, or should not be, simply a form of behavior modification. If the disorder is much more than the behavior that shows on the surface — and who can doubt this proposition — then an approach to treatment that is deeper than behavior modification should prove effective.

Recovery as a Goal in Stuttering Therapy

Consider the similarities between stuttering and addictions. It is not our belief that stuttering **is** an addiction, only that it has some characteristics in common with addiction, including the illusion of control, of shame and stigma, of avoidance and denial, of perfectionism, and most of all, a difficulty in assuming responsibility for one's own recovery. These similarities may arise because stuttering, like substance abuse, gambling, or codependency, gives the illusion of being controllable by will power, but it is only an illusion. Speech itself happens naturally without conscious control. It can be brought under conscious control but not for very long; much as the alcoholic can swear off for a while but, when he or she tries to stay sober by sheer will power alone, often fails in the attempt. What the alcoholic needs is support and structured recovery — mostly support from others with the same problem, or someone trained to deal with the problem. What the stutterer needs is the same thing — support from other stutterers, or support from an understanding and knowledgeable clinician. And beyond that, the stutterer and his or her clinician need to think in terms of recovery — in the sense that it is used in addictions — rather than in the simplistic terms of behavior modification.

We believe it is helpful to address stuttering for adults in terms of recovery rather than in terms of modification. Adults want to be able to make choices. For them, a recovery approach is, we believe, efficient and results in a more complete recovery, one that does not require constant monitoring of one's speech and one with less chance of relapse.

In recovery, the person who wants to change is responsible for establishing the goals and choosing the experiences that will lead to achieving those goals. A clinician familiar with this kind of treatment can be of great help in suggesting goals and experiences that can be helpful, but the final authority for making these decisions rests with the stutterer.

Recovery is ongoing; modification has a beginning, middle, and end. Often likened to a journey, recovery continues. It does not have, like modification, a set of preestablished criteria for termination. As is often said, it is a journey, not a destination.

Recovery is a search for understanding that will be a foundation for change, not an attempt to change without the foundation. This may be the most important difference between recovery and modification. In recovery, the person tries to become more aware of what it is they do when they stutter, of how they feel when they stutter, and what they are thinking about before, during, and after stuttering episodes. Through this increased awareness, they learn to accept those aspects of themselves for the moment, and then, through this increased awareness and acceptance, to discover that change happens with little or no effort. The foundation for change is the insights, altered perceptions, free-flow of feelings, and awareness of attitudes. Change is seen, in recovery, as a process that will naturally happen unless barriers are placed in its way. The foundation for change removes those barriers by first helping the person become aware of them, then by helping the person accept the reality of them.

Recovery is a journey of discovery that one takes into oneself. Much of the activity consists of removing the masks of denial and avoidance, learning to be honest with oneself, taking responsibility for oneself, and caring about oneself enough to be willing to bear the sometimes painful challenges of self-confrontation.

Recovery occurs in a linguistic domain. The changes that occur in recovery are mediated by language, by talking and listening. Although modification can also be mediated by language, it uses language only as a means to deliver behavioral consequences, and in fact, language is unnecessary for the direct application of learning processes to the modification of behavior. This is not true for recovery, where the process occurs through a conversation in which the stutterers' semantics change — they redefine themselves and their disorder; they discover new ways of thinking about stuttering and social interaction.

Awareness and acceptance are recurring themes in the process of recovery — whether from grief, addiction of one sort or another, or stuttering. Coping with new awareness is often awkward and acceptance is certainly not easy. But learning to accept what IS (especially when we don't like it very much) is empowering. We like to say that once we stop fighting those things we cannot change, we find new energy to change the things we can. if we are to become aware of the process of recovery that all stutterers are in, we need to rethink our role in dealing with them. In the recovery approach, we are not therapists, producing changes in people with modification techniques. Instead, we observe the process that is occurring. We bear witness to it when it happens spontaneously and when necessary, we help it to happen more smoothly or more quickly and with as little discomfort to the stutterer as possible. We are midwives to the process of recovery. We meet the person who stutters wherever he or she happens to be in the process of recovery and join them on the journey. Clinicians have seen others go this way and can therefore be helpful. But, in an important way, we are not therapists; we are not the ones who are responsible for making this process happen. It is the person who stutters who is the therapist, who decides what they should do to allow the process to continue, who evaluates the outcome of a particular strategy, and who plans for the next step of self-discovery that they are going to take.

CONCLUSION

From an examination of the way stuttering develops, several characteristics of the disorder become evident — it varies from person to person to an extraordinary degree; it is self-referential; much of it, and probably the most important part, is unobservable; it is a highly complex phenomenon that is influenced by many internal and external factors, often changing over time, and many of the factors are unknown and unobservable. Furthermore, therapy for stuttering is even more complex, varyings in its effectiveness as a result of many known and unknown variables, including characteristics of the client, the clinician, and the timing of intervention. Finally, no one has yet succeeded in devising an effective placebo against which therapy efficacy can be scientifically tested. There is good reason to believe that no such placebo will ever be devised. In conclusion, Horgan (1996) and Harris (1995) suggest seven criteria for nonscientific questions. In their opinion, a question is unsuitable for scientific investigation if any one of these criteria are met. The discussion here has shown that all but one of the seven criteria are clearly met by asking the question, "Is stuttering therapy efficacious?"

Finally, I have suggested that we may have been barking up the wrong tree in seeing stuttering as a condition that needs to be removed, like a disease. It may be more fruitful to see it as a process that can take helpful or harmful directions. By joining the client in a recovery process, rather than trying to change him or her, it may be that we can be more effective.

REFERENCES

Adelman, H., & Maatsch, J. (1956). Learning and extinction based upon frustration, food reward, and exploratory tendency. *Journal of Experimental Psychology, 50*, 61–65.

Amsel, A., & Roussel, J. (1952). Motivational properties of frustration I: Effect on a running response of the addition of frustration to the motivational complex. *Journal of Experimental Psychology, 43*, 363–368.

Amsel, A., & Ward, J. (1954). Motivational properties of frustration II: Frustration drive stimulus and frustration reduction in selective learning. *Journal of Experimental Psychology, 48*, 37–47.

Amster, B. (November, 1989). *Case studies in language overstimulation and stuttering.* Convention address, ASHA, Boston, MA.

Andrews, G., & Harris, M. (1964). *The syndrome of stuttering.* London: Heinemann.

Bloodstein, O. (1960). The development of stuttering I: Changes in nine basic features. *Journal of Speech and Hearing Disorders, 25,* 219–37.

Bloodstein, O. (1972). The anticipatory struggle hypothesis: Implications of research on the variability of stuttering. *Journal of Speech and Hearing Research, 15,* 487–499.

Bloodstein, O. (1987). *A handbook on stuttering (4th ed.).* Chicago: National Easter Seal Society.

Brauth, S. E., Hall, W. S., & Dooling, R. J. (1991). Plasticity of Development. Cambridge, MA, MIT Press.

Crowe, T. (1997). *Applications of counseling in speech-language pathology and audiology.* Baltimore: William & Wilkins.

Gregory, H., & Hill, D. (1984) Stuttering therapy for children. In W. Perkins (Ed.), *Stuttering disorders.* New York: Thieme-Stratton.

Harris, M. B. (1995). *Basic statistics for behavioral science research.* Needham Heights, MA: Allyn & Bacon.

Hofstadter, D. R. (1979). *Godel, Escher, Bach: An eternal golden braid.* New York: Basic Books.

Hofstadter, D. R. (1985). *Metamagical themas.* New York: Basic Books.

Horgan, J. (1996). *The end of science.* New York: Addison-Wesley.

Janssen, P., Wieneke, G., & Vaane, E. (1983). Variability in the initiation of articulatory movements in the speech of stutterers and normal speakers. *Journal of Fluency Disorders, 8,* 341–358.

Jezer, M. (1997). *Stuttering: A life bound up in words.* New York: Basic Books.

Krashen, S. (1973). Lateralization, language learning, and the critical period: Some new evidence. *Language Learning, 23,* 63–74.

Rollin, W. J. (1987). *The psychology of communication disorders in individuals and their families.* Englewood Cliffs, NJ: Prentice-Hall.

Schaef, A. W. (1992). *Beyond therapy, beyond science.* San Francisco: Harper.

Sheehan, J. (1970). Stuttering: Research and Therapy. New York: Haper & Row.

Sidman, M. (1960). *Tactics of Scientific Research: Evaluating experimental data in psychology.* New York: Basic Books.

Starkweather, C. W. (April, 1994). *Current practices in stuttering therapy.* Paper presented at the Special Interest Division on Fluency Leadership conference, Hilton Head, SC.

Starkweather, C. W., & Givens-Ackerman, J. (1997). *Stuttering.* In the Pro-Ed Series on Speech Pathology (H. Halpern, Ed.). Austin, TX, Pro-Ed.

Starkweather, C. W., & Gottwald, S. R. (1993). A pilot project of relations among specific measures obtained at intake and discharge in a program of prevention and early intervention. *American Journal of Speech Pathology, 2,* 51–58.

Starkweather, C. W., Gottwald, S. R., & Halfond, M. (1990). *Stuttering Prevention: A Clinical Method.* Englewood Cliifs, NJ: Prentice-Hall.

Stephenson-Opsal, D., & Bernstein Ratner, N0. (1988). Maternal speech rate modification and childhood stuttering. *Journal of Fluency Disorders, 13*(1), 49–56.

Van Riper, C. (1982). *The nature of stuttering (2nd ed.).* Englewood Cliffs, NJ: Prentice-Hall.

FOOTNOTES

[1] There are some exceptions to this — children who begin with laryngeal blocking particularly. In these cases, the onset seems to be associated with intense emotional experiences, fear, or excitement; the intensity seems to be critical.

[2] The theme of recursion is developed considerably in another book, *Metamagical Themas* (Hofstadter, 1985).

Author Index

A

B

Subject Index

A

ABA time series, 21–22
Affect, *see* Emotionality
Age
   and onset
      developmental patterns, 149, 158–159
      and neurobiology, 66–68, 69, 71
      and recovery, 48–49, 50, 148–149
American Speech-Language-Hearing Association (ASHA), 1, 3
Anger, 136
Anxiety, 135
Attractor states, 39–41
Autism, 68, 89
Avoidance, 134, 239–341

B

Behaviorism
   and componential analysis, 104–105
   and etiology, 159, 160t
   and integrative research, 7, 115, 123–125
      schism in, 119–120
      time-out procedure, 120–122
   and Lidcombe Program, 194–195
      maintenance procedures, 200–201
      praise/correction, 196–199
      speech measures, 199–200, 209n3
   and neurophysiology, 97–98

C

Clinical trials, 20
   randomized controlled, 20
Cognition
   and integrative research, 7, 115, 116, 117, 118, 119, 121–122, 123, 126
   in multifactorial model, 32, 34, 35
Componential analysis, 104–105
Control groups, 220–221
   matched randomized pre/posttest, 21

D

Delayed auditory feedback (DAF), 57–58
Demands and Capacity (DC) model, 85
Demands/capacities analysis, 105–107
Descriptive research, 17–18
   and disability, 18
   and handicap, 18–19
Developmental Sentence Analysis, 156
Diagnosogenic theory, 35, 117
Disability level, 2, 15–17, 18
Disconfirmatory strategy, 60–61
Disorder level
   as disability, 2, 15–17, 18
   as handicap, 2, 15–17, 18–19
   as impairment, 2, 15–17, 18
Down syndrome, 89, 176, 180
Dynamic theory
   attractor states, 39–41
   emergent property, 38–39
   and etiology, 37–42
   self-organizing systems, 39
   volcano analogy, 4, 27–29, 30, 34
Dysarthria, 64
Dyslexia, 68, 89
Dystonia, 66

E

Emergent property, 38–39
Emotionality, 8, 132–133, *see also* Shame
   anger, 136
   anxiety, 135
   avoidance, 134, 239–341
   denial, 239–241
   empathy, 131
      other-oriented, 135–136
   guilt, 137, 141
      nature of, 134
   and integrative treatment, 7, 115, 116, 118, 119, 121–122, 123, 126
   life events response, 8, 153–154, 158–159